MECHANICS OF PATENT CLAIM DRAFTING

(Second Edition)

MECHANICS OF PATENT CLAIM DRAFTING

(Second Edition)

Fourth Printing

John L. Landis

With the Collaboration of
John D. Kaufmann, Bryan W. Sheffield
and Myron Cohen

G1-0633
PRACTISING LAW INSTITUTE
New York City

Library of Congress Catalog Card Number: 74-77345

DEDICATION

This book is dedicated to the faculty of PLI claim-drafting tutors, who have given most generously of their time and talents over the last eleven years in the patent bar review course, helping the students to draft better claims.

Most particularly, I wish to thank Messrs. Myron Cohen, John Kaufmann, Martin Pfeffer, Bryan Sheffield, Maurice Stiefel, "Chick" Turner and Herbert Winegar, who have reviewed this text in many different forms over many years and contributed a great deal to the text.

Also, Ruth Druss, Program Director of the PLI; founder of the PLI patent and patent bar review courses; and Patricia Landis, grammarian and proofreader extraordinaire.

FOREWORD

The enthusiastic reception of the First Edition of this book both in America and at programs in Brussels, Copenhagen and Munich has led to this expanded, revised version, incorporating new cases, additional examples and further discussions of developing fields.*

Mr.Landis, long the chief lecturer for the Institute in the area of drafting patent claims, is General Patent Attorney of Teletype Corporation. John D. Kaufmann of Teletype, Bryan W. Sheffield of Bell Telephone Laboratories, and Myron Cohen of Hubbell, Cohen & Stiefel have contributed greatly to this revision.

The experienced patent practitioner will find this volume both a distillation of advanced technique and a review of the fundamentals of his field. The person new to patent practice will welcome the absence of jargon and the inclusion of texts of relevant statutes, rules and procedural interpretations. The attorney or businessman with occasional need to evaluate an existing patent should find the numerous claims, both court-approved and specially developed for illustrative purposes, convenient keys to understanding the result of the drafting process.

HENRY W. ENBERG II
Senior Legal Editor
Practising Law Institute

---

*This printing corrects errors called to our attention since publication. Mr. Landis is now Division Patent Attorney for Western Electric in New York City.—H.W.E. II

TABLE OF CONTENTS

Page

MECHANICS OF PATENT CLAIM DRAFTING

by John L. Landis
With the collaboration of
John D. Kaufmann and Bryan W. Sheffield

INTRODUCTION

The primary object of this book is to present a simple and direct approach to the mechanics of claim drafting. The major emphasis in Chapters I-VI is on practical techniques for composing claims to many different types of inventions. In Chapters I-VI, there is also emphasis on various preferred claim-drafting practices and techniques which have grown up over the years by case law,* Patent Office** rules and memoranda and, simply, custom, as well as definitions and preferred usage of stylized words and phrases in the patent law, such as "consisting," "means for" and "whereby."

There is also extensive discussion of many case law doctrines relating to nonart rejections,† both classic rules and modern trends. In many of these areas, there have been liberalizing trends

---

*Court or Patent Office Board of Appeals decisions. The Patent Office Board of Appeals in an administrative tribunal in the Patent Office that hears appeals from adverse decisions of the patent examiners on substantive issues. The Board usually sits in panels of three designated members, but sometimes convenes in an enlarged band to hear citizens involving important legal issues.

**Now, officially named the "Patent and Trademark Office."

†Rejections based on doctrines other than anticipation or obviousness over prior art.

by the CCPA** in recent years to overthrow or simplify rejections not based on prior art. In particular, this book covers both the classic and the more recent constructions of means clauses (Section 31), inherent function of the apparatus doctrine (Section 37), mental steps and computer programs (Section 41)), product-by-process claims (Section 43), claims referring to drawings (Section 51), new use claims and preamble limitations (Section 52), Jepson claims (Section 54), undue multiplicity (Section 59), old combination (Section 60), aggregation (Section 61) and printed matter (Section 62).

There are many examples of suggested claims to various types of inventions: machines (Chapter III), processes (Chapter IV), articles of manufacture (Chapter V), compositions of matter (Chapter VI), designs (Section 44) and plants (Section 45), as well as dependent claims (Section 53), Jepson claims (Section 54), generic and species claims (Section 55) and subcombination claims (Section 56).

Many quotations from claims on appeal and in litigation are given, so that the reader can see for himself which types of limitations and phrases have been judicially approved and which not.

Unfortunately, it is too often true that the inventor or patentee wins or loses, because of formal rules and language problems in the claims, not because of any lack of "Invention" over the prior art. This book is intended to help the practitioner in designing his claims around these myriad rules and doctrines, to draft the most effective types of claims for each type of invention.

**Court of Customs and Patent Appeals. A special five-judge Federal Court having jurisdiction over appeals from Patent Office administrative tribunals, as well as customs appeals.

Chapter I

STATUTORY PROVISIONS—SOME BASIC PRINCIPLES

Section 1—The Statute

In the beginning, 35 U.S.C. §112:*

> The specification shall conclude with one or more claims particularly pointing out and distinctly claiming the subject matter which the applicant regards as his invention.

This is the fundamental rule, with which all others must be consistent. It was almost ever thus; the patent act of 1836, which started the modern examination system, provided (5 Stat. 117) that the applicant ". . . shall also particularly specify and point out the part, improvement, or combination which he claims as his own invention or discovery." See *Robinson on Patents* §§504-38 (1890), for a thorough discussion of the history and philosophy of claims, as well as of patents in general.

Under this very broad and general statutory directive, various rules and practices have grown up by case law, commissioner's regulations and custom since 1836, as to how and how not to fulfill the statutory mandate of *particularly pointing out and distinctly claiming.*

In general, this means that the claims must define "the Invention," meaning the claimed subject matter, in such detail that

*This is the section of the basic patent statute (Title 35, United States Code) relating to the patent specification, including claims. Sections of the statutes and Patent Office Rules of Practice mentioned are reproduced in Appendix D, Part I and II.

the patent examiner and, later, the world of prospective infringers can understand what the claimed subject matter is; that is, what is forbidden territory and what is open, so far as this particular patent is concerned.

SUMMARY—Patent claims must particularly point out and distinctly claim what applicant (usually, you, the patent practitioner) regards as his invention after reading this book.

Section 2—Omnibus Claims

All of the specific rules and tests must be derived from, or at least not be inconsistent with, the dominating statutory provision. For example, a first rule is that "omnibus" or formal claims are not permitted in utility patents.* Such claims as: "My invention substantially as shown and described," or the classic and all-encompassing: "Any and all features of novelty described, referred to, exemplified, or shown," are not permitted in the United States, although they are allowed in some foreign countries. Obviously, these claims do not "particularly point out and distinctly claim" anything, certainly not the "invention." The examiner rejects such claims out of hand, as being "non-statutory."

If such claims were allowed in utility patents, the world of potential infringers would be left to guess what the patent covered. The basic concept of United States claims is that the inventor owes the public a duty to define the forbidden territory of the patent as precisely as the circumstances permit. Correspondingly, all features disclosed but not claimed are held to be dedicated to the public,† at least so far as that patent is concerned.

*Patents other than designs (Section 44) and plants (Section 45).

†Not normally through benevolence on the part of the patentee, but merely because the patent becomes prior art against the inventor one year after patenting, under 35 U.S.C. §102(b) and *In re* Gibbs, 168 USPQ 578 (CCPA 1971); and it becomes prior art against others as of its earliest

A customary analogy is that the patentee must stake out the precise boundaries of his claim, in a manner similar to the description of the boundaries of a plot of land. For this reason United States claims are sometimes referred to as "peripheral" claims, meaning the outer boundaries or periphery of the patentee's claim must be stated.

This concept of claim certainty is very useful to potential infringers, but often very hard on the patentee because the real "essence of the invention" is sometimes not fully understood until many years later—when the somewhat different structure of the accused infringer is known and when all of the prior art has become developed.

SUMMARY—Claims must define the invention with certainty and in detail. Formal or omnibus claims are not permitted in utility patents.

Section 3—The Statutory Classes

The statute, 35 U.S.C. §101, sets out four main categories or "pigeonholes" of technical subject matter for which utility patents can be granted. These are "process, machine, [article of] manufacture, or composition of matter," usually termed "the statutory classes." Many of the claim-drafting rules to follow stem from case-law definitions of the words "machine," "process," "manufacture," and "composition of matter" in the statute. No matter how novel or how valuable an "invention" may be, it cannot be patented if it cannot be made to fit within one of these classes. Thus, such things as mathematical formulas, bookkeeping systems and articles found in nature have been held unpatentable because

---

effective filing date in the United States, under 35 U.S.C. §102(e). This can include the date of an earlier U.S. application to which the patent is entitled, under 35 U.S.C. 120, but not the date of an earlier foreign application to which the patent is entitled under 35 U.S.C. 119.

they are not within the classes set up by Congress. The question of whether or when "computer program" inventions can be patented hinges largely on the interpretation of the word "process," as discussed in Section 41.

This leads to a second fundamental rule, that a claim, no matter how beautifully drafted, must define the invention in such a way as to fit it into one of these statutory classes, as construed by court decisions since 1790, when similar categories of patentable subject matter were established in the first patent statute.*

With these few basic principles in mind, the following chapter concerns some details and common practices for transforming inventions, generally, into claims, after which Chapters III-VI in turn cover particular problems encountered in the four statutory classes.

SUMMARY—Claims must fit within the "statutory classes" of patentable subject matter, as construed by court decisions. These classes are machine, process, (article of) manufacture, and composition of matter, for utility patents. Ornamental designs and certain agricultural plants, are separate statutory classes with different rules (Sections 44-45).

*The classes of 1790 were "art, manufacture, engine, machine or device." Designs were added in 1842 and plants in 1930.

Chapter II

CLAIM FORMS AND FORMATS IN GENERAL

Section 4—Single Sentence

The only known (or at least acceptable) way so far to "particularly point out and distinctly claim" an invention in a statutory class is by means of an English sentence. This is unfortunate, because many of the problems in claim drafting stem from problems in writing English and in the meanings of words.

To begin at the beginning, the standard custom as to sentence construction is that each claim must be the direct object of a single sentence, however long, beginning with a standard introductory phrase such as "I [or We] claim" or the equivalent "What is claimed is." See MPEP* 608.01(m) where this is called "present Office practice." The origin of this "single sentence rule" is unknown to this author, but it seems to have been standard practice for as long as anyone remembers. In filing an application with

---

*MPEP stands for a loose-leaf book *Manual of Patent Examining Procedure*, which is a Patent Office publication setting forth detailed instructions to the examiners on almost every conceivable point that could arise in practice before the Patent Office. Sections of the manual cited in this book are reproduced in Appendix D, Part III. The manual represents the official position or opinion of the office on practically every point of law and procedure, and is continuously amended and supplemented as changes occur. Since the manual ordinarily operates as the examiner's bible, its mandates should normally be followed to the letter except where one is convinced that the manual is wrong *and* one's client's interests are likely to be prejudiced. In that case, an appeal (35 U.S.C. §134) or petition to the commissioner (Patent Office rule 181) will usually be necessary, in effect to reverse the manual. When that occurs, the manual is amended to reflect the change.

more than one claim, the introductory phrase, such as "I claim," appears only once, before the first claim.

Standard office practice also is to insist that each claim begin with a capital letter and end with a period, so that each claim reads as a complete sentence when taken with the introductory words such as "I claim." Except for standard abbreviations such as °C.,† no other periods are permitted in the body of the claim.

Example:

> I claim: A pencil having an eraser fastened to one end.

The above claim is to illustrate layout and form only, not as an example of patentable subject matter. (A different claim to such a combination was held unpatentable by the Supreme Court in *Reckendorfer v. Faber*, cited and discussed in Section 61 on Aggregation.)

In connection with the single-sentence rule, it is important to watch grammer, particularly verb forms, to make sure the claim reads as a complete sentence. For example, "I claim: A pencil *comprises* . . . [parts A and B]*" does not form a complete sentence. However, the generally standard phaseology, "I claim: A pencil *comprising* . . . [A and B]" does form a sentence.

This is sometimes troublesome in long, complicated claims with many elements, subelements, and intricate relationships between elements; in dependent claims (Section 53); and in *Jepson* claims (Section 54).

SUMMARY—Make sure the claim forms a complete sentence forming the direct object of the phrase "I claim." Begin each claim with a capital letter and end it with a period. What goes in between causes the trouble.

Section 5—Numbering and Order

Section 112 of the statute, on utility patents, provides that the

---

*Letters "A," "B" conventionally stand for the "elements" of the claims, such as "pencil" and "eraser" in the above example.

†Modern practice does not use a period in °C.

"specification shall conclude with *one or more* claims. . . ." In design patents, Section 44, and plant patents, Section 45, only one claim is permitted. Almost always, more than one claim is submitted in a utility patent application (sometimes only one claim is allowed, and one is lucky to obtain that many).

When only one claim is presented, no numeral is used as in the above example to the pencil. When more than one claim is submitted, each claim must start with an Arabic numeral. The claims must be numbered consecutively, and good practice dictates that the claims be grouped and numbered in a logical order for consideration. The usual practice is to begin with the broadest claim and proceed to the narrowest, and to group similar types of claims together. Effective 24 Jan 78 required 75(f)

As to preferred order, a Patent Office notice "Guidelines for Drafting a Model Patent Application under the Revised Rules"* (Oct. 12, 1966), also MPEP 608.01(m), provides that:

> Claims should preferably be arranged in order of scope so that the first claim presented is the broadest. Where separate species are claimed, the claims to like species should be grouped together where possible and be physically separated by drawing a line between claims or groups of claims. . . . Similarly, product and process claims should be separately grouped.

In view of this notice, as well as general good sense, the claims should be grouped in what the claim writer thinks is the most logical order for consideration. The practice occasionally seen of trying to slip in an unusually broad claim as claim 17, out of nineteen claims, is condemnable.

Special rules apply to the numbering of certain dependent claims. (See Section 53.)

---

*Patent Office Rules of Pratice. The commissioner adopts rules of practice pursuant to the authority of Congress in 35 U.S.C. §6:

"He may . . . establish regulations, not inconsistent with law, for the conduct of proceedings in the Patent Office."

Such rules have the force of statute, *United States v. Marble*, 22 O.G. 1365 (1882). How far, if at all, the commissioner can go in amplifying the statute in substantive matters is not clear. See in particular the discussion in Section 59 of undue multiplicity.

How many claims may be presented, and how different they must be from each other is discussed in Sections 57-59.

Example of a complete claims layout:

I claim:
1. A pencil having....
2. A pencil as recited in claim 1, wherein . . . [more detail]
3. A pencil comprising . . . [the most detailed combination acceptable to the applicant].

SUMMARY—Present multiple claims in a logical order and number them consecutively.

Section 6—Preamble

Most claims have "preambles," or introductory statements, the purpose of which is to name or define the thing which is to be claimed. Preambles may be quite long or very short, depending on the type of claim one is using.

The best type of preamble for most claims is simply a general definition of the combination to be claimed, with whatever detail or length is necessary to match the body of the claim. One important point to remember is that the preamble and the body of the claim should be consistent one with the other, two parts making up a whole. The preamble cannot be written properly until the scope of the claim-to-be is determined, and the preamble should be checked for consistency after the claim has been finished. When a claim is revised or amended, the preamble should be rescrutinized for consistency. As to the effect of limitations in the preamble, see Section 52 on new use claims; preamble limitations. In general, one should avoid any unnecessary limitations or statements anywhere in the broader claims, even in the preamble.

Recommended preambles for different types of claims are set out in subsequent parts of this book.

SUMMARY—Use descriptive preambles defining the nature

of the combination claimed. Do not put unnecessary limitations even in the preamble. Assume every word you write in a claim is critical, and may some day be used against your client, to restrict the scope of his invention.

Section 7—Transition from Preamble to Body—"Comprising"

Most ordinary combination claims require a transitional phrase between the preamble (naming the thing to be claimed) and the body of the claim (defining what the elements or parts of the thing are). Two recommended forms of transition which can be employed for most claims are the phrases: "which comprises" or "comprising." The choice between the two is immaterial.

The word "comprises" has been construed to mean, in patent law, "including the following elements but not excluding others."*

For example, a claim to "A writing implement comprising a pencil with an eraser fastened at one end" covers any type of eraser-tipped pencil: wood, mechanical, etc., with or without a clip to hook it on one's pocket, and whether or not the additional features or additions are patentable to the later inventors. Thus, in patent shorthand, "the combination comprising A+B (individual elements or parts)" covers A+B+C . . . or A+B′ (a variation of element B falling under the claim definition). In general the technique of writing broad claims is to claim the minimum number of elements that will function in the combination, each defined as broadly as the prior art and claim-drafting doctrines will allow. In this manner the main "point of the invention," or "inventive concept"† should be crystallized in concrete terms.

**See Ex parte* Schaefer 171 USPQ 110 (Bd. App. 1970).

†Note, some attorneys sometime speak loosely of "the invention," as meaning the point of novelty or inventive concept, rather than merely to refer to the technical subject matter sought to be patented, as the word "invention" is defined in the statute. This double or triple meaning for the word "invention" is confusing and should be avoided, as pointed out by the CCPA in many recent cases.

Some form of the word "comprise" is practically always used for mechanical or method combination claims. Words such as "including" or "having" are sometimes used, and mean the same thing as "comprising"; however, "comprising" is recommended simply because it has become a standardized word of the patent art.

SUMMARY—Use the transition "comprising" or "which comprises" except in very unusual cases.

Section 8—"Consisting"—"Consisting Essentially of"

The following transitions have more limited meanings, and are used primarily in chemical cases, where the art or other reason requires limitation:

"consisting of"—excluding more than traces of other ingredients;

"consisting essentially of"—excluding other elements of any essential significance to the combination.

For example, in *In re Garnero*, 162 USPQ 221, 223 (1969), the CCPA ruled that the phrase "consisting essentially of" excludes ". . . additional unspecified ingredients which would affect the basic and novel characteristics of the product defined in the balance of the claim." These meanings were discussed by the Patent Office board of appeals in *Ex parte Davis*, 80 USPQ 448 (1948), as a "code" adopted by a group of primary examiners for their guidance. These meanings are now quite stylized in the patent law.

These more limited claims are spoken of as "closed ended," because other elements or other material elements are excluded from the combination. Of course "consisting" should be avoided in the broader claims wherever possible as it is severely limited. The test of when "consisting essentially" is required instead of the broad "comprising" is not clear.

There may be other, hybrid phraseologies acceptable having

a scope somewhere between "comprising" and "consisting essentially." For example, Natta *et al.* patent 3,112,301 has a claim that reads, "consists prevailingly but not essentially of. . . ."

In Ziegler v. Phillips Petroleum Co., 177 USPQ 481 (5th Cir. 1973), the court on a specific factual situation held that "consisting essentially" permitted material additions so long as the consisting essentially ingredients were "necessarily present," and the composition with the added ingredient still used the "real invention." This sounds like the best interpretation to this author.

SUMMARY—Do not use the expressions, "consisting" or "consisting essentially" unless the examiner requires them. Then, consider whether you really have to or whether some other expression will do. Watch for new cases on these expressions and what these words mean.

Section 9—Body of the Claim

The body of a combination claim, meaning the part which follows the preamble and the transistional phrase, comprises:

(a) a recitation of the "elements" of parts of the combination; and

(b) a description of how the elements cooperate with one another to make up the operative combination recited in the preamble.

The body of the claim is written in narrative expository prose, perhaps somewhat hampered in long claims by the single-sentence rule. The claim must be limited to a description of the technical subject matter, and surplus or laudatory statements, such as "novel," are not permitted, nor are statements of objects or advantages. Thus a claim to "A combination steam and dry iron comprising [A, B and C], thus to iron clothes more effectively than heretofore" would be objectionable in the last quoted clause.

In terms of English grammar, the body of a combination claim in a series: A and B, A, B and C, etc. The letters A, B and C conventionally stand for the "elements" of the claim, by which is meant the main structures, steps, parts or ingredients which form the machine, process, article of manufacture, or composition of matter recited in the preamble. See as an example, claim 1, Section II.

In the rare case of a single-element claim (as distinguished from a combination claim), the single element, be it a mechanism, step, article or composition, is merely described. Example, claim 5, Section 39. Since practically all claims are to combinations of one sort or another, this book will deal primarily with combination claims except where specifically noted.

Of course,, clear and intelligible wording should be used in describing the elements and how they cooperate or function, to make sure the claim "particularly points out" the invention and "distinctly claims" it, Section 1. Avoid "ambiguities, vague or clumsy expressions, and unnecessary repetition of language." This latter advice is from Patent Office's guidelines in reviewing claims written by applicants for admission to practice before the Patent Office in a written examination known as the Agent's Exam.

SUMMARY–The body of the claim lists the main elements of the combination (parts, steps, chemicals, etc.) and tells how they work together or are related to each other. Most claims are directed to combinations of two or more elements. Stick to technical description, and eschew unnecessary, redundant surplusage and any laudatory statements. Tell what the invention is, not how good it is. The claim must be readily understandable, and clear as to what it covers

Section 10—Format and Punctuation—Subparagraph Form

Since a combination claim is a grammatical series, if three or more elements (A, B and C) are described, which coincide with the clauses of the series, they must be set off at least by commas. Even with two-element claims, punctuation should be used unless the first element contains very few words, so that it is clear where the description of the second element starts. As in any writings, semicolons should be used to set off the clauses whenever one or more of the clauses contains internal punctuation. Other punctuation, such as parentheses, dashes, etc., is not ordinarily needed or used in claims, although there is no good reason why such techniques should not be used in appropriate cases.

The single paragraph form of claim (see Claim 1A, Section 11), with commas between the elements and with no indentation, letters or numerals to identify the elements, is the form which was used almost exclusively by practitioners in the past. It is still accepted by the Patent Office, and may be preferable for very simple claims, such as a five-line claim with only two or three elements.

Because claims are often complex and difficult to follow, various other formats are being widely used today to make claims easier to follow and understand. The Patent Office is known to favor most such attempts at clarity, and therefore it is recommended that some format other than a single paragraph be adopted.

One such format, the subparagraph or tabular form, is strongly favored by the Patent Office and is recommended for most if not all claims. (See Claim 1, Section 11.) This form actually helps the apprentice claim drafter, since it is easier to use and he is less likely to make mistakes in recognizing and setting out the elements of the claim. In the subparagraph form, the first word of each element, or main clause, of the claim is indented so as to distinguish clearly between each of the claimed elements. The examples of claims in this book use versions of the subparagraph form.

The colon-semicolon form, in which a colon is inserted after the transitional phrase and semicolons are used between the elements as in Claim 1, is also recommended, particularly with subparagraph claims.

Another form, termed the "outline form," involves using identifying letters, (a), (b) (c), as in an outline, before the recitation of each element, or main clause, whether or not the subparagraph form is used. While this technique is helpful, and is recommended if the subparagraph form is not used, it ordinarily adds little to comprehension where the subparagraph form is used. Wherever the claim drafter believes letters would help in understanding the claim, particularly in complex claims, they should be used. Sometimes letters may help in referring back to elements of previous claims. For example, given a method comprising steps (a) through (e), one might refer in a dependent claims to performing an added step "after step (c)."

SUMMARY—Use the subparagraph form for claims. Make claims as easy as possible for readers to understand and to follow what the elements are. The Examiner will appreciate it, as well as everyone else who ever reads the patent.

Chapter III

APPARATUS OR MACHINE CLAIMS

Section 11—In General

The general rules and procedures discussed in Chapter II will now be illustrated as they pertain to apparatus claims. The word "apparatus" is used generically to denote various machines and devices, including electrical circuits, having cooperating parts which accomplish some useful result, usually some act or operation on an article or workpiece.

Example I–Shaker

Referring specifically to the form of shaker illustrated in Figs. 1 and 2 of Appendix A, Example I, a sample claim specific to that structure (as distinguished from the structure in Fig. 3) reads as follows:

(Preamble)	**1. Apparatus for shaking articles,**
(Transition)	**which comprises:**
(Body of Claim)	**(a)** *a container* for the articles; **(b)** *a base;* **(c)** *a plurality of parallel legs,* **each of which is connected pivotally at one end to the container and at the other end to the base, to support the container for oscillating movement with respect to the base; and** **(d)** *means for oscillating the container* **on the legs to shake the articles.**
(Elements in Subparagraph Form)	**[NOTE — The "elements" of the claim are in italics for illustrative purposes only. The introduction "I claim" is understood, and is not normally written, except as part of a patent application.]**

For comparison, the same claim in single paragraph form (Section 10) reads:

> **1A. Apparatus for shaking articles which comprises a container for the articles, a base, a plurality of parallel legs, each of which is connected pivotally at one end to the container and at the other end to the base, to support the container for oscillating movement with respect to the base, and means for oscillating the container on the legs to shake the articles.**

Note that Claim 1A is much more difficult to follow than the same claim in subparagraph form.

SUMMARY—Use the subparagraph or outline claim form, and watch formal problems, punctuation, grammar, etc., as outlined in Chapter II.

Section 12—Preambles for Apparatus Claims

Claim 1 illustrates one simple type of preamble which is quite common and which can easily be used for most mechanical combination claims. Generally, this type of preamble follows the pattern: "*Apparatus for* performing a specified act or operation on a particular article or workpiece, which comprises:"

The article to be worked on need not be defined in detail, unless such description is important to the functioning of the apparatus or made necessary by the prior art.

The word "apparatus" is frequently used by patent practitioners as a sort of generic expression covering machines or other mechanical devices which perform operations on workpieces; however, phrases such as "a machine," "a device" or "a circuit" may be used where appropriate.

It should be apparent that the drafting of the body of the claim is simpler, and the claim is easier to follow, when the specific operation to be performed and the specific workpiece on which such operation is to be performed are clearly set out in the preamble.

Further examples of this type of preamble follow:

> Apparatus for coating the inside of a tubular workpiece with a liquid thermoplastic resin

> Apparatus for transferring articles from a first conveyor belt to a second conveyor belt running parallel to the first but in the opposite direction

> A device for simultaneously attaching axial leads to opposite ends of an electrical component

> A circuit for detecting discontinuities in the insulation of an insulated wire

In cases where the apparatus has a generic name, that may be used; for example:

> A binary counter

> A self-propelled lawn sprinkler

> A carburetor

> A shaker for articles [an equally acceptable preamble for Claim 1]

Other types of preambles are used for special situations, as discussed in Chapter VII, and in some chemical compound cases (Chapter VI).

Occasionally, one sees a claim such as "In combination, [an A, a B and a C].' This type of preamble should be reserved for inventions so broad that any attempt to name the thing to be claimed would be too narrow. Of course, if Claim 1 on the shaker started out only "In combination," this would be uselessly misleading since the claim itself was intended to be limited to an apparatus for shaking articles. Therefore, there is no reason for not using a normal preamble.

Also, recent cases such as *In re Duva*, 156 USPQ 90 (CCPA 1967), have held that statements in the preamble may not be disregarded in determining patentability. Thus, descriptive preambles can be quite helpful in obtaining allowance of the claim.

The *Duva* case is discussed in more detail in Section 52 on new use claims; preamble limitations.

SUMMARY—Select a descriptive preamble describing the over-all function of the machine to be claimed, either a distinctive name such as "power lawn mower," or a made-up phrase such as "apparatus for [doing a job]."

Section 13—Elements of Apparatus Claims

The "elements" of an apparatus claim are the main structural parts which together make up the combination claimed. As illustrated in Claim 1, the complete description of each element forms the subject matter of a separate clause, or subparagraph, of the claim. The workpiece ("articles" in Claim 1) should be recited in the preamble of the claim, not made an element of the claimed combination.*

One of the most important technical "rules" of form in drafting claims is that it is never proper to introduce a new element of the claim in the middle of the clause describing another element, sometimes called "inferential claiming." Each element must be positively set out in a separate clause. Thus, while it may be quite natural, and good practice in the descriptive portion of the specification, to state: "a container which is connected pivotally to a plurality of parallel legs," it is improper in the claim. The legs are separate elements of the combination, and thus should be positively set out and defined in the claim, as in Claim 1.

Another example:

Wrong: "A lever having a forked end pivoted on a pin mounted between the furcations of the forked end"

---

*Even if it were proper to make the workpiece an element of the combination, one would rarely wish to do so as it would unduly narrow the claim. A machine manufacturer would rarely sell the workpiece along with the machine, thus he would not be a direct infringer [35 U.S.C. §27(a)] of the claim.

Note, the pin is not part of the lever; it is a separate mechanical element.

Correct: "(a) a lever having a forked end; and
(b) a pivot pin mounted between the furcations of the forked end"

Four essential elements *(italicized)* were selected for the combination of Claim 1—(a) the container, (b) the base, (c) the legs and (d) the oscillating means. Note that all of these parts are essential, within the framework of the scope of claim desired, to accomplish the shaking of the articles, and that nothing more is needed. If a narrower claim were desired, the motor, cam and cam follower linkage (together making up the oscillating means) could be made elements of the claim.

For the writing of broad claims, one concentrates on the minimum number of elements essential to the invention. It is also wise, at least in the broadest claims, to concentrate on what a potential infringer might sell, and leave out conventional elements such as power supplies, water supply hoses, compressed air sources, etc., which might not be sold as part of the combination.

There are usually three important things to tell about each element:

(1) What is its name?

(2) What are its constituent parts, if any, or distinctive features; that is, what features are necessary for the purposes of this claim to distinguish this element from any other element of the class?

(3) How are it and its parts cooperatively associated with the other elements or parts to accomplish the desired result? Or, what is the necessary connection and cooperation between the elements and parts? Where pertinent, what does each element do and how does it do it?

One analogy is to think of (1) the elements as islands, (2) the parts of elements an peninsulas, and (3) the statements of connection and cooperation as bridges. When the claim is done, all islands must be connected by bridges. Thus one composes a claim to a complete mechanical combination, or "machine."

SUMMARY—Find the main elements or parts of the machine to be claimed. Make each element the subject of one clause of the body of the claim. The claim must name the elements and tell how they are related to each other physically and co-operatively to do the job stated in the preamble.

The following sections focus on how to do all this.

Section 14—Negative Limitations

In the past, negative limitations, telling what an element is not instead of what it is, were generally considered improper except in unusual cases. However, a notice entitled "Practice Re: Technical Rejections," dated April 30, 1965 (814 O.G.* 715), states that:

> The inclusion of a negative limitation shall not, in itself, be considered a sufficient basis for objection to or rejection of a claim. However, if such a limitation renders the claim unduly broad or indefinite or otherwise results in a failure to point out the invention in the manner contemplated by 35 U.S.C. 112, an appropriate rejection should be made. See also MPEP 706.03(d).

There normally would be no problem that a negative limitation per se would make a claim too broad, indefinite, etc.

Under this practice, descriptions such as "halogen other than fluorine" would presumably be acceptable. Expressions such as "noncircular," "nonmagnetic" or "colorless" have always been accepted, on an emergency basis, because there is no other practical way to state the concept. In view of the former antipathy, it is suggested the negative statements still be avoided except

*O.G. stands herein for the *Official Gazette*, a weekly publication of the Patent Office containing abstracts of patents granted, as well as official notices and other information concerning patents and trademarks. The O.G. is now issued in two separate volumes, one for patents, the other trademarks, with the notices appearing in both.

where it seems the only way, or by far the clearest way, to state the limitation.

In *In re Duva,* 156 USPQ 90, 94 (CCPA 1967), a negative limitation, "absent sufficient CN [cyanide] ions to prevent deposition . . ." was held proper even if a positive expression could have been employed, which was disputed. Further, it was held proper to claim a negative limitation even at the "point of novelty," but there were other points of novelty.

Perhaps negative limitations, under the *Duva* case and the notice cited above, could be used in some cases to avoid the limiting language "consisting" or "consisting essentially" in Section 8. For example, if one's claim covered the combination comprising A+B+C, and the examiner cited A+B+C with a large amount of D, and if it were unobvious to eliminate D, the claim could perhaps be amended to read "comprising A+B+C and absent sufficient D to . . . [hurt the combination]," as in *Duva,* rather than switching to "consisting" or "consisting essentially." Then the claim would cover A+B+C+E, where E is not equivalent to D.

SUMMARY—Avoid negative limitations except in unusual cases where you think they are the clearest way to state the limitation; if questioned, cite the *Duva* case. But in general, tell what an element is, not what it is not.

Section 15—Support in Specification and Drawings

All terms and phrases used in the claims must find ". . . clear support or antecedent basis in the description so that the meaning of the terms in the claims may be ascertainable by reference to the description." Patent Office rule 75(d). That is, the claims must clearly "read on"* the remainder of the specification,

*Patentese, meaning that each technical phrase in the claim must literally describe a corresponding element or connection, etc.,found in the description. Frequently, the claim is literally read word-by-word and the corresponding things found and checked off in the specification, or in an alleged infringing product or drawing of the product. Thus, our client's claim "reads on" an adverse party's product.

with consistent terminology being used so that no ambiguities are present.

This rule traces from the statutory requirement that the claims "particularly point out and distinctly claim"; if it it not followed, the claim will be rejected under section 112 of the statute as "indefinite" or "vague and indefinite." Thus, one must be able to understand what the claim means, and how it is related to the example described in the detailed description.

Generally, best practice is to use the identical words of the claim somewhere in the body of the specification to insure that this requirement is met. For example, if a fastener is used in the machine, comprising a rivet in the specific example illustrated in the application, but one wishes to claim it in some or all claims broadly as "a fastener," the descriptive portion of the specification should so describe it: such as, "a fastener, such as a rivet 10. . . ." Thereafter it is proper merely to refer to it as "the rivet 10." It would be poor practice to refer to a certain element as a lever throughout the detailed description and then call it a bar in the claims.

Similarly, rule 83(a) provides that "the drawing must show every feature of the invention specified in the claims." Thus, for machines, articles of manufacture, or other inventions where an element is capable of illustration in a drawing, it must be shown; however, symbols or labelled boxes, etc., may be used if the element per se is conventional.

On prior Patent Office Agent's Exams, examples of lack of support have included:

1. Parts or features in the claims not described at all in the description;
2. Inconsistent descriptions of parts;
3. Misdescriptive wording in the claims;
4. Ambiguities, where it is not clear which of several elements in the description is intended by a word in the claim.

For special problems in block diagram disclosures in electrical cases, see Sections 32 and 41 (computer programs). The key test is whether or not ". . . a person skilled in the art could make and use the invention without undue experimentation." *In re Scarbrough*, 182 USPQ 298 (CCPA 1974). In theory, this test applies equally well in all classes and types of inventions, mechanical, electrical, chemical; but the problems most frequently arise in complex electronic circuits, particularly block diagram, mean-type disclosures, and most particularly, disclosures concerned with computers.

SUMMARY—Have clear and unambiguous support in the detailed description for all words and phrases in the claim, so that anyone can understand how the claim reads on the description. Also, all structures described in the claim must be illustrated in the drawing, even old or conventional things.

Section 16—Naming the Elements

It is good practice to analyze the structure and select the essential elements to be claimed, with whatever scope is desired, before starting to write a claim. The elements must be assigned names, such as base, container, legs and oscillating means in Claim 1.

The exact name selected for each element is often not critical, as long as the claim drafter is not mistaken. While applicant in theory has the *Alice through the Looking Glass* privilege of making words mean what he wants them to mean, no term may be given a meaning repugnant to its usual meaning. This rule is often stated as "applicant may be his own lexicographer,"* but

---

**See, e.g., In re* Rohrbacker and Kolbe, 128 USPQ 117, 119 (CCPA 1960):

> Within reasonable limits an applicant is his own lexicographer and words used in his claims are to be interpreted in the sense . . . used in his specification. Kennicott v. Holt, 230 F. 717; and Wheeler Salvage Co. v. Rinelli, 295 F. 717.

See also Minneapolis Honeywell Regulator Co. v. Midwestern Instruments, 131 USPQ 402 (7th Cir. 1961).

within limits. Of course, the words used must have "clear support or antecedent basis" in the specification, as mentioned in Section 15. It is very important to make all parts of the specification consistent with the claims. When one wishes to impart a special meaning to a word or phrase appearing in the claims, he should define that word or phrase in the specification; for example "As used in this description and in the appended claims, the word '______ ______' means ______________________." However, do not use ridiculous words such as "gizmo," "widget," or "dingle arm."

Frequently there are various expressions which could be used. For example, in Claim 1, the base could have been called "a support," "a mounting plate," or the like. The container might have been designated "a box" or "a holder."

In most cases, the inventor or a mechanical dictionary can supply the precise name for a part in any specific embodiment. Appendix C contains a glossary of many mechanical terms commonly used in patents. For the broader claims, a generic word is usually needed. If no concrete generic name is available, often a home-made name indicating the function of the part may be used, such as "a rotary member" or "a holder," together with as much description of the part and its function as is necessary. Also "means" clauses are often used to describe an element broadly (see Section 31). Where practical, it is best to give two similar but different elements distinct names, such as "a holding member" and "a support member." In other cases, this is not possible, in which case designations such as "first" or "second" should be used: "a first rotating member, . . . a second rotating member. . . ." Each element must always be described in such a distinctive manner as to clearly distinguish it from other similar or identical elements, as covered in Section 15.

SUMMARY—Select a clear-cut name for each element, based on the detailed specification description where given. Where a broad name is desired functional names such as "a fastener" or "means for moving . . ." should be used.

Section 17—Plural Elements

The number of elements of a given type, if more than one, should also be stated where the number is material to the claim:

> A pair of arms . . .
>
> Three springs . . .
>
> A plurality of rods . . . (used for an indefinite number, two or more). [The word "multiplicity" is often used also, but this may tend to connote a fairly large number, such as "a sieve having a multiplicity of perforations."]
>
> At least five fingers . . . (used where there must be at least five but more would do).

The minimum number of elements necessary for the combination to function properly should be recited. This then covers a larger number where, as is customary, the word "comprising" is used (Section 7). The term "a pair" will cover two or any number greater than two, but it will not cover only one. Where one or more will function, then one merely claims "a" member (singular) and this covers more than one. Optionally, one sometimes sees "at least one ______" or "at least two ______," which is also correct. An alternative statement "one or more" would ordinarily be considered improper under the rule against alternative claiming discussed in Section 21. However, one case, *In re Pavlecka*, 138 USPQ 118 (CCPA 1963), allowed a claim including "a spline or splines."

SUMMARY—State the minimum number of similar elements needed where more than one is *necessary* to the claim. If any number more than one will do, use the phrase "a plurality."

Section 18—Double Inclusion of Elements

One should be careful that precisely the same element is not included in the claim twice under two different names. This is an error known as "double inclusion." Sometimes the problem arises in writing dependent claims (see Section 53), where one might inadvertently add as an apparently new element something already in the parent claim, or one of several earlier claims in a chain of dependent claims. If two elements of a claim contain some or much common structure, it is not double inclusion so long as at least some structure is different. See further comments on this, with respect to "means" clauses, in Section 31.

Example, Claim 1 (Section 11) calls for "means for oscillating the container." If claim 2 recited "A combination as recited in Claim 1, *further comprising* a motor, . . ." it would be improper since the motor is part of the means for oscillating in Claim 1.

This problem comes up rarely in practice, but has been an occasional subject for Agent's Exam questions.

SUMMARY—Do not put the same element in the claim twice under two different names. Watch dependent claims so as not to add as a further element something already included in a previous claim from which the new claim depends.

Section 19—Use of Reference Numerals in Claims

Reference numerals corresponding to the specific elements or parts shown in the drawings may be used in claims. This practice, common in some foreign countries,* has been very rare in the United States. The Oct. 12, 1966, Notice "Guidelines for Drafting a Model Patent Application . . ." (846 O.G. 685) provides for this practice on an optional and nonlimiting basis as follows:

> Reference characters corresponding to elements recited in the detailed description and the drawings may be used in conjunction with the recitation of the same element or group of elements in the claims. The reference characters, however, should be enclosed within parentheses so as to avoid confusion with other numbers or characters which may appear in the claims. The use of reference characters is to be considered as having no effect on the scope of the claim.

---

*For example, Japan and Sweden require numerals throughout the claim, and the Netherlands and Germany in the body of the claim.

See also MPEP 608.01(m). While this technique may seem helpful in interpreting claims as long as the claim scope is not limited by the parenthetical numerals, it is almost never used at present and many attorneys probably consider the practice unsafe. This may well be made mandatory in the future as it obviously would be helpful in interpreting claims.

SUMMARY—Do not use reference characters from the drawings in claims, but it is not wrong to do (if placed in parentheses).

Section 20—Antecedents—Indefiniteness

The first time an element, or part, is mentioned, the indefinite article "a" or "an" should be used, as in Claim 1 "a container," "a base," etc. This practice merely follows normal rules of grammar. A "means for" clause requires no article: "means for oscillating. . . ." When each element or part is referred to again, the definite article should be used as "the container," "the base" or "the oscillating means" in Claim 1. The word 'said" is used by many practitioners rather than "the" to refer back to previously recited elements, sometimes to a previously recited anything. This practice is unobjectionable, although perhaps overly legalistic. If "saids" are used, one should be consistent in the usage. One common style is to use "said" only for the elements themselves, and "the" for everything else. The expression "the said" one sometimes sees is a patent redundancy and should be avoided.

When referring back to an element, it must be perfectly clear which element. The claim must be consistent with itself. For example if two gears have been described in the claim, it is improper to refer back to "said gear"; refer to "said first gear," 'said drive gear," etc. Similarly, if a motor has been recited, do not refer back to "said drive means." In another example, the claim recited "a handle" and then something connected to "a handle"; thus it was not clear whether the first handle was meant or a different one. Such descriptions are "indefinite." It is also improper to describe additional details of an element when referring back; for example, if "a gear" has been recited, it would be improper to refer to "said *plastic* gear." This is also called an "indirect limitation" in MPEP 706.03(d).

In dependent claims, one must be careful to avoid confusion between elements in any parent claim(s) and elements added by the dependent claim.

So far as the CCPA is concerned, all such rejections or objections on matters of claim form must trace from 35 U.S.C. §112, that the subject matter has not been "particularly pointed out and distinctly claimed," meaning that the examiner cannot tell what the claim covers. In *In re Miller,* 169 USPQ 597, 600 (CCPA 1971), the court held that an "indefiniteness" rejection must be based on section 112, and held that the Patent Office could not reject the claim under section 103 (obviousness) and ignore the allegedly indefinite words, citing *In re Wilson,* 165 USPQ 494 (CCPA 1970). Note the *Miller* court's quote:

> *All words* in a claim must be considered in judging the patentability of that claim against the prior act.

This question arises in many contexts, such as preamble limitations (Section 52), mental steps (Section 41), functional language (Section 28), printed matter (Section 62) and others.

Ex parte Schaefer, 171 USPQ 110 (Bd. App. 1970), holds that:

> Omission of some elements of the device [the complete device described in the specification, through the use of the preamble "comprising"—Section 7] makes the claim broad, but not vague, indefinite or misdescriptive.

In other words, the Court and board are saying to the examiner: "reject broad claims on prior art, if you can find any, but not under section 112 as 'indefinite,' etc. Section 112 applies only where you cannot understand what the claim covers." See also "incomplete" claims, Section 63.

In *Norton Co. v. Bendix Corp.,* 171 USPQ 449 (2d Cir. 1971), a claim was held invalid for indefiniteness in the phrases "closely spaced" and "substantial distance." Apparently, these features or relationships were important to novelty, and the specification did not define them. The testimony showed that a potential infringer could not tell, nor could the patentee, just what infringed and what did not.

The cases on indefiniteness can be confusing and may turn on specific facts adduced at trial, long after the claim was written and patented.

SUMMARY—Use "a" or "an" the first time you mention an element or part in a claim, where grammar rules dictate. Use "the" or "said" after that, when referring again to the same element or part. Make sure the claim is consistent with itself, that each "the" or "said" element has one and only one clear antecedent in the claim, and that consistent, definite phraseology is used throughout the claim. In general, make sure the claim is definite and clearly understandable as to what it covers and how it reads on the detailed description and drawing.

Section 21—Alternative Expressions

It is ordinarily improper to use alternative expressions for an element or part in a claim. Thus, it is improper to state: "a spring or a weight for urging the carriage against the stop." (Assume the carriage and stop had been defined.) In effect, this would be two claims. The way to avoid alternative expressions is to find or invent some expression which is generic to both embodiments or species, such as "means for biasing" in the above example. See Section 47 on Markush expressions for a limited exception in certain types of chemical cases.

A Patent Office Notice dated July 23, 1968 "Rejections Not Based on Prior Art," appears to permit some limited use of alternative expression, MPEP 706.03-d:

> Alternative expressions such as "brake or locking device" may make a claim indefinite if the limitation covers two different elements. If two equivalent parts are referred to such as "rods or bars," the alternative expression may be considered proper.

Since the precise boundaries of this are not clear, and since alternatives were previously considered improper per se, it is suggested this device not be used pending further clarification. Note also, the *Pavlecka* case (Section 17) sanctioning "a spline or splines."

Similarly, attempted alternative or hedged expressions like "a drive means, such as a motor," or "a holder, preferably a perforated box," are considered improper. These are alternative and really an attempt to present two different claims, one broad, one narrower, at the same time. Each claim must cover a single combination with an ascertainable scope, not several combinations of different scope. The solution, of course, is to use a broader word for the first claim and, if important, the narrower words or alternate structure in other claims.

This so-called 'rule against alternatives" in claims may have no statutory basis to support it, and thus might fall under a growing line of CCPA cases requiring an express statutory basis for every ground of rejection. (See the discussion of statutory vs. case law grounds of rejection in Section 60 on old combination.)

In *In re Wolfrum and Gold*, 179 USPQ 620 (CCPA-1973), the Court expressly held that a Markush claim to "patentably distinct" species A and B could not be rejected under Section 112. See further discussion of this case in sections 47 and 64. The claim in question was very definitely an alternative claim to groups of compounds A or B, but the Court held that Section 112 would not support such a rejection since it was clear what the applicant intended to claim, and that is all Section 112 requires. Note, there would never be any indefiniteness problem per se in an alternative claim, applicant would clearly intend to claim combination A or combination B, assuming each of the alternatives was clearly defined by itself.

In *In re Haas*, 179 USPQ 623 (CCPA 1973), the Court held that such claims could not be rejected under 35 U.S.C. 101, defining the statutory classes of patentable subject matter. (See discussion of this case, Section 47.)

It is not clear what other statutory clause might support a rejection of an alternative claim, and if all bases for rejections of claims must be based on a specific section of the statute, the Wolfrum and Gold case might open up claim drafting practices to any and all definite forms of alternative claims, such as "a spring or a weight for biasing." There would be no question as to what applicant regards as his invention, either a spring or a weight. The Wolfrum case could terminate the so-called "rule against mechanical Markush groups" (Section 47). By extension, one might be allowed to claim a lawn sprinkler or a popcorn popper, totally different inventions, so long as each was defined clearly, so far as Section 112 is concerned. Whether some other statutory provision would bar this is not known and will await the outcome of the "patentably distinct Markush" cases cited at the end of Section 47.

Even under such a doctrine permitting express alternatives, alternative expressions such as "a spring or the like" might be barred because it would not be definite as to what "or the like" is.

SUMMARY—Avoid alternative expressions, particularly names of parts, like the plague. Make claims definite as to what they cover.

Section 22—Parts or Features of Elements

It is necessary to describe everything about each element that is pertinent to a claim of the scope to be drafted. That is, *where material to the claim,* one must describe such features as (1) the constituent parts of the element and how they are related; (2) details of construction such as apertures, rounded ends, etc.; (3) the size, shape and geometry of the element or any of its parts and (4) the materials of construction used. If the orientation of an element (horizontal, vertical) or its location (above or below some other element) is important, this should be stated.

The foregoing list is illustrative not exclusive. The rule is to describe everything about the element *that is necessary to the claim* and no more. Of course, the claim drafter must distinguish between the elements of the claim and the parts of elements; sometimes an item of structure may be made either a separate element or a part of an element, depending on how the elements are defined. In case of doubt, make the item a separate element.

One problem comes with unbased comparatives, such as "thick," "heavy," "small." These will frequently be considered vague and indefinite by the examiner. The remedy here usually is to relate the property to some other element or to an external standard, such as ". . . smaller than the ———" or "having a specific gravity greater than one." In this area, there is a "rule of reason," and qualifiers such as "resilient," "flexible," etc., are usually accepted without question.

If many features of elements are essential to the claim, they should be described in some logical order usually a matter of choice, using subordinate clauses as necessary. But, watch out for grammar, particularly verb tenses, and make sure the claim continues to read as a proper sentence (Section 4). One example of a description of a moderately complex element follows:

> A carriage on which the bending fingers and the article holder are mounted, the carriage being mounted in the guideway of the base for sliding movement between the first and second stops, the carriage having a transverse guide slot in its upper surface in which the article holder is mounted for relative sliding movement toward and away from the bending fingers, . . . [Note the "the bending fingers," etc., would have been described in previous clauses.]

As much detail is stated as is necessary, in the easiest way possible.

It is ordinarily best to describe all of the salient features of each element in the clause pertaining to that element, even though the purpose for a feature does not appear until later in the claim. However, this is not mandatory, and sometimes other techniques made the claim easier to understand and should be used. Similarly, it is usually best to tell how an element moves or cooperates with other elements at the point where all of the background has been described, rather than waiting until the end of the claim.

It should be noted that Claim 1 does not include any features of elements, as this was not necessary to describe the simple shaker claimed. However, assume that the shaker is a popcorn popper and is to be so claimed, and that the holes in the container (Fig. 1) are important and must be defined.

Clause (a) of Claim 1 might read:

> A container for receiving kernels of corn to be popped, the container having a perforated bottom with apertures smaller in size than the kernels;

Other examples of expressions defining features of elements:

> a disc of resilient material having a peripheral groove . . .
> a relay having two windings . . .
> a lever having a forked end and a rounded end . . . [If only the forked end is important to the combination being claimed, do not mention the rounded end.]
> a gear of electrically insulating material . . .

If an element by definition inherently includes a certain feature, such feature need not be recited and it is proper to refer, without previous mention, to such features as:

> the end of the lever . . .
> the periphery of the disc . . .
> the tines of the fork . . .

In case of doubt, positively describe the feature or part.

SUMMARY—Select those parts or features of each element that are essential to the combination being claimed. Then, describe them in a logical order, preferably following the main description of the element in the same clause of the claim. How many features need to be described and how broadly each should be recited is a matter of claim scope (based largely on the prior art), but the principles are the same as used in selecting the elements and naming them.

Section 23—Claiming Holes

In the situation where a hole is to be described it must not be recited positively. That is, instead of stating "a hole, groove, aperture, recess, slot, etc., in the lever," one must state ". . . the lever having a hole, groove, etc." Thereafter, one can refer to "the hole" or "said hole." This "rule" may seem to make little sense, but it is another founded in antiquity like the single-sentence rule. Maybe someone thought that a hole is nothing—and people shouldn't claim nothing?

Another approach to describing holes is an expression such as ". . . the level having portions defining a hole, groove, etc." The hole is thus defined in terms of the structure which forms it.

One case *In re Newton,* 163 USPQ 34 (CCPA 1969), held that it was proper to claim a hole and its function as a means for performing a function, specifically "means for providing fluid communication between . . . [two members]."

SUMMARY—Do not claim holes positively or make them claim elements. Holes are nothing; you cannot claim nothing. Claim "a [member] having a hole," groove, slot, aperture, etc.

Section 24—Order of Elements

The elements of the claim should be presented in some logical order. Often, there are several orders that make sense, and any one may be selected. The order used in Claim 1 is a "functional" order, starting with the element which first contacts the workpiece (the container) and proceeding along functional lines to describe the remaining elements.

Another order which is often used is a "structural" order, starting first with the base, or the source of power, and proceeding along structural lines to describe the remaining elements. In structural order, Claim 1 would read:

> **1B. Apparatus for shaking articles, which comprises:**
> **(a) a base;**
> **(b) a plurality of parallel legs, each of which is connected pivotally at one end of the base;**
> **(c) a container for the articles connected pivotally to the other ends of the legs, so that the legs support the container for oscillating movement with respect to the base; and**

(d) means for oscillating the container on the legs to shake the articles.

It should be noted that exactly the same structure and movements have been described, only more words are required. The structural order is very common, and is a fairly easy order to follow. It may be used always, or, preferably, whenever no more logical order occurs to the claim drafter. With long mechanical drives, and various electrical circuits, it is often preferable to start with the motor or power source and work toward the end of the drive or circuit, describing the motions or functions as one proceeds. It is equally proper, and sometimes convenient, to start at the output and work backwards.

It should be noted that Claim 1 would be illogical and difficult to follow if one attempted to start with the legs or with the means for oscillating.

SUMMARY—Describe the elements in some logical order.

Section 25—Tying the Elements Together

It is very important that the essential cooperation between each element of the claim and the other elements with which it cooperates be specified. When complete, the claim must define the direct or indirect cooperation of each element with every other element of the combination. If no such cooperation is stated, the claim will usually be rejected for this reason alone; for example, as being drawn to "a mere catalog of elements" or, more graphically, as "reading on so many parts lying in a box." This is sometimes called an "aggregation," but what is really meant in such a rejection is that the combination is aggregative *as claimed.* A real "aggregation" relates to a defect in the structure (the parts do not cooperate) rather than any problem in claim drafting. (See Section 61.) The claim must be to an assembled, operable combination, not to a mere parts list such as one might find in the corner of a production drawing. The words of connection, cooperation, etc., may well be regarded as the glue which must hold the claims together.

This rule follows from court decisions construing the word "machine" in the statute, now 35 U.S.C. §101, setting out the classes of things that can be patented, as explained in Section 3. Machines can be; parts in a box cannot.

Of course, if one part were novel, it could be patented by itself, but not in aggregation with other parts. A "machine" is an assembled, operate combination of parts or machine elements in place ready to do a job.

Example—Claim 1 drafted as an aggregation or catalog of elements:

> Apparatus for shaking articles, which comprises: a container, a base, a plurality of legs, and means for oscillating the container.

A proper claim *includes* and starts with a parts list, as above, involving the selection and naming of the elements, as described in preceding Sections 13-24; but it must also tie the elements together so as to make up a complete, operable machine. See the *Adams* case and others cited in Section 61 on aggregation to the effect that the necessary cooperation need not be "direct mechanical interconnection"; the elements may function independently "so long as the over-all result has utility and is unobvious."

While it is difficult to set out ground rules for writing machine claims *in vacuo*, a good general rule might be that each element or part of an element must be connected or related functionally to at least one other element or part, and all elements must tie together into a unit through one or more such individual connections between elements. Thus, one might have five elements A to E connected many ways, such as

```
A—B—C
  |
  |
  D—E.
```

In this example, it is necessary to connect the group D–E to the previous group A–B–C, such as by connecting D to B as well as to E. There are often many connections, such as

Do not leave even one element or part hanging in air with no apparent connection to anything else, and no apparent function in the combination. For example, do not describe "a lever having a forked end," and then fail to recite any purpose for the forked end. It is better to err on the side of stating too much connection and cooperation between elements, rather than running the risk of defining an unintegrated or incomplete structure. Think of the elements as islands, the parts of elements as peninsulas, and statements of connection or cooperation as bridges; then, make sure when the claim is done that each island and peninsula is connected directly or indirectly to every other island or peninsula by bridges.

One trick in making sure the elements are tied together is to draw a diagrammatic sketch, or "stick picture," of what the claim states, and only that. Make the picture as different from the specific example in the drawings as the words permit. The picture should depict more clearly than words if some element, feature or "glue" is missing,* or if necessary features have been omitted, or unnecessary features included, etc.

---

*The Patent Office also suggests that the examiners do this in making their search. See MPEP 904.01, 01(a), (b) and (c)—Appendix D. They must search for undisclosed structures which the claim also covers, in addition to the disclosed structure. Most mechanical claims cover many, usually an infinite number of, possible structures.

Example, stick picture of Claim 1, Section 11, to the shaker:

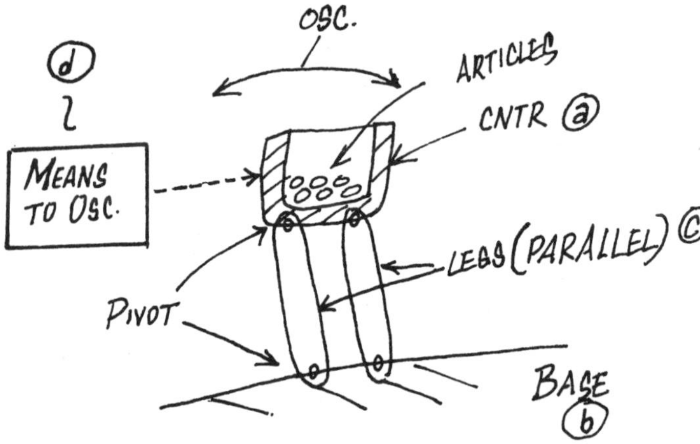

This crude sketch diagrams one simple example of the elements of Claim 1, and shows how they are connected.

SUMMARY—Tie the elements together in the claim; claim machines, not parts. Do not leave even one element with no connection to another, or with no apparent purpose in the claimed combination. If it has no purpose in the combination claimed, it can probably be left out.

Section 26—Structural Connection

A structural connection between the elements (a), (b) and (c) of Claim 1 is found in the expression "each of which is connected pivotally. . . ." This ties the first three elements together mechanically. The "means" clause automatically carries its own inherent structural and operational connection with whatever element is the object of the means clause. Thus, it is implicit in the recitation "means for oscillating the container" that some part of such means must engage the container or something connected to the container to accomplish the function. This need not be stated expressly, such as "means engaging the container for oscillating. . . ."

Some examples of structural connection statements:

> a turntable *on which* the barrel is *mounted;*
> a rotary cam *fixed to* one end of said shaft;
> a cam follower *engaging* said cam . . .
> a capacitor *electrically connected* to the emitter of said transistor . . .
> a coil spring *positioned between* said clutch plate and said base . . ..
> means for mounting the bending fingers on the base *for lateral movement* with respect to the first and second clamps . . . [Note the means for clauses inherently contain and define the necessary physical connections, thus are very frequently used to set out connections, particularly conventional connections, such as mounting, guiding, fastening, etc.]
> a worm gear *in mesh with* the drive gear . . .

Normally, statements of physical or mechanical connection are fairly easy to write. A problem, as with elements or parts of elements, is how broadly to claim the connection, and this of course depends largely on the prior art. In most mechanical cases, the precise manner—or srtucture—of a connection is not critical to novelty or unobviousness, in which case relatively broad words are used to state the connection, such as "mounted on" rather than "fixed to" or "bolted to," etc. Very often means clauses (Section 31) are used for conventional mountings, connections, etc. in both machine and electrical circuit cases (Section 32).

SUMMARY—Connect the claim elements structurally, as required to make up a complete and operable combination. Use relatively broad words of connection where the prior art permits.

Section 27—Functional or Operational Expressions

In addition to the structural cooperation, it is good practice to specify the functional or operational cooperation between the elements, where this can be done without unduly limiting the claim. When this is done, the claim not only tells what the parts are and how they are mechanically interconnected or associated, it tells how they function together and operate on the workpiece to accomplish the result stated in the preamble.

Functional, or operational, connective in claim 1 are such expressions as "for the articles" in clause (a), "to support the container for oscillating movement with respect to the base," in clause (c), and "to shake the articles" in clause (d).

Try to make each independent claim a complete, self-contained unit, comprehensible by itself.

The reader may have heard statements derogatory of functional expressions, and may wonder if they should be avoided altogether. The answer is—definitely no! When properly used, statements of function or operation are usually welcomed by the Patent Office. When not used to excess or to introduce unnecessary limitations into the claim, they make the claim more definite and easy to understand without referring to the specification.

Most problems with so-called "functional statements" come when an attempt is made to predicate patentability on a purely functional statement, or to present extremely broad claims.

There is never any objection to functional statements that merely set forth the movements, actions or results which necessarily follow from the structure previously recited. Thus, in claim 1, the capability of the container for oscillating movement follows once the double-pivoted mounting of the container on the base has been stated. No magic words are necessary for functional statements. Such expressions as "so that," "for," "in order to" are typical. The words "whereby" and "thereby" are often used, but have assumed stylized meanings described in Section 29. Also, "means for" clauses are very commonly used, Section 31.

Some examples of straightforward, noncontroversial functional or cooperative statements:

a container *for* the articles . . . ["for" is very commonly used] to *support* the container *for oscillating movement* . . .

a turntable [element] on which the barrel [workpiece] is

mounted [structural connection] *for rotation therewith* [cooperation or function] . . .

means for *reciprocating* the strand guide *so that* it moves . . . [in a stated way]. [means clauses are very common in stating cooperative relations (Section 31)].

a pulse counter *responsive* to each pulse of current . . . *for counting* . . .

There are many different forms for this, some special ones of which will be covered in the following sections and further examples. As usual, and as with virtually *every word in the claim*, the scope should be checked carefully. Make sure every word is really needed, in the broader claims.

Watch vague and indefinite statements of cooperation, particularly the phrase "adapted to," which is likely to be objected to by the Patent Office as "insufficient structure to support functional statement." This phraseology has been criticized on Patent Office Agent's Exams. The remedy is to use a more specific word such as "mounted on," or often simply "for" doing something. Alternatively, use a "means for" clause under the guidelines in Section 31. In *Ex parte Roggenburk*, 172 USPQ 82 (Bd. App. 1970), the board held that a functional expression, "sealingly engaging," was an improper functional statement, but that a "means for" clause of exactly the same scope would have been all right. Whether such seemingly formalistic Patent Office "rules" could stand up to recent CCPA cases cited at the end of Section 28 is doubtful, but it is best to comply with the older doctrines and forms, where possible without sacrificing real scope.

SUMMARY—Relate the claim elements functionally to each other. That is, tell how the parts move or cooperate with each other to accomplish the overall result stated in the preamble. Tell the following things where applicable about each element:

a) What is it? (name, Sections 13 and 16; and parts, Section 22);
b) Where is it? (physical cooperation or location, Sections 25-26);
c) What does it do? (Sections 27-31); and
d) How does it do what is does? (Sections 27-31).

But, beware of functional statements that make the claim overly broad (Sections 28, 29, 31) or violate other rules, as by being vague and indefinite (Section 20).

Section 28—Claiming Desired Results; Overly Broad Functional Statements

The main problem with so-called "functional statements" comes when one attempts to use them to present ultra-broad claims. One example of this is when one is trying to claim a desirable end result broadly. detached from the specific mechanisms or steps for achieving that result. An example cited by the Patent Office* is a claim reading: "A woolen cloth having a tendancy to wear rough rather than smooth," meaning that it will not become shiny as a result of wear! This tells what the cloth does, the desirable end result, but not how the result is accomplished (decreasing the animal grease content and adding silk threads). The court held, "This claim . . . describes, imperfectly and too broadly. . . . It is also functional, describing a result only and not a process." This type of claim may be variously rejected as being "functional," "too broad" or "nonstatutory" (it does not "particularly point out and distinctly claim" under 35 U.S.C. §112).

It may be unfortunate that the phrase "functional" is sometimes used for this type of rejection, which really concerns over-claiming and not anything wrong with the functional statement itself. For example, if the claim to the woolen cloth had first described its physical structure or novel properties, or the process of manufacture if the physical structure could not be defined (see Section 43 on product-by-process claims), there would have been no objection to the functional statement about "wearing rough"; in fact, that statement would have been most helpful to understanding the claim and, most likely, in showing unobviousness.

---

*MPEP 706.03(c) from *In re* Fuller, 1929 C.D. [Decisions of the Commissioner of Patents] 172; 388 O.G. 279; 35 F.2d. 62 (CCPA 1929).

Another example: in *Knapp v. Morss*, 150 U.S. 221 (1893), the Supreme Court stated:

> The use and purpose sought to be accomplished by the Hall patent was the radial expansion of the dress form, but it is well settled by the authorities that the end or purpose sought to be accomplished by the device is not the subject of a patent. The invention covered thereby must consist of new and useful means of obtaining that end. In other words, the subject of a patent is the device or mechanical means by which the desired result is secured.

Thus, the problem is not with functional statements per se but with claiming too broadly. In particular, in mechanical claims, the examiner will usually argue that the recited structure itself must contain novelty over the prior act. Unquestionably functional recitations help to sell the claim in many cases once novel structure has been described.

These principles were well stated by Robinson in 1890, sec. 150:

> Thus excluding from the sphere of the invention
>
> (a) the principle or force which it employs,
> (b) the function it performs, and
> (c) the effect which it produces,
>
> we see that the complete result of an inventive act consists in
>
> (d) an idea of means, embodied in some instrument [machine, article of manufacture or composition] or operation [method], and capable, when brought in contact with its proper object [workpiece], of performing certain functions and thereby producing in the object certain definite effects. If any of these essential requisites are wanting, there can be no [patentable] invention.

Probably the classic case in claiming too broadly, and claiming only desired results, is *O'Reilly v. Morse*, 56 U.S. (15 How.) 62 (1853), on the printing telegraph. Morse's claim 8 covered:

> . . . the use of the motive power of the electric or galvanic current, which I call electro-magnetism, however developed, for marking or printing intelligible characters, signs, or letters, at any distance. . . .

This was held invalid by the Supreme Court; one cannot merely claim the desired end result to be accomplished, divorced from the means for accomplishing the result.

A fairly recent example of this doctrine, by the Patent Office board of appeals, is *Ex parte Slub*, 157 USPQ 172 (Bd. App. 1967). In the *Slub* case, the expression "a liquefiable substance having a liquefication temperature from about 40° C. to about 300° C. and being compatible with the ingredient in the powdered detergent composition" (broadly stated in the claim as "a powdered detergent composition") was rejected as "too broad," as "functional," and also as "vague and indefinite," citing cases.

While this was a processes claim involving a key functional description of a composition of matter used in making a new composition of two elements, the principles of the case apply to any kind of claim: that is, any kind of technology and any class of claim. The board held this bad for several reasons:

1. Improper to recite compounds by what they do rather than what they are [*cf.* CCPA cases cited later in this section]
2. Reads on inoperative species—materials that would not work in the composition such as low-melting metals (see Section 46)
3. Claim not supported by the disclosure since only ten limited examples of compounds were given.

A good example of the difference between claiming a function added to a system and claiming merely the desired end result is given by Donald R. Johnson in *The Art of Drafting Patent Claims* 111-12: (Jackson *et al.*, eds., PLI 1966)*:

> I will illustrate by referring to the precipitation of solid wax from an organic solution. This precipitation of the wax is accomplished by cooling the solution in a heat exchanger. How-

*This excellent book resulted from a PLI seminar on claim drafting in 1962, representing the combined efforts of twenty-nine skilled patent attorneys. It is now out of print.

> ever, a problem is involved in the deposition of solid wax on the heat exchanger surfaces and in some cases the plugging up of the apparatus.
>
> What the inventor conceived as a solution to the problem was an incorporation into the system of a surface active agent which would form a film on the heat exchanger surface and prevent the deposition of the wax. The inventive concept here was in the form of a function to be added to the system. . . .
>
> However, the prior art situation in this case did not show the use of any surfactant in the particular system claimed. The art did show a surfactant in a related system, in which solid wax was precipitated from a liquid by cooling, but in which there were two immiscible liquid phases, and in which the surfactant and the solid wax were concentrated at the interface between the two liquid phases. In this circumstance it was, of course, necessary for the inventor to distinguish the system to which the surfactant was added from that disclosed in the art. Once this was done, it was possible to claim the surfactant generally, as one capable of forming a film on the heat exchange surface.
>
> This illustrates a proper case of functional claiming. It also illustrates a case where the inventive concept is initially in terms of a function to be added to the system. This is a strong argument in favor of defining the added material functionally. However, it is necessary to distinguish between a function of this sort and the ultimate desired effect. In this case the ultimate desired effect was preventing the deposition of wax, and it certainly could not be claimed in this fashion, i.e., as simply a means for preventing such deposition.

Within these general rules of ultra-broad or indefinite claims, claiming only end results or desired principles, the law is not very clear as to just what kinds of broad functional statements can be permitted (patentable), and what cannot. The Patent Office tends to reject broad "functional" claims for any of several reasons, but the CCPA has been increasingly liberal lately in allowing relatively broad functional statements and, in particular, requiring the Patent Office to be very specific as to exactly which section of the statute the rejection is based on. General "catchword" rejections such as "too broad," "unduly functional," "not fairly based on the disclosure," etc. will no longer suffice.

In *In re Echerd*, 176 USPQ 321 (CCPA 1973), the court held

that "there is nothing inherently wrong in defining something by what it does rather than what it is." The key limitations in question were:

> having sufficient flexibility and wet strength to permit . . .

and

> having sufficient adhesive characteristics to firmly bond . . .

To the same effect are *In re Swinehart and Sfiligoj*, 169 USPQ 226 (CCPA 1971); *In re Fuetterer*, 138 USPQ 217 (CCPA 1963); and *In re Ludke and Sloan*, 169 USPQ 563 (CCPA 1971). The court has been holding recently that no limitation or wording anywhere in the claim can be ignored in determining patentability. In the *Echerd* case, as typical of a great many cases in the past, the Patent Office rejected a claim as anticipated by prior art, or obvious, where all of the specific *structure* claimed was old and the novelty resided solely in function (or other objectionable) statement, such as negative limitations (Section 14), or mental steps (Section 41). The court is now holding all such rejections improper as not consistent with the statute.

In the *Ludke* case, the claim was directed to a parachute canopy comprising old elements A and B, with:

> . . . said plurality of the lines [B] *providing* a radial separation between each of said panels [A] upon deployment [of the parachute] *creating* a region of high porosity between each of said panels *such that* the critical velocity . . . will be less than . . . *whereby* said parachute will sequentially open and *thus* gradually deaccelerate.—
>
> [Note the claim form uses almost all of the functional expressions known (except "means for") one after the other (in paraphrase):]
>
> [said B]
> *providing* . . . [a stated physical relationship, in operation],
> *creating* . . . [a physical property]
> *such that* . . . [a functional relationship is achieved]
> *whereby* . . . [an effect happens]
> *and thus* . . . [a desired end result is achieved].

This may be a classic in functional language.

The court held that there was nothing wrong with the functional language, citing the *Swinehart* case, but affirmed a different (anticipation) rejection that applicants had not proven that the same functions did not happen in a prior art reference. Thus, even with broad functional language acceptable under these cases, the claim must still pass other tests, particular prior art tests, and one must be prepared to prove that his new functions are novel in view of the prior art; that is, not inherently present in the prior art.

See also Section 64, vague and indefinite claims, and In re Wolfrum and Fold, discussed therein.

In *In re Halleck*, 164 USPQ 647 (CCPA 1970), a chemical-new-use type of case, the phrase "an effective amount of [compound X] for [performing a desired function]" was held proper. See new use claims, Section 52.

In the *Kockum Industries* case, cited in Section 31, the court held that functional expressions were proper at the point of novelty, so long as the specification was clear as to what the words meant and how the function was achieved. See discussion of "functional at the point of novelty" rejections in Section 31, on means claims.

Exactly how far such doctrines can be carried, and whether other courts will follow the apparent nullification of old case-law claim doctrines is not certain. See further comments on such trends by the CCPA under Section 60 on old combination.

See also specific comments under Section 31, means clauses.

SUMMARY—Beware of overly broad functional statements, particularly those claiming only desired end results. In practice, scrutinize this topic and the prior art carefully, as many kinds of functional statement may now be permissible under recent CCPA cases, particularly defining an element or feature by what it does rather than by what it is.

Section 29—"Whereby" Clauses

"Whereby" and "thereby" clauses have come in for quite a bit of judicial construction. They are entirely unobjectionable when properly used, and are really quite helpful. A whereby clause is proper when it merely describes a function or operation which *necessarily* follows from the previously recited structure. Such a clause is improper if the function does not necessarily follow, as in such a case the claim drafter is trying to imply structural or cooperational relationships. The cases are practically unanimous in holding that the function stated in a whereby clause cannot be considered to determine patentability of the claim. Therefore, equate "whereby" with "it follows from the foregoing that. . . ."

A safe rule for whereby clauses is to delete the clause and substitute a period; then ask, does the claim still have structural novelty and adequate cooperation among elements? If so, the clause is probably good.

One example of a whereby clause, used in connection with the popcorn popper discussed in Section 22:

> A container for the articles, having apertured walls, the apertures of which are smaller in size than the articles to be shaken *whereby the articles are retained in the container as they are shaken;*

The retaining function necessarily follows, *whereby* the clause is proper. Contrast the foregoing clause with the following: "an apertured container for the articles *whereby the articles are retained in the container as they are shaken.* Even though the same whereby clause is used, it is now improper because it attempts to define a structural relationship (the relative sizes of the apertures and the articles) in purely functional terms.

Whereby clauses, and other functional clauses, can be used (or avoided) equally well in method claims; see Claim 6 in Section 40 for an example of a "method whereby."

The Patent Office does not always object to "bad (or structure-implying) wherebys," and one sees them fairly often in issued patents. In another example, the invention involved the discovery that a metal article would stick to a sheet of a particular resin, if pressed against the sheet, by a vacuum effect not clearly understood. The claim recited: "Placing the article against the sheet of . . . (X resin) whereby the article adheres. . . ." Note this "whereby" is implying the manner of placing, which implies pressing or some similar positive step. "Placing the article against the sheet . . . in such manner that. . . ." would be an equivalent functional expression. Note that this latter expression might conceivably be objected to as too broad or functional, but at worst it would be no more objectionable on that score than the same type of expression via a whereby clause. But the whereby clause might also be objected to as a matter of form or, worse, might not be considered in determining patentability.

This "rule" seems entirely a matter of form not substance, based on an arbitrary definition of the word "whereby." The same claim scope can usually be obtained with other expressions, such as "so that," "for," or "means for." Such a doctrine might not stand up under recent CCPA cases cited in Section 28, but there is no point in generating controversy where none is needed.

SUMMARY—Either avoid whereby clauses completely, or make sure the function stated as the object of the whereby clause absolutely, 100 percent necessarily follows from the previously recited structure in the claim. Other words will do the same job, and do it as well or better in most instances.

Section 30—Location of Functional Clauses

As to claim form, cooperative or functional clauses (such as "so that," "for," "whereby" clauses) may be used either:

(1) at the end of the description of a particular element, provided everything necessary to the functional clause has then been set out; or

(2) at the end of the claim where all that is necessary to the statement has not been set out until the last element has been described.

Type 1 is preferred, where applicable, as it makes the claim easier to follow. Also, one is less likely to be accused of functional claiming when the functions are set out one at a time, rather than, for example, when a long whereby clause is placed at the end.

SUMMARY—Put functional clauses where you think most logical.

Section 31—"Means" Clauses

The reader will note that the following "means" clause has been used in Claim 1: "Means for oscillating the container on the legs to shake the articles."

Means clauses have come under some criticism in the past, particularly when used as a vehicle to present ultrabroad or functional claims.

One Patent Office example of a means clause being too broad is the claim: "In a device of the class described, means for forcing a flow of air while preventing injury to the operator." (From the August 1963 agent's examination.) The device disclosed was a fan with soft rubber blades. This claim is similar to the "woolen cloth" claim described in Section 28: too broad—it does not particularly point out and distinctly claim the invention. It is attempting to claim the desirable end result only, not the way in which the result is accomplished. This type of case is less an adverse decision on means clauses than on overly broad claims generally. In general, one cannot use a means clause to do what one cannot do otherwise; obtain fantastic claims far broader than the invention.

With such outer "No-No" boundaries in mind, it is clear there is no particular problem in using means clauses to describe generally conventional elements of a mechanical combination, and such clauses are very widely used. The outer periphery of permissible uses for means clauses is somewhat uncertain, and new cases on the subject appear frequently.

As a starting point, there is no possible objection to means expressions per se. They are expressly authorized by the statute (35 U.S.C. §112), third paragraph:

> An element in a claim for a combination may be expressed as a *means* . . . *for performing a specified function* without the recital of structure . . . in support thereof. (Emphasis added to illustrate the form.)

Note the statutory language "claim for a *combination.*" Thus, a single element claim such as the following cannot employ means plus function language.

> Apparatus for shaking articles in a container, which comprises: means for oscillating the container to shake the articles.

Note that the "means for forcing air" claim was a "single means" claim, and would also be objectionable on that score. But, adding "a base" or other conventional element would not have helped that claim.

This is also discussed in MPEP 706.03(c), where the following claim from *Ex parte Bullock*, 1907 C.D. 93, 127 O.G. 1580, is stated to be improper:

> In a device of the class described, means for transferring clothes-carrying rods from one position and depositing them on a suitable support.

By statutory construction (35 U.S.C. §112), the means clause ". . . shall be construed to cover the corresponding structure . . . described in the specification and equivalents thereof." Thus, the scope of the claim is as broad as the invention. Note that this is the broadest protection one would ever be entitled to in any event. However, this is for the purpose of determining what *infringes* the claim after granting, not what anticipates for the purpose of patenting, according to *In re Lundberg and Zuschlag*, 113 USPQ 530, 534 (CCPA 1957). There, the court concluded that applicant's claim read on the prior art, thus applicant could not argue that the prior art was not equivalent. The court ruled that this would not be "distinctly claiming" under the second paragraph of 35 USC §112.

Most mechanical claims are, or can be made to be, directed to a combination of elements, in which case there is no problem on this score. A possible problem in this area is with an improvement of Jepson-type claim (see Section 54), where, in the body of the claim, a single new element might be claimed which cooperates with several old elements in the preamble to make up a complete machine or apparatus. As noted in Section 54, it is thought that such a claim is truly a claim to a combination, so that the body of the claim could properly consist of a single means expression. However, there may be some difference of opinion on this score, so it might be good tactics to put at least one other element, means or otherwise, in the body of the claim.

As to overly broad means claims, the Supreme Court held in 1946 that a claim was invalid as indefinite and too broad where it used broad means plus function language at what the court considered to be "the precise point of novelty" of the claim. *Halliburton Oil Well Cementing Co. v. Walker*, 329 U.S. 1, 71 USPQ 175 (1946).

The clause in question read:

> means associated with said pressure responsive device for tuning said receiving means to the frequency of echoes from the tuning collars of said tuning section to clearly distinguish the echoes of said couplings from each other.

While the stated function apparently was technically novel, the court felt the patentee should be limited to claiming his specific means (a tuned acoustical pipe) rather than all possible means, some of which might be later invented.

Note that this case came up before the 1952 statute, and was undoubtedly one of the items which led to the new paragraph of section 112 dealing with means clauses. Means clauses were common before the statute, as a matter of practice which had grown up, but the *Halliburton* case cast doubt as to their worth. Many commentators believe the statute was intended to overrule the *Halliburton* case.

For example, Judge Giles S. Rich* of the CCPA in *Encyclo-*

*These remarks were written before Judge Rich was appointed to the CCPA. As an attorney, he was a member of the drafting committee which wrote the 1952 patent statute.

pedia of Patent Practice and Invention Management 17 (R. Calvert, ed., 1964), said:

> And I would assume that this [means clause in a combination claim] is authorized even if the particular element or step is at the exact point of novelty. You will recognize its applicability to *Halliburton* . . . *v. Walker*. . . .

In *In re Lundberg and Zuschlag,* cited earlier, the CCPA came close to holding that 35 U.S.C. §112 overruled the *Halliburton* case, though this was not necessary to the decision:

> As correctly stated by appellants in their brief, this paragraph was designed, at least in part to modify or overrule such decisions as Halliburton. . . .

In *Ex parte Ball and Hair,* 99 USPQ 146, 148 (Bd. App. 1954), the board indicated, vaguely, that ". . . some measure of greater liberality in the use of functional expressions in the definition of elements in proper combination claims is authorized by section 112 than has been permitted by some of the stricter decisions of the courts in the past." Some means-plus-function claims were allowed, where the function stated in the claim was "distinctly unlike any function which is or could possibly be performed" by the reference. This seems to be allowance of a means-plus-function claim at the precise point of novelty. Other means claims were rejected, primarily because the function was not clearly stated, and thus did not comply with the second paragraph of section 112.

In *Ex parte Mayer,* 111 USPQ 109 (Bd. App. 1956), the board expressly held that there is no objection to a means plus function clause ". . . merely because it is at exact point of novelty in a combination claim . . . ," citing the *Ball and Hair* case. In this case the acceptable clause was:

> means responsive to said residual of potential to disable said discharge means for a period greater than the interval between pulses and sufficient to permit normal voltage on said network to be restored before said network is again discharged by said discharge means.

See also *Ex parte Roggenburk*, 172 USPQ 82 (Bd. App. 1970), for another board of appeals case expressly so holding, but noting that "some circuit courts" may have doubts on the question. Also, *Kockum Industries, Inc. v. Salem Equipment, Inc.*, 175 USPQ 81 (9th Cir. 1972), held that the revision to 35 U.S.C. §112 overruled *General Electric Co. v. Wabash Appliance Corp.*, 304 U.S. 364 (1938), on a claim apparently using functional language other than "means for." Note that the statute gets around what seems to be the Supreme Court's main reason for objecting to the broad clause: that it would cover nonequivalent structures, in that the coverage under 35 U.S.C. §112 is expressly limited to the specific means shown, plus equivalents. At best, this point may be regarded as unsettled.

One CCPA case, *In re Chandler*, 117 USPQ 361 (1958), goes one step further than allowing a means plus function clause at the point of novelty. The *Halliburton* case was not mentioned. This case holds that a "means for doing something . . . so that" clause is proper and patentable where the sole point of novelty follows the expression "so that." In other words, the general idea of means for doing the thing was old, but not for doing it in the specified way. This case may represent the outer border of permissible means clauses.

The clause in question read:

> . . . and *means* responsive to said movement *for regulating* the propulsive power of said engine, in accordance with said movement, *so that* said aircraft is propelled at a definite, selected speed, corresponding to the position of said engine relative to said aircraft, throughout the speed range of said aircraft. (117 USPQ at 361, emphasis added.)

In holding the claims patentable the court stated,

> Accordingly, if claim 2 distinguishes patentably over Goddard, it must be because of the recitation, in its final lines, of "means responsive to said movement for regulating propulsive power of said engine, in accordance with said movement, so that said aircraft is propelled at a definite, selected speed" . . . 117 USPQ at 364.

> The examiner held that the words beginning with 'so that' in the quoted expression were merely a functional expression equivalent to the "whereby" clause considered in *In re Lamb*, 64 U.S.P.Q. 241 (C.C.P.A. 1944), and hence could not have patentable significance. [Note Section 29.]
>
> We are of the opinion that the expression beginning with "so that" is not merely functional, but constitutes a part of the definition of the "means responsive to said movement." . . . Such a definition conforms to the provision of 35 U.S.C. 112 that an element in a claim for combination "may be expressed as a means or step for performing a specified function without the recital of structure, material or acts in support thereof." The instant situation differs from the presented in *In re Lamb*. There the "whereby" clause did not constitute a part of the definition of any means but merely stated a function which did not necessarily follow from the apparatus recited in the claim. [Note how this decision highlights the difference between "means" and "whereby."]

Similarly, in *In re Wilson and Hutton*, 149 USPQ 523, 527 (CCPA 1960), the court held "means for delivering materials" at stated pressures was a positive limitation which had to be considered (favorably to applicants).

See also *Ex parte Roggenburk*, cited above and in Section 27, that a means for clause would be allowable, but not an equivalent functional clause without the magic words "means for." See also *In re Atwood*, 148 USPQ 203 (CCPA 1966).

Because of the previous controversy, and the fact that this area of the law should be regarded with caution (the Supreme Court has not spoken on means clauses since 1946), it might be wise to avoid means plus function language, where possible, at what might possibly be construed to be the "precise point of novelty" of the claim. For example, if all but one of the elements of a claim are old and if a similar combination is old in the art, the point of novelty in the claim probably resides in the construction of one element. In this type of situation, means expressions may well give trouble.

On the other hand, means clauses are routine where it is the function of the element which is important *and* where various other specific constructions could be used. Thus, in Example I, the oscillating means illustrated includes a motor, cam and cam-follower linkage, but it is obvious that various other common arrangements would be equally suitable, such as a piston and cylinder. It should be clear that the essential thing to the combination is *that* the container be oscillated, not how. Since many common structures could be employed to do this job, this is the ideal time for a means clause.

In this example, it is difficult to draw a generic expression, other than a means clause, covering both the motor-cam arrangement and a piston-cylinder arrangement, as well as any other conventional arrangement for oscillating a member. As was mentioned in Section 21, an alternative expression such as "cam or cylinder" cannot be used, even if that were considered broad enough. A generic expression must be found. Other attempted generic expressions such as "a mechanism for oscillating . . ." or "a mechanical device for oscillating . . ." are just as subject to an objection, if any, for undue breadth as is a means clause. However, the means clause has the express sanction of the statute, whereas the other expressions do not. Therefore, in this type of situation, it is recommended that means clause be used.

In writing means clauses, as many qualifying words or expressions should be employed in the means clause as are necessary to limit the claim to the scope desired. Thus, one might recite such expressions as:

> resilient means, connected between the carriage and the base, for urging the carriage against the stop;

or

> means, actuated by the carriage at the end of its forward movement, for moving the bending fingers into contact with the carriage.

In these fragmentary expressions, it should be noted that such elements as "the carriage" and "the bending fingers" must have been recited in previous elements of such claims, as mentioned in Section 20 on antecedents. Where no such qualifying expressions are important, none should be used.

It is recommended that one use the exact statutory language "means for . . . (performing an act)" rather than possibly equivalent expressions such as "fastener means." One board of appeals case, *Ex parte Klumb*, 159 USPQ 694 (1967) held that "wing means" was improper as there was no function stated as performed. "What is means for winging?" the board wanted to know.

Although one should avoid the practice where possible, it is permissible to claim "means for [doing thing A], including means for [doing thing B]" if B is a part of A. For example, in patent 1,971,193, we find:

> Means for causing oscillations to be produced in said polyphase circuit having a frequency dependent on the tuning in said polyphase circuit said means [assume no unclarity] including means for producing a magnetic field between said anodes and cathode.

This may be necessary to avoid double inclusion of elements (Section 18) where they are partially overlapping or where one means includes another.

In referring back to a previously recited means element, later in the claim (see Section 20—antecedents), one merely gives it a convenient distinctive name such as "the reciprocating means" or "the container-reciprocating means." The exact choice is not critical as long as there is no possible confusion with other means elements. Wherever possible, it is best to avoid identifying a means only as "first means," "second means," etc.

It is recommended that means expressions be avoided where there is a definite generic word of the same scope available. Thus, in Example 1, "a base" is fully generic, and there is no need to say "base means," "means for supporting" or the like. Also, "a container" is generic, so there is no need for "container means" or "means for containing." Note that, in these situations, the word "means" does not add a thing; "container means" is not a bit broader than "a container."

As for the recitation of the "legs" in claim 1, a problem in scope of claims is presented. The legs could have been more broadly expressed as "means for mounting the container on the base for oscillating movement with respect thereto." This expression is, of course, much broader than pivoted legs for doing the same thing and it is interesting to note that the claim now reads on the spring mounting of Fig. 3 (Appendix A). However, a line was drawn for purposes of illustration to include the pivoted legs as elements of the claim. Fig. 3 shows a simple mechanism by which the wording of claim 1 may be circumvented.

As to what specific elements are included in a means clause, the clause includes whatever elements or parts of elements are disclosed in the specification to perform the recited function. In the "means for oscillating" clause stated in claim 1, it covers the motor, the cam, and the cam follower attached to the container. A means clause may read on a single element or part of an element, even a hole (Section 23), or a train of fifty cooperating elements—whatever is needed to do the job.

In *In re Prater and Wei* (on rehearing), 162 USPQ 541 (CCPA 1969), the court held that a means clause did not cover a human being (a possibly mental step in that case), but that it may properly cover a programmed general purpose computer. In the *Prater* case, the clause in question of the apparatus claim was:

> means for determining that one of said scalar functions of greatest magnitude for identification of . . . [a desired mathematical relationship].

This holding was affirmed and amplified in the subsequent case of *In re Bernhard and Fetter*, 163 USPQ 611 (CCPA 1969). See Section 41.

Further, there is no objection to having one or more specific elements of structure included as a part of two different means clauses, as long as the entire train of parts to perform each function is not identical.

For example, in *Reed v. Edwards*, 40 USPQ 620, 622 (CCPA 1939), the court held that different parts of a single element could support two means clauses, quoting with approval the following language from the board of appeals decision:

> It has long been recognized that one element of a claim may be relied on for performing different functions. . . . [W]e can see no reason why one side of a tongue or a groove in the Edwards device may not be regarded as the means for advancing the cutter, and why the other side may not be regarded as the means for limiting the rate of travel.

Note that these questions most frequently arise in interferences where a first party claims two separate elements which perform two separate and distinct functions, and the second party discloses only one element performing both functions. Then, the question is whether party number two can make the claim of party number one, which is the same question as whether his specification supports the claim. Usually, the first party has a patent so that the language of the proposed interference counts tends to be fixed by the claims of the patent.

If the disclosure of party number two has truly one completely indivisible element for performing both functions, then classic textbook law is that he cannot make the claim to separate means because of double inclusion, or double reading of elements. For example, in *Holdsworth v. Goldsmith,* 54 USPQ 90, 94 (CCPA 1942) the court stated:

> [There is] . . . fairly well settled law on the question. If a patent disclosure shows two elements to perform two different functions and the patent claim is drawn to define both as separate elements, a disclosure which has only one element performing both functions, will not be regarded as supporting the count. (Citing cases.)

These rather peculiar cases may not arise too often any more because of rule 205, which now provides for interferences with patents where one cannot quite copy the claim; "immaterial limitations" may be excluded.

SUMMARY—Means clauses are perfectly proper in *combination* claims. They are probably the simplest way to define functions performed, broadly. Beware of a means plus function clause "at the precise point of novelty" in the claim, although this may be proper today. Stick to the statutory language "means for performing a specified function"; that is, an act or operation, such as "means for reciprocating the container." Such a clause may cover one element, 10,000 elements, half of one element, or even a hole; it covers whatever is described in the specification, plus equivalents.

* * * * *

Example II—Take-Up Barrel

In this example (see Appendix A, Example II), the object is to collect an advancing strand 11 in a barrel 12. The strand is advanced toward the barrel by a conventional advancing means known as a "capstan" 13. The barrel is rotated on a turntable 14 by a motor 15, pulley 16, belt 17 and pulley 18. This operates to vary the point of strand collection circularly with respect to the bottom of the barrel, as shown in Fig. 2. An eyelet 20 is reciprocated by the same drive motor 15, a pulley 21, a belt 22, a pulley 23, a cam 24 and a cam follower 25 on a shaft 26 of the eyelet 20. This varies the collection point radially with respect to the barrel bottom. The particular strand is a flexible "tinsel" conductor, which forms itself into loops, as shown, as it hits the bottom of the barrel; however, the invention would be useful with other types of strand which would form other patterns.

A fairly broad claim to the combination follows:

> **2. Apparatus for collecting an advancing strand in a barrel, which comprises:**
> **(a)** *a turntable* **on which the barrel is mounted for rotation therewith;**
> **(b)** *a strand guide* **positioned above the barrel for guiding the advancing strand into the barrel;**
> **(c)** *means for rotating the turntable* **so that the point of collection of the strand varies circularly with respect to the bottom of the barrel; and**
> **(d)** *means for reciprocating the guide* **so that the point of collection varies radially with respect to the bottom of the barrel.**

This claim illustrates the use of two means clauses having some common elements. That is, both the rotating means (c) and the reciprocating means (d) include the motor 15 and its shaft. However, they also include many different elements, starting with the two pulleys 16 and 21 on the motor shaft. For this reason, two separate clauses are proper.

From a function standpoint, the elements (c) and (d) could equally well have been driven from separate motors. Therefore, the claim would be unnecessarily limited if a single drive motor for both were recited. The invention obviously is not in using a single drive motor to drive two moving parts synchronously—that is a common industrial expedient. The invention must relate to the fact of simultaneous rotation and reciprocation, not how the same is accomplished.

Claim 2 further illustrates such general principles of mechanical combination claims as preparing the preamble, selecting the essential elements (including means expressions), listing them in a logical order, and tying them together structurally and functionally to accomplish the result stated in the preamble.

These are the most important elements of mechanical claim drafting.

Further examples of mechanical claims of various kinds are presented in Appendix B, along with helpful advice by Myron Cohen in Chapter X.

Section 32—Electrical Circuit Claims (Bryan W. Sheffield & John L. Landis)

Substantially all of the precepts discussed in this Chapter III on apparatus claims apply to electrical circuits. The major difference is that the elements, or some of them, are electrical devices instead of mechanical parts, and the association or cooperation is or may be electrical, not mechanical. One simple example follows:

3. A circuit for counting the number of faults in the insulation on an insulated wire, which comprises:

(a) means for applying a test potential between a selected portion of the insulation and the underlying wire;

> **(b) means for moving the insulated wire relative to the potential-applying means; and**
> **(c) a pulse counter, associated with the potential-applying means and responsive to each pulse of current between the insulation and the underlying wire, for counting the number of faults in the insulation.**

generic expression

Means clauses are frequently used in electrical cases, both for the electrical elements and for associated mechanical structure, even to cover portions of a programmed general purpose computer. Note that the above claims covers a combination of electrical and mechanical structure. This is quite common and normally presents no problem.

In writing broad claims in electrical cases, it is desirable where possible to focus on what combination a prospective infringer might sell, and to avoid including as elements conventional items such as power sources or batteries which such person might not include with the device. This theory applies to all types of cases. One would always rather catch a direct infringer under 35 U.S.C. § 271(a) than a contributory one under 35 U.S.C. § 271(c).

Thus, in Claim 3, above, element (a) is recited as:

> means for applying a test potential between a selected portion of the insulation and the underlying wire.

and *not,* for example,

> a d.c. battery for applying a test potential between a selected portion of the insulation and the underlying wire.

As another example, if one were writing a broad apparatus claim to the simple radio receiver shown in Example IV of Appendix A, one should not write:

> an antenna connected to the tuning coil of said receiver . . .

because ordinarily such a receiver would not be sold with an antenna attached. It would be much better practice to claim:

> means for supplying the radio frequency signals to be detected . . .

which, of course, reads on the antenna input terminals, etc. without an antenna attached, as well as reading on the complete, operating combination with the antenna attached.

The importance of not positively reciting conventional elements, or elements which are not customarily sold with the claimed apparatus, cannot be overstressed; this is a common mistake with beginners. Not claiming power supplies, signal sources and other conventional elements is in many respects analogous to not claiming the workpiece in a machine claim. See Section 13.

A Cautionary Note—In complex electrical cases, for example, in telephone switching or computer applications, it is customary to use block diagrams of the claimed circuitry rather than describe in detail each resistor, capacitor, etc. (See Section 15 on support for claim elements in the specification and drawings.)

This is a practice of long standing and is perfectly acceptable provided that the requirements of 35 U.S.C. §112 are at all times satisfied. The patent attorney who uses such block diagrams must always be prepared to demonstrate to the examiner that what is contained within each block is per se known in the art, for example, by reference to another issued patent or to a publication, such as a textbook.

Of course, a block diagram should *never* be used when what is inside the block is novel and comprises the invention or a subelement thereof.

Another problem arises when what is inside the block is a programmable logic element or computer, admittedly old, but the novel program itself is not disclosed. Such was the case in *In re Brandstadter*, 179 USPQ 286 (CCPA 1973), which dealt with a message retrieval system for a store and forward communications system. A key element of the invention, which was recited in each of the apparatus claims, was a programmable control circuit which the specification stated could be the stored program controlled structure disclosed in a copending "jumbo" patent application.

The patent office rejected the claims, under 35 U.S.C. § 112, stating:

> . . . How and by what means (specifically) are the rectangles shown . . . caused to perform their functions, and (to) do so at the appropriate time? . . . A review of the instant disclosure reveals little more than a system diagram consisting of three sheets of labeled rectangles, accompanied by statements of a myriad of desired results. . . .The instant disclosure is completely devoid of any . . . program or even a flow chart to indicate the functions to be performed, the sequence in which they are to be performed, and the conditions which must be present at the time of performance. . . .

The applicants submitted affidavits from three experts stating that, in their opinion, it would be readily apparent to systems and circuit designers of ordinary skill in the art how to build *and program* the disputed control unit. Importantly, the applicants failed to supply the missing software stating that, "More information regarding these programs is not submitted herewith because the detailed information is considered proprietary. . . ."

Not surprisingly, the CCPA affirmed the rejection of all claims, stating:

> The Affidavits . . . do not convince us that the Examiner's challenge to enablement was unreasonable or has been met. Appellants have not submitted to the Examiner even flow charts of the programs which they admit . . . (they have) developed for the practice of their invention, and the Examiner correctly observed that he (has) been given to circumstances pertaining to this accomplishment . . . such as the number of programmers involved, the number of man-hours involved and the level of skill of the programmers involved.

Thus, to satisfy the standards laid down in *Brandstadter*, any application involving a programmable logic element or computer should, *as a very minimum*, include a flow chart and, preferably, the entire program listing if the claims, apparatus or method, are to satisfy section 112.

See also Section 40 on electrical methods, and Section 41 on computer programs for further discussion of questions and problems in electrical claims.

Further Examples—Other examples of typical electrical circuit elements and connections:

—first and second field effect transistors having gate, source, and drain electrodes; means for connecting the drain electrode of the second transistor to the gate electrode of the first transistor; a first capacitor connected to the source electrode of the first transistor; means for connecting a source of clock pulses to the gate of the second transistor;—[Note, these claim elements are specific circuit components.]

—a shift register connected to [or responsive to] said data input signal—; [Note, the shift register is a complex element, like a "means for."]

—means for sensing a difference between the output voltage from the capacitor under test and that from the reference capacitor, and for providing an error signal proportional to the difference [Note, a double means plus function for a complex element]; a servomotor responsive to the error signal for . . .;

—means, responsive to a change in light intensity between the light source and the photocell, for generating an output signal rleated to the—[electro-optical cooperation].

Considering the familiar Wheatstone Bridge circuit of Appendix A, Example III, a fairly specific claim to the circuit illustrated reads as follows:

3A. Apparatus for measuring the electrical resistance of an unknown resistor R_X, which comprises:

a four-terminal electrical network (A, B, C, D) including a first resistor having a known resistance R_1 connected between network terminals (A) and (B), a second resistor having a known resistance R_2 connected between network terminals (B) and (C), the resistance of said second resistor being selectively variable in value up to the maximum resistance R_2, a third resistor having a known resistance R_3 connected between network terminals (C) and (D), and said unknown resistor being connected across network terminals (A) and (D) for measurement;

means for impressing a source of potential from an external source across network terminals (A) and (C); and

means, connected across network terminals (B) and (D), for detecting when the voltage developed thereacross falls to zero, as the resistance of said variable

second resistor is adjusted, whereby the resistance of said unknown resistor is determined from the equation:

$$R_X = \frac{R_1 R_3}{R_2}$$

Note the specific language connecting the four resistors into the bridge circuit, combined with the broad "means for impressing" and "means for detecting" language for conventional circuit elements such as batteries and meters. Note the "whereby" clause is proper (Section 29) because the functional relationship and equation necessarily follows from the previously recited structure and connections. Note the use of reference characters (A), (B), etc. from the drawing (Sec. 19), these must be placed in parentheses.

A sample claim to the basic radio receiver (crystal set) shown in Appendix B, Example IV, follows:

3B. A radio receiver, which comprises:

a radio-frequency transformer having a primary and a secondary winding, said primary winding being connected between an external antenna and ground to receive radio frequency signals transmitted through the aether;

a variable capacitor connected across said secondary winding to form a tuned L-C circuit which rejects all but the particular radio-frequency signal to which the circuit is tuned;

means, connected to said tuned L-C circuit, for rectifying said particular radio-frequency signal;

transducing means, serially connected with said rectifying means, for rendering audible audio-frequency signals priorly modulated on said radio-frequency signal; and

a capacitor, connected in parallel with said transducer, to prevent the a.c. component in said rectified radio-frequency signal from passing therethrough.

This claim further illustrates the selection of elements, broad ("transducing means") or narrow ("a capacitor"), and connecting the elements together both structurally ("connected to said tuned L-C circuit) and functionally ("for rectifying") to do the job stated in the preamble.

Further examples of electrical circuit and structure claims are given in Appendix B.

SUMMARY—Electrical circuit claims follow the same rules as machine claims. The claim elements can be circuit components, or partly circuit components, partly mechanical structure. Means clauses are used frequently. For broader claims, focus on the combination as it would likely be sold. The connection or co-operation between elements can be electronic, electromagnetic, electroöptical, mechanical, or any mixture. Be careful of block diagrams in the drawings, and attendant lack of description in the specification—the man skilled in the art must know how to build each block, without exercising ingenuity *and* without undue experimentation. On support in specification (Section 15) for block diagram, means-type disclosures, see *In re Scarbrough*, 182 USPQ 298 (CCPA-1974) and cases cited in Section 41 on computer programs.

As with mechanical claims, one recites in broad claims the minimum number of elements that will work in the combination, defining each element and the necessary connections as broadly as the prior art will permit.

Chapter IV

METHOD OR PROCESS CLAIMS

(John D. Kaufmann & John L. Landis)

Section 33—In General

Method, or process, claims are generally easier to write than mechanical claims. The reason for this is that method claims by their very nature do not require as much structural "connecting up" nor as many detailed statements of the mechanical cooperation of parts as do mechanical claims. Also, selecting the elements (steps) is easier, and there is less problem in giving the elements names, broad or narrow.

As to form, the body of a method claim is rarely much more difficult to write than a cookbook recipe: "Preheat an oven to 350°F; sift 1½ cups of sugar; sift 1 cup of cake flour; sift together the sugar and the flour; add ½ teaspoon of salt to the sifted sugar and flour; beat . . . eggs . . .; add the beaten eggs; . . .; bake in the preheated oven for 45 minutes." As easy as pie (or angel cake)!

The words "method" and "process" are interchangeable in the patent law, although "process" is perhaps more frequently used in chemical cases, while "method" is more usual in mechanical and electrical cases. Before 1952, the word "art" was used in the statute, and was construed to mean "method" or "process." This former use of the word "art" is hopefully (although not certainly) now obsolete, because today "art" normally means "technology" or "field," as in the phrase "a person having ordinary skill in the *art*" in 35 U.S.C. §103. To provide uniformity, this statutory class is now called "process" in 35 U.S.C. §100(b) and is defined therein to mean "process, art or method."

Most of the general rules previously given apply also to method claims. They may be broad or narrow; chemical, mechanical or electrical; and may have most of the other variations (*e.g.*, genus/species) found in mechanical claims. The terms therein must find support in the specification; reference numerals may be used; appropriate antecedents are necessary; logical order is also necessary; steps must be "tied" together; "whereby" clauses may be used.

A very important rule to remember is that the "elements" of a method claim, instead of being structural parts, are, and must be, *acts* or manipulative steps which are performed upon an article, workpiece or chemical substance. It is the transformation or reduction of the article, workpiece or chemical substance to a different state or thing that is the essence of a method claim—and the key to its patentability. This is especially true when the claimed method includes no particular machine or apparatus.[*]

There is no per se objection to claiming a single-step method,[**] except where a broad functional step is claimed, as noted in Section 34. However, most claimed methods do involve combinations of steps, as is the case with machines and circuits. Of course, the claim must *particularly point out and distinctly claim* what the applicant regards as his invention (Section 1), which is the basic requirement of 35 U.S.C. §12. See Section 28.

In re Kuehl, 177 USPQ 250 (CCPA-1973), announced a liberal philosophy toward granting method or process claims of various kinds, even where the point of novelty appears to the examiner to reside in other statutory classes (new compound in that case). See further discussion of this case in Section 36.

SUMMARY—Method claims involve one or more acts or steps performed on an article, workpiece or chemical substance to achieve some result in the useful or technical arts. The elements of a method claim must be steps or acts, expressed as verb statements or phrases.

---

[*]Gottschalk v. Benson, 409 U.S. 63, 175 USPQ 673 (1972) (discussed in Section 41).

[**]*Ex parte Kelly,* 173 USPQ 743 (Bd. App. 1971); *Ex parte* Britton, 154 USPQ 321 (Bd. App. 1967); *Ex parte* Macy, 132 USPQ 545 (Bd. App. 1960); *Ex parte* Ford, 173 USPQ 743 (Bd. App. 1971).

Section 34—Elements of Method Claims

Generally, the verbs in a method claim need *not* be phrased in any particular voice or tense as long as there is no ambiguity and the requirements of Section 112 are met.* Nevertheless, it must be remembered that the elements of a method claim are method *steps,* which should usually be verbal (gerundial) phrases, introduced by a gerund or verbal noun (the "-ing" form of a verb), such as (the gerunds are italicized):

(a) *reciprocating* the guide** . . .
(b) *punching* a series of holes . . .
(c) *impressing* a signal . . .
(d) *coating* the sheet with an adhesive . . .
(e) *heating* the mixture to a temperature of . . .
(f) *separating* the alcohol from the aqueous solution . . .
(g) *distilling* the aqueous solution to separate the alcohol therefrom . . .
(h) *fractionally crystallizing* the aqueous solution to separate the alcohol therefrom . . .

The last three steps ("separating," on the one hand, and "distilling" or "crystallizing," on the other) illustrate, respectively, a generic and two-species method steps (see Section 55).

One should be aware that as to the format of step (g), above, examiners sometimes express a preference for language similar to the following: "(g′) *separating* the alcohol from the aqueous solution *by distilling* the solution. . . ." The argument favoring such wording is along these lines: "Regarding the phrase 'distilling . . . to separate,' [as in step (g)] one *could* distill the solution, yet never achieve alcohol separation. Such separation being the ultimate goal of the step, it (separation) should be *more positively recited* by being made the introductory gerund of the clause ["separating . . . by distilling," as in step (g′)] which sets forth the step."

**Ex parte* Lewin, 154 USPQ 487 (Bd. App. 1966).

**As in apparatus claims (Section 20), antecedents are important. Support for "*the* guide" must have been provided in a previous clause of the claim.

It is believed that this is fallacious reasoning. First, steps (g) and (g′) may be seen to cover exactly the same territory logically and semantically. Second, an objection to the *form* of a step written as step (g) ignores the expressly stated *substantive* limitation therein of "distilling . . . *to* separate." This limitation *requires* that the distillation effect the separation. Third, any administrative preference for one or the other form of the step ignores the reasonable latitude permitted by decisions such as *Lewin*, cited at the beginning of this Section. Fourth, seemingly ignored are the principles set forth in the next paragraph.*

The choice of which word (gerund) to use for introducing a method step is similar to the choice of which word to use for describing elements in apparatus claims. Generally, one chooses the broadest word the prior art will allow. Thus, in step (g), "distilling" is narrower than step (f) "separating." One may recite a generic or broad step, such as "separating," which is really a function or result of a more specific act such as "distilling" or "crystallizing." Moreover, it is permissible for a method step to recite some condition or property without reciting in the claim every step necessary to obtain or achieve that condition or property.** For example, "distilling" alone in step (g) should be sufficient. There should usually be no need, in place of "distilling" to recite "*placing* the aqueous solution in a (certain) container . . ."; "*heating* the solution to a (certain) temperature . . ."; "*condensing* the alcohol vapors . . ."; etc.

Pragmatically, the choice of what gerund to use is really of little moment as to the form of the claim. Moreover, the statute in Section 112 states (in the same paragraph sanctioning "means plus function" clauses) that:

*However, if the two formats, (g) and (g′), truly *are* the same, one would usually be foolish to "fight" the Examiner on the point. There are usually more important issues present, and a firm stand by the applicant on one particular format may not, in the words of Cicero, "render the audience [here, the Examiner] benevolent" as to more substantive issues.

***In re* Roberts and Burch, 176 USPQ 313 (CCPA 1973); *In re* Alul and McEwan, 175 USPQ 700 (CCPA 1972); *In re* Rainer, 134 USPQ 343 (CCPA 1962). Of course either the specification must disclose or a man skilled in the art must know, how to achieve the condition or property.

> An element in a claim for a [method] combination may be expressed as a . . . step for performing a specified function without the recital of . . . acts in support thereof, and such claim shall be construed to cover the corresponding . . . acts described in the specification and equivalents thereof.

Thus, the statute expressly sanctions the use of broad functional steps, such as "separating," where the prior art permits, rather than the specific *act*, "distilling." The interpretation of this language is similar to that described under "means claims" in Section 31: the claim ". . . *shall* be construed to cover the corresponding . . . acts described . . . and equivalents. . . ." Consequently, as with means clauses, the scope of protection afforded is exactly as broad as "the Invention"; thus, such "step of" clauses should be used whenever the prior art permits. This distinction between acts and steps is probably more academic than real, as very few if any cases focus on the difference in concept between a functional step and the act done to perform the step. As with "means claims," such functional step clauses must be limited to claims to *combinations*. In concept, a single-step method claim is all right (see Section 33) only when the step is an act.

The preamble of a method claim may be almost the same as that of a mechanical claim. Generically, the following preamble format is usually appropriate: "A *method of* (or process for) performing a specified act (or operation) on a particular article (or workpiece or chemical substance), which comprises: . . ." Except for the words "a method" this format is identical to the format proposed in Section 12 for apparatus claim preambles. Note that the workpiece is properly placed in the preamble, just as it is in apparatus claims (see Section 13). In the broader claims, avoid describing the workpiece or article any more narrowly than the prior art requires, which would be an "unnecessary article limitation" in the words of the Patent Office comments on grading Agent's Exam method claims.

Another similar preamble format ends with the words ". . . which comprises *the steps of:* . . ." The choice between these and equivalent forms is a matter of style.

Referring again to the take-up barrel of Example II (Appendix A) a method claim relating thereto might read:

> **4. A method of collecting an advancing strand in a barrel, which comprises:**
> **(a) *guiding* the advancing strand into the barrel;**
> **(b) *rotating* the barrel so that the point of collection of the strand varies circularly with respect to the bottom of the barrel; and**
> **(c) *reciprocating* the guide point above the barrel so that the point of collection varies radially with respect to the bottom of the barrel.**

Note the similarity in form to the apparatus claim in Section 31. If the title of Claim 4 were changed to "Apparatus for . . ." and the phrase "means for" were inserted before each step, one would have a proper apparatus claim (at least as to form). This is typical of most method claims: Add the words "means for" to transform a method step into an apparatus element. Similarly, where an apparatus element is expressed in "means for" fashion, deletion of that phrase usually results in a proper (as to form) method step.

Further examples of method claims of many kinds are given in Appendix B.

SUMMARY—The elements of a method claim are acts or steps, customarily phrased as gerunds ("heating"). They can be broad or narrow, depending on the prior art, and functional step clauses ("separating") can be used, corresponding to means clauses where the function performed, not the act used to do it, is the important thing. Single-step method claims are permitted where the step is an act, not a functional step.

Section 35—Order of Steps

The elements (steps) of a method claim must, of course, also be set forth in some logical order. The order of listing the elements in method claims is usually clearer than in mechanical claims. In the method of Claim 4, all three steps ("guiding," "rotating" and "reciprocating") occur simultaneously to accomplish the intended result so that, as written, either clause (b) or (c) could immediately follow step (a). It would be illogical to put step (a) last or in the middle.

Quite often, the steps, or some of them, *must* be performed in a given sequence. In this event expressions indicative of the order should be used, such as: "first," "second," "then," "subsequently," "after the embossing step," "between steps (c) and (d)," etc.*

Sometimes the description of a particular step inherently implies the order, such as "(a) depositing a film of zinc on a substrate; (b) depositing a film of platinum *on the zinc film.*" In this case, the order need not be further expressly stated, because step (a)'s timewise precedence over step (b) is *required* by the phrase "on the zinc film" in step (b). Step (b), therefore, cannot, within the wording of the claim, be performed until the zinc film is deposited by step (a).

Where all of the steps must be performed in a specific order, then all should be tied in timewise, either by sequence words associated with the description of each step, as previously discussed, or by a preamble statement such as: "A method of ————, comprising the following steps in the order named: . . ." or ". . . in the sequence set forth: . . ." These are useful ways of stating a necessary order of steps, particularly for claims with many steps.

Where the claim does not expressly state or necessarily imply the sequence of all or some steps, it covers the steps performed in any order or simultaneously. Then, as with the barrel take-up method, the order of description is a matter of logical convenience.

SUMMARY—Where the steps, or some of them, must be performed in sequence, one after the other, the sequence should be described. Otherwise, the steps should be set out in any logical order with no sequence stated. As with all other limitations in

---

*Note that use of the outline form of claim, with each step labeled with a number or letter, permits reference back to, *e.g.*, "step (c)" instead of "the mixing step."

any claim of any kind, make sure every word and every phrase is necessary in the broader claims. Consequently, do not state the sequence unless it is important to the claim.

Section 36—Claims to Both Method and Product —Obvious Method of Making an Unobvious Product

Part I–Patent Office Practice prior to April, 1974

According to a prior, classic Patent Office practice, a claim which recites "nothing more than the *obvious method* of producing an article, a product or a chemical," is not patentable despite the fact that the article or chemical itself may be patentable. The CCPA has held, over vigorous dissent by the late Judge Smith, that a generally "conventional-by-analogy" method of making a new chemical is not patentable, even though the chemical might be. See, among other cases, *In re Larsen*, 130 USPQ 209 (1961); *In re Albertson*, 141 USPQ 730 (1964); and *In re Kanter*, 158 USPQ 331 (1968). There must be "an Invention," meaning unobviousness, in each statutory class in which claims are sought. *In re Susi*, 169 USPQ 423 (CCPA 1971), questions this doctrine but expressly does not decide the issue. See also *In re Hoeksema*, 141 USPQ 733 (CCPA 1964).

Part II–New Tests: April, 1974

In April, 1974, the Patent Office formally gave up on the Larson test, or at least the prior interpretation of such test discussed above, as overruled by *In re Kuehl.* In revision 40, the Manual was rewritten as follows:

"**706.03(q) Obvious Method** [R-40]

" In view of a decision of the U.S. Court of Customs and Patent Appeals, process claims should no longer be rejected on a theory that once the article or composition produced thereby is conceived, anyone skilled in the art would at once be aware of a method of making it, *In re Kuehl,* 177 USPQ 250 (1973).

"A process may be unpatentable, however, even if the product produced therefrom is patentable, *In re Kanter,* 158 USPQ 331 (CCPA 1968). The mere substitution of a new starting material in an otherwise conventional process may well be obvious in the absence of some unobvious result in the process itself, *In re Kanter,* 158 USPQ 331; *In re Neugebauer et al.,* 141 USPQ 205 (CCPA 1964); *Corning Glass Works et al. v. Brenner,* 175 USPQ 516 (D.C. Cir. 1972).

"However, the use of a specific mineral oil in a process was held to be material in *In re Schneider et al.,* 179 USPQ 46 (CCPA 1973)."

What all this means, and how these somewhat cryptic phrases will be interpreted, time will tell. However, it seems clear to this author that all such cases should in the future be decided under the doctrine of the *Kuehl* case, and any following cases. *Kuehl* is decidedly liberal on process claims for using patentable compounds, and by direct statement *in dicta,* on processes of manufacture claims also. Further, *Kuehl* presents a liberal philosophy of allowing claims in all statutory classes *applicant* chooses to select, particularly all types of process.

As the *Kuehl* court points out, process of use (or manufacture) claims are really worth very little extra, if compound claims are allowed, since the compound claims cover *any* method of making, and *any* process of using; thus, allowing claims to a specific process of making or using do not really add to the scope of the patent. But the public gains because allowing such claims tends to increase the amount of disclosure in the patent, on specific details of how to make and how best to use, to furnish better support for the process claims.

While the court did not approve, and in fact expressly rejected, a per se rule that product patentability always provides process patentability, it is hard to imagine a case where, if X chemical is unobvious, any process at all for making an unobvious thing could be obvious. This is the theory strongly espoused in the Judge Smith dissent in the *Larson* and following cases.

The *Kuehl* case seems fairly strong in this direction: he had invented and got allowance of pure product claims to zeolite X, a new family of chemical compounds; now he wanted claims to cracking gasoline comprising the single step (Sec. 33) of "*contacting* a hydrocarbon . . . with the composition of claim 6" (see Sec. 53 on dependent claims crossing statutory classes). The single step "contacting with a catalyst" was notoriously old (see Sec. 39 on chemical process claims and section 52 on new use claims), but the novelty can reside in performing the process with a new material, as it is in fact a new process. The prior art taught cracking gasoline with all manner of zeolites of this general type and applicant did not show any particular advantage or unexpected results from using this particular zeolite. Thus, if the man skilled in the art *were given* applicant's zeolite X, as sanctioned in the *Larson* case, he would know at once what to do with it. But the key point of the *Kuehl* case is that the man in the art *was not given* zeolite X; zeolite X is not prior art against the applicant, as 35 U.S.C. 103 says that one must look at the prior art "at the time the invention was made" to determine obviousness. When or under what circumstances a method of making, or process of using, an unobvious compound could be obvious the court did not say in *Kuehl*, nor does the new Manual section quoted above.

SUMMARY—A prior, classic Patent Office rejection of method claims as drawn to the "obvious method of making a patentable product or compound" has been virtually overruled by recent CCPA cases. What if anything remains of this doctrine is obscure, but the cases cited above and any new ones should be studied carefully if the question arises.

Section 37—Claims to Both Method and Apparatus —Method Functional of Apparatus

Until 1968, there was a fundamental principle that, to be

patentable, a method must be more than the "inherent function of the apparatus" that was disclosed to effect the method. As stated in the first "Guidelines of Patentability" memorandum, dated June 17, 1963 (792 O.G. 3):

> A rejection on this ground is proper where the disclosed machine will inherently carry out the steps of the process set forth in the process claims regardless of whether an apparatus claim is allowed, unless it appears that the process claimed can be carried out by some machine which is not the functional equivalent . . . or by hand. . . .

Many, many cases had construed this doctrine over at least the preceding fifty years.* In 1968, the CCPA threw out the entire ground of rejection in *In re Tarczy-Hornoch*, 158 USPQ 141, and *In re Bekey*, 158 USPQ 260; followed by the board of appeals in *Ex parte Birnbaum*, 161 USPQ 635 (1968). In *Federal Sign & Signal Corp. v. Bangor Punta, Inc.*, 177 USPQ 737 (S.D.N.Y. 1973), the *Tarczy-Hornoch* decision was followed by a federal district court in New York. The Patent Office has indicated in MPEP 706.03(r) that it follows the decision. What, if anything, is left of this hoary doctrine remains to be seen; possibly examiners will find some other ground for rejecting method claims directed to what they think are clearly machine inventions.** It should also be noted that only the CCPA† has authoritatively spoken on the subject. Some other court might "reactivate" the doctrine.

At least for historical background, one should know that there was once "black letter" law on the subject, but that there *may* no longer be. In any event, the previous Claim 4 (Section 34) would easily satisfy even the old rule, because the strand could be manually guided, and /or the barrel could obviously be turned by hand, and/or the guide could be similarly reciprocated.

SUMMARY—According to the CCPA, and Patent Office, method claims cannot be rejected as merely drawn to the inherent function of a machine. (There once was law to this effect, and

---

*Robinson §518 cites this principle as established law as of 1890.

**Many feel this was the real reason for the doctrine.

† One federal district court has also spoken authoritatively on the subject.

may still be in other courts.) Where possible, detach the method from the machine so far as possible and try to define novelty in the steps performed.

Section 38—Apparatus Limitations

While there is no per se objection to including structural (mechanical and/or electrical) apparatus limitations in the elements (steps) of method claims, when the steps are properly phrased in method language, the use of such limitations should be avoided insofar as possible for at least two reasons.

First, apparatus limitations will often unduly limit the claim. Second, and more important, the "black letter" law is that the patentability of a method claim cannot be predicated *solely* on the structure of a mechanism used in practicing the method.* Accordingly, there is usually no point in including the structure except where the method necessarily involves manipulation of apparatus. There is no objection to including composition-of-matter or chemical limitations in method claims, and in fact these are frequently relied on for patentability, as noted in Section 39.**

In using dependent method claims (Section 53), avoid adding *only* apparatus limitations. Limitations added in dependent method claims should always be phrased as method steps, except where further defining compositions of matter or chemicals (Section 39). Thus, it would be poor form to depend a claim from the take-up method in Claim 4 setting forth: "A method . . . as recited in Claim 4, further comprising a *turntable*. . . ." One example of proper form along this line would be: "A method . . . as

*See *Ex parte* Dammers, 155 USPQ 284 (Bd. App. 1961), which nevertheless points out that structural apparatus limitations are not per se objectionable, and, to the extent necessary to carry out the claimed method, are permissible in a method claim.

***In re* Kuehl, 177 USPQ 250 (CCPA 1973), where the claim was to an old method of cracking gasoline, so far as the steps were concerned, using a new catalyst.

recited in Claim 4, wherein the step of rotating the barrel includes mounting the barrel on a turntable and rotating the turntable."

Note that this is primarily a matter of form not substance: one is entitled to include the turntable in the claim if one wants to, but there is no good reason to do so in a broad claim, because it is not essential to the method. Thus, Claim 4 might have included:

> rotating *a* turntable on which the barrel is mounted . . .
>
> reciprocating *a* strand guide positioned above the barrel . . .

Note the form (inferential) for bringing in apparatus limitations where they are used, such as "rotating a turntable . . ."

See also Section 52 on new use claims, for method claims where the novelty resides in a new use for an old material.

SUMMARY—Avoid apparatus limitations (machine or circuit) in method claims so far as possible. When necessary, bring them into the claim inferentially, *i.e.*, "rotating *a turntable*." There is no problem with chemical or materials limitations and these can be relied on for patentability, and frequently are in "new use" type claims, such as killing insects by exposing them to DDT.

Section 39—Chemical Processes

An example of a chemical process claim follows:

> **5. A process for treating the surface of a polyethylene article to increase its receptivity to printing ink, which comprises:**
>
> **exposing the surface of the article to a saturated solution of sodium dichromate in concentrated sulfuric acid.**

As previously noted in Sec. 33, there is no objection to a single-step method. Claim 5 illustrates the rare case of a claim that is not to a combination.

With chemical processes, it is proper to add a dependent process claim adding only details of the materials used. For example, if Claim 5 had recited "an acid," a dependent claim could cover: "A process . . . as recited in Claim 5, wherein the acid is sulfuric acid."

It is standard in chemical process cases that the process may distinguish by the compositions recited, as well as the actual manipulative step, which is often trivial per se. In the example of Claim 5, the manipulative step "exposing" an article to a reagent is of course prehistoric; the sole novelty resides in the composition of the reagent. Eminently logically, it is considered that exposing to reagent X is not the same step as exposing to reagent Y. See also Section 52 on new use claims.

Where the process can be practiced, or used, with more than one related material or chemical, Markush phraseology may be used under the rules set out in Section 47. Also, alternative expressions (A or B—Sec. 21) may sometimes be permitted in describing different chemical substances that can be used in the process. In *Ex parte Pantzer and Feier*, 176 USPQ 141 (Bd. App. 1971, 1972), during prosecution, Claim 16 was rejected under Section 112, without the citation of any references. Claim 16 recited a method of dyeing fibers wherein the dye used to prepare the dyeing solution was defined as the product of the reaction of "one *or* both of [A′] and [B′] with [C] under [certain] alkaline conditions." Other claims used the phrase "one *or* more of." Claim 1, from which all of the claims ultimately depended (see Section 53), recited A and B, certain amino phenols, of which A′ and B′ were species. Claim 1 was not limited to only one of A or B, because it called for a method which "comprises" dispersing A and B in an aqueous medium. The board reversed the rejection, holding that the phrases "one *or* both" and "one *or* more" were not so broad as to be indefinite and did not encompass "an infinite number."* etc.

Chemical processes can be to methods of treating something, as in Claim 5 above; methods of making chemical compounds (new or old); methods of using chemicals, such as killing insects or treating baldness; or any other process or subject having industrial utility.

**See, e.g., Ex parte Pontius*, Endres and Van Akkeren, 169 USPQ 122 (Bd. App. 1970).

A typical method/use claim:

> **5A. The method of treating baldness, which comprises applying to the scalp an aqueous solution of sodium chloride* having a concentration of 30-40 percent by weight** of sodium chloride.**

A typical claim to a method of making a chemical compound:

> **5B. The method of manufacturing sodium hydroxide, which comprises electrolyzing an aqueous solution of sodium chloride at a current density sufficient to decompose the sodium chloride into elemental chlorine and sodium, the sodium reacting with the water present in the solution to form sodium hydroxide and hydrogen gas.**

Note this process is one of the oldest, and still most common, ways to make sodium hydroxide, as well as chlorine and hydrogen gas. Since the circuit parameters would not be critical, they can be stated broadly (Section 28).

Other examples of chemical process claims are given in Appendix B, cases 13, 18, 20, 21 and 24.

In re Kuehl 177 USPQ 250 (CCPA 1973), discussed in Section 36, is a further case clearly holding that patentability of a process can reside in the use of a novel and unobvious material in the process, though the single process step (Section 33), contacting X with catalyst Y, is notoriously old per se. In *Kuehl,* one of the claims in question read:

"A hydrocarbon conversion process which comprises contacting a hydrocarbon charge under catalytic cracking conditions with the composition of claim 6."

Claim 6, a composition of matter claim to a group of new zeolites, had been allowed. The court held it would be unobvious to crack gasoline with the new zeolite, even though cracking with other, generally similar zeolites was very well known in the prior art and would have been obvious *after* one knew about appli-

---

*Salt water.

**This avoids reading on ocean bathing.

cant's new zeolite. However, one's own invention and allowed claims, are not prior art against one's process claim and one is entitled to both types of claim when he invents (a) a new compound, and (b) an unobvious process using that compound.

SUMMARY—Chemical process claims are the same as other method claims as to claim-drafting techniques. Often the novelty is in the chemicals used, not the act itself (treating, exposing).

Section 40—Electrical Methods (Bryan W. Sheffield & John L. Landis)

As an example of an electrical method, the following claim covers the use of the Wheatstone Bridge shown in Example III of Appendix A to measure an unknown resistance.

6. A method of measuring the electrical resistance of an unknown resistor R_X, which comprises:

connecting the unknown resistor R_X between terminals (A) and (D) of a four-terminal electrical network (A,B, C,D), said network including a first known resistor R_1 between terminals (A) and (B), a second known resistor R_2 between terminals (B) and (C), and a third known resistor R_3 between terminals (C) and (D), at least one of said known resistors being a variable resistor;

impressing a potential across terminals (A) and (C) of said network;

detecting the voltage developed across terminals (B) and (D) of said network as a result of said impressed potential; and

varying the resistance of at least one of said known resistors until the voltage detected across terminals (B) and (D) falls to zero, whereby* the resistance of the unknown resistor R_X is determined from the equation:

$$R_X = \frac{R_1 . R_3}{R_2}$$

---

*Note the proper "whereby" clause (Section 29), since this function indubitably follows from the previously recited steps. Whereby clauses can be used as well in method claims as in apparatus claims.

Claim 6A is another example of an electrical method claim and covers use of the Marconi crystal radio illustrated in Example IV of Appendix A.

> **6A. A method of demodulating a radio frequency carrier wave priorly modulated with an audio frequency signal, which comprises:**
>
> **applying said modulated carrier wave to a resonant L-C circuit;**
>
> **adjusting the resonant frequency of said L-C circuit until it equals the frequency of said carrier wave;**
>
> **rectifying the voltage developed across said resonant L-C circuit to recover said audio-frequency signal;**
>
> **passing said rectified voltage through a transducer to render said audio-frequency signal audible; and**
>
> **filtering-out the radio-frequency components present in said rectified voltage to prevent same from entering said transducer.**

Years ago, the Patent Office was sometimes chary about allowing electrical method claims, at least in certain arts, and "function-of-the-apparatus" rejections were quite prevalent in this area (Section 37). However, with the demise of the "method functional" doctrine reported in Section 37, it seems likely that greatly expanded use of electrical method claims will be possible in the future, unless countervailing forces intervene such as in the area of programmable process reported in the next Section.

SUMMARY—Electrical methods present no special problems so far as claim-drafting techniques are concerned. The only difference from mechanical methods is that the steps, or some of them, are electrical rather than mechanical. Typical steps or acts are "amplifying," "charging," "connecting," "impressing a potential," "detecting," "rectifying," "sensing," etc. The acts (amplifying) need not be do-able by a human being, circuit components do nicely.

Section 41—Mental Steps—Computer Programs (Bryan W. Sheffield & John L. Landis)

There was once textbook law that "mental steps" or "mental processes" could not be patented, meaning relied on for patentability in a method claim, the main reason being that such steps were not considered to be within the case-law construction of the word "process" in the statute, or the equivalent word "art" in earlier statutes. (See Section 33.) One of the leading cases was *In re Abrams*, 89 USPQ 266 (CCPA 1951). That case involved an oil-prospecting method where the critical, for novelty, steps were:

> (5) determining the rate of pressure rise in said bore hole . . ., and
> (6) comparing the rates determined in step (5). . . . 89 USPQ at 267.

In *Abrams*, the specification disclosed no apparatus, computer or otherwise, for performing the novel steps. They could only be done mentally, including use of paper and pencil, as far as the specification stated. The claim also involved normal or "good" method steps (digging a hole, sealing it, reducing the pressure and measuring the pressure change); the trouble was that these steps were all old. After much discussion and citation of cases, the *Abrams* court stated:

> Citation of authority in support of the principle that claims to mental concepts which constitute the very substance [novel or unobvious part] of an alleged invention are not patentable is unnecessary. It is self-evident that thought is not patentable. 89 USPQ at 269.

Abrams was commonly understood for the proposition that mental steps could be included (at least steps having industrial utility in a process, such as "determining," "registering," "counting," "measuring," "comparing") in a process claim along with ordinary physical steps, but that the novelty of the claim could not reside solely in the mental steps.

This commonly accepted view of the mental step doctrine was

challenged in 1968 when the CCPA handed down the first of two important decisions dealing with the patentability of "mental steps" and computer software in general. In the first *In re Prater and Wei* case [159 USPQ 583 (CCPA 1968)], herein called *Prater I*, the court held that steps which *could* be performed mentally ("comparing") can be included in the claim and relied on for patentability *if* apparatus such as a programmed computer is disclosed to perform the method.

The steps involved in *Prater I*, Claim 17, were:

> generating physical representations . . . [of coefficients of certain equations],
>
> generating from said physical representations . . . the magnitude of the determinant . . . [of certain simultaneous equations],
>
> comparing . . . for identification of the set of said equations whose determinant has the largest magnitude, and
>
> generating physical representations of the concentration of each said component . . . [of a mixture of gases being analyzed spectrographically.] 159 USPQ at 586.

The examiner alleged, and it seems undisputed, that the method could (probably with great difficulty) be performed mentally, including writing on paper and using one's eyes. However, in *Prater I*, a special-purpose computer was specifically disclosed to perform all of the steps, and the specification also disclosed in passing that a properly programmed general purpose computer could also be used(which is pretty apparent).

The court distinguished and severely limited the *Abrams* "rules" to cases where there was no disclosure of how to perform the "possibly mental" step mechanically, noting that, at the time of Abram's invention, ". . . programmable general purpose computers for calculations of this nature were still in the future." 159 USPQ at 590. (Today, most inventions of this type, "possibly mental steps," could be performed with a properly programmed computer.)

This cleared up the law very nicely and for almost nine months the law, at least in the CCPA, on mental steps was fairly certain. However, the commissioner of patents petitioned for reconsideration, which was granted by a 3 to 2 decision (160 USPQ 230), with a strong dissent by Judge Rich on the merits of reconsidering decided cases with different judges. (Judge Arthur Smith, who wrote the opinion in *Prater I*, died the day the decision was handed down.)

In the second *Prater* decision [162 USPQ 541 (CCPA 1969)], the *Prater I* decision on the method claims was withdrawn and the board's decision, "unpatentable," affirmed on a new ground, that the claims did not "particularly point out and distinctly claim" the invention under 35 U.S.C. §112 (see Section 1). The question involved was not mentioned by the *Prater I* court or the board of appeals.

On rehearing (*Prater II*), the question was raised whether the method claims, if allowed as a result of *Prater I*, *would in fact* cover the process performed mentally. If so, the Patent Office argued this would interfere with freedom of speech, etc. In arguing against rehearing, applicants stated that the claim did *not* cover mental infringement, no court would so hold, and *they did not intend* the claim to be so construed.

In view of this, the court held that the claims were unpatentable under 35 U.S.C. §112 since they read on things (the mental process) the applicants did not wish covered; therefore, they should go back to the Patent Office to amend the claims so that uncertain or ambiguous claims would not be granted.

Thus, the decision was made on a primarily technical or nonsubstantative ground, and the court found it was unnecessary to decide the mental steps question in this case, although the court reviewed the question and *Prater I* in great detail, and affirmed the *Prater I* reasoning, if the claims were limited to "machine processes":

> . . . it would appear that the *disclosure* of apparatus for performing the process wholly without human intervention merely shows that the *disclosed* process does not fall within the so-called "mental steps" exclusion. 162 USPQ at 549.

The court reserved for future decision whether "purely mental steps" can contribute to patentability, or whether claims as in the *Prater* application which cover either mechanical or mental processes are patentable subject matter, assuming the applicant wanted to cover process when performed mentally.

Many patent attorneys viewed the *Prater and Wei* cases as supporting the proposition that computer programs were proper subject matter for patents, if phrased as methods. *Prater I* does not expressly consider the question, while *Prater II* expressly states this although the question was not essential to the decision. Footnote 29 states:

> . . . No reason is now apparent to us why, based on the Constitution, statute, or case law, apparatus *and* process claims broad enough to encompass the operation of a programmed general purpose digital computer are necessarily unpatentable . . . once a program has been introduced, the general-purpose digital computer becomes a special-purpose digital computer . . . which, along with the process by which it operates, may be patented subject, of course, to the requirements of novelty, utility and non-obviousness. Based on the present law, we see no other reasonable conclusion. 162 USPQ at 549.

Thus, the court went out of its way in the footnote quoted above, to tell the Patent Office what it thought of computer program patents, if phrased as processes or machines. When claimed as machines (circuits, Sec. 32), the claim elements are usually "means for [performing step A], means for [doing thing B]," etc., which are really about the same as method claims, as explained in Sec. 31, except that such claim elements do not cover human beings, eyeballs, brains, etc. So with means for claims the mental step problem disappears.

For a thorough analysis of the *Prater* decisions and a host of pre-*Prater* cases on mental steps and related subjects, see an excellent review by Samuel J. Sutton, Jr., *The "Mental Steps" Doctrine: A Critical Analysis in the Light of Prater and Weil,* 13 *IDEA** Magazine, No. 3 at 458 (Fall 1969).

*IDEA originally was a quarterly journal published by the Patent, Trademark, and Copyright Research Institute of the George Washington University. It contains a wealth of scholarly material and much original research on all phases of the patent system and industrial property law.

IDEA is now published by the PTC Research Foundation affiliated with the Franklin Pierce Law Center, Concord, New Hampshire.

A subsequent case, *In re Bernhart and Fetter*, 163 USPQ 611 (CCPA 1969), affirmed *Prater II* law on computer programs and included comments on many other nonart rejections such as mental steps, printed matter (Section 62), scientific principles (Section 3) and old combination (Section 60). In general, this case severely limited all nonart rejections mentioned, which coincides with many other recent (late 1960's) cases by the court.

The case involved automatically making two-dimensional drawings of three-dimensional objects from different viewpoints. This involved a programmed general purpose computer operating an automatic drafting machine in a generally known way.

A typical method claim included:

> 13. A plotting method . . . comprising:
> (a) . . . programming the computer to compute . . . [certain axes];
> (b) . . . programming the computer to compute and produce an output defining . . . [certain coordinates]; and
> (c) . . . applying the computer output to the input of a planar plotting apparatus adapted to . . . [draw the picture]. 163 USPQ at 613.

This was held proper as to form. It does not define mental steps (quite obviously), affirming *Prater II*. Programming a computer to do a desired thing is not a mental step, and is also not unstatutory nor improper for any other reason:

> . . . the disclosure shows only machinery for carrying out the portrayal process. . . . Accordingly, a statutory process is here disclosed. Looking then to method claim 13, we find that it in no way covers any mental steps but requires both a "digital computer" and a "planar plotting apparatus" to carry it out. To find that the claimed process could be done mentally would require us to hold that a human mind is a digital computer or its equivalent, and that a draftsman is a planar plotting apparatus. . . . We are unwilling to so hold. 163 USPQ at 617.

After this brightening of the hearts of the program patent attorneys, the court then looked at the claim and held it obvious over the (highly relevant) art cited by the examiner. Broad apparatus claims were also held proper but obvious, while narrower apparatus claims including a specific equation which the computer was programmed to follow were allowed because the equation was unobvious, hence the Court reasoned that it was obviously unobvious to program the machine to implement the equation.*

A typical one of the broader (and obvious) apparatus claims reads:

> 18. A system for providing a planar illustration of a three-dimensional object . . . comprising:
>
> signal means providing a first group of signals representing the three dimensional co-ordinates of the location of the observation point and a second group of signals representing the three dimensional co-ordinates of a series of points on the object, . . . ;
>
> electronic digital signal processing means [a fancy name for a computer] coupled with said signal means and programmed to provide a series of third groups of signals corresponding to . . . [specified things]; and
>
> planar illustration means coupled with said signal processing means and responsive to said series of third groups of signals to provide a planar illustration of the object.

This was held proper subject matter; certainly, the court concluded it did not involve mental steps, nor "any elements requiring or even permitting the incorporating of human facilities in the apparatus." The claim could not read on humans, as discussed in Section 31 on means clauses.

Somehow, a series of cases involving "printed matter" (Section 62) was raised by the Patent Office, but these were held not applicable (obviously).

With respect to nonstatutory subject matter, the court repudiated what it believed was the office's position in generalized form: "If . . . the novelty is indicated by an expression which

---

*This reasoning may be suspect in view of the Supreme Court's decision in the Benson & Tabbott case cited later in this Section.

does not itself fit in a statutory class . . . , then the whole invention is non-statutory since all else in the claim is old."

The court held that one *could* rely on mathematical formulae for novelty, if the claim limited their use to use in a stated machine. One was not patenting the new equation, only a computer programmed to use the equation in a certain way.

As in *Prater II*, the court held that a differently programmed computer was a physically new machine. This is unquestionably correct. However, the court cautioned that:

> It may well be that the vast majority of newly programmed machines are obvious . . . under 35 U.S.C. 103. We are concluding here that such claims are statutory under 35 U.S.C. 101, and, that claims defining them must be judged for patentability in light of the prior art.

So saying, the court then held Claim 18 obvious over the art.

Claims 19-21, which specifically recited the new equation, were held patentable. The equation was held unobvious.

The key element of Claim 19 was

> "electronic digital computer means programmed to respond to applied signals (X_e, Y_e, Z_e) and a series of groups of signals (X_1, Y_1, Z_1) to provide a corresponding series of pairs of output signals (V_1, W_1) with the relationship between signals . . . being defined as follows: — — — [equation given and terms defined]."

Interesting side notes are (1) that the equation was merely an (unobvious) simplification of the prior art equation, (2) the specification did not disclose how to program the computer (the court held this would be obvious to those skilled in the art, thus disclosure in detail was not necessary) and (3) the court revised an old combination rejection (discussed in Section 60).

In *In re Mahony*, 164 USPQ 572 (CCPA 1970), the court further construed these doctrines and the *Prater* and *Bernhart* cases. As an extension or clarification of the *Prater* doctrine, the court held that, if the preamble inherently describes a process incapable of mental performance, then the body of the claim need not expressly state that the steps are performed by a machine or computer even though the steps, considered alone, ostensibly could be performed mentally.

In a typical claim, 19, the preamble covered: "The method of establishing which *bits in a bit stream* are data bits and which are framing bits. . . ." (Italics added.)

The court held, as a fact, that at least within the framework of this claim, "bits" are electrical pulses, not "1's" and "0's" written on paper as a translation. Therefore, the human mind could not sense the pulses or perform the method. The steps in the method, held patentable, were:

> (1) comparing to one another the values of bits in respective bit positions in successive equal length groups of bits,
> (2) registering which respective positions in said groups of bits have a sequence of bit values inconsistent with said predetermined framing sequence as ascertained by repetitions of the comparing step, and
> (3) counting the number of successive bit positions in the bit stream wherein the sequence of bit values has been ascertained as inconsistent with the predetermined framing sequence, whereby the framing bit positions are established when the number of successive bit positions counted is equal to the total number between the framing bit positions.

Strictly speaking, neither *Prater*, *Bernhardt*, nor *Mahoney* were computer program applications. Both *Prater* and *Bernhardt* included process claims which were carried out in specifically disclosed hardware and, while it is true that *some* of the process steps could have been carried out in a suitably programmed general purpose computer, the overall process could not have. *Mahoney*, on the other hand, claimed a process that was, in effect, an algorithm—that is to say, a sequence of steps to accomplish a particular end result, in this instance, establishing which bits in a bit stream were framing signals and which were data signals. Like *Prater* and *Bernhardt*, *Mahoney* disclosed a particular hardware configuration, but the method claims were not limited to that hardware. Indeed, the claims in *Mahoney* could be practiced in a general purpose digital computer. However, because the claims in *Mahoney* were drafted in terms of operations performed on "bits," *i.e.*, on tangible physical representations of information, they could not be said to be computer program claims, that is to say, claims directed to a *pure* algorithm.

Whatever was left of the so-called "mental step" doctrine was all but demolished in two subsequent CCPA decisions, *In re Musgrave*, 167 USPQ 280 (CCPA 1970), and *In re Foster*, 169 USPQ 99 (CCPA 1971), both of which dealt with seismic exploration, more particularly, with the processing of seismic data. Claim 60 of Musgrave, set forth below, claims:

> In seismic exploration where a family of seismograms are produced . . . , the method which comprises:
>
> (1) generating signals from each of said seismograms,
> (2) applying to said generated signals a succession of dynamic time-adjustments, one for each seismogram . . . ,
> (3) time-shifting said generated signals . . . in accordance with a plurality of approximately hyperbolic functions of different eccentricities, and
> (4) adding together said generated signals for the production of summation signals . . .

All the method steps, except the first, which was clearly old, were to be carried out by computer. The Patent Office rejected the claims as unpatentable under 35 U.S.C. §101 citing *Abrams* and the "mental step" doctrine. The CCPA disagreed, however, stating ". . . recent cases before this Court have made it clear that there is now only a very narrow scope to this 'fearful' mental steps doctrine." Discussing the *Bernhart* and *Mahoney* decisions, the court went on to say that a *reasonable* interpretation of the claims did not include within their coverage mental implementation of the process.

The court continued, "All that is necessary, in our view, to make a sequence of operational steps a statutory process within 35 USC 101 is that it be in the technological arts so as to be in consonance with the constitutional purpose to promote the progress of 'useful arts.'. . ."*

---

*As discussed hereafter, this broad statement of the law is probably invalid under the Supreme Court decision in the Benson & Tabbott case.

Thus was the stage set for the next important software decision to come before the CCPA, *In re Benson and Tabbot,* 169 USPQ 548 (CCPA 1971), which, as we shall later see, the Patent Office subsequently appealed to the Supreme Court, with most unfortunate results for those patent practitioners who favored the protection of computer software by patent.

The *Benson and Tabbot* application involved a method for the programmed conversion of numerical information from one form to another. More specifically, the inventors claimed a method of converting binary coded decimal [BCD] signals into binary signals (claim 8).† A companion claim (claim 13) was directed to the conversion of BCD representations into binary representations, without specifically defining what those representations might be. Claim 13 of the application is set forth below:

> 13. A data processing method for converting binary coded decimal number representations into binary number representations comprising the steps of:
>
> (1) testing each binary digit position i, beginning with the least significant binary digit position, of the most significant decimal digit representation for a binary "0" or a binary "1";
> (2) if a binary "0" is detected, repeating step (1) for the next least significant binary digit position of said most significant decimal digit representation;
> (3) if a binary "1" is detected, adding a binary "1" at the (i + 1)th and (i + 3)th least significant binary digit positions of the next lesser significant decimal digit representation, and repeating step (1) for the next least significant binary digit position of said most significant decimal digit representation;
> (4) upon exhausting the binary digit positions of said most significant decimal digit representation, repeating steps (1) through (3) for the next lesser significant decimal digit representation as modified by the previous execution of steps (1) through (3); and
> (5) repeating steps (1) through (4) until the second least significant decimal digit representation has been so processed.

---

†For those not familiar with this terminology, the process would be like converting Roman numerals into Arabic numerals (VII = 7).

Not unexpectedly, the Patent Office rejected the claims as non-statutory, stating that they were drawn to "mental processes" and "mathematical steps." The CCPA reversed, however, rejecting the Patent Office argument that the claimed process was not a "process" within section 101 because a programmable computer is merely a "tool of the mind." The court also rejected the further Patent Office argument that the method was basically "mental" in character because the "workstuff" of the method was numbers, which are mathematical abstractions. As the court pointed out, cash registers, bookkeeping machines and adding machines also work only with numbers, but this has never been considered a ground for taking them out of the machine category of section 101.

The court concluded by stating that the claimed process had no practical use other than the more effective operation of a digital computer and hence, it was beyond question that since computers are in the technological field, the process itself was in the "useful arts" rather than the "liberal arts."

The Patent Office was extremely unhappy with this decision, as well as with all prior CCPA decisions in this field, beginning with the *Prater and Wei* cases. The Patent Office, thus, petitioned the Supreme Court for a writ of certiorari, which was granted. Because of the importance of this case, amicus curiae* briefs were filed by no less than thirteen interested corporations, trade associations and individuals.

In a fairly short decision, the Supreme Court reversed, in *Gottschalk v. Benson and Tabbot,* 175 USPQ 673 (Sup. Ct. 1972), ruling that the claimed subject matter was indeed non-statutory. Mr. Justice Douglas read the opinion of the Court and stated that, "Phenomena of nature, though just discovered, mental processes, abstract intellectual concepts, are not patentable, as they are the basic tools of scientific and technological work."

*Latin for "friend of the court." Amicus briefs are often filed in the Supreme Court by groups or parties concerned with the legal questions involved but not with the specific controversy between the parties. For example, patent lawyer associations and industry associations frequently file such briefs in patent cases when they think important legal principles are involved.

Justice Douglas continued, "It is conceded that one may not patent an idea. But in practical effect that would be the result if the formula for converting binary code to pure binary were patented in this case. The mathematical formula involved here has no substantial practical application, except in connection with a digital computer, which means that if the judgment below is affirmed, the patent would wholly pre-empt the mathematical formula and in practical effect would be a patent on the algorithm itself." The fundamental basis for the decision was that the claim did not define a statutory "process" (see Section 3 on statutory classes), based on a host of prior Supreme Court decisions including the *Morse* telegraph case cited in Section 28.

This is by no means the end of the story, however. Mr. Justice Douglas continued, "We do not hold that no process patent could ever qualify if it did not meet the requirements of our prior precedents. It is said that (this) decision precludes a patent for any program servicing a computer. *We do not so hold . . .*" (emphasis added).

Thus, the law regarding which computer programs are patentable and which are not is as confused now as it ever was. Certainly if the algorithm is useful *only* in a computer, it is unpatentable. But what unobvious algorithms will ever be of use outside a computer? No one knows.

In any event, the CCPA felt constrained to follow *Benson* and deny a patent in a subsequent case, *In re Christenson* 178 USPQ 35 (CCPA 1973).

The inventor claimed a method of determining the porosity of subsurface geological formations. The claim read:

> The method of determining the porosity of a subsurface formation *in situ* comprising the step of:
>
> forming a fluid filled hole through said formation,
> measuring the density of said formation,
> generating both compression and shear waves in said formation,
> computing compression and shear wave velocity from said waves,
> determining the bulk modulus of said fluid, and
> computing the porosity of the formation from the relation . . . [equation].

The examiner rejected the claim under 35 U.S.C. §103 stating that the applicant himself conceded all steps were old except the last and that mathematical equations were non-statutory under 35 U.S.C. § 101. The CCPA agreed, dismissing the applicant's arguments that *Benson* was restricted to computer programs and that the applicant's invention, being a process carried out *in situ*, was not a computer program and hence not covered by the *Benson* decision.

Citing *Benson*, the CCPA stated, "Given that the method of solving a mathematical equation may not be the subject of patent protection, it follows that the addition of the old and necessary antecedent steps of establishing values for the variables in the equation cannot convert the unpatentable method to patentable subject matter.

To further confuse the issue we must also mention two important post-*Benson* CCPA decisions that have been described by some wags as "overruling the Supreme Court." These cases both involve apparatus claims of the "means plus function" type and might appear out of place in a chapter dealing with process claims. However, if you will recall the discussion at the end of Section 34 and the Supreme Court's position on process claims *qua* process claims, you will appreciate that efforts to disguise computer process claims as apparatus claims are of interest.

In the first case, *In re Knowlton*, 178 USPQ 486 (CCPA 1973), applicant filed claims directed to a system for computer processing of list information. The specification included a rudimentary drawing of a computer but mentioned an IBM 7094 computer as being suitable for performing the invention. A detailed program listing was also included. The Patent Office rejected the claims on several grounds, one of which was the fact that, as the examiner put it, the applicant had specifically stated, ". . . that his invention (was) a program or series thereof, but . . . (was) confusing the issue by couching his claims in means plus function language." The examiner went on to say, "Such disclosed programming must be changed to method steps to be properly claimed."

The CCPA reversed, stating that even if the applicant had admitted that his invention was in the procedure or method "at best that admission constitutes *some* evidence that the claims were directed to something other than what applicant regards as his invention, and such evidence would be completely refuted by the rest of the application, including the claims as filed, as well as by appellant's position throughout the prosecution of this case. . . ."

Of course, claiming a computer program or an algorithm as a piece of hardware, that is to say, claiming a computer which has been programmed with the particular program or algorithm which is regarded as novel, is not without its perils. Among these are the "sufficiency of disclosure" and the "best mode" requirements of 35 U.S.C. §112. The case of *In re Comstock*, 178 USPQ 616 (CCPA 1973), while not directly in point, is illustrative. The applicants disclosed and claimed a desk-top calculator which apparently had not yet actually been constructed, but which had been simulated on a suitably programmed IBM 1620 computer which was disclosed as a series of block diagrams. The program, admittedly novel, was designed to achieve first-in, first-out (FIFO) storage of data from the calculator keyboard and, if successful, was to be embodied in a hard-wired form in the calculator when actually built.

Claim 1 is illustrative of the claimed invention and reads as follows:

> 1. In a calculator, the combination comprising:
>
> (a) an arithmetic and control portion;
>
> (b) keyboard means coupled to said arithmetic and control portion for manually entering data into said arithmetic and control portion;
>
> (c) a storage coupled to said arithmetic and control portion having more than one register;
>
> (d) said storage including means to enter data therein and retrieve data therefrom in a first-in, first-out arrangement;
>
> (e) and said keyboard having means for providing access to said storage to store data therein and to recall such data therefrom.

The novel element of the claim, *i.e.*, the FIFO algorithm disguised as hardware, is clearly the data entry and retrieval means set forth in paragraph (e).

The Patent Office rejected the claim under 35 U.S.C. §112 on the asserted failure of the applicant to disclose particular structure conforming to the claimed calculator. The examiner stated, "It is submitted that the IBM 1620 is made up of a multitude of circuits and logic functions, and that a program is not a teaching of the precise structure being used. . . . The Applicant is putting the burden on the public of determining the specific structure to be used, which he himself has failed to disclose or is unable to disclose. . . ."

The CCPA reversed, citing, *inter alia*, the *Knowlton* and *Bernhart* cases discussed above. The court said, "We think that . . . the specification does disclose structure supporting those elements of the combination of means appearing in the appealed claims. The specific computer itself, physically altered by the operation of the disclosed specific modifications and especially as altered by the operation of the disclosed program, is the structure to which appellants properly direct attention as the actual, practical embodiment of the invention."

The matter of computer programs thus rests, somewhat uneasily, as of January 1974. In time more cases will undoubtedly be decided by the CCPA; it is hoped these will clarify what the Supreme Court meant in the *Benson* decision.

SUMMARY—There are no special problems in drafting claims to programmable processes (see above examples). Getting them allowed is something else. If faced with such a situation, read the cited cases and any new ones carefully. Present "means for" claims instead of or in addition to process claims; where applicable, tie the claim to a specific industrial utility, such as prospecting for oil or chemically analyzing gasses. Try to avoid predicating patentability solely on a mental step or equation. Be careful you have enough disclosure to support the claims (Section 32); black boxes may not be good enough. If all else fails, appeal to the CCPA unless your case falls 100 percent under the facts of *Gottschalk v. Benson.*

See Sections 53 and 54, for comments on dependent method claims and Jepson-type method claims.

Chapter V

ARTICLE OF MANUFACTURE CLAIMS

(John D. Kaufmann & John L. Landis)

Section 42—In General

Claims to an article of manufacture (termed a "manufacture" in 35 U.S.C. §101)* differ little in principle from apparatus claims, and most of the general rules previously given apply. Basically, the article will ordinarily be a combination of elements, which must be named and tied together as with the elements of a mechanism. Articles of manufacture usually have no moving parts—examples are an ash tray or a hammer—whereas machines (even though they *are* manufactured articles) generally have moving parts as well as some "rule of operation"—examples are a stapler or a typewriter. In some borderline cases, it may be hard to tell whether a specific structure is an article of manufacture or a machine. Which (an article or a machine) is a pair of scissors? Fortunately, the difference is academic only, as no one ever questions whether an invention is in the class "machine" or the class "manufacture" for claim purposes.

Ordinarily, the preamble of an article claim merely names the product to be claimed, such as:

A resistor
A soap dish
A girdle

*"Manufacture" and "article of manufacture" mean the same thing. *In re Hruby*, 153 USPQ 61 (CCPA 1967); *In re* Hadden, 20 F.2d 275 (D.C. Cir. 1927).

If there is no generic name, one can use a functional preamble such as "a device for ____________," similar to machine claims.

The elements of an article claim are the constituent parts that go to make up the article being claimed. One simple article claim follows:

> **7. A resistor which comprises:**
> **(a) a ceramic core;**
> **(b) a coating of carbon on the core; and**
> **(c) a stripe of conductive material at each end of the core in electrical contact with the carbon coating.**

Further examples of article claims are given in Appendix B, cases 22 and 23.

Means-plus-function clauses (Section 31) may also be used in article claims, such as "means for attaching element A to element B . . . [in some particular manner, or perhaps so that some function is accomplished]."* However, the means-plus-function

*There is nothing intrinsically wrong in defining something by what it does (*i.e.*, functionally) rather than by what it is (*i.e.*, structurally). (See Section 28.) The third paragraph of 35 U.S.C. §112 specifically allows the use of such functional language as a claim limitation in defining an invention to distinguish over the prior art. *In re* Roberts and Burch, 176 USPQ 313 (CCPA 1973) (Claim 1: "Corrugated polyethylene terephthalate film having a surface coefficient of friction of less than about 0.40 *as determined by the Bell test.*"); *In re* Echerd and Watters, 176 USPQ 321 (CCPA 1973) (Claim 12: "A . . . pipe lagging material . . . having sufficient flexibility and wet strength to permit [it] to be wrapped when wet around insulated pipe surfaces . . . and having sufficient adhesive characteristics to firmly bond itself to such surfaces upon subsequent drying. . . ."); *In re* Swinehart and Sfiligoj, 169 USPQ 26 (CCPA 1971); *In re* Ludtke and Sloan, 169 USPQ 563 (CCPA 1971); *In re* Fuetter, 138 USPQ 217 (CCPA 1963). The Patent Office may however properly require proof that the functional limitations are not inherent in the prior art. *Swinehart* and *Ludtke, supra.* Moreover, such functionality may be expressed *negatively,* such as in "formed by mixing together A and B at a temperature whereat A and B are *incapable* of forming (certain undesirable compounds). . . ." *In re* Barr, Williams and Whitmore, 170 USPQ 330 (CCPA 1971); *In re* Wakefield, 164 USPQ 636 (CCPA 1970); and see Section 14 and MPEP 706.03(c). One should be aware, however, of the many non-CCPA infringement decisions which seem to state that the language, to be "accorded structural significance," must encompass a means "which possesses a *presently existing* function *[in the article]* or a *presently existing capability* to perform [the stated] function *[in the article].*"*

An article claim may distinguish from the prior art by the shape or arrangement of parts, by the materials used in construction† and sometimes even by the manner in which it was made,**

---

patentability of apparatus and article claims depends on structural limitations, and not on "mere" statements of function, whatever that means. *See, e.g.,* Scott Paper Co. v. Fort Howard Paper Co., 167 USPQ 4 (7th Cir. 1970); Galland-Henning Mfg. Co. v. Dempster Bros., Inc., 165 USPQ 688 (E. D. Tenn. 1970).

**In re* Bozek, 163 USPQ 545 (CCPA 1969). In *Bozek* a "rib means" in a pull-tab type can top was claimed as performing the function of absorbing excess metal resulting from the formation, during the manufacture of the can top, of the score line defining the pull tab. The score line formation was effected by pressing the can top between two dies which extruded metal (*i.e.,* caused it to flow) out and away from the formed score line—thus, the excess. The only function served by the rib means *in the completed top* was to strengthen the top; the prior art showed similar strengthening ribs in can tops. The excess metal absorption function was accorded no structural significance, because the rib neither performed its absorbing function *in the completed top* nor had the capability of *presently* so performing that function. No cases were cited by the court on this point.

†See further discussion in Section 52 on new use claims. *In re* Andrews, 168 USPQ 360 (CCPA 1971), the court held that the rejection of a claim because it set forth a "device according to Claim 1 . . . made from CR-MO-W steel material" was impermissible where the specification asserted that the use of such materials gave the device improved properties, and where the examiner had neither questioned the assertion nor shown the obviousness of the improved properties.

**Article claims are not indefinite simply because they include process limitations. *In re* Brown and Saffer, 173 USPQ 685 (CCPA 1972), stating: "In order to be patentable, a product must be novel, useful and unobvious. In our law, this is true whether the product is claimed by describing it, or by listing the process steps used to obtain it."; *In re* Pilkington, 162 USPQ 145 (CCPA 1969); *In re Garnero,* 162 USPQ 221 (CCPA 1969); *Ex parte* Clark and Sumerling, 174 USPQ 40 (Bd. App. 1971). Moreover, to the extent such process limitations distinguish the article from the prior art, they must be given the same consideration relative to patentability as traditional limitations. And this is true even though what the process uses or operates on is not present in the final article. *In re* Luck and Gainer, 177 USPQ 523 (CCPA 1973). Accordingly, where an article claim includes elements A and B "bonded as discussed in the next section. Special considerations apply when it is attempted to distinguish an article from the prior art by printed matter appearing on the article (see Section 62).

SUMMARY—Article of manufacture claims list the parts of the article and connect them where applicable. Means clauses and other permissible function descriptions can be used.

Section 43—Product-by-Process Claims

Part I—Patent Office Practice prior to April, 1974

Note: The following text refers to standard Patent Office practice prior to April of 1974, at which point the rules were changed nearly completely, as set out in Part IV, to follow court decisions set out in Part II.

According to the prior, classic standard Patent Office practice, this type of claim is permissible as to form only where the product "... cannot be described in any other manner" than by the process by which it was made.*

---

together by being contacted in the presence of X at a temperature of 200°F.," the process limitation ("by being contacted . . .") is entitled to patentable significance even though X is not present in any form in A, in B or in the A/B bond.

While the existence of an old or obvious method of producing an article does not *necessarily* negate the article's patentability, such a method is a factor to be considered along with similarities in and differences between the structure and properties of the article and the prior art. *In re* Lewis, 172 USPQ 238 (CCPA 1972); *In re* Hoeksema, 158 USPQ (CCPA 1968). On the other hand, the general rule is that, for an article to be patentable, it must *itself* meet the tests of 35 U.S.C. §§102 and 103. It is usually insufficient for patentability that the article is manufactured by a novel and unobvious method. Thomson Indus., Inc. v. Nippon Thompson Co., 160 USPQ 318 (E.D.N.Y. 1969); *In re* Pilkington, 162 USPQ 145 (CCPA 1969); *Ex parte* Edwards, 162 USPQ 64 (Bd. App. 1968).

*See MPEP 706.03(e), citing *In re* Moeller, 48 USPQ 542 (CCPA 1941); see also *In re* Dreyfus, 24 USPQ 463 (CCPA 1935).

As an example, assume that in the resistor of Claim 7 the carbon coating was deposited on the ceramic core by decomposition of a hydrocarbon gas. In this instance, Claim 7 might read:

> **7A. A resistor which comprises:**
> **(a) a ceramic core;**
> **(b) a coating of carbon** *deposited* **on the core by** *decomposition of a hydrocarbon* gas; **and**
> **(c) a stripe of conductive metal . . . etc.**

(Italics indicate typical product-by-process phraseology.)

This type of description would be necessary to define the novel feature if carbon coated resistors were old with the carbon applied in some other way, such as by lacquering. It would be permissible as to form *if* the carbon coating produced by decomposition of the hydrocarbon gas were different mechanically and/or electrically to the prior art coating, and if the nature of the mechanical or chemical differences was not known or could not be stated.

This type of claim covers the product *only* when made by the specified method, so the claims are not as broad as regular or "pure product" claims. In the past, Patent Office practice has been to limit these claims to hardship or emergency cases only where there seemed to be no other way to claim the invention. As noted in the prior versions of MPEP 706.03(e), applicant is not allowed such claims where he also presents regular product claims. This seems unreasonable in that one might have a patentable invention on two levels, one on a generic level, covering the article produced by any method, and one on a specific level, covering the article produced by the particular method. For example, in the carbon resistor example, one might have invented the basic carbon-coated resistor of Claim 7 and also the deposited-carbon resistor of Claim 7A. This would be one typical example of generic and species inventions (Sec. 55). If only Claim 7 were patented, and the lacquered resistor prior art did not come to light until after the patent issued, Claim 7 would be invalid and Claim 7A, which presumably would have been allowed had the examiner known the art, would not be in the patent. Perhaps the product-by-process claim could be obtained by reissue, but this would be a needless expense and intervening rights could arise, 35 U.S.C. §252.

In *Leutzinger v. Ladd,* 139 USPQ 196 (D.D.C. 1963), the court allowed both a straight product claim and dependent product-by-process claims, such as:

> 7. The subject matter of claim 1, in which the linseed oil is heated to 200°F.; the waxes are then added and the temperature is held for four to nine days.

The court found that the product of Claim 7 was not the same as the generic product of Claim 1, and both were patentable. Thus, the Manual citation above seems not only illogical, it is out of round with the law, at least in the District of Columbia.

Since the Patent Office considers that product-by-process claims are for emergency use only, the prior version of MPEP 706.06(e) states that:

> As a rule, the product-by-process claims should be limited to one, unless . . . there are material differences between the products produced by the processes recited in the different claims.

This allows some latitude, but might also be overly limiting, particularly if the processes are different, since the claim covers only the product made by the stated process. In *Ex parte Pantzer and Feier,* 176 USPQ 141 (Bd. App. 1971), eight product-by-process claims were allowed where they "vary in scope and are substantially different in coverage" (Section 58).

Part II—Further Development in the Courts

A 1969 CCPA case (*In re Pilkington,* 162 USPQ 145) casts grave doubt on these restrictions, among other reasons, on the theory that 35 U.S.C. §112 states that the claims shall particularly point out and distinctly claim what ". . . *the applicant* regards as his invention," not what some Government official regards as his invention. Note there would per se be no problem in "particularly pointing out and distinctly claiming" in this area, since the product-by-process claims are narrower than pure product claims.

The *Pilkington* case involved a claim to "a sheet of glass . . . produced by" a method described in detail and claimed in a patent issued on a parent application, of which this application was a divisional application required by the Patent Office. The glass differed from prior glasses by a fire finish on both surfaces, as well as a superior flatness and freedom from certain imperfections. Pure product claims had been presented, were finally rejected as unpatentable because of certain prior art, and were cancelled.

The examiner and board of appeals held the claim unpatentable as an improper product-by-process claim since the product could be claimed without resorting to a product-by-process claim. Note, this whipsawing of the applicant by the examiner seems intolerable: the pure product claims are obvious, but I will not look at the product-by-process claim because you could present a regular product claim. Nobody in the Patent Office ever told applicant *how* to present a pure product claim *that would be allowable.* (He probably would have, quickly.) The *Pilkington* court said:

> In considering the problem presented in claiming a product by a recital in the claim of the process by which it is made, we observed in *In re Steppan* . . . 156 U.S.P.Q. 143, 148 (CCPA 1967):
>
> "The problem, in essence, is thus one of determining who shall decide how best to state what the invention *is.* By statute, 35 U.S.C. 112, Congress has placed no limitations on *how* an applicant claims *his invention,* so long as the specification concludes with claims which particularly point out and distinctly claim that invention."
>
> With that in mind, it appears that appellant has distinctly pointed out and claimed what he regards as his invention in accordance with 35 U.S.C. 112. 162 USPQ at 148.

It is not clear whether this language was intended to abrogate the doctrine altogether, or merely to liberalize it substantially. The court went on to state that:

> . . . the differences between that [applicant's] glass and the prior art do not appear to us to be *particularly susceptible* to definition by the conventional recitation of properties or structure. *(Id.)*

As a minimum, the test would seem now to be *particularly susceptible* in the judgment of *applicant*, rather than "cannot be described" as in the MPEP.

As to unobviousness of a product-by-process claim, it must reside solely in the product, not the process. The process is immaterial except as it affects the characteristics of the product. The court quoted from *In re Dilnot*, 133 USPQ 289, 292 (CCPA 1962):

> "The addition of a method step in a product claim, which product is not patentably distinguishable from the prior art, cannot impart patentability to the product." Citing *In re Moeller*, 48 U.S.P.Q. 542; *In re Lifton*, 89 U.S.P.Q. 641; *In re Shortell*, 81 U.S.P.Q. 359; and *Tri-Wall Containers, Inc. v. U.S.*, 161 U.S.P.Q. 116. (Parenthetical remarks by court, 162 USPQ at 147.

The *Steppan* case, cited in *Pilkington*, involved a claim to:

> 25. An acid phosphate of *a condensation product of* formaldehyde with a salt of a compound selected from the group consisting of . . . [A and B], the acid phosphate having the general formula* . . . [C]. (156 USPQ at 147 emphasis added.)

Pure product (structural formula) claims were also presented, but were held obvious by the court, affirming the examiner and the board.

As to Claim 25, the court held it was not a product-by-process claim at all. Words such as "condensation product," while telling the process (condensation) are not purely process limitations;

*A general formula tells what elements are involved and in what proportions, but not how connected.

they are also structural. (Obviousness was not considered as the claim was rejected only as being an "improper" product-by-process claim.)

In addition to the language quoted above in the *Pilkington* opinion, the court reviewed the history and philosophy of the rejection, tracing it back at least as far as 1891, in *Ex parte Painter*, 1891 C.D. 200, 57 O.G. 999.

The court points out that there is no statutory basis for the rejection, and strongly implies that it would not sustain one in a future case:

> Assuming arguendo that the practice of rejecting claims as drawn to an "improper product-by-process" is somehow implicity permitted by the 1952 Act, without citation or reliance upon a stated statutory basis for the rejection, . . . [The claim in question here is O.K. anyway]. 156 USPQ at 148.

See further discussion of the rejection of many of the old formal doctrines by the CCPA as not based on statute in Sections 60 (old combination) and 52 (new use product claims). Since the claims involved in that case were held to satisfy the existing Patent Office tests for such claims, the majority of the court did not reach the basic question of whether such extra-statutory rules or doctrines for disallowing claims can lawfully be created by the Patent Office. The concurring judge was vehement in his condemnation of the existing practice as an unreasonable restriction by a government bureau, not sanctioned by Congress.

Part III—Some Restrictions on the Prior Doctrine and Further Examples

Some apparent process limitations, such as "etched," "welded," "interbonded by interfusion" are considered structural limitations not subject to the product-by-process rules. See *In re Garnero*, 162 USPQ 221, 223 (CCPA 1969) where the following claim was considered:

> A composite, porous, thermal insulation panel characterized by dimensional stability and structural strength consisting essentially of expanded perlite particles which are *interbonded one to another by interfusion* between the surfaces of the perlite particles *while in a pyroplastic state* to form a porous perlite panel. (Emphasis added to stress limitations in question.)

The court held that:

> . . . the recitation of the particles as "interbonded one to another by interfusion between the surfaces of the perlite particles" is as capable of being construed as a structural limitation as "intermixed," "ground in place," "press fitted," "etched," and "welded," all of which at one time or another have been separately held capable of construction as structural, rather than process, limitations. [Citing an article by Saxe and Levitt, *Product by Process Claims and Their Current Status,* 42 JPOS* 528 (1960.]
>
> The correct inquiry therefore, it appears to us, is whether the product defined by claim 1 is patentably distinguishable over the disclosures of Thomas and Pierce in view of the structural limitation defining the panel as "consisting essentially of expanded perlite particles . . . interbonded one to another by interfusion between the surfaces of the perlite particles.

With respect to the further process limitation, "while in a plastic state," the court found it unnecessary to be considered because the claim was already held unobvious in view of the "interbonded" limitation. However, with respect to process limitations generally the court remarked:

> . . . the mere presence of a method limitation in an article claim which is otherwise allowable would not so poison the claim as to render it unpatentable. *Ex parte Lindberg,* 157 U.S.P.Q. 606, 607 (P.O. Bd. App. 1967).

**Journal of the Patent Office Society,* a monthly periodical containing articles concerning patents and related matters. The Patent Office Society is an association of examiners and others interested in the patent system. The Journal is the main source of law review-type articles and other commentaries on the patent system.

Another example where a product-by-process claim could be used is in the treated polyethylene article of Claim 5 (Section 39) where the surface was treated with a solution of sodium dichromate in sulfuric acid. One might claim:

8. A polyethylene article having a surface treated in accordance with the process of Claim 5.

This claim also illustrates claims in two statutory classes for the same invention, and a dependent claim which crosses statutory classes (see Section 53).

Part IV—New Practice

In April, 1974, the Patent Office capitulated to the Court decisions discussed in Part II, and revised product-by-process practice completely, eliminating virtually all of the stringent "rules" or nonrules set out in Part I. Specifically, the Office eliminated the "emergency doctrine," the rule that one could not have both regular product claims and product-by-process claims, and the doctrine that such claims should be limited to one in most cases.

Specifically, in April, 1974, the Manual section 706.03(e) was completely rewritten as follows, revision 40:

706.03(e) Product by Process [R-40]

"An article may be claimed by a process of making it provided it is definite. In re Moeller, 1941 C.D. 316; 48 USPQ 542; 28 CCPA 932; In re Luck, 177 USPQ 523 (CCPA 1973); In re Steppan, 156 USPQ 143 (CCPA 1967); and In re Pilkington, 162 USPQ 145 (CCPA 1969).

"When the prior art discloses a product which reasonably appears to be either identical with or only slightly different than a product claimed in a product-by-process claim, a rejection based alternatively on either section 102 or 103 of the statute is appropriate. As a practical matter, the Patent Office is not equipped to manufacture products by the myriad of processes put before it and then obtain prior art products and make physical comparisons therewith. A lesser burden of proof is required to make out a case of prima facie obviousness for product-by-process claims because of their peculiar nature than when a product is claimed in the conventional fashion. In re Brown, 59 CCPA 1936, 173 USPQ 685 (1972); In re Fessmann, 180 USPQ 324 (CCPA 1974).

"The fact that it is necessary for an applicant to describe his product in product-by-process terms does not prevent him from presenting claims of varying scope, Ex parte Pantzer and Feier, 176 USPQ 141 (Board of Appeals, 1972)."

In the judgment of the author, this now follows the Court decisions very nicely and brings Patent Office practice into line with the law on the subject. Basically, this says that one can present product-by-process claims any time he wants to, under the strong CCPA doctrine enounciated in the Pilkington case for product-by-process claims, and many other cases in other contexts, that claims should cover what "*the applicant* regards as his invention," as expressly spelled out in 35 U.S.C. 112, not what the patent examiner thinks it is. The examiner's job is to make sure he can understand what the claim covers, in which case the claim is "particular" and "distinct" under Section 112; this is rarely a problem in product-by-process claims.

How many claims applicant wants to present, and how many different types of claims, are covered by the general rules set out in Sections 58 and 59, not by any special rules for product-by-process. The CCPA has also been increasingly liberal in these areas, that it is up to the *applicant* to determine how many claims and what types of claims are desired to protect what he, the applicant, regards as his invention.

Therefore, the thrust of new Manual section 706.03(e) is that the examiner should not worry about formal things in these areas; he should consider whether the product is novel as made by X process and, if so, then whether such new product would have been obvious. Of course, these are merely the standard statutory tests for patentability of any claim on the merits, once the formal barriers have been passed. Let us concentrate in substance, not form, says the Court.

Paragraph 2 of the new Manual section says that the Patent Office is not equipped to analyze such claimed products to determine whether there are technological differences between the claimed product made by process X and prior-art products made by process Y. Where the prior art products appear close to the examiner, "prima facie obvious," then he can put the burden on the applicant to prove that there is a difference, and an unobvious difference, as by affidavits under Rule 132. This seems eminently reasonable, and should be familiar to chemical practitioners, as similar tests are used in proving patentability of chemical compounds closely related to prior art compounds; the so-called rule of "structural obviousness," earlier known as the "homolog rule." But proving that the product of process X is different should be relatively easy in most cases, compared to cases under the homolog rule where unexpected properties are usually required.

But, the basic rule remains that the product itself must be novel and unobvious, when made by process X, and the fact that process X may be patentable is not material to patentability of the product per se. This conforms to the basic rule of Section 3, and other sections, that there must be novelty and unobviousness in each statutory class of subject matter in which claims are sought.

SUMMARY—Product-by-process claims may be obtained whenever the product has novelty and is unobvious over prior art products. Prior rules and practices relegating such claims to emergencies, and restricting their use, were abrogated in April, 1974. These are claims reciting a product or composition of matter by the process by which it was made, rather than by its structural or chemical characteristics. Mixed claims are also permitted, defining some features in "regular product" phraseology, and one or more features in product-by-process language. It is up to applicant to describe what he thinks his Invention is, and he can use product-by-process language whenever he thinks necessary or best for a particular claim.

Section 44—Design Claims

For design patents (35 U.S.C. §§171-73), only one claim, in

formal terms, is permitted: "The claim shall be in formal terms to the ornamental design for the article (specifying name) as shown, or as shown and described. More than one claim is neither required nor permitted" (Rule 153).

Thus, a design claim attempting to describe the article verbally is improper. The claim may only incorporate the specification (drawing) by reference.

One example, from Design Patent No. 215,546:

> **9. The ornamental design for a cover for data communications apparatus, substantially as shown and described.**

As with any other claimed invention, a claimed design must be novel, useful and unobvious. The overall esthetic effect (*tout ensemble*) of the design must be viewed as a whole in determining whether these qualities are present.

It has been held that a portion of a water fountain which is composed entirely of water in continuous motion (*i.e.*, the spray!) is an "article of manufacture" within 35 U.S.C. §171 and may be the subject of a design patent. *In re Hruby*, 153 USPQ 61 (CCPA 1967).*

Section 45—Plant Patent Claims

A rule similar to that for design claims holds for a plant patent claim (35 U.S.C. §§161-64). Only one claim is permitted, except that ". . . the principal distinguishing characteristics" may be recited (Rule 164) and usually are, in rather flowery language. The following example is from plant patent 2,866 (Feb. 25, 1969):

*". . . the permanence of any design is a function of the materials in which it is embodied and the effects of the environment thereon. Considering the fact that the Romans and the French built now-famous fountains hundreds of years ago which still produce the same water designs today, the notion that a fountain is 'fleeting' [and, therefore not an article of manufacture] is not one which will 'hold water' " *id.* at 64.

10. A new and distinct variety of chrysanthemum plant of the thick decorative class, substantially as herein shown and described, characterized particularly as to novelty by the unique combination of a hardy and free habit of growth, a large bloom size, a very durable flower petalage, and a distinctive and attractive general color tonality of the flowers corresponding to Apricot Yellow, very lightly overcast with Light Cadmium.

Plant patent claims frequently appear to violate the general rule that laudatory statements are not permitted therein.*

---

*The disclosure of a plant patent may not fully comply with 35 U.S.C. §112, but yet be adequate under the statute pursuant to 35 U.S.C. §162. For example, plant patents require no "how-to-make" disclosure. *In re* LeGrice, 133 USPQ 365 (CCPA 1962). Nevertheless, there must be a sufficient disclosure (*e.g.*, of alleged characteristics present in the plant which are absent in closely-related varieties of the prior art) to establish the inventive characteristics. *In re* Greer, 179 USPQ (CCPA 1973). The scope of a plant patent differs from that of other patents, because an infringer must not merely copy; he must use stock obtained from, presumably directly or indirectly, the patentee. *Ex parte* Weiss, 159 USPQ 122 (Bd. App. 1967), and cases cited at page 124 thereof.

Chapter VI

COMPOSITION OF MATTER CLAIMS—CHEMICAL CASES

Section 46—In General

Compositions of matter are products where the chemical nature of the substances or materials used, rather than shape or form of a product, is the distinguishing characteristic. As with machines versus manufactures, there is no need to determine the statutory pigeonhole between manufacture and composition. If one had a situation where both the form and composition of a material were required for novelty, or otherwise to be claimed, it would not be necessary to designate into which class the claim fell.

As in the other classes, most composition claims are combination claims, except where a new compound or molecule per se is claimed. Even those involve combinations of the chemical elements, and groups of elements, or radicals. Composition claims are usually fairly easy to prepare, as to formulating *a* claim; the main problems relate to the allowable scope of the claims, such as: How many examples are needed to support a generic claim?* How close can one come to the prior art? Problems in broad functional definitions of materials (Section 28) are especially acute; see *Ex parte Slub*, discussed in Section 28.

**See In re* Marzocchi *et al.*, 169 USPQ 367 (CCPA 1971); *Ex parte* Laiderman, 175 USPQ 575 (Bd. App. 1971). Note also the possibility of "reading on inoperative species," *In re* Cook and Merigold, 169 USPQ 298 (Bd. App. 1971). While this is not a "chemical case" (optical lens), the problem most often arises in chemical-type cases.

One simple example of a composition claim to a combination of materials follows:

11. A zinc electroplating solution, comprising:

(a) an aqueous solution of zinc acetate, from 30 to 90 grams per liter;
(b) citric acid, from 1.5 to 3 times the zinc acetate concentration; and
(c) an alkaline pH-modifying substance in an amount sufficient to adjust the pH* to a value of from 4 to 5.5

Note that the "elements" of a composition claim are chemical elements or compounds, described either broadly (element c) or narrowly (elements a and b), depending on the prior art. Note that the "pH modifying substance" clause is very similar to a "means clause" in that it tells what function the element performs, not what it is. Presumably, any alkaline substance would work in the combination, and the point of invention concerned establishing the stated pH range, not how to establish it. Means clauses are not often if ever used in composition claims, but the author sees no theoretical reason why they could not be, as: "means for adjusting the pH of the solution to a value of from 4 to 5.5. As described in Sec. 31, the statute says "an element in a claim for a combination"; it does not limit this to any particular type of combination.

In a composition claim, it is usually not essential to state the intended use for the composition in the preamble. Under classic rulings, a label such as "zinc electroplating solution" will not save the claim if the composition per se is old for another use. (See further comments in Section 52, new use claims.)

A composition of matter, claimable under the patent law, may be a new molecule, compound, solution, mixture, etc., although, in the case of a mere physical mixture of materials, an obviousness question is very likely to be raised. However, the test should be whether it would have been obvious to associate

---

*A measure of acidity, numbers below 7 being acid.

the materials, not *how* they are associated. *Ex parte Dubsky and Stark*, 162 USPQ 567 (Bd. App. 1968), is one case allowing claims to a physical mixture. Although the components of the mixture (a polymerizable compound and a chelate) were intended to react to form a compound, the mixture had a substantial shelf life and thus could be claimed. The board implied that, if the reaction were instantaneous, the mixture could not be claimed because it would have no substantial existence.

Special problems came up in the metallurgical arts in claiming new alloys, usually nowadays including changes in proportions of known ingredients to achieve new properties or advantages. For further information, see an outstanding discussion of this subject and the special rules developed by the Patent Office in *The Art of Drafting Patent Claims* 161-198. Also, as discussed in Section 51, it is often permissible to refer to an area of a component diagram shown in the drawings to define proportions of ingredients in metallurgical cases.

In the early 1960's, the board of appeals settled a long-standing philosophical debate by allowing claims to new atoms. Claim 1 of patent 3,156,523 reads "Element 95" (now called americium) and Claim 1 of patent 3,161,462 reads "Element 96" (curium). See two cases *In re Seaborg*, 140 USPQ 659 and 662 (CCPA 1964). The board of appeals* had held that the claims were directed to proper statutory subject matter, but that both elements were anticipated as having been inherently produced in the prior art (Enrico Fermi *et al.* patent), etc. The CCPA held the elements were not anticipated nor obvious in view of the prior art, and that any prior production was miniscule and unknown. (Many might question the basic conclusion as to the obviousness of a new atom per se.)

A typical type of claim to a new organic molecule:†

12. A compound having the formula:
R-CH = N-S-X,

---

*These decisions are unpublished, but available in the patent files.

†See also 47 for further example of formula claims to organic molecules, and groups of molecules.

wherein

R is an alkyl group selected from the group consisting of methyl, ethyl and isopropyl; and

X is a halogen selected from the group consisting of chlorine and bromine.

Note that the foregoing claim covers a total of six specific compounds, for any use to which they can be put. This illustrates the very common class of inventions where new molecules are claimed by structural formula. It also illustrates the use of what is termed "Markush," or alternative, terminology to cover several different compounds with a single claim. (See Section 47.)

See Sec. 53 for comments on dependent composition claims, and Sec. 54 on Jepson-type claims in this area.

SUMMARY—Composition of matter claims list the chemical ingredients (compounds, elements or radicals) making up the composition or compound. The ingredients or elements may be claimed narrowly (specific named components), with intermediate scope (a group of similar elements functionally equivalent), or broadly as to function performed, where the prior art permits. Where necessary to novelty, etc., the proportions or other conditions or parameters of the compound are stated, usually in ranges of concentration of ingredients. The intended use for the composition (rust inhibition, antibiotic) may or may not be stated in the preamble. (See Section 52 for details on the effect of preamble limitations.) The problems in chemical practice come primarily with obviousness questions over prior art and how much disclosure is needed in the specification, not primarily in the techniques of drafting claims.

Section 47—"Markush" Expressions

This type of expression, from a commissioner's decision, *Ex parte Markush,* 1925 C.D. 126, 340 O.G. 839, where permitted, may be used in "chemical type" cases only. It is a sort of a home-made generic expression covering a group or two or more different materials (elements, radicals, compounds, etc.) which will work in the combination claimed.

A typical example, from the previous section, Claim 12: ". . . *a* halogen *selected from the group consisting of* chlorine and bromine."

Note that this covers either chlorine or bromine, either of two specific elements out of five in the halogen group, in apparent violation of the "rule" against alternative claiming discussed in Section 21. The Markush doctrine originated out of necessity. In the previous example there is no generic word for the specified group of two halogens out of five. To refuse a generic claim because of a paucity of language seems unreasonable. Thus, Markush language is used to create an artificial generic expression.

Mr. Markush's claim in question involved: "a material selected from the group consisting of aniline and halogen substitutes of aniline."

Markush terminology may be used in claims in any of the statutory classes of utility patents; wherever several alternative types of material are involved. As an example of an article of manufacture, in the resistor of Section 42, if the only materials that would work for the terminal stripes were copper, silver and aluminum, or if for any other reason a claim limited to those three materials were desired, clause (c) of Claim 7 could read as follows: "a stripe of *a conductive metal selected from the group consisting of* copper, silver and aluminum at each end of the core in electrical contact with the carbon coating."

For a process claim, consider the example in Section 39 of treating polyethylene articles, and suppose that the acid could be only concentrated sulfuric, nitric or phosphoric acid.

The claim then would read:

5A. A process for treating the surface of a polyethylene article to increase its receptivity to printing ink, which comprises:

exposing the surface of the article to a saturated solution of sodium dichromate in *an acid selected from the group coisisting of* **concentrated sulfuric, nitric and phosphoric acids.**

In the foregoing examples, the italics indicate the Markush phraseology. It should be followed exactly: "Never "comprising"; never "or"; always "A ——— selected from the group consisting of ——— . . . and ———." Note that the word "consisting" limits the claim to the named group, as mentioned in Section 7. An interesting example is from Stebbings patent 3,234,948 on a cheese filter cigarette: "2. A cigarette filter according to Claim 1, in which the cheese comprises grated particles of cheese selected from the group consisting of Parmesan, Romano, Swiss and cheddar cheeses." This illustrates the use of a Markush expression to define one element of an article of manufacture claim.

The rigidity of this possibly artificial language was liberalized by a 1965 Notice on "Technical Rejections," MPEP 706.03(y), which permits claiming in the alternative *if* a Markush group would have been proper:

> When materials recited in a claim are so related as to constitute a proper Markush group, they may be recited in the conventional [Markush] manner, or alternatively. For example, if "wherein R is a material selected from the group consisting of A, B, C and D" is a proper limitation then "wherein R is A, B, C or D" shall also be considered proper.

Apparently, under this "modified Markush practice," in the example of Claim 7, one could recite a "stripe of copper, silver or aluminum. . . .' This is much simpler and covers the same thing as the regular Markush form. Note that this "liberalization" is only a matter of words, not substance; thus one might suppose that many attorneys will continue to use the classic Markush phraseology for an indefinite time because they are used to it and the examiners are accustomed to seeing it.

There once was a policy against Markush claims of diminishing or varying scope (Claim 1—the group A, B, C and D; Claim 2 —A, B and C), but this is now considered proper *unless* ". . . such a practice renders the claims indefinite [this would be rare] or if it results in undue multiplicity" (MPEP 706.03(y); Section 59). Markush claims also may be allowed as subordinate ("subgenus") claims under a broader ("genus") claim not naming particular materials (see Section 55 on generic and species claims). Under this liberalized practice, for example, Claim 1 could cover conductive materials broadly, Claim 2 a Markush group of 5 materials, Claim 3 a limited group of three preferred materials, etc.

When claiming specific compounds per se (that is molecules), questions have arisen in how closely related the members of the Markush group must be for the claim to be proper: could one claim such disparate things as air, earth, fire or water? Polypropylene, benzene hexafluoride, tantalum sesquinitride, or element # 117. Until the early 1970's Patent Office policy was that the materials in the Markush group must ordinarily "belong to a recognized physical or chemical class or an art-recognized class," according to prior standard Patent Office policy, as stated in MPEP 706.03(v). Air, earth, fire and water would not suffice. In the early 1970's, the Office began to crack down on this, particularly with formula claims (Sec. 46) covering thousands of new compounds involving many radically different substituents.

In *Rohm & Haas v. Commissioner*, 177 USPQ 625 (D.D.C. 1973), the District Court for the District of Columbia affirmed a Patent Office Board of Appeals ruling* that a Markush claim to two different compounds is improper where the claim includes two "patentably distinct" inventions. This apparently means that if compound A were prior art, compound B would be unobvious over A, and vice versa, then a Markush claim to the group A or B is improper. The theory is that, here, there are two "independent and distinct" inventions, thus restriction into two patents must be required under 35 U.S.C. §121. Therefore, the Markush claim covering either A or B is improper. This is apparently a new doctrine as far as the court is concerned, and it remains to be seen how far the Patent Office will pursue this reasoning in restricting Markush claims. There is some doubt as to whether the CCPA would follow the *Rohm & Hass* decision.

In November, 1973, the CCPA cast great doubt on the Patent Office policy of rejecting or otherwise refusing to act on Markush

---

**Ex parte Haas*, 175 USPQ 217 (Bd. App.—1972), a 10-5 decision by an augmented, special panel, with six different opinions on the subject.

claims covering species A or B, where the Examiner thinks A and B are "patentably distinct" inventions. The Court did not mention the *Rohm & Haas* case. In *In re Wolfrum and Gold,* 179 USPQ 620 (CCPA-1973), the Court held that Markush claims could not per se be rejected under 35 U.S.C. 112; and in *In re Haas,* 179 USPQ 623 (CCPA-1973), the Court held that a "withdrawal" of the Markush claim from further consideration after a restriction requirement was a "rejection" of the claim on the merits, thus both the Board of Appeals and the CCPA had the jurisdiction and the duty to review the decision. The sum of these two cases is that the CCPA will eventually decide for itself the "patentably distinct Markush" question decided adversely to applicants in the Rohm and Haas case by the District Court for the District of Columbia.

In the Wolfrum case, the head or generic claim was "an azo dyestuff selected from the group consisting of . . . [A and B]," where A was any of a great many complex organic tertiary amine molecules, and B was the quaternary ammonium salts of the same group of molecules. Restriction had been required between groups A and B on the theory that these were "patentably distinct inventions." The Markush claim to A *or* B was rejected on various grounds, but the only ground (statutory basis) actually decided and affirmed by the Board of Appeals was that the claim was improper under 35 U.S.C. 112:

> . . . and appellant does not definitely and accurately point out his invention when he assembles a plurality of different inventions in a single claim.

The Court held only that Section 112 will not support such a rejection, and left the question open whether some other section of the statute would. This is in keeping with (1) the Court's long-standing insistance that *all* rejections stem from some specific section of the statute (see comments in Section 60 on statutory vs. case law rejections in general); and (2) the Court's traditional unwillingness to decide any issue other than whether the Board was right or wrong on the exact rejection and ground of rejection they decided.

In other words, the Court did not hold that Markush claims to two different inventions were proper, only that Section 112 was not a proper ground of rejection.

On Section 112, the Court followed a growing line of its cases (see Section 64) that Section 112 requires only that the Examiner be able to understand what *the applicant* regards as his invention; that is, that the claim be "precise and definite" as to what it covers. This would normally be no problem with a Markush claim per se; the claim covers either compound(s) A or compound(s) B. Whether or not A is "patentably distinct" from B is obviously immaterial to the question of whether the claim is definite; that is whether it "particularly points out and distinctly claims what *the applicant* regards as his invention." Clearly, applicant here, thought he invented A or B and wanted to claim it so.

In *In re Haas*, the CCPA held that both it and the Patent Office Board of Appeals has the power (jurisdiction) and the duty to review a patent Office refusal to consider a Markush claim covering what were alleged to be "patentably distinct" inventions. Even though the refusal came up in connection with a restriction requirement, as in the Rohm and Haas case discussed above, and was stated to be a "withdrawal of the claim from further consideration," the Court held that it was still a rejection of substance, since the Examiner had refused to act on the claims. Thus, the Markush claim was rejected on a substantive ground, regardless of the words used by the Examiner.*

But the Court did not decide the question on the merits; it merely remanded the case to the Board of Appeals for the Board to decide the question on the merits. (An earlier, split decision by a special 15-member Board, that it had no jurisdiction to pass on the merits, *Ex parte Haas*, 175 USPQ 217 (Bd. App. 1972), was reversed. (See that case for a detailed discussion of the issues.)

In the Haas case, the claim in question was a typical Markush claim, in this case covering any of a large number of specific compounds. The claim read:

---

*Note—Neither the Board nor the CCPA has the power to review a pure restriction requirement, as noted in *In re Hengehold*, 169 USPQ 473 (CCPA-1971).

1. A compound of the formula:*

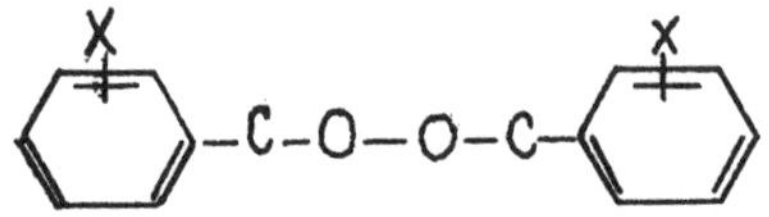

wherein X is a reactive functional group selected from the group consisting of monosubstituted chloro, bromo and fluoro alkyl groups containing from 1 to 3 carbon atoms, inclusive; formyl; formyl substituted alkyl groups containing from 1 to 4 carbon atoms inclusive; isocyanate; and isocyanate substituted alkyl groups containing from 1 to 4 carbon atoms, inclusive.

Thus, the claim covers di-substituted benzoyl peroxides, with any of some 25 different substituents in each of the X positions, or some 625 different compounds as to basic chemical ingredients, and many thousands of specific compounds, counting all of the isomers.

The Examiner's problem is that some of the X substituents are radically different from each other; haloalkyl such as $-CH_2Cl$ is quite different from formyl $-CH{=}O$, or isocyano $-N{=}C$. Therefore, the Examiner believed that Mr. Haas made more than one invention and should not be entitled to claim all of these separate inventions in a single patent solely because his attorney was skillful enough to write a single Markush claim covering compound A or compound B, or C, D, E . . . etc.

The Patent Office, examining branch, would like the rule to be that one cannot use a Markush, alternative form of claim, to do what he cannot otherwise do, claim two independent and distinct inventions in one patent. The statute, 35 U.S.C. 121, gives the Commissioner power to forbid that, via a restriction requirement, and the Office sees the Haas type of claim as a way around the basic law that if one has two Inventions, he should get two patents.

In a footnote (4 on page 625), the Court reversed a rejection by the Examiner under 35 U.S.C. 101, although the Board didn't

*See section 46 on formula claims to organic molecules.

consider it. The Court held that "the purpose of §101 is to define patentable subject matter, not to limit a patent to one invention."

The net result of this case, plus the *Wolfrum and Gold* decision discussed above, is that the Patent Office must find some *statutory* basis to reject Markush claims to different inventions if it wants to continue this practice, and that neither Section 101 nor Section 112 is any good. Also, the CCPA has served notice that *it* will decide this question for itself the next time it comes up.

Since the CCPA (in all but obviousness-type double patenting rejections discussed in Sec. 60) requires an express statutory basis for all rejections, it seems clear that "improper Markush claim" will not be good enough. The Office must point to some section of the statute that forbids it, and it cannot be Section 112 or Section 101. Presumably, this will have to be 35 U.S.C. 121, the restriction clause, "if two or more *independent and distinct* inventions are claimed in one application, . . ." the Commissioner *may* require restriction. But how can a claim to A or B be independent and distinct from a claim to A alone or B alone?

This author predicts the CCPA will not follow the Rohm& Haas case when it gets a crack at the question.

In May, 1974, the following Patent Office Notice was released (922 O.G. 1016), following the Haas case and setting out further details on implementation:

May 1, 1974

PRACTICE RE MARKUSH-TYPE CLAIMS

This notice deals with Markush-type claims which include a plurality of alternatively usable substances or members. In most cases this recitation by enumeration is used because there is no appropriate or true generic language.

Where an application claims two or more independent and distinct inventions, the Commissioner, under the provisions of 35 U.S.C. 121, may require the application to be restricted to one of the inventions.

"A Markush-type claim is directed to "independent and distinct inventions," if two or more of its members are so unrelated and diverse that a prior art reference anticipating the claim with respect to one of the members would not render the claim obvious under 35 U.S.C. 103 with respect to the other member(s).

If the claim is of that nature, the examiner is authorized to reject it as an improper Markush claim and for misjoinder under 35 U.S.C. 121 and to require the applicant to restrict the application to a single invention. In making such a requirement, the examiner will (1) clearly delineate the members or groups of members believed to constitute improperly joined inventions, and (2) state reasons fully explaining why they are independent and distinct. Applicant's response to such a requirement should be an election of a single adequately disclosed and supported invention, with or without restriction of the claim(s) to that invention. Of course, the response must not introduce new matter into the application. See 35 U.S.C. 132 and *In re Welstead*, 59 CCPA 1105, 463 F.2d 1110, 174 USPQ 449 (1972). A refusal to elect a single invention will be treated as a non-responsive reply.

If the members of the Markush group are sufficiently few in number or so closely related that a search and examination of the entire claim can be made without serious burden, the examiner is encouraged to examine it on the merits, even though it is directed to independent and distinct inventions. In such a case, the examiner will not follow the procedure outlined in the preceding paragraph and will not require restriction.

Where the examiner has rejected the claim and required restriction and the applicant has responded without restricting the claim(s) to a single invention, the examiner shall, if the position is adhered to, again reject the claim and any other Markush claims not restricted to the elected invention. No further examination of these claims is required unless and until such rejection has been overcome. However, if the search of the single elected invention develops prior art which would render both the elected invention and the improper Markush claim(s) unpatentable, such prior art may be applied in rejections of both without a complete search of the subject matter of the improper Markush claim(s).

Otherwise, only true generic claims and those restricted to the elected invention will be examined in the usual manner.

"Review of the rejection will be by appeal to the Board of Appeals under 35 U.S.C. 134."

With this Notice, the Rohm & Haas rule is made discretionary with the Examiner. But the last paragraph, appeal to the Board of Appeals, means that the CCPA will now get a chance to review the question as the Court stated in the Haas case that it would.

The above rulings, at least through 1974, appear to relate only to claims for two different compounds. When claiming a process or a combination of materials, standard Patent Office practice is more liberal:

> it is sufficient if the members of the group are disclosed in the specification to possess at least one property in common which is mainly responsible for their function in the claimed relationship and it is clear from their very nature or from the prior art that all of them possess this property. This test should be applied as liberally as possible. MPEP 706.03(y).

Also, where a Markush expression is applied only to a portion of a chemical compound (for example, Claim 12, a radical such as methyl, ethyl, etc.), the propriety of the grouping is determined by consideration of the compound as a whole, and does not depend on there being a community of properties in the members of the Markush expression per se. See *Ex parte Price*, 150 USPQ 467 (Bd. App. 1965), for further discussion.

It has consistently been held improper to extend Markush claiming to process steps or mechanical elements, such as "a fastener selected from the group consisting of nails, rivets and screws." In mechanical cases, there would usually be some generic word available, often a "means for" clause.

SUMMARY—Markush claims define alternative chemical ingredients that can be used in a compound, composition, process or article. Where claiming alternative compounds, they must not be "patentably distinct" under present office practice; otherwise, they need only have a common property useful in the combination claimed. The standard format is "a ______________ selected from the group consisting of A, B and C." There are many detailed rules on Markush practices described in the preceding section, and modern Patent Office practice may be to restrict use of Markush claims and to require restriction between inventions the examiner thinks are independent and distinct. The CCPA will probably speak on this shortly, and very possibly will reverse.

Section 48—Trademarked Materials—Arbitrary Names

Where an ingredient in a composition to be claimed is known only by a trademark or by an arbitrary name used in trade, according to the Patent Office, MPEP 608.01(v), such names may be used in the application and claims *only* where the term has a fixed and definite meaning, either well known in the literature or defined in the application, if necessary by describing the process of manufacture. Where available, a generic name should be used. If the description is not sufficiently definite to enable one skilled in the art to practice the invention (35 U.S.C. §112), the claim may be rejected. There has been much controversy over this, and the law should be regarded as unsettled.

In *Ex parte Steigerwald*, 131 USPQ 74 (Bd. App. 1961), the board rejected an application because the specification used various trade names ". . . without precise identification of the composition thereof at the time of filing," citing MPEP 608.01(v) and *Ex parte Bickel*, 122 USPQ 27 (Bd. App. 1957).

In the *Bickel* case, the board rejected a claim including the key limitation

> absorbing sodium from the spent solution with a synthetic resin base carboxylic acid ion exchange material in the hydrogen form....

The specification identified the class of materials similarly to the description in the claim and gave one specific example: "Amberlite IRC-50 available from the Rohm and Haas Company." This much appeared in a chemical dictionary, but the formula, process of making, etc., Amberlite were unknown to applicant. (A later filed patent was held unavailable to augment the disclosure.)

The claims were held unpatentable because the specification did not satisfy rule 71(b). (See Appendix D.) The board held:

> It is believed self-evident that the naming of a class will not serve as a specific embodiment. The designation of a compound solely by its arbitrary trade name without more is not a proper identification of that compound under the patent statutes. *Lamn v. Watson,* 108 USPQ 203 [D.D.C. 1955]. A manufacturer may arbitrarily alter such composition and thus leave the public or anyone later practicing the invention without sufficient information to carry it out.

In the *Lamm* case, the court held improper the inclusion of a generic term "a polymerized acrylic ester" having defined properties, where the only example in the specification was "Acryloid 710."

In *Leutzinger v. Ladd,* 139 USPQ 196 (D.D.C. 1963), the use of a well-known trademarked material "Carnuba" was approved on the theory that the substance was generally known to those skilled in the art at the time the application was filed.

In an article, *Rules Defining the Use of Trade Terms in Patent Applications,* 51 JPOS 339 (June 1969), Mr. F. Prince Butler reviews many prior cases and publications on the subject, and deduces the following general rules and summary:

> Rule #1—A Trade Term is properly used in a specification if those skilled in the art can make the product designated by the trade term at the time the application is filed, using the specification and/or published literature that is implicated by the specification.
>
> Rule #2—A trade term is also properly used in a specification if the product is generally known to persons skilled in the art and is readily obtainable at the time the application is filed, provided the composition of the product is a trade secret and there is reason to believe that whenever the composition of the product is mofied the trade term will also be changed.

> Rule #3—A trade term is also properly used in a specification if it designates a component of the embodiment which is not essential to the invention.
>
> Rule #4—A trade term can be used in a claim only if its meaning has been adequately defined in the specifications, whereby it imparts specific limitations to the claim.
>
> SUMMARY*
>
> Generally, it is undesirable to use trademarks and trade names in patent applications; however, courts have allowed their use under a variety of factual circumstances. Because of the divergence of such decisions it is difficult for patent attorneys and patent office examiners to appraise whether or not particular trade terms have been properly used in patent applications. This note presents four rules which embody all the known cases involving the use of trade terms in patent applications.

While the author of this book believes this JPOS article goes a long way in synthesizing a set of reasonable rules for future reference, he also believes the law should go still further in providing protection.

The proper test should be the rule of reason, derived only from 35 U.S.C. §112. Has applicant disclosed everything about the material he reasonably can? If so, that is enough.

If "Amberlite IRC 50" is a critical material in a process or composition, and if the applicant does not know what it is and the trademark owner will not say, why should he be denied a patent, assuming the invention is unobvious, etc.? If, as the board or courts worry, the trademark owner goes out of business or so modifies the formula that the invention no longer operates, then the patent would be useless. Validity would not come into question, because no one could practice the invention. However. if, as more normally happens, the trademark owner does not go out of business, the patent would then remain operative and useful as long as the material stayed available. A patent with an effective life of five years is preferable to no patent at all. Samples

---

*From Butler article.

of the trademarked material, as it existed at the application date, could be deposited with the Patent Office, or other depository, along the lines of microorganisms. Also, since the disclosure of the trademarked material by name is a description of an existing thing, it should not be held "new matter" to add a further description of that material if it subsequently becomes available any time before the patent is granted and perhaps even after grant of the patent. The only thing that should be required is an affidavit or statement of *identity*—that the later description indeed describes the composition mentioned in the applications—nothing else. The rule against new matter* should really have nothing to do with this mere identification question.

The basic rule should be:

> Applicant must particularly point out and distinctly claim what he regards as his invention, as particularly and distinctly as is reasonably possible under the circumstances. Liberal rules should be applied in hardship cases to avoid unpatentability of unobvious inventions on nonsubstantive grounds beyond applicant's control.

Of course, trademarks should always be properly designated. See MPEP 608.01(v) and other sources on correct trademark usage for details.

SUMMARY—Avoid defining compositions used in practicing an invention by trademark or trade name so far as possible. Where there is no other way, describe everything known about the material in the application. If rejected under 35 U.S.C. §112, appeal.

Section 49—Special Claims for Chemical Cases —Fingerprint Claims

In chemical composition claims, special forms of claims are sometimes permitted on an emergency basis. One important situation is where a new composition has been produced, such as

*35 U.S.C. §113: "No amendment shall introduce new matter into the disclosure of the invention."

a new or modified form of a material, but where the differences from previous forms *cannot* be explained in terms of physical or chemical structure. In this situation so-called "fingerprint" claims are sometimes permitted, defining the material in terms of its properties, such as X-ray diffraction patterns, solubility, melting point, etc.

One famous example follows, from the Aureomycin patent, Duggar 2,482,055. Claim 1 reads:

> Substances effective in inhibiting the growth of Gram positive and Gram negative bacteria selected from the group consisting of a substance capable of forming salts with acids, containing the elements carbon, hydrogen, nitrogen, chlorine, and oxygen, being very soluble in pyridine, soluble in methanol and in acetone and being slightly soluble in ethanol and in water, its crystals having a refractive index parallel to elongation between about 1.674 and 1.694, and exhibiting characteristic absorption bands in the infra red region of the spectrum when suspended in a hydrocarbon oil in solid form at the following frequencies expressed in reciprocal centimeters: 3420, 1643, 1609, 1580, 1523, 1302, 1231, 1209, 1121, 1080, 1050, 969, 943, 867, 844, 825, 805, 794, 788, 733, 713 and the acid salts of said substance.

This was a new chemical compound, but the inventors did not know what the structure was at the time. They described it as to every property known, as well as providing considerable detail in the specification on methods of production with a newly discovered strain of bacteria named "*Streptomyces aureofaciens*," because it produced the new chemical Aureomycin.

Note that the proper test for this type of claim should be whether it "distinctly claims" the invention under Section 112 of the statute. In other words, do the listed properties so uniquely identify the novel composition, as do fingerprints, that they (1) distinguish from old compositions and (2) cover the new composition with sufficient certainty that potential infringers can tell when they have the patented compound and when they do not.

In *Benger Labs, Ltd. v. R. K. Laros Co.*, 135 USPQ 11, 14 (E.D.Pa. 1962), the court held:

> . . . nothing in the law requires the courts to deny a patent to the inventor of a new and useful product merely because . . . the chemical structure cannot be recognized and described. All that is necessary is that the patentee make as full disclosure as he reasonably can and that he describe the product with sufficient particularity that it can be identified and that those who are interested in its manufacture are enabled to determine what will and what will not infringe.

Claim I in question was: "A composition comprising a substantially nonionic complex of ferric hydroxide with a dextran having an average intrinsic viscosity at 25°C. at about 0.025 to about 0.25, said complex being stable in contact with water." 135 USPQ at 13.

The court held this precise enough: ". . . whatever its chemical formula may be, it can be distinguished from both mixtures and compounds." 135 USPQ at 14.

In at least some cases, the claim may be simplified by referring to a spectrum shown in a drawing. For example, Donouick *et al.* patent 2,982,689 (May 2, 1961):

> A substance effective in inhibiting the growth of gram-positive bacteria, selected from the group consisting of thiostrepton and the salts thereof, said thiostrepton being
>
> a weakly basic substance
> having the following elementary analysis . . . ;
> has an antibacterial spectrum including . . . ;
> possesses a crystalline structure in the pure state;
> is substantially soluble in . . . ,
> and relatively insoluble in . . . ;
> darkens at . . . and
> melts at . . . ;
> has an absorption spectrum . . . ;
> and an infra spectrum when suspended in hydrocarbon oil in solid form substantially as shown in the drawing.

See Section 51 on claims referring to drawings generally, and Section 50 on coined name claims. This seems to be a hybrid claim, defining first the coined name and then its distinctive properties, telling what the coined name means.

See also Waksman *et al.* patent 2,992,162 (July 11, 1961) and

Cataldi *et al.* patent 3,015,607 (Jan. 2, 1962) for further examples. See also the discussion in Jackson and Morris, *The Art of Drafting Patent Claims* 220-226, 333-335.

See also *In re Miller*, 169 USPQ 547 (CCPA 1971), cited in Section 20, for an allowable fingerprint claim to polytetrafluoroethylene particles defined by size, molding properties (use), strength, and many other factors. Note this claim is to the form of a product, as a molding compound, not to its chemical composition.

Section 50—Coined Name Claims

A somewhat similar form of claim is the "coined name" claim. For example, in Conover patent 2,699,054, Claim 2 simply reads "Tetracycline."* While this patent has been much in litigation, the form of claim—one word—was not attacked. Tetracycline was alleged to be a new organic molecule (whether or not it was new was part of the dispute), which was identified in the specification as to structure, properties and method of production. Of interest, it was a chlorinated form of Aureomycin discussed in Section 49, discovered in the course of research which finally determined the structure of Aureomycin. Presumably, the antibiotic tetracycline had become known by that name in the literature, so that the mere name did identify the compound, and drawing the long organic molecule was unnecessary.

Apparently, the Patent Office has held that coined name claims are proper only where the name was known to the art before the application was filed. This would be rare.

In *Ex parte Brian*, 118 USPQ 242 (Bd. App. 1958), the board held that a claim to: "An alkali metal salt of gibberellic acid" was improper since the coined name was not art recognized, although defined in the specification.

Citing authority, the board stated: "Since these claims do

---

*Its full name is "4-dimethylamino-1, 4a, 5, 5a, 6, 11, 12a-octahydro-3, 6, 10, 12, 12a-pentahydroxy-1, 11-dioxo-2-naphthacenecarboxamide."

not recite the . . . necessary physical and chemical characteristics [as in other "fingerprint" claims] . . . to properly identify the acid, they do not adequately define the invention." 118 USPQ at 245. Fingerprint claims, to the unknown structure, were allowed as discussed in Section 49. Product-by-process claims (Section 43) were rejected because the material could be otherwise defined, by the fingerprint claims.

It is not clear whether such a claim could be used instead of a fingerprint claim in a case such as Aureomycin, where the structure was unknown at the time, but the name was known. The method claims in the Duggar patent do refer to "A process for the production of Aureomycin," without repeating all the characteristics. Perhaps a coined name claim to an unknown structure, if allowable, would not be as valuable as a fingerprint claim because, from the claim, it would not be clear which of all the properties listed in the specification would be required to infringe the coined name claim, whereas each of the fingerprint claims lists specific key properties which must be met, but not all properties mentioned in the specification. If the claim is to one specific molecule, the number of properties listed would presumably be immaterial because the compound is the same regardless of the number of properties listed.

In a somewhat similar case, Altman *et al.* patent 3,382,053, May 7, 1969, the office allowed both a coined name claim "A composition of matter comprising beta tantalum" and several fingerprint claims describing the material in terms of its properties and characteristics. This involved a new form of the element tantalum of unknown physical structure, but the distinct properties could be stated in terms of crystallographic analysis, etc.

In all of these situations, where the structure is unknown, a product-by-process claim might also be proper, as noted in Section 43—to define the new material. Note the process would necessarily be different, and almost always unobvious, if a new material were produced. However, such a claim would not necessarily be as valuable as a fingerprint or coined name claim, since the product-by-process claim would cover the material only when made by that process, and there might be other processes to produce the material. Sometimes, fingerprint and product-by-process recitations are combined in a single claim further to identify the material.

As to presenting more than one type of claim to the same material, the board in the *Brian* case, previously discussed in this section, rejected all claims for "undue multiplicity" (Sections 58-59), since applicants were attempting to claim the same material three different ways (coined names, fingerprint, and product-by-process). This ruling seems unduly harsh, and may not be proper today.

Section 51—Claims Referring to Drawings

Another example of an emergency situation, wherein special rules are allowed in chemical cases, is a claim referring to a drawing. This comes up particularly in three-element compositions, such as alloys, where the proportions of each element may be varied and the other two may then be varied for each concentration of the first element. This can readily be depicted on a three-element triangular diagram, but is extremely difficult to define in words. Thus, where practical necessity dictates, claims with limitations such as the following have been allowed: ". . . with said manganese content restricted to amounts beneath the curve in the accompanying diagram. . . ." *In re Tanczyn*, 97 USPQ 150 (CCPA 1953). The diagram was a series of curves in a drawing showing maximum amounts of manganese for various amounts of chromium.

Similarly, in a process, Claim 1 of Stauch patent 2,248,173 (April 26, 1966) reads:

> A process for testing female urine to determine pregnancy which comprises heating in the urine at a pH below 6.5 a paper strip impregnated with a predetermined amount of iodine, the amount of iodine being related to the specific gravity of the urine sample and to the volume thereof in the manner shown on the accompanying graph, to produce a raspberry pink color on said strip indicating pregnancy when the test is positive.

The graph was a three dimensional perspective drawing, depicting operable amounts of iodine as a function of volume and specific gravity.

In 1961 this doctrine was extended to a mechanical case.

In *Ex parte Squires*, 133 USPQ 598 (1961), the board of appeals allowed a claim to "A font of numerals as shown in Fig. 1," reproduced below:

(Squires patent 3,034,806) *Fig. 1*

As is apparent, it is extremely difficult, probably impossible, to describe the characteristics of the numerals in words.

Applicant alleged that this font was particularly superior to previous numerals in low intensity red light encountered in submarines, which increased the readability of the numerals. This was not denied by the examiner.

The board found this to be: "the best, most accurate way of defining the invention which depends on . . . the precise configuration of the numerals and their interrelation in a set." 133 USPQ at 600. Claim 2 of the Squires patent (the only other claim allowed) reads: "In an environment of low brightness of red light, a font of numerals as shown in Fig. 1."

As to what equivalents are covered by such a truly "picture claim," no one may ever know, since it is a United States government patent intended for use in submarines. For further discussion of the principles, see an article by the attorney for Mr. Squires, L. B. Applebuam, *The One Line Picture Claim,* 44 JPOS 379 (1962).

In 1966, the board of appeals in *Ex parte Lewin,* 154 USPQ 487, refused to extend the *Squires* doctrine, holding that this is a necessity doctrine only, not for applicant's convenience. In *Lewin,* a claim to an electrical method as "The method set forth in Fig. 15 of retrieving words from a content-addressed memory" was held improper. Fig. 15 was a block diagram depicting the steps in the method. The reasoning was that this method of claiming was not necessary, and could not be used merely for convenience.

The board held:

> Concerning the incorporation by reference of subject matter outside the claim, we are in agreement with the examiner that this device is properly used only where it can be shown that it is not possible or feasible to appropriately define the invention within the confines of a claim.
>
> We note that certain exceptions have become recognized in the case of inventions in which the only, or only feasible mode of definition is by an incorporation by reference from outside the claims, as for example microphotographs of metallurgical grain structures or irregular areas of a graph, such as a phase diagram. Ex parte Squires, 133 USPQ 598, is a similar exception based on the specific nature of the subject matter of that invention, a font of numerals, which the Board found to be the most accurate way of defining the invention in view of the "poverty of words to properly point out and distinctly claim the invention."
>
> In the record of the instant appeal we find no showing that such a "poverty of words" exists but, on the contrary, we find other claims to appellant's method in which no such poverty is

> evident and we note also that the material sought to be incorporated from Figures 3 and 15 of the drawing is not the appearance of some tangible object but is the meaning or sense conveyed by words alone, of which these figures of the drawing essentially are composed.
>
> On the particular facts of the instant case we find no exceptionable problem of definition of the invention nor do we consider it proper to make an exception solely for an applicant, to display multiple techniques of grammatical composition.

SUMMARY—(Sections 49-51) In emergency cases involving impossibility of words to accurately define an invention, special techniques may be employed, such as the fingerprint claim (Section 49); more rarely, the coined name claim (Section 50); or claims referring to drawings (Section 51). These are emergency doctrines only, and normally one has to show there is no other possible or practical way. Normally these are limited to chemical cases, although there is no necessary reason they have to be, as in the "font of type" case, only chemistry is more mysterious.

Section 52—New Use Claims—Preamble Limitations

At least until 1969, standard textbook law and routine Patent Office rulings have been that one cannot rely for novelty on a statement of intended use in the preamble of a composition claim, sometimes called a "label claim."

For example, if the zinc-electroplating solution of Claim 11 (Section 46) were old for some other (and hopefully unrelated) purpose, the label "a zinc electroplating solution" would not render the claim to the old material patentable. Instead, one would need to employ a "new use" claim, which is nothing more than an ordinary method claim, the main difference being that the novel feature is not, or need not be, in the manipulative steps of the method. Rather, the novelty may reside in the use of the old composition for a new purpose. Such a claim might read:

13. A method of electroplating zinc, which comprises the step of electrolyzing a solution comprising:

(a) an aqueous solution of zinc acetate, from 30 to 90 grams per liter;

(b) citric acid, from 1.5 to 3 times the zinc acetate concentration; and

(c) an alkaline pH-modifying substance in an amount sufficient to adjust the pH to a value of from 4 to 5.5.

Note that this claim recites the same composition defined in Claim 11, but the invention is now phrased as a method. The test of patentability becomes obviousness of the new use, since a novel process is defined. Even though the only manipulative step, "electrolyzing," is notoriously old, the novelty of a process step may reside in the material being treated as well as in the nature of the step itself. (See Section 39.) If the composition were previously used as a cleaning solution, it presumably would be unobvious to employ it as an electroplating solution.

This doctrine, that one cannot claim an old material as a composition by stating an intended new use in the preamble, has sometimes been stated that one cannot patent a new use for an old material. This is misleading because new uses have long been patentable as methods; in fact many method claims inherently involve new uses for old materials. Since 1952, the statute, 35 U.S.C. §100(b), has expressly covered this by stating that the word "process" includes "a new use of a known process, machine, manufacture, composition of matter, or material." See Gottchalk, *The Term "Process" Includes a New Use,* 40 JPOS 451 (1958), and Hewitt, *The New Use Patent,* 51 JPOS 634 (Oct. 1969), for a detailed discussion of the cases.

As another example of a new use for an old material, the method of treating polyethylene of claim 5 (Section 39) is also a new use claim if the treating solution (sodium dichromate and sulfuric acid) is known for other uses, such as cleaning test tubes.

While the statute expressly refers only to new uses for old materials, etc., a new use for a new material is equally patentable as a process under standard interpretation of the term "process." In other words, as far as a process claim, like claim 13, is concerned, it matters not whether the material is old or new. For the composition claim, claim 11, the composition per se must be novel under conventional tests.

Where the new use is properly claimed as a process, the claim must be written as a normal process or method claim (see Sections 33-34), including steps or acts. In *Clinical Products, Ltd. v. Brenner*, 149 USPQ 475 (D.D.C. 1966), an attempted hybrid claim to "the use of X (an old chemical) as a Y (use)" was held improper as not a true process claim. A proper method claim would have been: "the process of (doing thing Y), which comprises administering (compound X) to the body (or object in question)."

Perhaps the leading case on the "new use" product claim is *In re Thuau*, 57 USPQ 324 (CCPA 1943), where the court held that a claim to a therapeutic agent, which was an old compound for tanning, was not patentable as a compound. A typical claim read: "A new therapeutic product for the treatment of diseased tissue, comprising a condensation product of metacresolsulfonic acid condensed through an aldehyde." Method claims were not involved or mentioned in the decision. This case led to the "Rule" that "a new use of an old compound, without modification, is not patentable," meaning as a composition. How much "modification" is needed is a subject of much controversy, and many cases have appeared on the details. For example, is it enough to:

1) **Add a carrier or a solvent?** Generally, no, unless perhaps some particular solvent cooperates specially with the composition. *In re Rosicky*, 125 USPQ 341 (CCPA 1960). Note also the Müller DDT claim discussed later in this section.

In *Ex parte Douros and Vanderweff*, 163 USPQ 667 (Bd. App. 1968), the board considered a claim to:

> A composition for use as an effective algaecide which comprises . . . [a named compound] dissolved in a solvent selected from the group consisting of water, ethyl alcohol and mixtures of water and ethyl alcohol.

The compound was held obvious over the art, but the use was not. With respect to the solvent, the board held: "It is clearly obvious to add a carrier or a solvent to an unpatentable compound, [citing many cases]." With respect to the statement of use, it held: "The recital in the claims of the intended use of the composition does not patentably distinguish it from an aqueous solution thereof. *In re Sinex* . . . 135 USPQ 302." 163 USPQ at 668.

In *Ex parte Billman*, 71 USPQ 253 (Bd. App. 1946), claim 24 read:

> A plant stimulant composition containing as an essential active ingredient . . . [X chemical] in a water soluble diluent selected from the class consisting of . . . [generally old materials] . . . in the proportions of 10 to 20 grams for each pound. . . .

X chemical was old for other (unstated) purposes, selection of the solvent apparently was trivial, and the proportions were not alleged to be critical (nor probably were they). The claim was rejected as a direct consequence of *Thuau*. One could not, at least in 1946, avoid the *Thuau* doctrine by adding obvious limitations so as to define a technically novel chemical composition.

2) **Make the material into a tablet or capsule**—the so called "dosage-form" claims? Probably not if the tablet is the pure material, but if the dosage form requires a particular unobvious concentration of the pharmaceutical, effective for a certain disease, then, often, yes.

In re Craige, 90 USPQ 33 (CCPA 1951), considered:

> 13. A veterinary antihelminthic [tapeworm killer] composition containing an essential active ingredient [X, an old chemical] and a solid carrier therefor and in the form of a compressed tablet.

The court held that: 1) The label was no help under *Thuau*, which was merely "a restatement of the well established rule 'that a patent for a new use for an old substance quite unchanged is not authorized.' . . ." 2) Adding a carrier and/or making into a tablet were not inventive.

> While it is true that in certain cases invention might be present in a very slight alteration and the *Thuau* doctrine avoided, such alteration must always amount to more than mechanical or professional skill.

But, in *In re Halleck*, 164 USPQ 647 (CCPA 1970), the court allowed a claim to "an improved *growth stimulating* composition for animals which comprises an animal feed and *an effective amount* of [old compounds] contained therein for *growth stimulation*." Other than the *italicized* phrases, the mixture was old.

For a learned exposition, and perhaps the most famous quotation on the new use doctrine, see *Old Town Ribbon & Carbon Co. v. Columbia Ribbon & Carbon Mfg. Co.*, 72 USPQ 57 (2d Cir. 1947):

> The Constitution (Art. I, §8) gives Congress power to grant limited monopolies for "discoveries," and there is no antecedent reason for saying that Congress might not, if it chose, issue a patent for a new use of an old physical object, which is in fact closely akin to, if not identical with, an "art," like a process. There would be nothing unreasonable in so doing; substantially no "machine, manufacture of composition of matter" is ever new throughout; usually it is a combination of elements, all of which are severally old, and the invention consists in the mental act of fabricating the combination. Nevertheless, since 1793, unless a patent disclosed a "new and useful art," a new "machine," a new "manufacture," or a new "composition of matter," it has not been a valid patent. If it be merely for a new employment of some "machine, manufacture or compositoin of matter" already known, it makes not the slightest difference how beneficial to the public the new function may be, how long a search it may end, how many may have shared that search, or how high a reach of imaginative ingenuity the solution may have demanded. All the mental factors which determine invention may have been present to the highest degree, but it will not be patentable because it will not be within the terms of the statute. This is the doctrine that a "new use" can never be patentable. In this circuit we have many times applied it, and it has been recognized elsewhere. As we have said in earlier cases, this does not mean that very slight physical changes in a "machine," a "manufacture," or a "comsition of matter" may not be enough to sustain a patent; the act of selection out of which the new structure arises, is the determinant, and small departures may signify and embody revolutionary changes in discovery; but the law does not protect the act of selection per se, however meritorious, when it is not materially incorporated into some new physical object.

It is suspected that these sympathetic statements by Judge Learned Hand in 1947 helped pave the way for the statutory change in 1952 that new uses are expressly patentable as processes.

All of this has been very confusing, and involves hypertechnical consideration of apparent flyspecks. Note that the method new use claims are usually far less desirable, in many cases worthless, because the patentee, to enforce the patent, would have to sue each individual farmer, doctor, etc., which would normally be impractical. These users are usually also the customers of the patentee, and who wants to sue a customer. For additional discussion of these problems, see Fellner, *Method Claims for New Use and Their Enforcement*, 41 JPOS 54 (1968).

For a further detailed discussion of these and other special problems in pharmaceutical practice, see the excellent article "Pharmaceutical Patent Practice," by I. Louis Wolk, in the Calvert *Encyclopedia of Patent Practice* (1964) at 622.

In 1967, the CCPA cast grave doubt on the entire basis of the *Thuau* doctrine. In *In re Duva*, 156 USPQ 90, the court held that one could not ignore the preamble limitation "a composition *for* chemically deposting gold," and that *all* statements in the claim must be considered in determining obviousness.

The court stated:

> Thus, all *factual* differences which may be properly noted in any portion of a claim must be included within the basis for comparison with the prior art if we are to properly evaluate the *differences* between the invention defined in a claim and the teachings of a reference. The command of 35 U.S.C. 103 is to compare the invention *as a whole* with the prior art. Absent a failure of the applicant to comply with 35 U.S.C. 112, we think every portion of the appealed claims must be considered in determining the invention as a whole in arriving at our decision as to obviousness required by a rejection under section 103. 156 USPQ at 94.

See also *In re Miller* and *In re Wilson,* cited in Section 20, that "*All words* in a claim must be considered in judging the patentability of that claim. . . ." While those cases arose in other contexts (indefiniteness, etc.), the quoted language fits exactly with the

Duva case, and should be applicable in many situations. In *Union Carbide v. Filtrol*, 170 USPQ 482 (C.D. Cal. 1971), the district court expressly followed the *Duva* case and held that "non-obviousness of novel compositions requires consideration of limitations in the preambles of the claims." The claims in question were not quoted.

In this case, the body of the claim also contained some novelty, so it might not have been necessary for the court to throw out, if they did, this ancient doctrine. In view of this case, the future of "label claims" is uncertain. It might be dangerous to rely on any silent overruling of the old *Thuau* doctrine, thus it is recommended that claims of the various types permitted be sought.

Suppose one were permitted simply to claim: "An insecticide comprising . . . [DDT],"* DDT being known for other uses. When another party merely makes DDT, it *is* an insecticide comprising DDT, but this cannot be an infringement because DDT is old. It might be difficult to tell when infringement arises: When sold to a farmer in a bottle labelled DDT, but no instruction as to what to do with it? Would whoever put a label "insecticide" on the bottle be an infringer?

The DDT patent, finally Re. 22,922, was involved on a second application for reissue in *Ex parte Müller*, 81 USPQ 261 (1948) before the board of appeals. At issue were new use claims sought for the first time in the second reissue application, such as Claim 5:

> "The method of killing insects which comprises dissolving the chemical compound [DDT] in a solvent liquid and spraying the liquid so as to bring the [DDT] into contact with the insects." 81 USPQ at 261.

This claim, and a somewhat broader one were allowed as proper new-use method claims. The original and first reissue claims were for "A contact insecticide composition comprising"

---

*The broadest label claim, claim 4 actually reads: "A contact insecticide comprising the chemical compound . . . [DDT] in an aqueous emulsion."

a similar composition, the scope being narrowed in the first reissue. After the first reissue, the patentee learned that the composition was old, in an obscure thesis at the University of Basel, Switzerland, use as an insecticide not being suggested. The board held that this was a proper reason for reissue since the product claims were doubtful at best. Interestingly, the product claims were not rejected, although one concurring board member would have taken these away under the *Thuau* case.

The object of the claim drafter in these cases should be to get as many different types of claims as possible. For example, in Buzas *et al.* patent 2,827,418 (Mar. 18, 1958), Claim 2 covers a new compound per se (but this might be found in obscure prior art); Claim 3 is to an intermediate (which could be unobvious if the compound turns out to be old); Claim 4 is for the process of making the intermediate (in case that material turns out to be old, the process might not be); Claim 6 is for an injectable preparation containing a certain amount of the compound of Claim 2 in water; and Claim 7 is for a tablet containing the required dose (0.15 gram) of the compound of Claim 2. Any of these different claims, as well as use claims, might be very important, depending on prior art later developed and on the court's feelings about the *Thuau* case and extensions to compositions and dosage form claims.

It is interesting to note that the "new use" doctrine has been held not to apply to cases where the use results in a technically novel article of manufacture.

This "technical novelty" doctrine was promulgated chiefly by Judge Learned Hand in *Traitel Marble Co. v. Hungerford Brass & Copper Co.*, 18 F.2d 66, 68 (2d Cir. 1927) and *Old Town Ribbon & Carbon Co. v. Columbia Ribbon Mfg. Co.*, 72 USPQ 57, 60 (2d Cir. 1947).

These cases hold that, as long as there is *any* structural change, the patentable concept can reside in the realization of the new use.

As to the materiality of preamble limitations generally (prior to the *Duva* case), this was a matter of great confusion. No one could say with any degree of certainty whether a particular preamble limitation was to be counted or not, and the test might be different depending on whether the applicant/patentee wanted the words counted to make the claim patentable, or ignored so as to copy some one else's claim for interference, or to catch an infringer.

In *Kropa v. Robie and Mahlman*, 88 USPQ 478 (CCPA 1951) the court tussled with the question of whether or not the phrase "abrasive article" in a claim to "an *abrasive article* comprising abrasive grains and . . . [a certain resin]" was an express limitation. . . .

This was for purposes of whether the claim could be copied for interference (if material—no, if not—material—yes). One would think that, for patentability, the court would have disregarded the limitation under the *Thuau* case, as it is merely a label.

The court considered and cited thirty-seven of its prior cases on preamble limitations, in twenty-seven of which (including *Thuau*) the words were held *not* to express a limitation and in ten of which they were. After due struggle, the court held that "abrasive article" was material. The full text of the court's analysis is reproduced below.

APPENDIX [to Kropa v. Robie]

A. Ex parte cases in which preamble held not to express limitation in claim.

No.	Case	USPQ Vol.	USPQ Page	Introductory Clause
1.	In re Dawe	11	181	A driving wheel for tractors and similar agricultural implements
2.	In re Abrahamsen	13	96	A moulding scraper
3.	In re Weingartner	13	199	A stoker-drive power box
4.	In re Garratt	16	369	In a device of the class described
5.	In re Wolfe*	21	105	In a refrigerator cabinet
6.	In re Schoenky	21	236	In a shoe-conveying system
7.	In re Beplate et al.	25	386	In a carrying apparatus for use in the drying of a plurality of rows of filaments in skin form

*semble

No.	Case	USPQ Vol.	USPQ Page	Introductory Clause
8.	In re Allen†	33	160	A cutting tool for high speed rotary cutting of non-metallic materials
9.	In re Mason	36	337	In separating apparatus for separating the silicious and phosphatic constitutents of oiled fine mineral phosphates
10.	In re Walker et al.	39	485	A blowpipe nozzle for removing surface metal from ferrous metal bodies by reaction with an oxidizing gas stream applied to the surface thereof
11.	In re Crabbs**	37	740	In an asbestos cement shingle
12.	In re Waldron	48	381	A rock splitting tool
13.	In re Jannell	50	51	Apparatus for the manufacture of thread or the like in which the thread or the like is at all times accessible from a working face defined as a vertical plane paralleling the longtitudinal axis of the apparatus as a whole
14.	In re Stacy	57	307	In a fluid operated motor for drawing metal blanks where if the resistance of the blank to the drawing operation suddenly lessens during the drawing operation, the ram element may jump ahead
15.	In re Thuau	57	324	A new therapeutic product for treatment of diseased tissue
16.	In re Lamb	64	241	In a scaffold the character described
17.	In re Jacobson et al.	65	425	Apparatus for selective testing of combustible gases with different ignition temperatures including
18.	In re Rockwell	66	215	A power unit for intensifying and modulating hydraulic pressure . . . said power unit comprising

†While the introductory clause may have been considered a limitation, it was not a patentable limitation.

**semble

No.	Case	USPQ Vol.	Page	Introductory Clause
19.	In re Hutchison	69	138	As an article of manufacture, adapted for use in the fabrication of a metal template or the like suitable for metal-working operations
20.	In re Dense	70	212	A floor mat
21.	In re Benner et al.	82	49	A ball mill lining element
22.	In re Hooker	82	190	In photo-electric target apparatus
23.	In re Hansen et al.	86	390	In apparatus for measuring high frequency power
				The method of measuring high frequency power by means of a bridge circuit having one element variable in resistance in accordance with excitation thereof

In the foregoing cases (A-1 through 23) the following were the principal reasons advanced for not considering the introductory clause to be a limitation in the claim:

In combination claims the invention must be found in the combination of elements making up the device. An introductory phrase is merely the title of the invention defined in the part of the claim following that clause. (Case A-1).

The introductory clause merely indicated a field of use different than the field of use of prior art devices, but the structure defined in the body of the claims following the introductory clause pertains to the same art as the prior art devices and is not inventive over that art. While the field of use of the respective devices differs, the art is the same. (Case A-3).

Where the structure is completely defined independently of the preamble of the claim and can be constructed from the description given, the preamble does not constitute a limitation upon structure but merely states a purpose or intended use of the structure. (Case A-7).

The introductory clause merely recites a property inherent in the old composition defined by the remaining part of the claim. (Case A-15).

In a process claim, where every physical step is anticipated by a reference, the introductory clause stating the purpose of the process is not a limitation, as it is immaterial what purpose the patentee had in mind. (Case A-23).

B. Ex parte cases in which the preamble either expressly or by necessary implication was considered to be a limitation upon the subject matter defined by the claim.

No.	Case	USPQ Vol.	Page	Introductory Clause
24.	In re Fawick*	13	92	In a transmission In an automobile vehicle having a spring supported frame
25.	In re Covey*	17	240	In a tire
26.	In re Bennet	17	485	A sheet steel barrel construction for barrels formed of heavy gauge sheet steel and adapted for shipment of heavy contents weighing in the hundreds of pounds
27.	In re Buttolph	24	85	A discharge tube for positive column light
28.	In re Reichel	30	74	An expansible diaphragm device
29.	In re Krasnow*	68	210, 212 -213	In an apparatus for measuring radioactivity within a bore-hole

In the foregoing cases (B-24 through B-29) the following were the principal reasons advanced for considering the introductory clause a limitation in the claim:

The applicant was the first to provide the article described in the introductory clause comprised of the elements recited in the remainder of the claim (Case B-24) the existence of which latter, while previously known was not obviously useful in the environment specified in the introductory clause, and which use solved a problem, the solution of which had been sought for years by the industry. (Case B-25).

Where there inhered in the article specified in the introductory clause a problem whose solution transcended that before prior artisans, the nature of that problem characterizes the elements comprising the article, recited in the body of the claim following the introductory clause, and distinguishes the claim over the prior art. (Case B-26).

The introductory clause constituted an essential element in the novelty of the device and constitutes a limitation in the claim (Case B-27).

C. *Interference cases in which introductory clauses were held not to express a limitation in the counts.*

---

*semble

No.	Case	USPQ Vol.	USPQ Page	Introductory Clause
30.	Braren v. Horner	8	455	In an engraving machine and the like
31.	Deutsch et al. v. Ball	25	470	A collapsible top for vehicle bodies of the cabriolet or convertible coupe type
32.	Marden et al. v Braselton	49	256	An ultraviolet lamp
33.	Bartsch v. Baker	57	143	A dish for maintaining food at a desired temperature

In the foregoing cases (C-30 through C-33) the following were the principal reasons advanced for considering the introductory clause not to be a limitation in the count:

The structure recited in the count following the introductory clause was a self-contained description and did not depend for completeness upon the introductory clause. That clause merely stated the particular use to be made of an otherwise integral apparatus or mechanism (Case C-30).

The structure defined in the counts exclusive of the preamble was a complete and definite invention irrespective of the intended use recited in the preamble (Case C-31).

D. Interference cases in which introductory clauses were expressly or impliedly held to express a limitations in the counts.

No.	Case	USPQ Vol.	USPQ Page	Introductory Clause
34.	Hall v. Shimadzu	13	259	A process of manufacturing a fine powder of lead suboxide intermingled with powder of metallic lead
35.	Smith v. Bousquet	45	347, 352	An insecticide An insecticide composition
36.	Kenyon v. Crane	49	707	A directional indicator for aircraft showing the direction and amount of deviation from course
37.	Lawson v. Davis	54	405	In an article of hosiery A knitted article of apparel

In the foregoing case (D-34 through D-37) the following were the principal reasons advanced for considering the introductory clause a limitation in the counts:

The introductory phrase is absolutely essential to point out the invention defined by the counts. The introductory phrase is necessary to give life, meaning, and vitality to the counts. Also, the counts originated in one party's patent where the entire object of the patent was expressed in the introductory clause of the counts, which objective nowhere appears in his opponent's disclosure. (Case D-34).

The preamble is a limitation where it specifies an article or composition in which there inheres a field of specific use, and the constituents of the article which are recited in the portion of the count following the preamble are old compounds not theretofore known to be useful in such an article (D-35).

The preamble is an essential element of the invention defined by the counts and not merely introductory for the purpose of explaining the environment in which the other structural elements of the count are designed to be used. Moreover where a vital term of a count is susceptible of more than one interpretation, the meaning must be taken from the application in which the counts originated. (Case D-36).

About all this author can deduce from this array of preambles cited in the *Kropa* case is that, in the CCPA, the odds prior to 1951 were 1.7 to 1 against the preamble limitation's counting. How can one possibly distinguish "a stoker-drive power box" (No) from "an expansible diaphragm device" (Yes) or "In apparatus for measuring high frequency power" (No) from "In an apparatus for measuring radioactivity. . . ." (Yes).

In a subsequent case, *In re Tanczyn*, 97 USPQ 150 (CCPA 1953), a claim in question called for:

> "*wrought and polished* straight chromium stainless steel *products* . . . substantially free of surface defacing complex silicate inclusions," comprising . . . [specified proportions of particular metals.]

Although the prior art showed two specific alloy compositions falling within the range, the claim was held patentable because of the italicized preamble limitations: "In these particular circumstances, we think such limitations are significant and give life and meaning to the appealed claims. . . . Here the claims are directed to an article of manufacture produced from an alloy composition . . ." not only the alloy. There are other uses for the alloy per se.

On obviousness, applicant had recognized a problem for the first time in understanding what caused certain surface defects, so the solution to the problem could hardly be obvious *once* the claim is held literally to avoid anticipation. See such cases as *In re Antonson*, 124 USPQ 132 (CCPA 1959); and *Eibel Process Co. v. Minnesota & Ontario Paper Co.*, 261 U.S. 45 (1923); for classic holdings that the "Invention" (unobviousness) can reside in recognizing the problem, as well as in providing a solution, as long as the claims are not literally anticipated by the prior art.

In *In re Szujna et al.*, 164 USPQ 632 (CCPA 1970), the court held that the preamble limitation "an insert *for converting* a mold . . ." must be considered in determining unobviousness, even though the structure in the claims was old in the prior art; the purpose was different, citing *Kropa v. Robie* and other cases. Note, in this case, the body of the claim referred back to the preamble statement *in two* places. This helped to make sure that the preamble statement was ". . . more than a *mere* statement of intended use since it gives 'life and meaning' to the recitations in the body of the claim." Thus, the statement of use was not "mere" and it gave "life and meaning"; which are inherently difficult tests to administer.

Hopefully, the *Duva* case may have terminated all this type of mental gyration as to whether a preamble limitation counts, by stating that *all* limitations count.

In re Kuehl, 177 USPQ 250 (CCPA-1973), discussed in Sections 36 and 39, holds that one may patent a new use for a new compound, even where that use would be very obvious to one skilled in the art *after* learning about the new compound. In that case, the applicant invented and had gotten allowance of claims to a new class of zeolites, and sought also new-use type process claims to cracking hydrocarbons with his new zeolite, this being very well known in the prior art with other, related but "patentably distinct" zeolites. The court held such a new use, but conventional-by-analogy, process claim patentable, ruling that knowledge of the new compound was *not* part of the prior art and could not be used against applicant. There is no "exhaustion of monopoly" doctrine that limits applicant to composition claims in such cases. In effect, the court is saying "if zeolite X is not obvious, how could cracking hydrocarbons with zeolite X be obvious?" Applicant can have claims in all statutory classes he wishes, given novelty and unobviousness in each class, and allowing him method of use claims does not really add very much to the patent.

SUMMARY—Classic law holds that one cannot patent (rely for patentability) on a statement of intended use for an old compound or material. In other words, a preamble limitation such as "insecticide" will not allow one to patent an old compound. New uses for old things, when the use is unobvious, are patentable as processes. These are ordinary method claims, such as "a method of killing insects, comprising exposing said insects to [X chemical]," where the novelty is in the material used. Prior to 1967, there was great doubt about the use of preamble limitations, whether or when one could rely on them; the *Duva* case may have ended this by stating that one can rely on *any* limitation *any*where in the claim. Patentability of new use inventions as products (articles or compositions) is preferred by patent owners where possible, particularly for consumer products (insecticides, antibiotics). Thus, applicants will continue to seek new ways to attempt to protect the product.

Chapter VII

SPECIALIZED FORMS OF CLAIMS

Thus far, we have been concerned primarily with independent claims for each of the statutory classes. The following sections will consider some specialized forms of claims, which may be used in any statutory class of utility patent.

Section 53—Dependent Claims

The statute, 35 U.S.C. §112, provides that "a claim may be written in independent or dependent form . . ."; the latter being defined in rule 75-(c) as claims which "refer back to and *further restrict a single* preceding claim [emphasis added]." Note the limitations: (a) *further restrict* and (b) *single* preceding claim. Thus, it is improper to use a dependent claim which omits something from the preceding "parent" or "base" claim, or is inconsistent with the parent. The following claims are improper.

(a) "Apparatus is recited in claim 1, wherein the biasing means is omitted."

(b) If claim 1 calls for a metal selected from the group consisting of copper, silver and gold, "A composition as recited in claim 1, wherein the metal is tantalum." This claim is inconsistent with the parent.

As to single preceding claim, the following type of claim is improper under rule 75, although permitted in many foreign countries: "Apparatus as recited in Claims 1 or 2 [or "Claims 1 and 2," or "any of the preceding claims"] further comprising. . . ."

These are generally called "multiple dependent claims." For a six-months' period (July 1 to Dec. 31, 1968), the Patent Office ran a trial program permitting limited use of multiple dependent claims, in which claims could be dependent from more than one preceding claim, none of which could also be multiply dependent. This was generally similar to Canadian practice. As a result of the trial, the Patent Office decided not to adopt this technique, first because it was little used in the trial (Notice of June 9, 1969; 864 O.G. 323) and, second, because the evaluators felt it took more time to examine such claims since the examiner had to figure out all of the different claim associations and what they covered, exactly as if the multiple dependent claims were submitted separately.*

A dependent claim incorporates by reference everything in the parent claim, and adds some further statements, limitations or restrictions. The statements added may be either (1) one or more additional elements and/or (2) a further description or limitation of one or more of the elements of the parent claim.

The Patent Office fee schedule, 35 U.S.C. § 41(a), adopted in 1965, provides for a surcharge of ten dollars for each independent claim in excess of one. The Patent Office strongly favored this proposal before Congress, over strong Bar Association opposition. For background on this controversy, and some theoretical opinions on this erstwhile burning issue, see this author's article "hypotelantilepsiphobia,"† appearing at 47 J.P.O.S. 337 (May, 1965). The main advantage of dependent claims, of course, is that they require far less time to examine, and those using them should be given a financial incentive. Note that, when any claim is allowed, all dependent claims can be allowed practically without study, other than to make sure they are dependent claims. In one case, *Ex parte Ligh*, 159 USPQ 61, 62 (1967), the board of appeals held that it was error to reject a dependent claim while allowing its parent.

Also, 35 U.S.C. § 282 was amended at the same time to provide that "dependent claims shall be presumed valid even though

---

*Letter to author.

†An unreasonable fear or loathing of dependent patent claims.

dependent upon an invalid claim" (in case there was any doubt previously). These statutory changes have resulted in a great increase in the usage of dependent claims, simplifying the jobs of everyone who must ever consider the patents. Some attorneys believed and testified that dependent claims were not so "good" as independent claims; however, with the new statute and the greatly increased use of dependent claims, it is likely that this fear will disappear with time.

Any attempt to avoid paying the $10 fee for independent claims by submitting an obviously unpatentable parent claim such as "A four-wheeled vehicle" is considered unethical practice according to a Patent Office notice. (June 8,, 1966; 846 O.G. 682.)

There is no objection to a dependent claim where the "single preceding claim" is also a dependent claim, and there is no limit to the length of a chain of dependent claims.

Identically worded dependent claims may be dependent from different parent claims. See *In re Flint*, 162 USPO 228 (CCPA 1969), discussed further in Section 59. In *Ex parte Primich et al.*, 151 USPQ 737 (Bd. App. 1966), it was held improper to reject a dependent claim as adding only old elements to an allowed parent claim, as long as the total number of claims was not "unduly multiplied" (Section 59).

In general, the dependent form should *never* be used unless one is sure that he really wishes to present a claim which includes every limitation of the prospective parent claim, but adds some significant element or feature. He must satisfy himself that every limitation in the first claim is also necessary in the second. There may be a tendency among some who use dependent claims extensively to overuse them, by failing to present a second independent claim, where appropriate, that does not include all the limitations of the first claim. U.S. practice has no requirement that any one claim be a "head claim," or otherwise dominate every other claim in the application. There may be as many head claims as the invention and the prior art permit, subject only to restriction requirements under 35 U.S.C. 121 and Patent Office policy implementing that Section (Rule 141 and MPEP 806.04

et seq.) However, once it has been determined that the claim scope desired *does* include all elements of a preceding claim, then it is recommended that the dependent form ordinarily be used.

There is no objection per se to a claim dependent from another claim in a different statutory class, as long as the dependent claim does include all the limitations of the parent claim: that is, "it shall not conceivably be infringed by anything which would not also infringe the basic claim" MPEP 608.01(n). This is the Patent Office's definition of whether a claim is in fact dependent, despite the fact that an alleged dependent claim might refer to another claim by numeral. With respect to claims crossing statutory classes, dependent "product-by-process" claims (Section 43) are very common: "A ________ produced in accordance with the method of claim 1." Similarly, a claim to "A method of making the ________ of claim 1" would be proper *if* it *could not* conceivably be infringed without infringing claim 1.

With respect to the numbering and order of dependent claims, the general rules set out in Section 5 should be followed, but in addition MPEP 608.01(n) states: "A claim which depends from a *dependent* claim should not be separated therefrom by any claim which does not also depend from said 'dependent' claim." This means that the following claim patterns are permitted (arrow indicates a claim dependent from earlier numbered claim; no arrow designates a second independent claim):

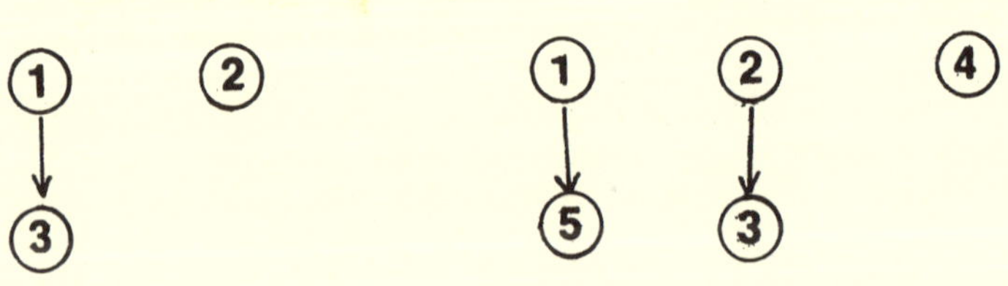

Dependent claims (3 and 5) separated from *independent* parent claim (1) by any number of other claims of any kind.

The following pattern is not permitted:

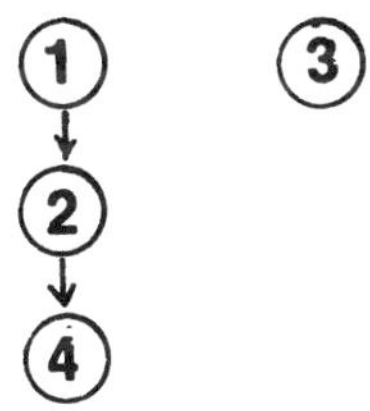

Claim 4, here, is a claim which depends from a *dependent* claim (2), but is separated therefrom (from 2) by a claim (3) which "does not also depend from said dependent claim" (Claim 2). This is bad.

The above rules set forth a *minimum* standard on placement of dependent claims. Beyond this, claims which depend from independent claims may be placed wherever the writer thinks most logical; however, unless unusual factors are present (such as claims in different statutory classes), it is best to group all claims dependent from a single independent claim after that claim.

One simple format for dependent claims follows (refer to Example I, Chapter III):

> **14. A shaking apparatus as recited in claim 1, in which the oscillating means comprises:**
> **(a) a motor;**
> **(b) a rotary cam driven by the motor;**
> **(c) a cam follower engaging the cam; and**
> **(d) a link pivoted at one end to the cam follower and at its other end to the container, to permit oscillation of the container on the legs.**

In claim 14, one of the elements of the parent claim is defined in greater detail; specifically, the "means" element is broken down into four constituent parts. Note that the new elements must be connected and related to each other *and* to the elements of the preceding claim, exactly as with independent claims (Section 25). With respect to antecedents (Section 20), it is proper to refer to an element of a parent claim as "the" or "said"; "the container" in claim 14 finds its antecedent in claim 1. One must consider all preceding claims in the chain to be certain it is perfectly clear that there is only one such element which fits the definition.

When preparing dependent claims, one must be careful not to add as an apparently new element an element already in the parent claim. This "double inclusion" of elements (Section 18). For example, in the previous claim 14, the motor cam, etc., added by the dependent claim comprise the oscillating means of the parent claim. It would be improper to add those elements as new elements without relating them to the oscillating means of the parent claim.

In order to illustrate a dependent claim that adds an element to a preceding claim, refer again to Example II, Appendix A, the take-up barrel. Assume that a photocell circuit (not shown) is provided to detect when the barrel 12 is full, and that this photocell operates (1) a pair of shears positioned between the barrel and the eyelet 20 to cut the strand 11, and also (2) an accumulator positioned between the eyelet and the capstan 13 to collect the strand for a short time while a new barrel is placed on the turntable. A dependent claim to this combination might read as follows:

15. A collecting apparatus as recited in claim 2, further comprising:

means for detecting when a predetermined amount of strand has been collected in the barrel;

a cutter, operated by the detecting means, for severing the strand when the predetermined amount has been collected; and

an accumulator, operated by the detecting means, for accumulating the strand after it has been severed.

Note that "a cutter" is as broad as "cutting means," so that the means expression, while possible, was avoided. However, a photocell is not as broad as "detecting means" so that the means expression was used. A weight-responsive switch could equally well have been employed to sense the time when the barrel was full.

Another format for adding an element to a claim follows: "A collecting apparatus as recited in claim 2, wherein means are provided for detecting when. . . ." There are many other acceptable styles for introducing a dependent claim.

One caution with dependent claims, particularly where elements are added, is to make certain that the larger combination is still consistent with the preamble, as discussed in Section 6. Sometimes the extra elements add so many additional functions that the old preamble is no longer suitable. While it is possible, and fairly common, to modify the preamble by a dependent claim, it is often best simply to use another independent claim.

For example, if the previous example also included automatic means responsive to the photocell to push the full barrel off the turntable and substitute an empty barrel, plus means for sensing the presence of the empty barrel on the turntable to reverse the accumulator and start collecting the strand in the new barrel, there is now significantly more than a *mere* "apparatus for collecting an advancing strand in a barrel." Instead, there is a much more impressive combination: "Automatic apparatus for continuously collecting an advancing strand in a succession of barrels." The continuous/automatic feature would undoubtedly be very important in such an invention, and should be written into the preamble. This is a main, overall feature of the combination claimed. As a dependent claim with a modified preamble, this could read: "A collecting apparatus as recited in claim 15, for automatically collecting an advancing strand in a succession of barrels, . . ."

Where the dependent claim modifies the preamble of the parent, this should be stated in the preamble of the dependent claim.

An example of a form for a dependent method claim:

> A method of ______ , as recited in claim ______ , wherein the separating step is performed by [or comprises] distilling the aqueous solution . . ." [defining a step in more detail].

When preparing dependent method claims, the added limitations must relate to variations in the method steps, or materials used in the case of a chemical process (Section 39). Dependent method claims should never add only apparatus (machine) limitations.

An example of a dependent method claim, adding steps:

> **15A. A method of collecting an advancing strand, as recited in claim 4, further comprising:**
> **detecting when a predetermined amount of strand has been collected in the barrel;**
> **cutting the strand when the predetermined amount has been collected; and**
> **accumulating the strand after it has been cut.**

Note this corresponds in scope to dependent apparatus claim 15.

For a chemical process, see claim 5, Section 39 as the parent claim:

> **5A. A process as recited in claim 5, wherein the solution is heated to a temperature of 80° to 90°C.** [adding preferred process conditions].
> **5B. A process as recited in claim 5, wherein the solution also contains between 1 and 5% by weight of sodium chloride** [telling more about the composition].

With respect to composition claims, dependent claims may add further materials to the composition or define one or more of the elements or radicals more specifically. For example, in the zinc-electroplating solution claim (claim 11, Section 46) one could claim:

> **11A. A zinc electroplating solution as recited in claim 11, wherein the pH modifying substance is ammonium hydroxide** [specifying one ingredient in greater detail].

Note it would be wrong to add "further comprising ammonium hydroxide" if this is the pH modifying substance.

Another example:

> **11B. A zinc electroplating . . . , further comprising 0.5 to 1 gram per liter of boric acid** [adding a material].

One could also specify the concentrations of ingredients in more detail:

> **11C. . . . , wherein the concentration of zinc acetate is 50-60 grams per liter, and the citric acid 100-150 grams per liter.**

In Claim 12 to the new molecule, one could specify the radicals in more detail:

> **12A. A compound as recited in claim 12, wherein R is methyl and X is chlorine** [Note this is a claim to one specific compound, sometimes called an "ultimate species." See Section 55 on genus and species claims.]

SUMMARY—Use dependent claims extensively, most of the time when you wish to present a second claim that adds elements or features to a prior claim, whether the prior claim is dependent or independent. Either tell more about elements in the previous claim, or add elements to that claim, or both. But you must *further restrict* a *single* previous claim in some manner. Be careful, in practice, with dependent claims, particularly those adding detailed features, that you really need for patentability every feature of the main claim. If not, stop and write a new independent claim: there is no law against it, and it only costs $10 to present a second independent claim.

Section 54—Improvement or "Jepson-Type" Claims

This type of claim recites all or some of the old elements of a combination in the preamble to the claim, while the body of the claim recites only the new or modified elements, or tells of new forms of connection or cooperation between old elements. Such claims are frequently used where there is an improvement in one or more elements of an otherwise old and unchanged combination, or if one or more new elements are added to an old combination. This type of claim should avoid or help avoid an "old combination" rejection. (See Section 60.)

Versions of general approach to claims are frequently known as a "European-type" claim, inasmuch as such claims are very common in Europe and are required in some countries. For example, in the Netherlands, the preamble must relate all elements and relationships in common with the closest single reference. Effective January 1, 1967, a new rule 75(e) was enacted by the Patent Office:

> Where the nature of the case admits, as in the case of an improvement, any independent claim *should* contain in the following order, (1) a preamble comprising a general description of all the elements or steps of the claimed combination which are conventional or known, (2) a phrase such as "wherein the improvement comprises," and (3) those elements, steps and/or relationships which constitute that portion of the claimed combination which the applicant considers as the new or improved portion. (Emphasis added.)

The word "should" was apparently meant to be strongly urging, but not mandatory. At a hearing on the proposed rule, Assistant Commissioner Reynolds stated that it was not intended as compulsory. However, in view of this urging by the Patent Office, *it is recommended that "Jepson-type" claims be used whenever the quoted language of the rule clearly fits.*

In *In re Bernhart*, 163 USPQ 611 (CCPA 1969), this was considered optional with no mention of rule 75(e). See further discussion in Section 60.

The original Jepson claim (from *Ex parte Jepson*, 1917 C.D. 62, 243 O.G. 525) was:

> [16.] *In an* **electrical system of distribution of the class wherein a variable speed generator charges a storage battery and when the battery becomes sufficiently charged a voltage coil becomes effective to regulate the generator for constant potential,** *the combination with* **said voltage coil** *of* **a coil traversed by current flowing to the battery which is acted upon by decreasing battery current to reduce the potential maintained constant by the voltage coil.** [Emphasis added.]

Generalized, the original Jepson form is "In a ________ having [old elements A, B, C] the combination with [A] *of* [new element D]." Note that the new element is defined both as to structure and how it cooperates with the old elements A, B or C to accomplish a useful result.

In long claims, the original Jepson format is sometimes hard to follow as the body of the claim begins with the key word "of," and there may be several other "of's" in the claim. Various other formats (known as "Jepson-type") are permissible, no magic words being necessary. One suitable and straightforward form follows: "In combination with an [A] of the type wherein [conventional elements B and C are provided for doing something], the improvement which comprises: . . ."

The new or modified elements then follow as in any other claim, related structurally and functionally both to each other and to the elements in the preamble. It is advantageous to work the word "combination" into the preamble somewhere.

Another equally good, perhaps preferable, style is to use the specific language from rule 75(e)—"wherein the improvement comprises," for example, "An improved A of the type having a B and a C, wherein the improvement comprises. . . ." Other possibilities are: "In a machine of the type having . . . , the improvement which comprises: . . ." or "A machine having [old elements named], characterized in that: . . . ."

This latter is the "characterized" form widely used abroad, and required in some countries. It is perfectly acceptable in the United States although not very commonly used.

Except when the "characterized" form is used, the body of the claim starts with the word "comprises" or "comprising" as in normal United States claims. Thus, that magic word is a code word or trigger, telling the reader where the allegedly novel part of the claim starts. For this reason, it is recommended that the word "comprising" not be used in the Jepson preamble; instead use "having," "including" or the like in the preamble. For example, "An improved A comprising B and C, wherein the improvement comprises D" could be confusing.

For a specific example, consider again the barrel takeup of Example II, but assume this time that all of the elements shown in the drawing are quite old and well known. Assume that the client's only invention is in the addition of the detector, cutter and accumulator of claim 15, Section 53.

A Jepson-type claim to the improved combination might read as follows:

> **17. An improved strand-collecting apparatus of the type in which an advancing strand is collected in a barrel mounted on a rotating turntable, and in which a reciprocating strand guide is positioned above the barrel to guide the advancing strand into the barrel, wherein the improvement comprises:**
>
> **(a) means for detecting when a predetermined amount of strand has been collected in the barrel;**
>
> **(b) a cutter, operated by the detecting means, for severing the strand when a predetermined amount has been collected; and**
>
> **(c) an accumulator, operated by the detecting means, for accumulating the strand after it has been severed.**

It should be noted that the body of this claim is identical with that of dependent claim 15, the only difference being in the preambles. It is a significant difference. In claim 15, the client invented both the basic system of claim 2 and the photocell system of dependent claim 15, whereas in claim 17 the client invented only the photocell system as an improvement on the basic system.

Note that the preparation of the body of a Jepson-type claim is very similar to a dependent claim, except that the part which would be the parent claim is the preamble of the Jepson-type claim, rather than a different claim.

The Patent Office interpretation of these claims is set out in the Nov. 1, 1966, Notice "Guidelines for Drafting a Model Patent Application," also MPEP 608.01(m).

> The form of claim required in Rule 75(e) is particularly adapted for the description of improvement type inventions. It is to be considered a combination claim. The preamble of this form of claim is considered to positively and clearly include all the elements or steps recited therein as a part of the claimed combination.

With this description of the entire claim as being a combination, there should be no objection per se to the body of the claim's comprising a single means element, as mentioned in Section 31.

Also, in Jepson-type claims, there is less need to tie the preamble elements together as described in Section 25, as long as the element of the body are adequately tied to each other *and to* the preamble elements with which they cooperate. However, a bald preamble catalog is not recommended as sound practice. (See Section 61 on aggregation.)

While the foregoing example relates to a machine claim, Jepson-type claims may also be used for methods, articles of manufacture and compositions.

An example of a method:

18. In a method of collecting an advancing strand in a barrel, of the type wherein the advancing strand is guided into the barrel and the barrel is rotated to vary the point of collection circularly with respect to the bottom of the barrel, the improvement comprising [or characterized by]:

reciprocating the guide point back and forth above the barrel so that the point of collection varies radially with respect to the bottom of the barrel.

Note that this claim covers the same combination as claim 4, Chapter IV, except that two of the elements of claim 4 now are old and have been put in the preamble.

A composition of matter:

19. An improved zinc-electroplating solution of the type containing an aqueous solution of zinc acetate, from 30 to 90 grams per liter; citric acid, from 1.5 to 3 times the zinc acetate concentration; and an alkaline pH modifying substance in an amount sufficient to adjust the pH to a value of from 4 to 5.5, wherein the improvement comprises:

0.5 to 1 gram per liter of boric acid.

Note the preamble of this claim is identical in scope to Claim 11, Section 46, with the added material being the same as in dependent Claim 11B, Section 53.

SUMMARY—Use Jepson-type claims extensively for improvement type inventions, where new or modified elements are added to an otherwise old and unchanged combination. Describe the old elements from the closest single reference in the preamble. Usually the old things can be described fairly broadly. Describe the new or modified elements in the body of the claim after a transistion such as "wherein the improvement comprises," or "the improvement comprising." Connect or relate the new elements to each other and to the preamble elements, as with any other claim, particularly in mechanical combination (machine) claims as outlined in Chapter II.

Section 55—Generic and Species Claim

In some inventions, there are two or more alternative and mutually exclusive embodiments of the invention; that is, where two or more different structures, steps, parts or compounds, called "species," may be used interchangeably to accomplish a desired result. Examples of this are the legs and springs in Figs. 2 and 3 of Example I (Appendix A); the copper, silver or aluminum stripe of the resistor in Section 47; the separation of alcohol from a water solution by fractional distillation or by solvent extraction in Section 34. A generic claim is one which defines the element in question with sufficient breadth to cover all of the disclosed species, and often also additional undisclosed species, while the species claims cover the separate embodiments one at a time. Note that, if no allowable generic claim is presented, a requirement for restriction among disclosed species is likely, called "election of species." 35 U.S.C. §121 and rules 141, 142 and 146. After election, all claims readable on the species are examined.

If no concrete generic word is apparent, a means-plus-function clause may be appropriate to provide a generic expression, as outlined in Section 31. In chemical cases, a Markush group is always a generic expression, as discussed in Section 47. Of course, alternative expressions cannot be used to make a generic claim, as set out in Section 21, except under the new Markush practice in Section 47.

There is no special problem in drafting generic and species claims. The species claims may be either dependent or independent, although the dependent claim form is especially useful and common in this situation. One makes an element of the generic claim more specific in one way for species I and in a different way for species II.

The words genus and species, in most cases, signify relative to a particular set of claims; a generic expression (electrically conductive metals) may be a species of a more generic expression (electrically conductive materials, which also includes carbon). The words genus and species in patent law can be totally arbitrary such as genus: mammals; species: man, cat, etc.—but genus: man; species: male, female. The breakdowns are made in whatever way suits the invention. Some species, which cannot practically be further divided (sodium chloride) are referred to as "ultimate species." In mechanical cases, there would theoretically never be an ultimate species because an element (a spring for example) could be a species of biasing means, but would be generic to particular kinds of springs (coil springs, leaf springs), and each of these could be further defined in parallel, mutually exclusive ways.

These distinctions are not too significant as far as writing claims is concerned. They relate primarily to the question of whether one can obtain one patent (with an allowable generic claim) or several patents (in most cases where no allowable generic claim is presented).

SUMMARY—Generic claims cover two or more mutually exclusive species, A or B, and possibly also C or D, etc., not all of which may be disclosed. Claims to the individual species cover less than the whole group of things, either one at a time, or less than all at one time. There are no special problems in writing such claims. Such claims may come up in any statutory class of utility invention: machine, process, article of manufacture, or composition of matter.

Section 56—Combination and Subcombination

Thus far, we have been considering primarily combination claims; that is, claims to complete machines, processes, manufactures, etc. A subcombination is some element or group of elements that forms a part of the main combination. If the subcombination has utility by itself, it may be separately claimed, although restriction will often be required if the combination is also claimed. (See Section 60 on old combinations as to when the combination may also be claimed and MPEP 806.05(c) as to restriction between combination and subcombination.) Subcombinations usually relate to machines, but may also be present in methods, compositions, or articles of manufacture.

As one example, the details of construction of the accumulator used with the barrel take-up arrangement of claim 14 of Section 53 would comprise such a subcombination. If new, it could be separately claimed. Such a subcombination claim might start out: "Apparatus for accumulating an advancing strand, which comprises: . . ."

Note that, in this case, the subcombination is a complete mechanism or machine in itself, serving its own function, but which would always be used with other machines to make a combination machine.

Restriction would probably be required since the subcombination may obviously be used in other combinations and is separately classified.

Other examples of subcombinations are a carburetor for a car, and other major subassemblies such as tires, headlights, etc. A subcombination method might be a method of accumulating strand in a take-up method, or a method of separating chemical X from Y as a part of a complete process for making Z, wherein X is a byproduct and useful to be recovered. In a composition, a subcombination might be a new compound per se, useful in killing insects, and a combination claim an insecticide containing the new compound with other materials.

Note that subcombination claims of this sort offer no special problems in claim drafting.

Another common format for subcombination claims is: "In an apparatus for doing something, an A, a B and a C."

Note that this type of claim is an exception to the general "Rule" about having a transition between the preamble and the body (Section 7). Also, in this type of claim, it is less important to list all elements necessary to make a complete combination, since by definition the claim need only be to some part of the combination.

The author is not certain how far one can go in drafting fragmentary "In a" claims, covering only certain portions of a combination, where less than a complete functional subcombination is claimed. It seems that such claims might be rejected as "incomplete" (Section 62) or lacking in utility in that they would lack sufficient structure to make a complete combination, machine or process, etc.

Another format which combines the subcombination with a Jepson approach (Section 54): "An improved A for an X-type system having old elements Y and Z, wherein the improved A comprises: . . . ." For example: "An improved accumulator for a strand-collecting apparatus of the type having a barrel . . . , wherein the improved accumulator comprises: . . . ."

See further discussion in Section 60 on old combinations, and the claim involved in *In re Rohrbacher and Kolbe*, 128 USPO 117 (CCPA 1960). This is to the effect that a claim to "a cooling liquid pump *for* engines" of a certain type, is properly a subcombination claim to the pump.

See also *In re Dean*, 130 USPQ 107 (CCPA 1961) discussed in Section 60, that a claim to "in a camera having . . . , a shutter-timing apparatus . . . comprising:" is a proper subcombination claim to the timer, not an (allegedly old) combination of the timer and a shutter. See also Section 52 on new uses and preamble limitations generally.

With respect to applicant's *right* to obtain subcombination claims, see *Special Equipment Co. v. Coe*, 64 USPQ 525 (U.S. Sup. Ct. 1945), discussed further in Section 63 on incomplete claims.

SUMMARY—Subcombination claims cover parts or portions of a complete combination or system, where the subcombination has utility in itself. There are no special problems in writing such claims, and they may be necessary in some cases to avoid an old combination rejection.

Chapter VIII

CLAIMS OF VARYING SCOPE

Section 57—In General

In drafting claims of varying scope, whether dependent or independent claims are used, the claim drafter should make certain that there is a significant difference between the claims, particularly if more than about ten claims* are presented. Of course, the differences between the claims need not amount to patentable differences, but they should be as substantial as the situation permits and related to the areas of novelty. Such practice ordinarily makes the problems of duplicate or redundant claims (Section 58) and undue multiplicity of claims (Section 59) fairly easy to avoid. Dependent claims also help in this regard.

The narrowest claim is usually a sound "picture claim," which should probably recite by name all of the significant structure disclosed, omitting only the nuts and bolts. This should describe the commercially most effective way to carry out the invention, including all preferred conditions.

This not only protects against the copyist, but wherever possible, it is desirable to assert a narrow claim against an alleged infringer because such a claim is harder to invalidate either on new prior art or on formal grounds (too broad, etc.).

The narrowest claim should be fairly easy to write if the structure and operation are understood. The broad claims are the

*Large numbers of claims are sometimes necessary for complex applications having many points of novelty; however, the office will look much more closely at the necessity of each claim (Sections 58 and 59) if many claims are presented.

most difficult to prepare, in that the claim drafter must analyze the structure and pick out its essential elements, and decide how broadly to state them. Intermediate claims should be fairly easy to prepare in that some significant elements and/or details of construction are either added to a broad claim or omitted from a narrow claim.

Any one of the claims may be written first, whichever seems easiest. Different practitioners advocate different methods of beginning. Perhaps a flexible approach is best: if the claim drafter has a clear idea for a broad claim, he should start with that; if not, he should simply write *a claim* and work it over. Having any claim done helps one think of variations. Then elements may be (1) added or described in more detail to make a narrower claim or (2) omitted, combined or broadened to make a broader claim. It is probably best if at least several, if not all, claims are prepared before starting to write the remainder of the specification, because then the specification can better be written to point out the claimed invention and the words in the claims will naturally find clear support in the remainder of the specification (see Section 15).

While it is important to provide significant differences between the claims, the terminology and form should be as consistent as possible except where the differences occur. Do not give the same part different names in two successive claims, except where this is done intentionally to change the scope of the claim. However, beware of a common limitation in all claims. If there is one, make certain that it is absolutely essential to patentability.

With respect to preferred numbering and order of multiple claims, refer to Section 5, numbering and order.

See also the discussion in Section 53, that there need be no one head claim, or dominating claim in the application. One is entitled to claim every possibly novel combination, subcombination, method, apparatus, etc., that he wants to, subject only to restriction practice that he might have to get two patents instead of one.

SUMMARY—Present a "reasonable" number of claims, given the nature and scope of the invention over the prior art. This varies widely from case to case. Avoid extra claims adding only things old in the art. The narrowest claim(s) should be quite detailed, including all significant structure, both to clearly catch copyist infringers and also to try to get some claims allowed on the first Office action. In this case, you will then be arguing only allowable scope of the invention, not whether or not it is patentable.

Section 58—Duplicate Claiming

"Duplicate claiming," MPEP 706.03(k), refers to two claims that are ". . . so close in content that they both cover the same thing, despite a slight difference in wording." The manual also provides that ". . . it is possible [although rare] to reject one claim on an allowed claim if they differ only by subject matter old in the art. . . . This rejection is usually not applied if there are only a few claims in the application." In *Ex parte Primich,* 151 USPQ 737 (Bd. App. 1966), the board seems to have renounced this doctrine, at least where the second claim is a dependent claim.

The basis for this ground of rejection is rule 75(b): "More than one claim may be presented *provided they differ substantially from each other* and are not unduly multiplied." (Emphasis added to indicate the basis for the duplicate, or redundant claiming doctrine.) This doctrine theoretically applies regardless of the total number of claims presented, although in practice it is not used often unless "too many" claims are also presented, as discussed in the next section.

SUMMARY—Avoid claims that are "substantial duplicates" as to what is covered, particularly independent claims. Avoid claims that differ only by items clearly old in the art, or highly conventional. This doctrine should be highly limited by the Patent Office, and appeal to the CCPA would often be successful.

Section 59—Undue Multiplicity

A separate, but related doctrine of "undue multiplicity" derives from the same rule, 75(b), second part: "provided . . . they *are not unduly multipled.*" Theoretically, this means that too many claims are presented, whether or not any two meet the "duplicate" test of the previous paragraph. According to MPEP 706.03(1):

> An unreasonable number of claims; that is unreasonable in view of the nature and scope of applicant's invention and the state of the art, affords a basis for a rejection on the ground of *multiplicity*. A rejection on this ground should include all the claims in the case inasmuch as it relates to confusion of the issue.

The boundaries of this rejection are not very clear and it is not used very often. When used, it is usually combined with a duplicate claims rejection.

In an undue multiplicity rejection, the examiner will set a number of claims* he thinks is reasonable under the circumstances, and one can then elect that many claims to prosecute on the merits. Then, after prosecution is completed on the elected claims, one can appeal the multiplicity rejection, along with any other rejections, if one still believes it is unreasonable.

In *Ex parte Birnbaum*, 161 USPQ 635, 637 (Bd. App. 1968), the board reversed an undue multiplicity rejection stating:

> All of the claims [twenty-four] have been rejected on the ground of multiplicity. While forty pages of claims may seem to be unnecessarily prolix, the mere psychological reaction to this amount of material does not, in and of itself, constitute a legal basis for rejection. The Examiner must show either that the claims are so unduly multiplied that they are difficult to understand, or that the claims are for the most part duplicates.

See also *Ex parte Joyce et al.*, 168 USPQ 373 (Bd. App. 1969), for a fairly recent board opinion affirming such a rejection and applying a "rule of reason" test (forty-two claims covering thirty pages for a "relatively simple and not complex" invention).

The CCPA, recently, has not been sympathetic to multiplicity.

---

*MPEP 706.03(1).

One case in 1969 (*In re Flint*, 162 USPQ 228) holds such rejection improper on the merits, with the concurring judge, Judge Neese, believing that the whole basis for rejection, rule 75(b), not being founded in the statutes, is illegal, and that the MPEP practice cited is even worse in eroding applicant's rights. This case reviews many previous cases on the subject.

SUMMARY—Avoid presenting "too many" claims total, and where a large number of claims must reasonably be presented, make sure there are clear-cut differences between the claims. Dependent claims will help in avoiding multiplicity rejections. Basically, be reasonable, particularly where more than ten claims are thought necessary. This doctrine may well not stand further CCPA scrutiny.

Chapter IX

NONART REJECTIONS

The following sections cover some formal rejections to claims not previously discussed in detail. By "formal" is meant rejections other than anticipation, obviousness, or lack of statutory subject matter (*e.g.*, rejections of methods of doing business, naturally occurring articles, scientific principles, etc.). See MPEP 706.03(a).

Section 60—Old Combination—Overclaiming

This "form" of claim, if used, is objectionable under present Patent Office practice. If the entire barrel take-up of Claim 15, Section 53, were old, and only a new type of accumulator were provided, it would be improper to claim the combination of the new accumulator with the barrel, rotary turntable, reciprocating guide, etc., unless the accumulator coöperated in some new way with the take-up, which it most probably would not. Since the only novel feature in such an invention would be the accumulator, it must be claimed per se.

The first "Guidelines of Patentability" memorandum, dated June 17, 1963 (792 O.G. 3) sets out the Patent Office's concept of general rules relative to old combination, also known as "exhausted combination." See also MPEP 706.03(j):

> The rejection is proper when a single reference discloses broadly a combination of elements functionally cooperating in substantially the same manner to produce substantially the same results as that of the claimed combination. . . . The fact

> that an applicant has improved one element of a combination which may be per se patentable does not entitle him to a claim to the improved element in combination with old elements where the elements perform no new function in the claimed combination. . . . The test to be applied to claims of this character is whether or not the action of any of the elements embraced by the claim is modified in any material manner by the fact that another element has the specific structure recited. . . .

This is an old, but not yet exhausted doctrine, dating from before 1890, as explained in *Robinson on Patents* §513. There has been little change in the basic theory of the doctrine over the years. A Patent Office example, from an old agent's examination (October 1953), concerns a man who invented a new composition for a searchlight mirror, but then claimed the mirror in combination with all of the old elements of a standard searchlight—obviously the mirror cooperated in no new way with the bulb, power source, etc.

This doctrine was originated by the federal courts in invalidating claims, sometimes under the name "overclaiming." One of the leading Supreme Court cases on old combination is *Lincoln Eng'r Co. v. Stewart-Warner Corp.*, 37 USPQ 1, 3 (U.S. Sup. Ct. 1938), where the patentee invented an improved gripping chuck for a grease gun, but claimed the entire grease gun in which the other elements performed no new function. The claim in litigation, letters and paragraphing added, was:

> 2. The combination with
> (a) a headed nipple for receiving lubricant of
> (b) a lubricant compressor having
> (c) a coupling member . . . comprising
> (1) a cylinder,
> (2) a piston . . . , and
> (3) having an aperture
> (4) an apertured sealing seat . . . , [and]
> (5) radially movable locking elements carried by the cylinder coacting with the nipple and actuated by said piston for compressively clutching the elements upon the nipple whereby . . .

The court found elements (a) and (b) to be old, with the *sole* novelty in the coupling member, element (c), which constituted 90 percent of the claim. But 90 percent was not sufficient:

> . . . having hit upon this improvement he did not patent it as such but attempted to claim it in combination with other old elements which performed no new function in his claimed combination. The patent is, therefore, void as claiming more than the applicant invented. The mere aggregation of a number of old parts or elements which, in the aggregation, perform or produce no new or different function or operation than that theretofore performed or produced by them, is not patentable invention. And the improvement of one part of an old combination gives no right to claim that improvement in combination with other old parts which perform no new function in the combination.

A more recent example, in 1963, is *Holstenssen v. V. M. Corp.*, 139 USPQ 401 (6th Cir. 1963), *cert. denied*, 377 U.S. 966 (1964). In this case, the patentees had invented the modern offset-spindle type of phonograph record changer, which replaced the prior slicer blade structure and achieved great commercial success. While the judge indicated this was a very significant invention, he held the claims not only included the novel record-dropping mechanism, but also included all of the old and unchanged elements of a complete automatic record player: turntable, pick-up arm and cycling mechanism. Neither did the specification point out what was old and what was new.

The claim in question called for the following elements (old except where italicized):

> 1. In a talking machine,
> (a) a rotatable *hollow* shaft,
> (b) a turntable . . . ,
> (c) *a post extending through the shaft and having an upper extension which is offset . . . for forming a shoulder for supporting a stack of records . . .*,
> (d) *steadying means . . .* ,
> (e) *a lever pivotally mounted in said supporting post . . .* ,
> (f) a pickup arm . . .
> (g) means . . . for swinging the pickup arm . . . , *said means* also rocking said lever, and
> (h) means for then returning the pickup arm inwards to playing position.

The five generally old elements (a), (b), (f), (g) and (h) were defined only very broadly, while the new elements (c), (d) and (e) were described in substantial detail. Unquestionably, the new record dropper cooperated with the old cycling mechanism in no basically new way.

An earlier patent to one of the patentees claimed the same general combination, with a different form of record dropper. The fact that there was a prior patent should theoretically have been immaterial to the overclaiming question, but it seems to have influenced the judge. The patented changer enjoyed great commercial success, all manufacturers but the defendant had taken licenses, the patent had previously been held valid and infringed in another circuit (Illinois), and the defendant did not even contest the district judge's holding that the invention was unobvious. The sole issue was the formal ground of old combination or overclaiming. The court even held that ". . . the spindle type record dropper was new and constituted invention [meaning it was unobvious]."

The court then held the claim invalid, citing Lincoln *Engineering v. Stewart-Warner*, previously discussed. The court held (emphasis added):

> We come, finally, to the critical question for our decision, namely, will the owner of a patent which, *in part, contains patentable invention,* be denied recovery from one who clearly infringes the part of the patent which is invention, merely because the patent is not a true combination and claims as part of the invention that which is old and disclosed in a prior patent? We are of the opinion that we must answer in the affirmative. Such a holding appears unfair unless there is a policy of patent law which, in its effect, visits total forfeiture upon a patent which attempts to extend its monopoly to something already patented. There is such a policy.

The court expressly considered whether the new statute (1952) was any different than the old statutes in this regard, and held there was no change, thus the old cases had to be followed. The court went on to state, at 413:

> In contemplating this seemingly drastic rule, we bear in mind that there is no natural or common law right to a monopoly of an invention. Robinson Treatise on the Law of Patents (1890) §24. By Constitutional grant, Article I, §8, Clause 8, Congress has power to give inventors, for a limited time, "the exclusive right to their respective discoveries." Applicants for such monopolies must comply with the requirements that Congress insists be met as a condition to exercising such monopoly. The seeming harshness of this rule [against overclaiming] is further ameliorated when we keep in mind that an inventor may gain monopoly for an inventive improvement to an existing device simply by limiting his claim to that which he did invent.

The expression "overclaiming" seems inaccurate, since a subcombination claim to A+B+C is *broader* than a combination claim to A+B+C+D+E+F, etc. Thus, it seems the big combination claim would be *under*claiming the invention. In fact, had Holstenssen *et al.* attempted to file for reissue, to eliminate the old elements, the Patent Office would have held this to be a *broadening* reissue.

Regardless of any theoretical discussion of the word "overclaiming," the *Holstenssen* case is a strict decision clearly teaching that one should be very careful to claim *only his new invention,* detached from a lot of old things. This type of case, as well as new rule 75(e), should point the way toward Jepson-type claims (Section 54) or subcombination claims (Section 56), whichever are appropriate. This is of the utmost importance in view of such language as "total forfeiture"!

It is a little difficult to understand why people insist on pursuing narrower claims to large combinations. Perhaps one factor is the thought that royalties or damages might be based on the value of the large combination instead of "the Invention." This is probably erroneous in theory, but may be significant in practice. See Crisman *et al., Vending an Old Combination: A Patent Misuse-Antitrust Problem,* 51 JPOS 649 (Oct. 1969), for further discussion of the doctrine and problems generated in licensing subcombination patents.

In keeping with its recent custom of discarding or drastically liberalizing nonart rejections* the CCPA threw out the classic "old combination" doctrine on Nov. 20, 1969, in *In re Bernhart and Fettter*, 163 USPQ 611. The invention is discussed in detail in Section 41 on mental steps and computer programs. Certain claims, given in essence in Section 41, were rejected as "drawn to the old combination of a programmed computer and a plotting device, which combination is shown to be old by . . . [a reference]." Here the novelty was strictly in the computer program.

The court quoted MPEP 706.03(j), stating that the MPEP ". . . statement has the support of many cases."

The court then held that there was no statutory basis for the rule, as stated, and rejected it. The court discussed the cases calling this "overclaiming" and rejected that, as suggested above by this author.

> Such statements [about overclaiming] are indeed puzzling in view of the fact that the addition of elements to a claim *narrows* its scope and thereby creates a lesser monopoly. Others have said that the combination is not new or is obvious, if no new coaction or result is obtained. This too is unsound, since it is not the result which is to be patented but the recited machine, composition, etc. If the prior art does not show or suggest the improved element itself, it defies logical reasoning to say that the same prior art suggests the use of the improved element in a combination.

The court next reasoned that, under the present statute, the old combination rejection could only be based on 35 U.S.C. §112, lack of "particularly pointing out and distinctly claiming." The court then held that the claims in issue were particular and distinct. Note, there is nothing peculiar about old combination claims that would make them as a class nonparticular or indistinct. The court thought that, if the plotter were put in the preamble, à la *Jepson* (Section 54), it would "greatly increase the number of words"; and, if eliminated (as a subcombination

---

*See method functional of apparatus (Section 37), product-by-process claims (Section 43), new use claims and preamble limitations (Section 52), mental steps (Section 54), aggregation (Section 61), printed matter (Section 62).

claim, Section 56), it would not make the claims "more particular or distinct, since the monopoly . . . would be substantially broadened."

A caution with this new doctrine, as with all other old rules and nonrules wiped out by the CCPA recently, is that other courts may disagree. Although one can presumably obtain old combination, aggregation, new use, function of the machine, etc., claims from the Patent Office, since it generally must follow the CCPA,* the status of such claims will be in grave doubt until other courts, notably the Supreme Court, have also spoken. In all such situations, it is recommended that all other forms of less controversial claims also be obtained just in case.**

While this author agrees with the *logic* of the court fully on old combinations, the ultimate basis for the decision—that the statute, *sub silentio*, threw out the old case law rejections—is tenuous and this author believes clearly wrong. (See also comments in Section 52.) Note the strong dissenting opinion by Judges Kirkpatrick and Worley in the *Tarczy-Hornoch* decision (Section 37) exorcising the "mere function of the machine doctrine," 158

---

*It would be pointless not to follow the CCPA, since applicant could and would appeal the next case to the same court. The only remedy if the Patent Office disagrees is petition for certiarari to the Supreme Court. The Patent Office has petitioned for certiorari recently in three cases where the office did not agree with CCPA decisions. In *Brenner v. Manson*, 148 USPQ 689 (1966), the Supreme Court granted certiorari, and by seven to two reversed a liberal CCPA decision on chemical utility. Later, the Supreme Court granted certiorari to review *In re Hofstetter*, 150 USPQ 105 (CCPA 1966). This case involved the CCPA's standard ruling that doubt should be resolved in favor of applicant, rather than in favor of Patent Office decisions, as the District of Columbia courts hold. However, the application was abandoned by the inventor (probably to avoid a test) and the case was dismissed without a decision. *See also* Gottschalk v. Benson, 175 USPQ 673 (Sup. Ct. 1973), where the Supreme Court reversed the CCPA in a computer program case, discussed in Section 41.

For further background on the recent CCPA's attempts to revolutionize or make sense of the law (depending on one's viewpoint), see an excellent review, *The CCPA: Evolution on an Activist Court,* by Stanley H. Liberstein in 13 IDEA 63 (Spring 1969).

**If faced with problems of "duplicate claiming," Section 58, by two different kinds of claims (for example, *Jepson* and regular) covering the same thing, probably the court can be prevailed on to throw out that doctrine also.

USPQ at 151. This dissent is to the effect that Congress intended no such thing in passing the 1952 statute. Congress intended only to codify the law, including judicial precedents. Judge Kirkpatrick cites the Supreme Court in *Graham v. John Deere Co.*, 148 USPQ 459 (1966), as expressly so holding (on the question of obviousness).

In fact, this theory that Congress threw out all the old case law doctrines by not writing them into the 1952 act* was expressly not followed by the chief promulgator of the theory, Judge Giles Rich, in double patenting cases. For example, in *In re Zickendraht and Buehler*, 138 USPQ 22, 27 (CCPA 1963), Judge Rich in a concurring opinion states that what is known as "obviousness-type double patenting"† is a case law judge-made doctrine which (somehow) survived the statute and is expressly not based on the statute.

The words of Judge Rich in the *Zickendraht* case in June 1963 are almost exactly the same as the words of Judge Kirkpatrick in the *Tarczy-Hornoch* dissent in June 1968:

---

*This reasoning may have started, as far as the cases go, with *In re Stempel,* 113 USPQ 77, 81 (CCPA) 1957), which involved a question of antedating a reference. But the language fits all of these nonstatutory situations:

> The patent statutes give to inventors the *right* to a patent upon compliance with *their* provisions, and neither the rules promulgated by the Patent Office nor the interpretation placed on them can detract from these rights. 35 USC 6. Under 35 USC 102 an applicant is '*entitled* to a patent *unless*' it is shown that one or another of the prohibitory provisions therein, or elsewhere in the statute, applies. (Emphasis supplied)

This language, establishing an overall test, has been cited in many subsequent cases, and is the basis of the rule that all rejections must be based on statute.

†"Obviousness-type double patenting" means that the claims of one application are obvious in view of the claims of an issued patent to the same inventor or owned by the same assignee, where the patent, *qua* patent, is not prior art under 35 U.S.C. §102. Regular prior art may be combined with the claims of the patent, if needed, to build an obviousness rejection exactly as if the prior claims were part of the "prior art."

> . . . [in a double patenting case] this statute would seem to be inapplicable and the . . . patent has to be denied on some other ground. . . . The basis for denial is not a statutory basis; rather, . . . it is clear that it [obviousness-type double patenting] has been a firmly established rule in this Court for over thirty years [at least 67 years in the machine-function case] . . .

This concurring opinion has since become the Court's standard unanimous opinion on what the court now calls obviousness-type double patenting.

Boldly to reverse an ancient doctrine because the doctrine no longer makes sense (and in fact never did) is one (highly laudable) thing; to say that Congress did so when it plainly did not is quite another. These decisions are also dangerous, particularly for younger attorneys who might not know about the Lincoln Engineering case, and use cases such as *Bernhart and Fetler* to compel the Patent Office to allow their clients totally invalid claims under the Supreme Courts "policy of patent law which . . . visits total forfeiture upon [such] a patent."

If *any* inference at all can be drawn about what Congress intended with the 1952 act, this author believes it should be that Congress intended to affirm all well-established case law doctrines by not reversing them or mentioning them in the statute. This seems a more legitimate construction. As a matter of purely practical fact, it is probably true that Congress intended to pass the bill the committee approved, and the committee intended to approve the bill the patent lawyers wrote, as explained by Judge Rich in speeches to Patent Law Associations.

To return to the classic "old combination" doctrine, this ground of rejection did not apply where the subcombination was only *intended* for use in the combination, but the old elements were not positively recited in the claim.

For example, in *In re Rohrbacher and Kolbe*, 128 USPQ 117, 119 (CCPA 1960), claim 1 in question was directed to a special cooling pump designed for use with a particular kind of engine, but the engine parts were not made positive elements of the claim. Claim 1 read:

1. A cooling liquid pump *for engines having parallel rows of liquid cooled cylinders* and comprising

an elongated pump casing *adapted to extend between said rows of cylinders and to be secured at the opposite ends thereof to the liquid cooling cavity walls of said rows of cylinders.*

said casing being formed to provide . . . [certain chambers defined in detail], . . .

said casing ends being formed to provide outlet ports . . . [defined] and being *adapted to provide communication between* said discharge chamber *and the cooling liquid cavities within said cavity walls of said rows of cylinders*, . . . (Paragraphing and emphasis added to show relation to the engine.)

In reversing an old combination rejection, the court held:

The first ground of rejection is based on the board's holding that the claims are not drawn merely to pump structure, as contended by appellants, but that the engine forms a part of the claimed combination.

It is clear that the engine is not positively recited as an element of any of the claims. It is referred to only by such statements as that the pump is "for" engines of a particular type and that the pump chambers are "adapted" to communicate with certain portions of the engine. We are of the opinion that such statements are intended merely to define the structure of the pump itself and that, as stated in appellants' brief:

"The pump defined by the claims may be separated from the engine and carried away from the engine. The claims still read on the pump after it has been carried away."

The appealed . . . claims do not state that the article claimed is an engine or includes an engine, but merely that it is for an engine or is adapted to be connected therewith. Such statements of adaptation for an intended use have been held not to limit the claims to the particular use specified. Brown Mfg. Co. v. Deere et al., 61 F. 972 (C.C.A. 7).

While the device recited in the appealed claims is intended to be used with an engine and has a particular structure adapting it for such use, the claims define only the structure of the pump itself and not a combination of the pump with an engine.

Another example of how to avoid "the old combination" doctrine, while retaining some aspects of the combination in the claim, is to use an "In a" claim discussed under Section 56 on combination and subcombination. One can claim the subcombination for use in the combination, with the subcombination elements *adapted* to do things to the elements of the combination. Dean's Claim 3 in *In re Dean,* 130 USPQ 107 (CCPA 1961) trod a very fine line to avoid old combination:

> In a camera having a shutter mechanism including two independently operable shutter-actuating elements, a *shutter-timing apparatus for* effecting a precisely predetermined camera exposure *comprising:*
>
> [1] a pair of electro-responsive devices adapted to be individually coupled to said [shutter-actuating] elements; . . . and
>
> [7] an electrical time constant circuit responsive to . . . for rendering said discharge device conductive to develop a delayed pulse . . . to cause its associated electro-responsive device to *complete an exposure.* (Emphasis and paragraphing added.)

The claim had been rejected, among other grounds, as drawn to an old combination of a timing circuit and an old shutter mechanism.

The CCPA ruled that the claim was a subcombination claim to the timer per se, not a claim to the combination of the timer and shutter. The preamble limitations "In a camera" and "for effecting a camera exposure" were not considered positive elements of the claim. With respect to "adapted to be coupled," the court stated:

> To state mere *adaptability* of these parts of the timer to perform the coupling function does not import into the claim the shutter. . . . The above clause is a limitation of elements [1] but not an inclusion of shutter elements.

Similar comments were made with respect to such clauses as "to cause its associated . . . device to complete an exposure." This was merely a statement of the *reason* why the pulse is developed at all, a statement which, together with the preamble, we think improves the clarity of definition of the elements of the timer, and nothing more."

These types of claims, then, are really only special forms of subcombination claims, sort of hybrids spelling out inferentially enough of the combination details to give meaning to the subcombination elements, but not including such details in the claim. This seems to be a highly useful type of claim in an appropriate case. See further discussion in Section 56—combination and subcombination. Compare also, with the discussion in Section 52 of new use claims, concerning preamble statements of intended use.

In 1971, the Seventh Circuit followed the *Lincoln Engineering* and *Holstenssen* cases on old combination, without any question, but held that the claim in question was not drawn to an old combination since all of the elements cooperated to perform a new function.

SUMMARY—Beware of old-combination claims. Claim the new things your inventor contributed, not in combination with a lot of old and unchanged things. Point out what your inventive contribution is, not old environment where it is used. Use Jepson claims (Section 54) or subcombination claims (Section 56) to avoid this problem. In addition to avoiding invalidity on a purely technical defense, claims to "the Invention" are better received by the examiner and more likely to be allowed.

Section 61—Aggregation

A claim to an aggregation is fairly easy to draft, but in the past has not been proper subject matter for a patent under longstanding doctrines. (See *Robinson on Patents* §154 (1890), citing a host of cases.) The word "aggregation" is used by various people to mean different things, and much confusion has resulted. In accordance with one meaning, espoused by MPEP 706.01(i), the statutory classes, particularly the class "machine," are limited by court decisions to "combinations": that is, structures where the parts cooperate to achieve a result. It has been said* that an aggregation is like a track team, while a true combination is like a football team. In a famous case, a pencil with an eraser on the end was held to be unpatentable, at least in part because it was an aggregation of parts and the statute did not authorize such claims, *Reckindorfer v. Faber*, 92 U.S. 347, 5 O.G. 697 (1875).

In the *Reckindorfer* case, the court stated:

> When the functions and uses of each [separate element] are unaffected by the union and the means of uniting [glue] has no novelty, it is not obvious, certainly, that anything of invention can be alleged of the combined elements. [Citing still earlier cases.] That the aggregated result may be very convenient . . . popular . . . find a ready sale . . . great demand does not determine the question. As suggested in several cases relating to aggregation as distinguished from patentable combinations, the aggregate result may be . . . better . . . and yet, for lack of novelty of device or new result . . . it may have no patentable quality.

Note that, while the court speaks of lack of novelty, it seems to say that aggregations are not patentable as a class and that one does not reach the question of novelty (admitted) in assembling the aggregation.

**Skinner Bros. Belting Co. v. Oil Well Improvements Co.*, 12 USPQ 61, 63 (10th Cir. 1931):

> A rough analogy, that cannot be pressed too far, has repeatedly occurred to me in considering this question. I think of a football team as a combination; one passes, one receives, another blocks, another runs, and still others hold the line. Eleven men are doing different things, each in his own way, and not always simultaneously; yet they are working to a common end, to advance the ball; and they co-act as a unit. I think of a track team as an aggregation; one runs, another hurdles, another jumps, another throws. They all work for a common general end, to amass points for their alma mater, but there is lacking the vital spark of cooperation or coordination. They work, not as one unit, but as several. In the case at bar, we have no doubt that the device is a combination and not an aggregation. A single object is to be accomplished—to prevent escape of the oil from the well. All the elements coordinate in working to that end. It is not a relay of horses from London to Bath; it is a three-horse hitch to the same coach. We conclude that the first patent is valid.

A true aggregation relates to a defect in the structure, and a well-written claim will not help. In Section 25, it was noted that a valid combination may be rejected as "aggregative as claimed" when the cooperation between the elements is not properly described in the claim.

The precise limits of an aggregation rejection are not too clear. The Patent Office position is set out in MPEP 706.03(i):

> Rejections on the ground of *aggregation* should be based on a lack of cooperation between the elements of the claim. . . . Confusion as to what is meant can be avoided by treating all claims which include more than one element as combinations (patentable or unpatentable) if there is actual cooperation between the elements and as aggregations if there is no cooperation.
>
> *Example of Aggregation:* A washing machine associated with a dial telephone. . . .
>
> A claim is not necessarily aggregative because the various elements do not function simultaneously. A typewriter, for example, is a good combination. . . .

In 1964, the CCPA in *In re Gustafson,* 141 USPQ 585, cast grave doubt on the propriety of aggregation rejections, suggesting that the sole test should be obviousness under 35 U.S.C. §103. However, the application was merely remanded to the board of appeals to clarify what it meant by "aggregation" in its decision: what statutory basis or bases for rejection were relied on?

In the *Gustafson* case, claims to a storage and display device for business cards had been rejected as being drawn to an aggregation. The court reviewed the leading cases and textbooks on this doctrine, prior to the 1953 statute, pointing out that "aggregation" had come to mean several things:

1. A non-cooperating assembly of parts, as (apparently) in *Reckindorfer v. Faber* cited earlier. This presumably is actually a rejection on nonstatutory subject matter under 35 U.S.C. §101, which was first mentioned by the Patent Office solicitor before the CCPA. This meaning was said in *In re Worrest,* 96 USPQ 381 (CCPA 1953), to be "the correct use of the term," but this has never been crystallized as the only meaning.

2. A combination which is not inventive, now an obviousness rejection under Section 103.

3. A combination which is not claimed with sufficient particularity and distinctness under Section 112.

In the first place, the court concluded that "aggregation" is a word of art in the patent law and does not have any specific meaning, such as (1) above. The main point to this case is that, therefore, an "aggregation" rejection, as here given, is improper because of indefiniteness; in that applicant is entitled to know the "true ground of rejection, including the statutory basis thereof." It did not appear that the Patent Office was certain what it really meant here, as they talked about lack of cooperation, unpatentability and lack of claim clarity under Section 112.

The strong inference is that an "aggregation" rejection, *in ipsissimis verbis*, even if limited to meaning (1), is not proper; that the rejection instead should be on one of the statutory bases. (The *Worrest* case seems to have been overruled.) Note the langauge, after reviewing all the pre-1953 meanings:

> On January 1, 1953, all this mental anguish ceased to be necessary. The test of the presence or absence of "invention" and along with it the subsidiary question of whether a device or process was or was not an "aggregation," or a "combination" or an "unpatentable combination for want of invention" was replaced by the *statutory test* of 35 USC 103.

The Patent Office evidently declined to pursue the subject of aggregation further in the *Gustafson* case, and the patent issued as 3,253,872, May 31, 1966.

In *Ex parte Nolden*, 149 USPQ 378, 380 (Bd. App. 1965), the board of appeals cited the *Gustafson* case as rejecting the old aggregation (lack of cooperation) doctrine stating that the court suggested that: ". . . the term 'aggregation' as a ground of rejection is nebulous and has no basis under the Patent Act of 1952."

The examiner had rejected the claim as an aggregation under Section 112 of the statute, saying that the lack of coaction made the claims indefinite, but citing the "classic aggregation" cases, including *Reckindorfer v. Faber*. This was, of course, the wrong section of the statute. The board quickly held that it was quite clear what subject matter (aggregation or combination) the applicant was claiming. There is nothing about an aggregation claim per se which makes it indefinite under 35 U.S.C. §112. But, just as plainly, there is no section of the statute that supports a pure aggregation rejection—it was a common law doctrine not mentioned in the statute.

In *Ex parte Dalton*, 152 USPQ 68 (Bd. App. 1966), the board followed *Gustafson* in reversing a rejection of a design claim as being drawn to an aggregation of designs.

In *Ex parte Davie*, 175 USPQ 122 (Bd. App. 1971), the board reversed an "aggregation" rejection by name, following the *Gustafson* case. But the board held the claim unpatentable under Sections 112 and 103 of the statute. Aggregations are often obvious. Note, this was a composition-of-matter claim, involving a non-cooperating mixture of compounds.

With respect to the philosophy of the recent CCPA decisions overturning ancient common law rejections as not based on stature, see the extended discussion in Section 60 on old combination. A note of caution is that this reasoning may not be accepted by the Supreme Court or other federal courts. In *Ansul Co. v. Uniroyal, Inc.*, 169 USPQ 759, 761 (2d Cir. 1971), the court held that "aggregation" applies to a chemical mixture of A and B, where no new function was performed by A or B (a wetting agent). A use (new use) claim was held patentable (Section 52).

As to a textbook aggregation, there is nothing one can do to improve the claim if the structure itself lacks cooperation. In marginal cases, include as much coaction and cooperation in the claim as the structure permits.

Note, as mentioned in the *Gustafson* case, that the word "aggregation," more frequently "mere aggregation" (implying that a nonmere aggregation is OK), has also been used to signify obviousness or lack of "Invention" under the pre-1952 tests—sometimes a mixture of both. Normally, an assembly of old parts brought together, and not cooperating, would be obvious. This is much like the old, so-called "negative rules of Invention," one will find in the old textbooks. If someone assembled an unobvious aggregation, that had industrial utility, why should he not be entitled to a patent? Is not the statutory class "manufacture" comprehensive enough to cover aggregations which may not properly qualify as machines?

Aggregation-like rejections, involving alleged lack of cooperation between elements (Sections 25 and 26), can come up in other frames of reference than a classical aggregation rejection. For example, in *Ex parte Adams and Farrari*, 177 USPQ 21 (Bd. App. 1972), a claim to a "combination" of a fireplace, damper, and assertedly novel means to indicate when the damper is closed was rejected as obvious over prior art under 35 U.S.C. §103, the examiner stating that "no cooperation is present between the fireplace and the pendant except for what the user may eventually choose to indicate. . . ." the board reversed, holding:

> We know of no requirement in the statute of direct mechanical interaction between the elements of a combination. As long as the over-all result has utility and is unobvious, the elements of a mechanical combination may function independently.

See also Sections 25-26 on tying the claim elements together.

In October, 1972, the Patent Office amended the Manual, MPEP 706.03(i), revision 34, to add the following paragraph to the text quoted above:

> A rejection on aggregation should be made only after consideration of the court's comments in *In re Gustafson*, 51 CCPA 1358, 141 USPQ 585 (1964).

About all this cryptic paragraph does is to alert a diligent examiner that there may be some sort of problem with aggregation rejections, but does not identify what it is nor attempt to say what the "new" rules or practices are. Apparently, the editor of the Manual couldn't figure out exactly what the *Gustafson* case stands for, nor what if anything may be left of the old common-law "aggregation" rejection.

SUMMARY—Avoid claiming "aggregations" insofar as possible, particularly in mechanical combination cases; combinations where the elements do not cooperate. Tie the elements together insofar as possible (Sections 25-27). If the invention *is* an unobvious aggregation, appeal any rejection to the CCPA under the *Gustafson* case.

Section 62—Printed Matter

One of the ancient general rules is that "printed matter" is not patentable, primarily because it is not within the interpretation of the class "manufacture"of 35 U.S.C. §101, discussed in Section 42. Clearly this means that such things as books, menus, tables of scientific data, etc., are not patentable subject matter even through, broadly, they are manufactured articles.

But when printed material is associated with a structural article for some utilitarian purpose, the rule becomes very cloudy. The manual states, MPEP 706.03(a), that: ". . . a mere arrangement of printed matter though seemingly a 'manufacture' is rejected as *not being within the statutory classes.*"

Note the omnipresent word "mere"; under this rule, the test is whether the printed matter is *mere* or not, similarly to the "mere aggregation" test of the previous section. "Nonmere" printing is O.K., whatever that is. At least until recently, this test was interpreted similarly to the "mental steps" rule of Section 41 and the philosophy still seems similar. It was permissible to include printed matter in the claim, but the patentably novel portion could not reside solely in the nature of the printed matter.

In *In re Miller,* 164 USPQ 46, 49 (CCPA 1969), the court clarified this" Rule" in what seems a clear and reasonable fashion: "The fact that printed matter *by itself* is not patentable subject matter, because non-statutory, is no reason for ignoring it when the claim is directed to a combination."

Claim 10 was directed to:

> A measuring device comprising:
> a *spoon* for measuring ingredients;
> volume measuring *indicia* . . . on said spoon . . . , and

> a *legend attached to said spoon.* . . . (164 USPQ at 47, emphasis added).

The spoon was ostensibly an ordinary measuring spoon, the indicia were things such as "1 teaspoon" and the legend was for example "½ recipe." The spoon marked "1 teaspoon" for "½ recipe" was really only ½ teaspoon. The novel feature resided solely in the proper relation between the indicia and the legend.

Thus, it seems the nature of printed matter on an article of manufacture can be considered in determining patentability. In this case, the court considered the printed matter and found the invention highly unobvious.

The "printed matter" rule is also discussed in detail in *In re Bernhart and Fetter*, 163 USPQ 611 (CCPA 1969), although the claims did not involve printed matter in any way. See the discussion of this case in Section 41 on mental steps. The general principles of this case, on nonstatutory class rejections, seem to apply equally to "printed matter" cases. The general import is that, even though certain items are nonstatutory by themselves, it is proper to include them and rely on them for novelty and unobviousness if combined with other items which are in the statutory class. The "other" items may all be old. The *Miller* case discussed above is a perfect example of this reasoning. If true, this is a new and rather beneficient "Rule" for inventors.

SUMMARY—Avoid including printed matter in claims where possible. Where necessary to patentability, include the printed matter in combination with mechanical elements under the *Miller* case cited.

Section 63—Incomplete

On completeness, the office states, MPEP 706.03(f):

> A claim can be rejected as *incomplete* if it omits essential elements, steps or necessary structural cooperative relationship of elements, such omission amounting to a gap between the elements, steps or necessary structural connection. Greater lati-

> tude is permissible with respect to the definition in a claim of matters not essential to novelty or operability than with respect to matters essential thereto.

No cases are cited for this proposition, and there have been very few, if any, in recent years. Presumably, if a claim were so rejected, it would be far easier to put in more elements or connections than argue the rejection. Also, if the *examiner* required additional elements, he would then be unlikely to reject the claim as an old combination (Section 60). This completeness doctrine, if applied, would set some sort of limit on subcombination or fragmentary claims discussed in Section 56, such as "In an A, a B and a C."

In view of this provision, and for general reasons as discussed in Sections 25-27, it is recommended that all claims define complete, operable combinations unless highly exceptional circumstances are present.

On completeness, the Supreme Court has held that it is not necessary to recite in the *claim* everything necessary to operate the device. As stated by Joseph Gray Jackson in *The Art of Drafting Patent Claims*, 59-60:

> One should refer to two decisions of the U.S. Supreme Court.
>
> In *Deering v. Winona*, [155 U.S. 286 (1894)], the device was an agricultural machine and lacked the support necessary for the board which was an element of the claim. The Supreme Court, said, "True that it is necessary and true it is not in the claim but it does not have to be; the claim does not have to include everything that is required to operate."
>
> The other case is *Special Equipment v. Coe*, [324 U.S. 370, 64 USPQ 525 (1945)], in which a subcombination claim was supported which related to a machine for cutting, peeling and coring pears, and there was no cutting knife involved in the claim. The Supreme Court said it is perfectly all right; you do not have to have everything required to operate this device in the claim.* Completeness is a much inflated "bugaboo" which is mainly of interest to certain examiners in the Patent Office,

---

*Note—this and the following quotes are by Jackson, interpreting what the Supreme Court held, not quotes from the Supreme Court decision.

> and should not really concern them. The claim is not a description of the device in any case. It is like a fingerprint which identifies the device. The fingerprint looks not at all like the person, but it is an identification of the person, and that is what we are interested in—identification.

See also *Ex parte Schaefer*, cited in Section 20, to the effect that omission of elements from claim makes it broad, but not vague, indefinite or misdescriptive. While the word "incomplete" was not used by name, it clearly was implied.

SUMMARY—To the extent feasible, claim complete combinations of elements. But, it is perfectly proper and advisable to claim novel subcombination under the cases cited above and in Section 56.

Section 64—Vague and Indefinite

In addition to being incomplete, a claim can be rejected or invalidated because it is vague and indefinite. This derives from 35 U.S.C. §112, that the claim does not particularly point out the invention or distinctly claim it. Various formal sources of indefiniteness were pointed out earlier, such as lack of antecedents (Section 20) or failure to read on the embodiments disclosed (Section 15).

The claim *in toto* may also be so peculiarly worded that it is unknown just what it covers, even though a patent lawyer may be able to read the claim word for word on the structure disclosed. It may bear no relation to the real point of the invention. This is somewhat similar to a rejection as being too broad, discused in various sections (particularly Section 28), but it is also somewhat different.

One recent example is *Laitram Corp. v. Deepsouth Packing Co.,* 162 USPQ 14 (E.D. La. 1969), involving what the judge considered to be a worthwhile and unobvious *invention* of a shrimp deveining machine. However, all but one of the claims of Lapeyre *et al.* patent 2,825,927 were held invalid as "hopelessly vague and indefinite."

Claim 12 was an example:

> A shrimp vein remover comprising: hook-like vein engaging means, shrimp moving means operatively associated with said vein engaging means, and means associated with at least one of said above named means for effecting relative movement therebetween.

The court held that such claims "do not accurately describe and are not limited to the scope of the . . . invention." Also, "a patent must be a certain guide; not a congeries [collection] of pregnant suggestions." Further "enterprise and experimentation must not be discouraged by an area of uncertainty as to the scope of the invention."

While this type of case could come up in any statutory class, it normally occurs primarily in the class "machine." In this case, structural and functional connections (Sections 25-27) were stated, but only in incomprehensible fashion. For example, the shrimp-moving means is "operatively associated" with the vein-engaging means How? Why? For what purpose? How does a shrimp get deveined? The "glue" mentioned in Section 25 is nominally present, but the wrong brand of glue was used.

Fortunately for the patentee, claim 1 was more specific; it was held valid and infringed. For comparison, claim 1 included:

> In a shrimp vein remover, a supporting member, a lip projecting at an acute angle from the supporting member and having a smooth rounded free edge for engaging beneath the vein of a shrimp and for wedging the vein between the lip and the supporting member, and means operatively associated with said supporting member for relatively moving the shrimp with respect to said member to cause separation of the vein from the shrimp meat.

While the judge thought that this "can claim no prizes for clarity or artistry," he also held the claim sufficiently definite:

> . . . it is impossible to suppose that anyone who really wished to respect the patent would have any difficulty in identifying what the claim covered. . . . (Quoting from *Musher Foundation v. Alba Trading Co.*, 66 USPQ 183 (2d Cir. 1945).)

This case well illustrates the point about obtaining intermediate and narrow claims, Section 57. In view of the ultrabroad claim 12, one might be tempted not to concentrate on the more pedestrian claims, such as claim 1; but ultrabroad claims can be shot down for a great many reasons; specific claims cannot.

In *In re Wolfrum and Gold,* 179 USPQ 620 (CCPA-1973), discussed in Section 4.7 on Markush claims, the Court held that a Markush claim to groups of compounds A or B was not rejectable under 35 U.S.C. 112, and that 112 rejections of claims were limited to cases where the claim is not "precise and definite" as to what it covers; that is, the examiner cannot understand what *the applicant* regards as his invention.

> "An applicant is free under that provision [Section 112] to set the metes and bounds of 'his invention' as he sees them," citing *In re Borkowski, In re Wakefield,* and *In re Swinehart.*

Thus, in effect, the Court held that Section 112 cannot be used as a basis for formal rejections of claims, such as the problem of Markush claims covering "patentably distinct" species.

See also, discussion of related topics in Section 28.

SUMMARY—Avoid "vague and indefinite" claims. Make claims certain as to what they cover and how they relate to the example(s) described in the detailed description.

Section 65—Prolixity

In the previous sections, we stated that claims must be complete and definite; now one must also learn that a claim can be *too* complete and *too* definite. According to a doctrine known as "prolixity," MPEP 706.03(g):

> Claims are rejected as *prolix* when they contain long recitations of unimportant details which hide or obscure the invention. *Ex parte Iagan,* 1911 Dec. Com. Pat. 10; 162 O.G. 538; expresses the thought that very long detailed claims setting forth so many elements that invention [now unobviousness] cannot possibly reside in the combination should be rejected as prolix.

While this doctrine is probably used relatively rarely, one should know it exists. A string of dependent claims might well help overcome the "problem," if one wanted to present such a total claim, in that no one claim would be all that long and detailed. Also, once one claim in the string was allowed, the further dependent claims would most likely be allowed without extensive consideration (Section 53).

SUMMARY—The overall rule on claim scope is simple to state but often hard to follow:

"The claim should not be too broad nor too narrow, not incomplete nor too complete; it should be just right."

Chapter X

REVIEW OF SOME BASICS

(Myron Cohen)

Preface

Mr. Landis: The following remarks were prepared by Myron Cohen of Hubbel, Cohen & Stiefel, as advice to our PLI Agent's Exam students at claim drafting clinics, where the students prepare claims to sample structures for criticisms by our tutors, including Mr. Cohen. Many such problems appear in Appendix B, *infra*.

Mr. Cohen's half-time pep talk to his students not only summarizes and highlights many of the most important portions of this book on how to write mechanical claims, it contains very sage advice on how to write broad claims generally. While some of the advice is intended for the rank beginner, and other parts focus on particular kinds of Agent's Exam questions, all can learn from these self-styled "random thoughts"* of Mr. Cohen.

Random Thoughts on How to Draft Claims to Mechanical Apparatus

Mr. Cohen: A claim is a one-sentence definition of the structure of the defined invention. It defines that invention with the

*These thoughts were composed over some ten years of practice in tutoring novice claim drafters. They are decidedly not random; they hit the students' problems on the head.

same particularity and precision as the description of a parcel of land in a deed. The analogy to the deed is a good one because United States claims serve to define the outer limits or boundaries of the invention in the same fashion as the description of land in a deed defines the outer limits of the land monopoly. Thus U.S. claims do not define the spirit or heart or central theme of an invention. Much of this does not shed any light on how to draft claims, but it is important to recognize that claim language must be extremely precise. The precision of the language has nothing whatsover to do with the breadth or narrowness of the claim, for the broad claim must be drawn with the same precision as the narrow claim. The point is that there are very few if any chores in the area of legal draftsmanship that are as demanding of language as the chore of drafting a claim.

Throughout the balance of these remarks, I intend to speak principally of apparatus claims. I will touch on method claims briefly and on composition claims not at all. However, the truly tough job in drafting mechanical claims is the preparation of a broad claim to apparatus and that is what we are going to concentrate on.

Most commentators in the field of U.S. claim drafting usually state that an apparatus claim is *not merely a catalog of parts.** They are absolutely correct in saying this. Unfortunately, they usually overlook the fact that while an apparatus claim is not *merely* a catalog of parts, it *absolutely must include a catalog of* parts. It is the cataloging of the parts which gives rise to what we call the positive recitation of elements. That is, each structural element in the claim must be set forth directly and independently of every other element.

Thus, if an apparatus is to be claimed which includes three elements, A, B and C, then the claim must have as a part of itself language that states "an A" and language that states "a B" and language that states "a C."

However, as the commentators told us, a U.S. claim is not merely a catalog of parts. What distinguishes a U.S. claim from

*Sections 25 and 26.

a mere catalog is the inclusion in the claim of language that directly or indirectly interrelates each element in the claim with each other element. The interrelationship can be (1) by connection, either a dynamic connection such as "rotatably mounted on," or by a static connection such as "fixed to"; (2) by definition of relative position between two elements such as element B being disposed above element A; or (3) by setting forth yet another element in the catalog which interrelates two elements, such as a gear train drivingly connecting element B to element A.

Thus, when one drafts a claim perhaps the simplest way to do it is first to set forth a catalog of the major parts. After this has been done, you can either add additional parts to interrelate the major parts or you can modify the major parts to put in language of relationship. For example, a claim can read as follows:

> A gadget comprising:
> an A;
> a B interrelated with A; and
> a C interrelated with B.

It will be seen in the example that by interrelating A with B and by interrelating B with C you have indirectly interrelated C with A. Thus all three elements A, B and C are directly or indirectly interrelated and you have a complete claim. If on the other hand the claim called for:

> A gadget comprising:
> an A;
> a B interrelated with A; and
> a C.

you would not have a complete claim as C would not be interrelated with either A or B. Such a claim would not be complete and would be rejected as being indefinite.*

---

* (Sec. 64; or "incomplete," Sec. 63; or drawn to an aggregation, Sec. 61; or not properly drawn to a machine, Sec. 25-26). Whatever the exact name of the ground of rejection, the examiner will usually object to such a claim. [JLL]

Perhaps a more common way of writing a U.S. claim is to interrelate the main elements with additional structural elements that must also be positively recited or catalogued. Thus a perfectly proper claim would be:

> A gadget comprising:
> an A;
> a B;
> a C;
> means interrelating A with B; and
> means interrelating B with C.

This example meets all of the tests of a complete claim in which all the elements are positively recited and each element is directly or indirectly interrelated with each other. The form of this last claim can prove rather sterile, and generally speaking a skilled claim draftsman would write that claim in slightly different form. The preferred form would probably be:

> A gadget comprising:
> an A;
> a B;
> means interrelating A with B;
> a C; and
> means interrelating B with C.

In apparatus claims we are concerned solely and exclusively with a definition of structure. By structure I mean hardware, something you can touch, something you can feel, something you can manipulate. We are not interested in function, and the function of an element cannot be used as a substitute for the definition of the structure of the element itself.

However, there is one exception to the rule concerning the avoidance of the definition of an element by virtue of its function. In the last paragraph of Section 112 of the Patent Act, there is statutory authority for defining an element as "a means for performing a function."* Now you may very well think that is

---

*See Section 31.

ridiculous, that merely saying "means for performing a function" is as functional as defining the element by the function itself. Well your logic may be good, but if you believe this you fail as lawyers. The Congress of the United States has said that "means for performing a function" is structural, it is not functional.* So, by act of Congress, such language meets all of the statutory requirements for the definition of a structural element. In this connection, I would like to urge you not to avoid the use of the expression "means for." It is a perfectly fine expression and gives rise to the writing of claims of substantial breadth.

Particularly, in taking the examination, we have found that more students lose more points by unduly limiting their broad claim than they ever do from writing a claim that is too broad. Thus I would urge you to not avoid the use of the expression "means for" in a claim in setting forth an element in a combination of elements.

There is one place that "means for" cannot be used. You cannot define a structure by a single element which is defined in terms of a means for performing a function. This is what is meant by a "single means claim" and it is regarded as being functional. However, when you have more than one element in a claim, there is nothing wrong with defining one, several or all of the elements in terms of "means for." I might say that there have been times when I have actually done this and have secured the allowance of such claims. When the prior art permits it, it is the best kind of claim you can get.

There are a couple of specific rules that I would like to set forth for your guidance in connection with taking the examination. These rules, in some instances, you may shed after you have become a licensed practitioner; but I think they should be followed at this point in your career.

The first rule is *never use the expressions, "adapted to" or "adapted for."* Both of these expressions tend to be somewhat functional and may lead to an objection on the ground of the claim's being indefinite.† There is a perfectly simple solution to

*See Section 28.

†See Sections 20 and 27.

the problem of proper language to be used in lieu of "adapted to" or "adapted for." The proper linguistic solution is the word "for." Thus never say, "a base adapted to support a table." It is much preferable to say, "a base for supporting a table."

The second rule which I think should be followed through the examination is *never use the word "whereby"* in a claim.* Now I know that you have been told that "whereby clauses" are perfectly good, and I for one use them regularly.

However, I think you have to know when to use them and when not to use them and I seriously doubt that you have reached the point in your development as claims draftsmen where you can use them with consistent propriety. Generally speaking, my experience has been that when a novice claim draftsman uses the word "whereby" he generally uses it to introduce a lengthy functional expression to cover up or blur the fact that he has not set forth the necessary structure. My advice to you is when you are drafting a claim and you suddenly see the word "whereby" jump out of that paper, stop! Go back and write the claim again. If the word "whereby" is going to be used, I think you are going to have a claim that is going to cost you a considerable number of points.

The third rule relates to the definition of holes,† grooves and other absences of material. Just as I have said that every structural element, every hardware element, must be recited positively, I can give you an equally inflexible rule concerning *holes, grooves, slits and slots. These cannot be recited positively;* they must always be recited inferentially. Thus you cannot say "a doughnut, a hole in the center of a doughnut." This would positively recite the hole in the doughnut and would be considered improper. The proper way to handle this is to write "baked goods comprising: a cylinder of dough having a hole in the center thereof." Note the hole just is not positively set forth or catalogued. It is impositively or inferentially recited by the use of the word "having." In the same manner, you might call for "a tube having

*Section 29.
†See Section 23.

a circumferential groove therein" or "a link having an axially extending slot therein."

Everything that I have discussed above relates to independent claims, that is claims which are wholly self-contained so far as the structure set forth therein. There is another breed of claim called a "dependent claim"* which is a claim of narrower scope than the claim from which it depends. A dependent claim is one which incorporates by reference all of the structure of the claim from which it depends. Thus, a dependent claim is not self-contained but relies for some of the structure defined therein on a claim which is referenced in the preamble of the dependent claim.

Now the Patent Office greatly prefers dependent claims to a series of ever narrower independent claims. They have found them easier to examine as such dependent claims highlight the points of difference between successive claims. For this reason the Patent Office charges only $2 for each dependent claim in excess of ten, but charges $10 for each independent claim in excess of one. This being the case, when you take the exam, if you are asked to write three claims of differing scope defining a particular structure, you should write one broad independent claim and two dependent claims. When you are asked to write "broad, intermediate and narrow," claims, you should make claim 2 depend from claim 1 and claim 3 depend from claim 2, whereby† claim 1 must logically be the broadest, claim 2 must be the intermediate claim, and claim 3 must be the narrowest.

But beware. The first rule of taking any exam is reading the exam carefully. One year, for no discernably good reason that I have ever conjured up, the Patent Office, notwithstanding its own preference for dependent claims, specifically instructed the examinees to write three *independent* claims of differing scope. Many of the students wrote a single independent claim and two dependent claims and lost many points on the two dependent claims. So, please read the exam and follow the instructions. If no

---

*See Section 53.

†Note purpose of "whereby" clause (Section 29), since the function necessarily follows from the previously recited structure [JLL].

instructions are given, then follow the formula given of one independent broad claim followed by a first dependent claim which depends on one and a second dependent claim which depends on two. Dependent claims are quick and easy to write as you will see in a moment and conform with Patent Office preference.

As I told you a dependent claim incorporates by reference the entire subject matter of the claim from which it depends. If a dependent claim depends from a dependent claim, then it incorporates everything set forth in the claim from which it depends and everything contained in the claim from which that claim in turn depends. The chain of incorporation by reference can go on indefinitely.

There are only three things which a dependent claim can do: a dependent claim can add structure to the claim from which it depends; a dependent claim can more particularly define structure already set forth in the claim from which it depends; or a dependent claim can do both of these things.

In order for a claim to add additional structure the dependent claim must have the following language:

> The gadget as defined in Claim 1, *further comprising* . . .

After the words "further comprising" you set forth the additional structural elements. Thus, for example, suppose you have a main or independent claim which states:

> A gadget comprising:
> an A;
> a B interrelated with A; and
> a C interrelated with B.

If in a narrower claim, you wish to add an element D to the claimed combination, then you would write a dependent claim in the following form:

> The gadget as defined in Claim 1, *further comprising* a D interrelated with (A or B or C).

Do not forget, even in a dependent claim every element must be directly or indirectly interrelated in some fashion with every other element that is contained in the claim either by express language or by incorporation by reference.

If however, rather than adding an additional element D, you wish to more particularly define that the element B is actually made up of sub-elements E, F and G, then you would be performing the second function of a dependent claim. You would be more particularly defining an element already set forth. To do this, the dependent claim would read as follows:

> The gadget as defined in Claim 1, *wherein* element B includes E, F, and G interconnecting E and F.

Please note this example sets forth more particularly just what is the construction of element B. Note that this dependent claim adds no additional element to the structure. Thus, when confronted with defining B as we have done in the immediately preceding example it would be improper to set forth this definition in the following fashion:

> The gadget as defined in Claim 1, further comprising an E, and F, and a G interrelating E and F.

The reason for this claim being improper is that E, F and G make up B. By using the further comprising language you have included element B twice in the structure, once as "B" and once as "E, F and G," when in fact B only appears once in the gadget. It is for this reason that the language "wherein" must be employed to more particularly define an already claimed element rather than "further comprising."*

All that I have said above relates to claims directed to structure, to apparatus. Apparatus claims are clearly more difficult to write than method claims. I am not going to spend much time on method claims other than to say that a method claim is merely a recitation of the manipulative steps necessary to perform the

---

*See Section 18 on double inclusion of elements.

process.* Note the emphasis on the word "manipulative." By manipulative steps we mean steps that can be performed directly or indirectly by hand or by machine controlled by the hand. Generally speaking you cannot include mental steps in such processes. In setting forth the manipulative steps you invariably use the "-ing" form of the verb such as "placing, gouging, sawing, heating, cooling, drilling," etc. In method claims you generally set forth the series of steps in the preferred sequence of performance.† However, be careful not to limit yourself to that sequence unless the particular sequence is critical. Be very wary of direct or indirect temporal limitations such as, for example, the word "then" preceding the verb at the beginning of the step. Also be wary of performing a particular step implicitly after another step. For example, if a method calls for hollowing out a bar, and also heating the bar, be careful not to call for the heating step as "heating said hollowed bar" because then you would be required to perform the heating after the hollowing in order to infringe the claim. However, if this particular sequence is necessary to a successful practicing of the process, then naturally you must include it.

Finally, I thought I might tell you just how I personally go about writing a broad claim in my day-to-day practice.** The reason I stress the broad claim is that once you have written a broad claim, that is a claim as broad as the prior art will permit, it really is very simple through the mechanism of dependent claiming to write narrower claims.

The first thing you must do in writing any broad claim is to arrive at a decision as to what is and what is not essential to "the Invention," meaning in this sense the patentable invention over the prior art. In this connection, and I speak principally to the chemists in the room, do not be afraid of making the wrong decision. If you do not know what really constitutes the Invention, then decide on something and write three claims to it. You will

*See Sections 33-35 on method claims, generally.
†Section 35.
**Sections 57, 13, 16, etc.

get points for doing that.* You will get no points if you leave your paper blank. As a matter of fact, I must tell you that when I took this examination, all too many years ago, I actually wrote three claims to a cutting machine having a shock absorbing means, when in fact, what I thought was a shock absorbing means was a safety guard. But I wrote three good claims and I passed the exam. So do not panic on the assessment of where the Invention is. Make a decision as to where the Invention is and then write a broad claim using the following technique.

After you have decided what the Invention is, what I do is, on a piece of scratch paper (do not put it in the notebook, or the exam book yet, put it on a piece of scratch paper) I write a claim of indeterminate breadth. That is, some of my elements come out very broadly and some of my elements come out very narrowly and I really do not care. All I am concerned with is getting something on paper from which to work. Once I have written down this claim of indeterminate scope I conduct what I call my schizophrenic dialogue. That is, I actually talk to myself and ask myself two series of questions. The first series of questions relates to each of the major elements in this claim of indeterminate scope. I read over each element and I ask myself is this element necessary to the invention as I have perceived it? Thus, if I have included as an element of my draft claim "a housing surrounding the drive shaft" and I know that the machine will work without the housing as well as with the housing, then I cross out that entire element. I do not need it and I do not want it to unduly limit my claim. By carrying on the first series of questions, I will get rid of any unecessary major elements in the claimed combination. Once I have done this I will go back and check to see that each element remaining in the claim is in fact interrelated with each other element. If it is not, I will add language to interrelate the unrelated elements.

*This advice applies to the type of Agent's Exam question given some years ago, where the examinee was required to write three claims to a mechanical structure (can opener, electric shaver, etc.) given only the drawing, with no description of the parts or how the device worked; and little if any indication of what might be the novel features. Examples of this type of question are given in Appendix B. [JLL].

Once I perform this second step to make sure that everything is interrelated, I go through the claim again. This time I go word-by-word and ask if the word is necessary. When I do this I look for all words of limitation such as "rigid, flexible, elongated, round," etc. Does the element have to be rigid? If it does, leave "rigid" in; if it does not, take it out. I look for "s's" on the ends of words because unless I need a plurality of the element, I have limited the claim to having the plural and have given up on the possibility of preventing someone from using the combination with a single one of those pluralized elements. In this fashion, I proceed through the claim word-by-word to measure the necessity of each word. If I do not need the word, I take it out. If I think that a given noun without modification is simply too broad or a modifier is necessary for the invention to be operative, I include the modifier.

When I get done with this second scanning of the claim, I have a broad claim, and it is as simple as that. Do not be bashful to talk to yourself and ask "is this element necessary" or "is this word necessary" and then say "yes" or "no." That is the way you are going to broaden your claim in the simplest, most direct fashion. After you have completed all of this crossing out and interlineating, then your claim is in shape to copy it into your exam answer book and you have yourself a broad claim.

With respect to the narrower claims I have already told you that I strongly urge you to write them in dependent form unless expressly told otherwise. I would also urge you, *if possible,* to narrow your claims in the area that you really consider to be novel in the combination. Thus, for example, if what is new is the addition of an element D to an old combination of A, B & C, then it is preferable for the second claim to more particularly define the new element D and the third claim to even more specifically define the same element. But in writing your narrower claims please be sure that there is *substantial difference* between them. For example, do not try to distinguish one claim from another by saying "wherein the means for securing element A to element B is a nut and a bolt." That is simply not a substantial limitation and you will lose points on it.

EXAMPLE I - SHAKER

FIG:-1

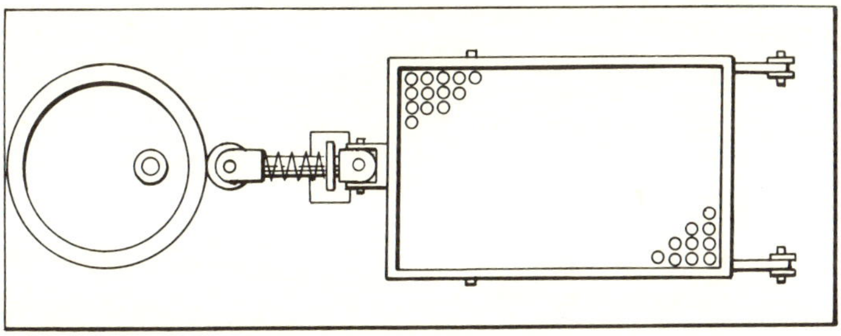

FIG:-2

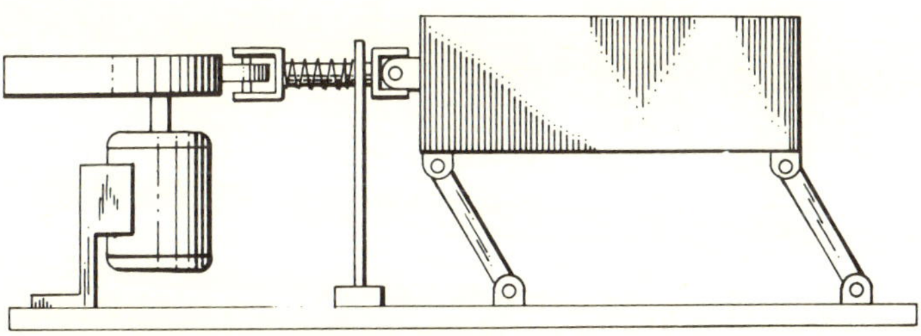

alternative embodiment

FIG:-3

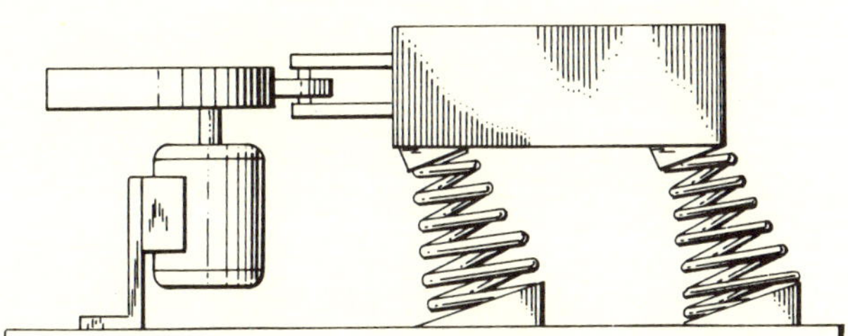

EXAMPLE II - TAKE-UP BARREL

FIG.-1

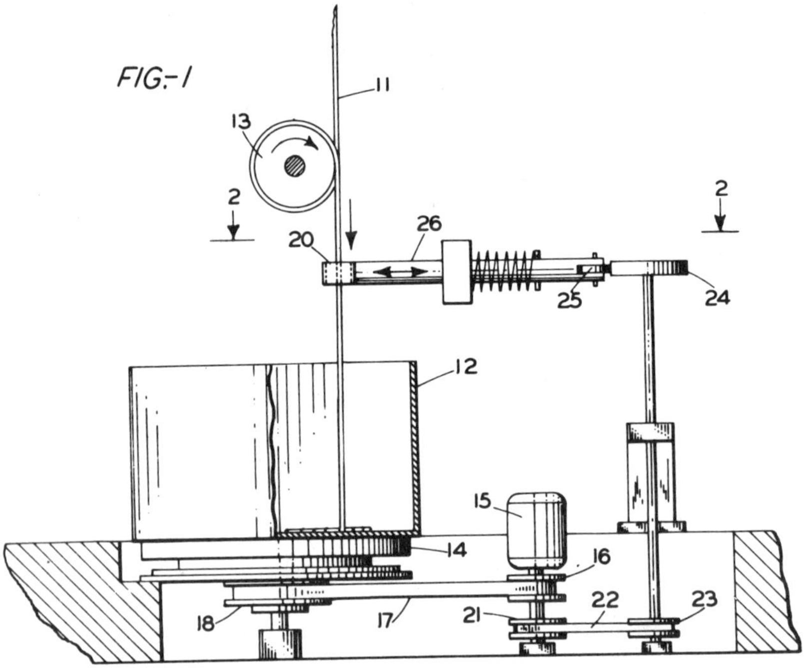

FIG.-2

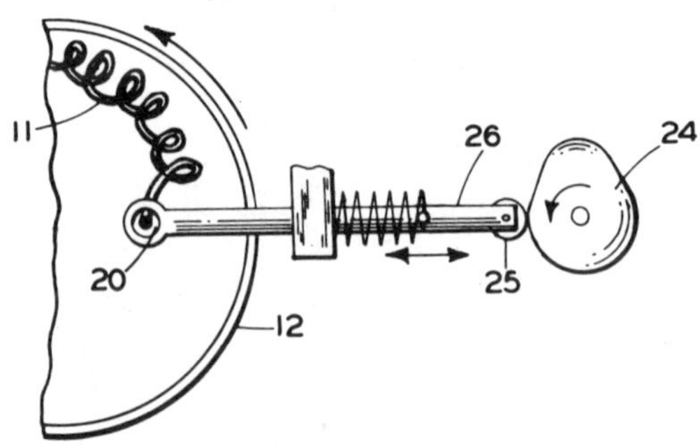

APPENDIX A

EXAMPLE III– WHEATSTONE BRIDGE

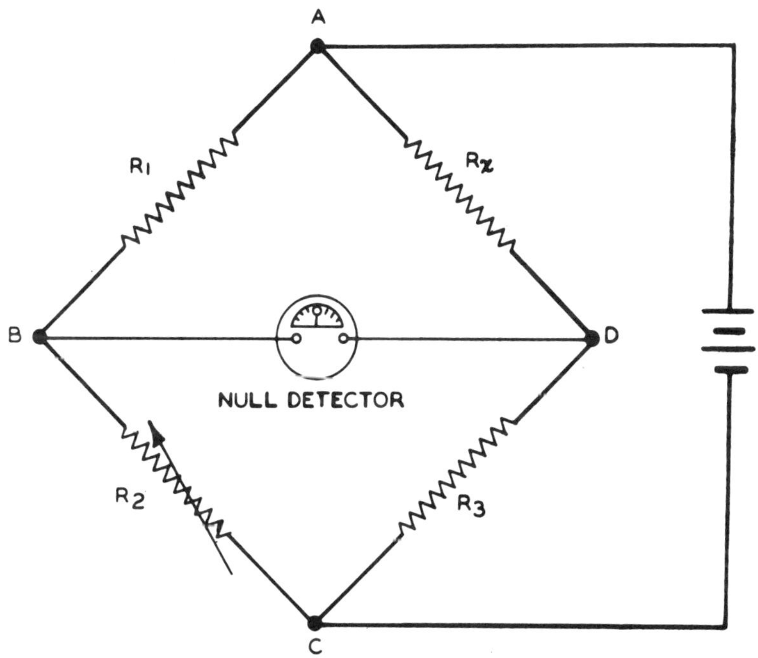

EXAMPLE IV - RADIO SIGNAL

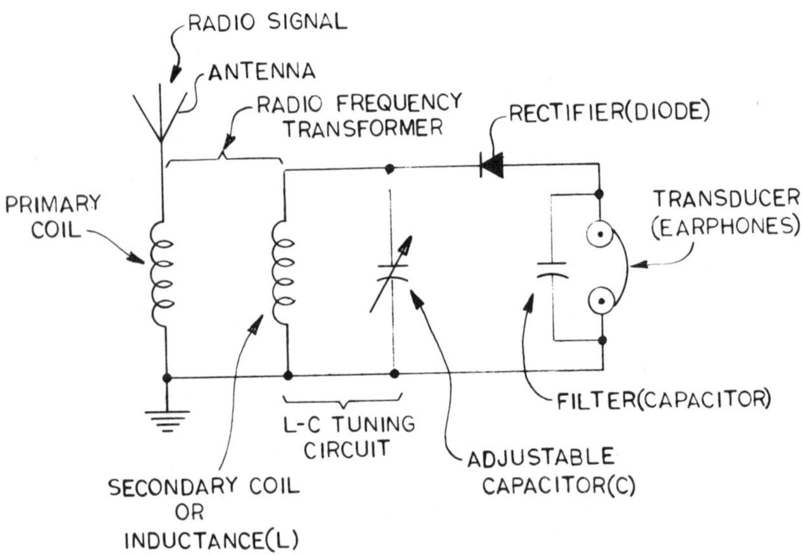

APPENDIX B

Further Examples of Claim-Drafting Principles, and Practice in Claim-Drafting Techniques.

The following material is selected from examples used in the Practising Law Institute's Patent Office Agent's Examination Review Course. These examples are intended to provide practice in drafting claims of various kinds, and in criticizing poorly written or "sloppy claims." Many examples are from prior Agent's Exam questions.

The sample claims and the comments are intended primarily for students planning to take the Agent's Exam, and do not represent sophisticated claim drafting practices or possibly controversial claim writing techniques that might be permissible and advantageous under modern court decisions cited in this book. The comments are intended to reflect Patent Office practices and preferences, as understood from the Manual of Patent Examining Procedure, Patent Office published remarks on acceptable answers to Exam questions, and generally conservative practice.

The sample claims in most cases are intended to be fairly moderate in scope, primarily to teach techniques of drafting relatively sound claims, in most cases not the broadest claims that might be allowable. In most real-life situations, drafting of really broad claims requires an exact knowledge of the prior art and, usually, a chance to argue such claims extensively in an amendment, because they are usually rejected the first time round. In all but a few of the examples, the prior art is not given or not given precisely; thus the object of these examples is to give an intermediate-scope sample claim that an Examiner reviewing a student's paper would like and be willing to accept fairly readily as allowable and conforming to good, standard claim-drafting techniques and practices.

If the student wishes to use these examples for practice, he should study the problem or question, then write claims or other answers as directed. Then he should compare his claims and answers with the sample claims and comments to look for major differences. In most cases, there are many acceptable claims and approaches, almost as many as there are patent attorneys. Thus there are no right or wrong answers. The best bet is to ask an experienced patent attorney to review your claim in detail. On the mechanical structure cases, particularly those given only a drawing, read again the advice in Appendix C on describing mechanisms and Chapter X on writing claims to mechanical structures.

The following is list of the cases in Appendix B and what problems they illustrate.

LIST OF CASES

PART I—DRAFTING OF CLAIMS

Case 1 — Stephen–Apparatus for Propelling Articles
Apparatus claims and relation of apparatus and method claims

Case 2 — Keltner–Traveling Lawn Sprinkler
Apparatus claims given the specification
Dependent claims

Case 3 — Tonn–Nutcracker
Apparatus claims given only a drawing

Case 4 — Wood–Hose Nozzle
Same

Case 5 — Brown–Glue Container and Spreader
Same

Case 6 — Chambers–Can Opener
Same

Case 7 — Washington–Sowing Device
Same

Case 8 — Wenstrand–Turntable
Same

Case 9 — Kokeisl–Apparatus for Storing and Delivering Granular or Like Flowable Materials
Apparatus claims given the specification

Case 10 — McBride–Power Propelled Water Craft
Apparatus claims, given a drawing.

Case 11 — Optical Sound Reproduction
Electrical circuit claim (mixed circuit and and mechanical structure)

Case 12 — Unijunction Pulse Generator
Detailed electrical circuit claim

Case 13 — Gunderman–Polymer Latex Films
Method claims given the specification
Markush claims–Generic and species claims

Case 14 — Bickel–Brush Making
Mechanical method claims, given specification Generic and species claims

Case 15 — Hiers–Straightening Flock
Method claims, given specification

Case 16 — Method of Making Foil
Method claims–Markush claims

Case 17 — Lippman–Determining Adhesion of Ice
Method claims

Case 18 — M. J. Brown–Plastic Encapsulation
Method claims

Case 19 — Coating Method
Generic and Species claims

Case 20 — Crowell–Maleic Anhydride Purification
Chemical Process

Case 21 — Purification of Phenol
Chemical Process

Case 22 — Morris–Soap Dish
Article of manufacture claims

Case 23 — Haslett–Coaster
Article claims

Case 24 — Parabanic Acid
Composition of matter claims
Chemical process claims–Manufacturing Compound
Method of use claims

PART II — CRITICIZING "SLOPPY CLAIMS"

Case 25 — Kohler–Suction Cleaner
(Also drafting machine claims given the specification.)

Case 26 — Voskresenski–Steam and Dry Iron

Case 27 — Bomb Proof Coating

Case 1

PREPARING APPARATUS CLAIMS—RELATION OF APPARATUS CLAIMS TO METHOD CLAIMS

July 25, 1961 W. F. STEPHEN **2,993,737**

APPARATUS FOR PROPELLING ARTICLES

Filed Feb. 23, 1960 3 Sheets-Sheet 1

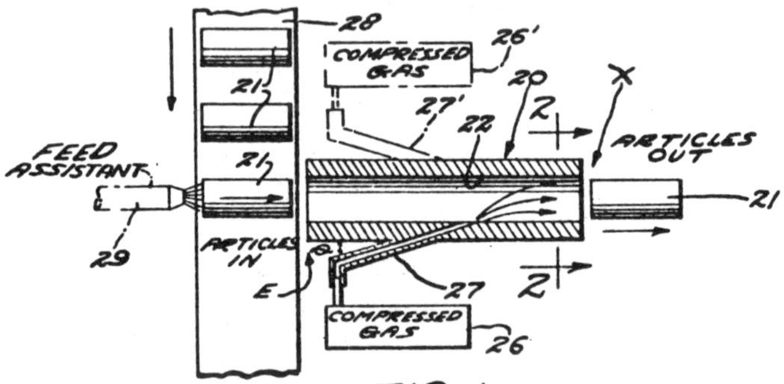

FIG. 1

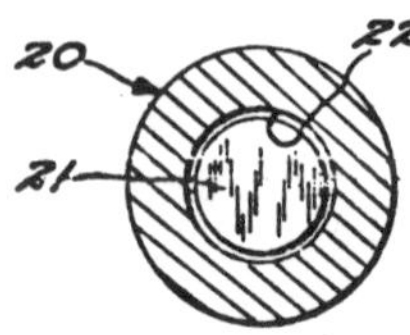

FIG. 2

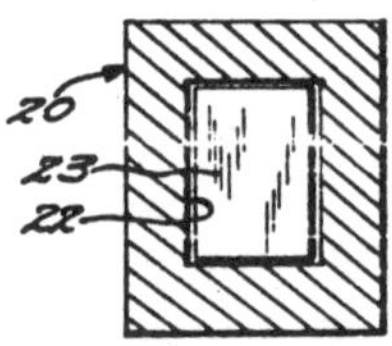

FIG. 3

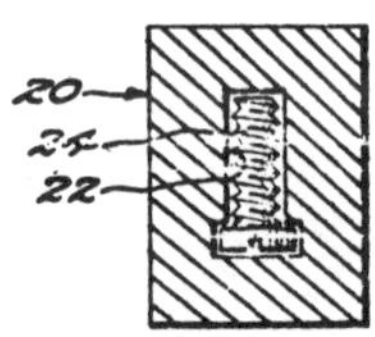

FIG. 4

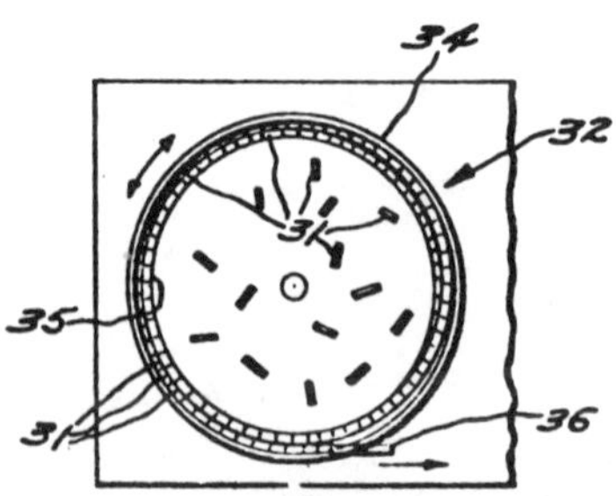

FIG. 7

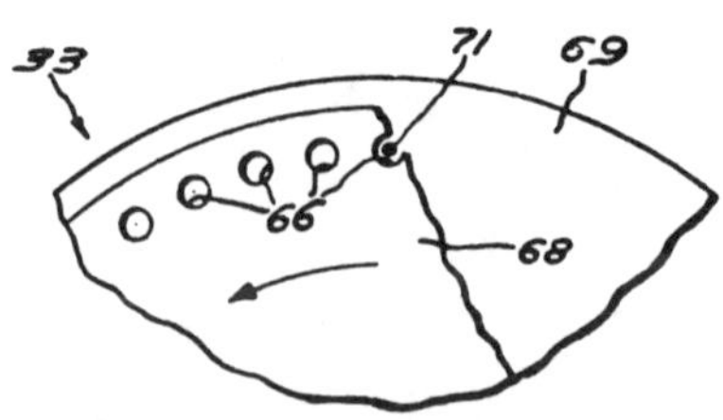

FIG. 10

PROBLEM

Draft an apparatus claim to the structure of FIG. 1 (assuming it to be new): A vacuum exists at the left end of tube 20, which tends to draw articles 21-21 into the tube, while high pressure exists at the right end thereof which forces the articles out of the tube. Assume the prior art is a standard blowgun or peashooter. Query: Would method claims be proper? If so, write a method claim.

Case 1

PREPARING APPARATUS CLAIMS—RELATION OF APPARATUS CLAIMS TO METHOD CLAIMS

SAMPLE CLAIMS— APPARATUS FOR PROPELLING ARTICLES

Moderate Scope

1. Apparatus for propelling an article, which comprises:

a tube having a bore extending therethrough from an entrance end to an exit end for closely receiving and passing the article therethrough;

a source of compressed gas;

a conduit extending from the source of compressed gas and terminating in the bore at an acute angle directed toward the exit end of the tube for discharging a stream of compressed gas into the bore and producing a partial vacuum at the entrance end of said bore; and

means for feeding the article to a position immediately adjacent to and in alignment with the entrance end of the tube to suck the article into the entrance end of the tube and blow it out the exit end.

Fairly Broad

2. Apparatus for propelling an article, which comprises:

a tube having a bore therethrough for closely receiving and passing the article through the tube; and

means for injecting a gas under pressure into the bore through a side wall of the tube at an angle such that a partial vacuum is

lots of functional language

created at a first end of the tube and the gas is discharged out the other end, so that an article placed adjacent to and in alignment with the first end of the tube is sucked into the tube and is blown out the other end.

COMMENTS

This is a simple example, not from an Agent's Exam, illustrating some of the main principles in drafting apparatus claims. Claim 2 is about as broad in scope as one would want to go, claim 1 about as narrow.

Note, "a tube having a bore," an example of how to claim holes, Section 23.

In claim 1, the source of gas and conduit can readily be combined into "means for injecting a gas," as in claim 2. In claim 2, the "means for injecting a gas . . . such that . . ." clause follows *In re Chandler*, cited in Section 31.

The "means for feeding" clause in claim 1 is obviously appropriate, particularly since the structure of the means (air blast 29) is probably not important to the inventive concept. This element is more broadly phrased in claim 2, which would be superior in practice "so that an article placed . . ." Thus, claim 2 would cover the case where a human places the article 21 in the appropriate position, as in a department store money and order transport system, which uses this principle. Literally, the "means for" clause does not cover a human being, as noted in Section 31.

ANSWER TO QUERY ON METHOD CLAIMS

Method claims would be proper, assuming the invention, with a scope such as in claim 2, is novel. Such a claim, following the scope of claim 2 could read:

3. The method of propelling an article, which comprises:

injecting a gas under pressure through a side wall of a tube having a bore therethrough for closely receiving and passing the article therethrough, the gas being injected at an angle such that a partial vacuum is created at a first end of the tube and the gas is discharged at the other end; and

placing the article adjacent to and in alignment with the first end of the tube so that the article is sucked into the first end of the tube and is blown out the other end.

Note how an apparatus claim (2) can be turned into a method claim by finding the actions or steps—"injecting gas" and "placing the article." Otherwise, claim 3 is of essentially the same scope as claim 2. Note how the minimum necessary apparatus limitations are brought into the claim (Section 38); for example; injecting a gas . . . through *a wall of a tube*." Of course the mechanical structure recited in the claim should be minimized so far as possible. It would seem that "a tube" of the right size is indispensible in practicing the method.

Case 2

PREPARING APPARATUS CLAIMS, GIVEN A SPECIFICATION—DEPENDENT CLAIMS

Sept. 22, 1959 | H. R. KELTNER | **2,905,392**

TRAVELLING LAWN SPRINKLER

Filed Dec. 16, 1955 | 2 Sheets-Sheet 1

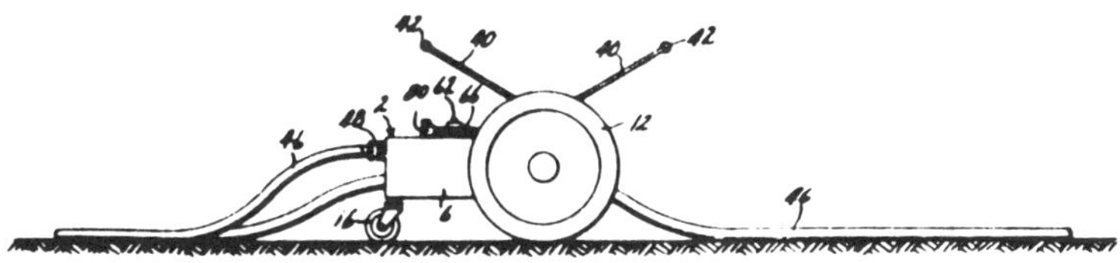

Fig. 1

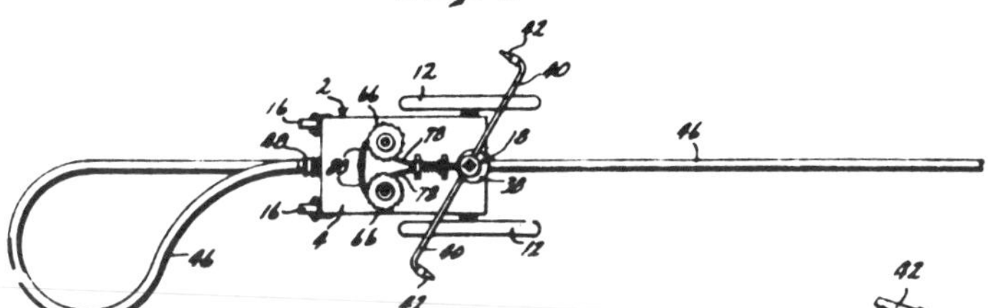

Fig. 2

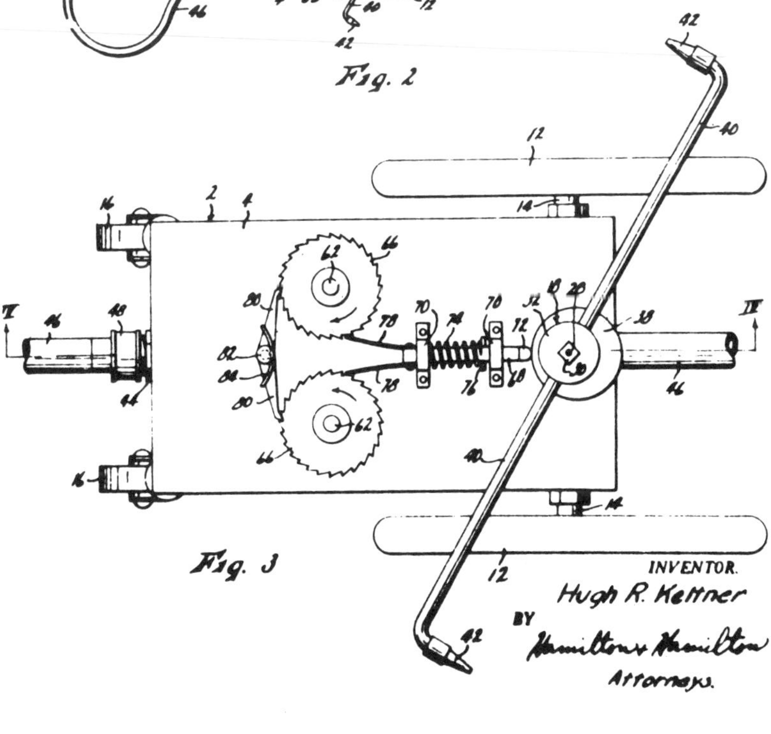

Fig. 3

INVENTOR.
Hugh R. Keltner
BY
Hamilton & Hamilton
Attorneys.

Sept. 22, 1959 H R KELTNER **2,905,392**

TRAVELLING LAWN SPRINKLER

Filed Dec. 16, 1955 2 Sheets-Sheet 2

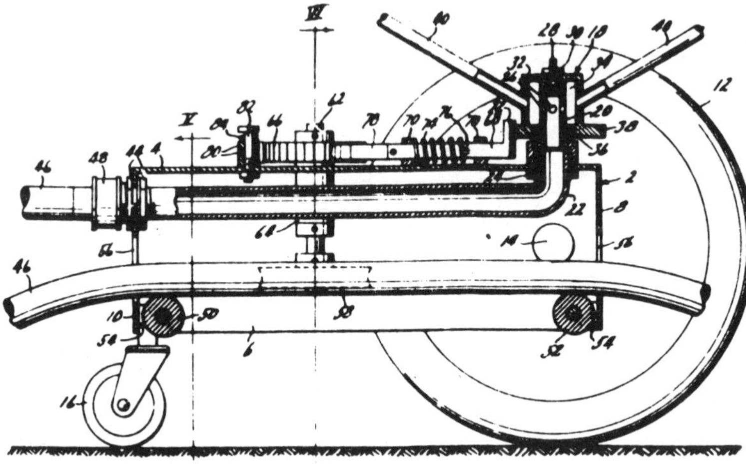

Fig. 4

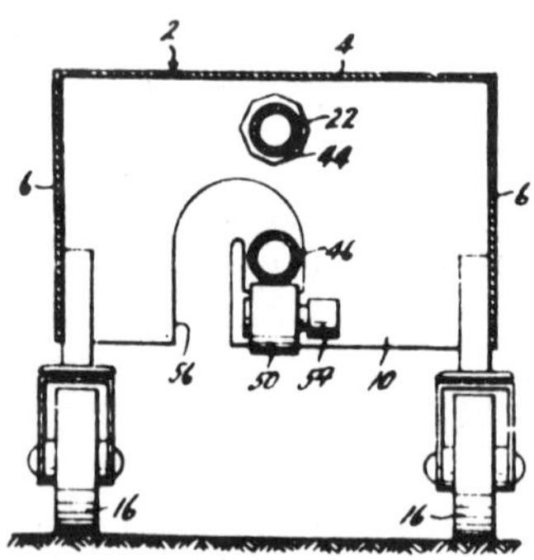

Fig. 5

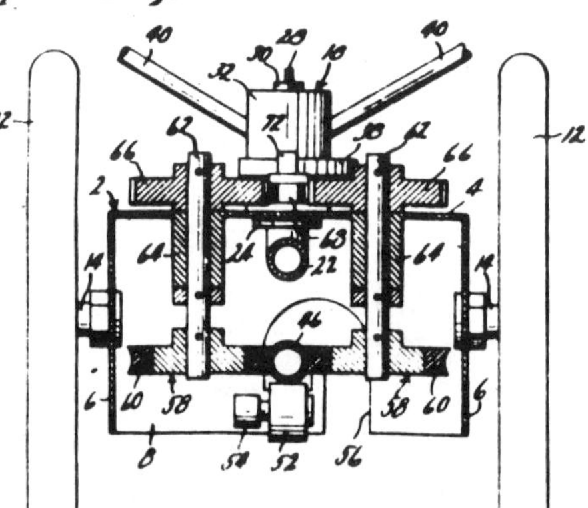

Fig. 6

INVENTOR.
Hugh R. Keltner
BY
Hamilton & Hamilton
Attorneys.

2,905,392
TRAVELING LAWN SPRINKLER
Hugh R. Keltner,
Johnson County, Kans.
Application December 16, 1955,
Serial No. 553,453
1 Chatm. (Cl. 239–110)

This invention relates to new and useful improvements in lawn sprinklers, and has as its principal object the provision of a lawn sprinkler comprising a sprinkler head mounted on a wheeled frame and attached to a pressure water supply, and having means operable by the pressure of the supply water to propel said wheeled frame over the ground.

Another object is the provision in a lawn sprinkler of the character described wherein the sprinkler head rotates to distribute water evenly over a wide area, and wherein said propelling means operates mechanically from the rotation of said head.

A further object is the provision of a lawn sprinkler of the class described wherein said propelling means operates by traction on an elongated member, which may be the water supply hose, laid out on the ground. The frame is steerable, so as to follow the elongated member around curves.

Other objects are simplicity and economy of construction, efficiency and dependability of operation, and adaptability for uses other than the watering of lawns.

With these objects in view, as well as other objects which will appear in the course of the specification, reference will be had to the drawing wherein:

Fig. 1 is a side elevational view of a lawn sprinkler embodying the present invention, shown in operative relationship to a water supply hose,

Fig. 2 is a plan view of the parts as shown in Fig. 1,

Fig. 3 is an enlarged plan view of the sprinkler,

Fig. 4 is a sectional view taken on line IV–IV of Fig. 3, and

Figs. 5 and 6 are sectional views taken respectively on lines V–V and VI–VI of Fig. 4.

Like reference numerals apply to similar parts throughout the several views, and the numeral 2 applies to a frame formed of sheet metal and having generally the form of a hollow rectilinear box. It has a top wall 4 and depending side walls 6, front wall 8, and rear wall 10, and is open at the bottom. It is supported at each of its forward corners by a ground-engaging wheel 12 rotatably mounted on a stub axle 14 fixed in the adjacent side wall 6, and at each of its rearward corners by a caster wheel 16, whereby the frame is rendered steerable.

Carried on top wall 4 of the

frame, adjacent the forward edge thereof, is a sprinkler head 18. As best shown in Fig. 4, said sprinkler head includes a vertical tubular body member 20 closed at its upper end and threaded at its lower end to a pipe 22, extending upwardly through said wall. Said body and pipe are fixed relative to the frame by a nut 24 threaded on said pipe below wall 4. Body member 20 is provided adjacent its upper end with a plurality of apertures 26, and at its upper end with a threaded axial extension 28. Mounted rotatably on said extension, and secured thereon by nut 30, is an inverted cup-shaped member 32 the depending skirt of which is disposed concentrically about body 20, and is of larger diameter than said body member whereby to form a chamber 34 therebetween. At its lower end, member 32 is provided with a sealing ring 36 which engages body member 20 to seal chamber 34, and with an external circular flange 36 which is disposed eccentrically to the axis of body member 20. Flange 38 serves as a cam as will be fully described below.

Fixed in the skirt portion of member 32, in communicating relation with chamber 34, are a plurality of upwardly and outwardly inclined tubes 40, at the outer end of each of which is mounted a nozzle 42. It will be noted in Figs. 2 and 3 that the nozzles are angled to direct streams of water substantially tangentially to the orbit of the nozzles, in the same relative angular direction. Hence when water under pressure is delivered to sprinkler head 18 through pipe 22, it passes outwardly through holes 26 of body 28 into chamber 34, and thence through tubes 40 to nozzle 42. The reactive force of the streams leaving the nozzles causes cup 32 of the head to rotate, this rotation being clockwise as shown although the direction of rotation is immaterial. This rotation distributes the water evenly over a relatively large ground area, and also causes rotation of cam flange 38, which operates the frame propelling mechanism to be described below.

Pipe 22 extends horizontally and rearwardly just below frame wall 4, and extends through rear wall 10, being secured therein by a pair of nuts 44. A flexible water supply hose 46 is secured to the outwardly extended end of said pipe by a suitable coupling 48. The hose is then looped as shown in Figs. 1 and 2 and passed beneath the frame 2 parallel to the line of travel thereof. The hose is then lifted from the ground and laid over a pair of rollers 50 and 52 carried rotatably at the inner face of rear wall 10 and front wall 8 respectively, said rollers being mounted on axles fixed to said frame walls by brackets 54. As best shown in Figs. 5 and 6, said rear and front frame walls are each provided with an inverted J-shaped notch 56 through which the hose may be moved transversely to engage the associated roller, and which serves to hold the hose centered over said roller.

Intermediate rollers 50 and 52, the hose is gripped between a pair of drive wheels 58, each of said wheels having a thick soft rubber facing 60 whereby to grip the hose frictionally. The drive wheel faces are concave whereby to conform closely to the hose. However, the wheel facings are sufficiently yieldable that the hose may be crowded therebetween. Each of the drive wheels is fixed on a vertical shaft 62 which extends upwardly through top frame wall 4 and is journalled in a bearing member 64 affixed to said frame wall. To the upper end of each of shafts 63, above wall 4, is affixed a ratchet wheel 66.

Ratchet wheels 66 are operated by a cam follower mechanism including a bar 68 disposed horizontally above frame wall 4 and carried slidably in a pair of brackets 70 fixed to said frame wall. Said bar is movable longitudinally along a line intersecting the axis of sprinkler head 18 and passing between ratchet wheels 66. It is provided at its forward end with an upright finger 72 which bears slidably against the rim of flange cam 38 of the sprinkler head, and which is urged yieldably against said cam by a coil spring 74 encircling bar 68. Said spring bears at one end against one of brackets 70, and at its opposite end against a pin 76 inserted transversely through bar 68. At its rearward end, a pair of leaf springs 78 are affixed to bar 68, and extend rearwardly therefrom. Said springs extend between ratchet wheels 66, and are tensioned outwardly so that each spring engages in the teeth of one of the ratchet wheels, as best shown in Fig. 3.

Thus it will be seen that as sprinkler head 18 rotates as previously described, cam 38 thereof will rotate and urge cam follower bar 68 rearwardly against spring 74, and leaf springs 78, acting as pawls, will turn ratchet wheels 66 in the direction indicated by the arrows in Fig. 3. The throw of cam 38 is such that the ratchet wheels will be turned one tooth for each revolution of the sprinkler head. The ratchet teeth, and the cam throw, may obviously be made much smaller than shown, in order to provide slower rotation of the ratchet wheels, but are enlarged somewhat in the drawing for clarity. Springs 18 are sufficiently stiff to function as pawls, but are also sufficiently flexible that they will be deflected transversely to ride over the ratchet teeth as the bar 68 is moved rearwardly by spring 74. The rotation of ratchet wheels 66 of course also turns drive wheels 58, and since the drive wheels are in frictional engagement with the hose, the frame is pulled forwardly along the hose. The hose may be laid out on the ground ahead of the sprinkler in any desired pattern, so long as any curves therein are of sufficiently large radius, and the frame will follow the hose. In this manner, even an irregularly shaped lawn may be watered thoroughly and evenly without necessity of attendance on the sprinkler.

It has been found that the work which must be performed by the frame in lifting the hose from the ground applies a braking force to the frame sufficient to prevent the frame from coasting forwardly by gravity, which could occur if the ratchet wheels overran the pawls 78, on any slope usually encountered in lawns. The ratchet wheels are secured against following pawls 78 on their retracting stroke, which could otherwise occur particularly on upslopes, by a pair of dogs 80 pivotally mounted on a bolt 82 fixed in frame wall 4 and engaging respectively the two ratchet wheels 66 (Fig. 3). Said dogs are urged yieldably into engagement with said ratchet wheels by a coil spring 84 disposed on bolt 82 and having its end portions extended to engage said dogs intermediate their ends.

Although I have shown and described a specific embodiment of my invention, it will be apparent that many minor changes of structure and operation could be made without departing from the spirit of the invention as defined by the scope of the appended claim.

PROBLEM

Given the specification, write three claims of varying scope, indicating "broadest," "intermediate" and "narrowest." Assume that it is old in the art to use the power provided by the rotation of the sprinkler head to cause movement of the sprinkler along the hose supplying water to the sprinkler. In narrowing your claims, do not rely on immaterial limitations.

Case 2

PREPARING APPARATUS CLAIMS, GIVEN A SPECIFICATION—DEPENDENT CLAIMS

SAMPLE CLAIMS—TRAVELING LAWN SPRINKLER

BROADEST:

1. An improved traveling lawn sprinkler of the type having a wheeled carriage, a rotary sprinkler head mounted on the carriage, and a fitting on the carriage to connect a water supply hose to the sprinkler head, wherein the improvement comprises:

(a) a pair of friction drive wheels mounted rotatably on the carriage for gripping the supply hose therebetween;
(b) a rotary cam mounted on the sprinkler head for rotation thereby;
(c) a cam follower mounted reciprocably on the carriage and driven by the cam; and
(d) a one-way drive linkage actuated by the movement of the cam follower in one direction to rotate the drive wheels intermittently in order to cause the carriage to travel along the hose.

INTERMEDIATE:

2. An improved traveling lawn sprinkler as recited in claim 1, in which the one-way drive linkage comprises:

a pair of ratchet wheels fixed to and rotatable with the friction drive wheels; and
a pair of spring pawls carried by the cam follower, each of which engages one of the ratchet wheels, for driving the ratchet wheels.

NARROWEST:

3. An improved traveling lawn sprinkler as recited in claim 2, in which the cam comprises an eccentric circular flange formed integrally with the sprinkler head and having an eccentricity designed to rotate the ratchet wheels through a distince equal to the space between successive teeth of the ratchet wheels for each revolution of the sprinkler head.

COMMENTS

This structure was used on the November 1962 Agent's Exam. When used on the Exam, the specification was not given and part of the problem was to figure out, at least generally, how the thing works. At that time (1962), the Patent Office was testing mechanical knowledge as well as claim-writing ability. The statement in the problem about "assume it is old" was given.

In view of the statement that traveling lawn sprinklers with rotary heads, etc., are old, an improvement or Jepson-type claim would appear preferable. (See new Rule 75(e), discussed in Section 54.)

It is difficult in this case to tell what specific structure to put in claim 1, and what to leave for claims 2 and 3. This is particularly tough in this case, since there is no real "summary of the invention" in the specification, and the statements in the object clauses (col. 1, lines 15-25) are generally old according to the question.

It appears that the purpose in stating that "it is old to use the power, etc." was to force the student to claim at least some mechanical structure, and not present merely "means responsive to . . . for driving . . ." types of claims. Sample claim 1 is only one of several possible arrangements, specifically reciting some of the mechanical details; many other combinations seem equally good. Note that, if too much structural detail is put in claim 1, then the student is hard put to add *significant* details for claims 2 and 3. (See Section 57.)

These claims further illustrate principles of selecting and naming claim elements (Section 22), and connecting or relating the elements (Sections 25-27) to make up a complete combination. For example, the friction drive wheels are "mounted rotatably on the carriage" "for gripping the hose." This relates them both structurally and functionally to the cooperative preamble elements, carriage and hose (the workpiece).

Claims 2 and 3 illustrate dependent claims, adding further detail of element from the parent claim 1 (Section 53). Note, claim 2 defines element (d) of claim 1 in more detail, while claim 3 tells more about element (c) of claim 1, and ties this structure in with the material added in claim 2. This is perfectly proper, and would be proper even if the matter added in claim 3 did not cooperate with the structure added in claim 2. Then, it would be the claim drafter's option whether to make claim 3 depend from claim 2 or claim 1.

Since the question asked one to label "broadest," "intermediate" and "narrowest," claim 3 must depend from claim 2, not claim 1. Otherwise it would not necessarily be narrower than claim 2.

Case 3

PREPARING APPARATUS CLAIMS GIVEN ONLY A DRAWING

Dec. 10, 1940. G. J. TONN 2,224,415

NUTCRACKER

Filed April 29, 1938

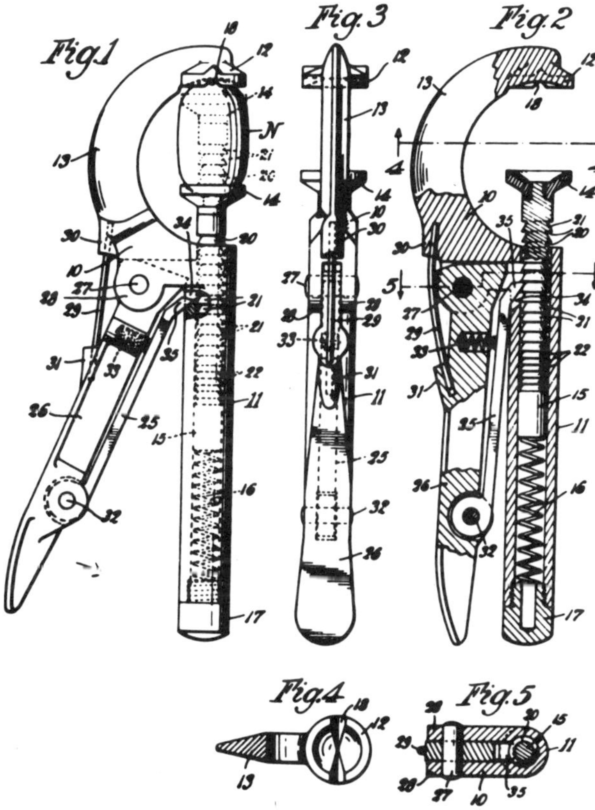

Spring 16 urges plunger 15 "up" to hold nut between jaws. Ratchet 20 and Pawl 25 operate to advance Jaw 14 one small step at a time to crack nut without crushing.

PROBLEM

Prepare three claims of varying scope.

Case 3

PREPARING APPARATUS CLAIMS GIVEN ONLY A DRAWING

SAMPLE CLAIMS—NUTCRACKER

1. A nutcracker, which comprises:

a frame;

a pair of opposed jaws mounted on the frame, at least one of the jaws being mounted for movement toward the other to crack a nut placed between the jaws;

a pair of operating handles mounted on the frame and movable toward and away from each other; and

a ratchet-and-pawl drive linkage connected to one handle and one jaw for closing the jaws a limited amount each time the handles are closed to crush a nut positioned between the jaws.

2. A nutcracker as recited in claim 1, further comprising:

a spring mounted in one handle for urging one jaw toward the other to clamp a nut placed between the jaws.

3. A nutcracker as recited in claim 2, wherein:

a first one of the handles comprises a cylindrical member having a cylindrical bore closed at one end;

the spring comprises a compression spring positioned in the bore against the closed end of the bore;

a first one of the jaws comprises a cylindrical member having a shaft portion slidably received in the bore against the spring and a jaw portion protruding from the first handle, the cylindrical member having a ratchet surface formed along a portion of its length and comprising part of the ratchet-and-pawl drive linkage;

the second jaw is pivotably mounted to the second handle; and

a pawl is pivotably mounted to the second jaw for engagement with the ratchet surface.

COMMENTS

From the February 1962 Exam. No description was given. Claim 1 illustrates one of several possible approaches, picking out 3 or 4 main elements, defined fairly broadly, and then connecting them together to form an operatable nutcracker. Then picking out relatively significant details for claims 2 and 3.

Case 4

PREPARING APPARATUS CLAIMS GIVEN ONLY A DRAWING

May 14, 1957 H. A. WOOD **2,792,260**

HOSE NOZZLE

Filed Dec. 12, 1956

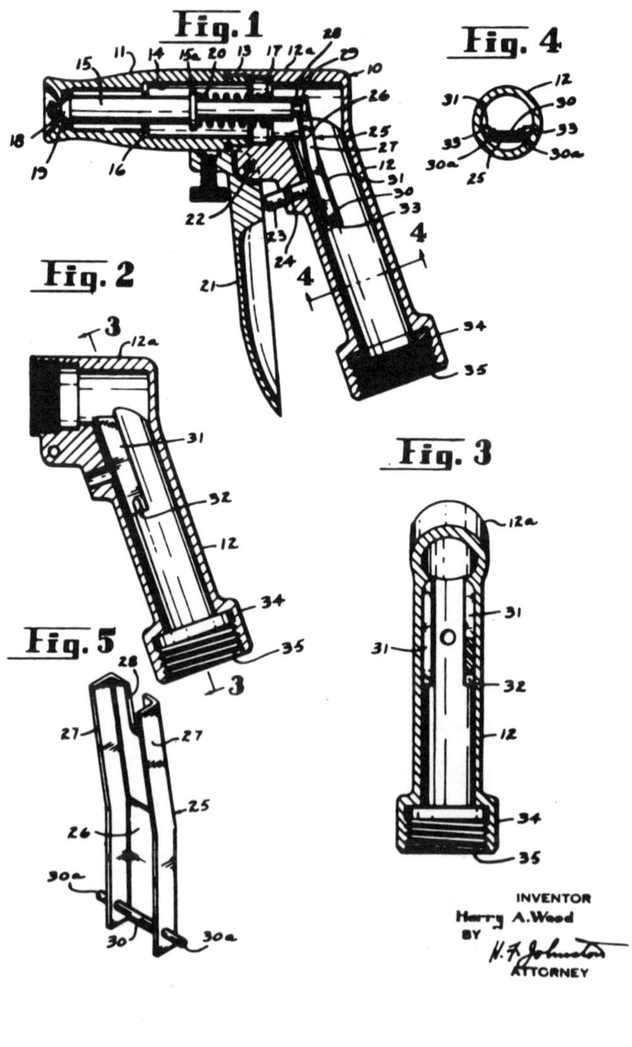

PROBLEM

Write three claims of varying scope, indicating "broadest" "intermediate" and "narrowest." Hand-held, trigger-operated hose nozzles are old.

Case 4

PREPARING APPARATUS CLAIMS GIVEN ONLY A DRAWING

SAMPLE CLAIMS—HOSE NOZZLE

BROADEST:

1. A trigger-operated hose nozzle, which comprises:

(a) a casing having a barrel section and a handle section so connected that, in use, the handle section depends from the rear end of the barrel section, the two sections having a continuous passage therethrough designed to permit flow of fluid into an entrance end of the handle section and out through the front end of the barrel section, the barrel section having a valve seat near the front end;

(b) a valve member slidably mounted in the barrel section and having a front portion designed for reception in the valve seat;

(c) resilient means for urging the valve member into engagement with the seat to seal the nozzle against discharge of fluid;

(d) a trigger pivotably mounted to the casing and spaced from the handle section a distance such that the handle section and trigger may be gripped and the trigger squeezed toward the handle section;

(e) a lever pivotably mounted within the handle section and engaged with a rear portion of the valve member; and

(f) means for translating movement of the trigger toward the handle section into pivoting movement of the lever to open the valve.

INTERMEDIATE:

2. A hose nozzle as recited in claim 1, wherein:

the valve member includes an elongated cylindrical stem centered within the barrel section, the stem having a circumferential groove near the rear end thereof and an enlarged flange near the center thereof;

the resilient means comprises a coil spring mounted within the barrel section between an inwardly projecting portion of the barrel section and the flange of the valve stem; and

the lever comprises a flat bar mounted wholly within the handle section and having a U-shaped groove at its upper end designed to receive the groove of the valve stem.

NARROWEST:

3. a hose nozzle as recited in claim 2, wherein:

a pair of pivot pins are secured to the lever and extend transversely therefrom near the lower end thereof;

the handle section is provided with a pair of internal projections having U-shaped recesses in which the ends of the pivot pins are received to permit pivoting of the lever;

the movement-transmitting means comprises a cylindrical plunger engaging both the trigger and a middle portion of the lever; and

the handle section is formed with a cylindrical bore in a front wall thereof, for receiving the plunger closely but slidably through that wall, the bore also being provided with a fluid tight seal about the plunger to prevent leakage of fluid between the plunger and bore.

COMMENTS

This structure was used on the November 1965 Exam.

As usual, it is difficult or impossible to tell exactly what if anything is *the* point of novelty. To do this, one would really need to know the exact state of the trigger-type hose nozzle art as of December 1955.

On reading the patent, one discovers that the primary point of novelty apparently resided in the specific construction of the pivot mounting for the lever 25 inside the handle 12. This is seen at best only dimly in FIG. 4. This the examinee could not possibly realize.

Therefore, the only sensible approach is to recite what appear to be the main structural parts of the combination in claim 1, leaving some structural details for claims 2 and 3. Sample claim 1 represents one such approach, but many others would be equally good, depending on the way the reader viewed the structure. Some details should be regarded as obviously noncritical and thus left out of claim 1, such as whether the casing is one piece or two, the angle of the handle to the barrel, or the shape of the valve seat.

In view of the statement in the question, we cannot assume that this is *the* basic patent on the trigger-operated squirter and claim it as broadly as

—a casing, a valve, and a trigger for operating the valve.—

The point of the question was to force us to claim some details of structure, not merely means for A, plus means for B. Claims to specific structure are harder to write than "means for" claims, which are really about the same as method claims.

It is recommended that at least some structural details be put in claim 1; however, such details as the structure of the plunger 23 for converting motion of the trigger 21 into movement of the lever 25 are presumably not critical, and could well be expressed as "means for translating . . ." as in sample claim 1.

Claim 1 is one typical example of many claims that could be written, and is on the narrow side. Substantially broader claims could be written, so long as some significant structural detail was included.

Case 5

PREPARING APPARATUS CLAIMS GIVEN ONLY A DRAWING

Jan. 14, 1936. S. A. BROWN **2,028,084**

GLUE CONTAINER AND SPREADER

Filed April 3, 1933

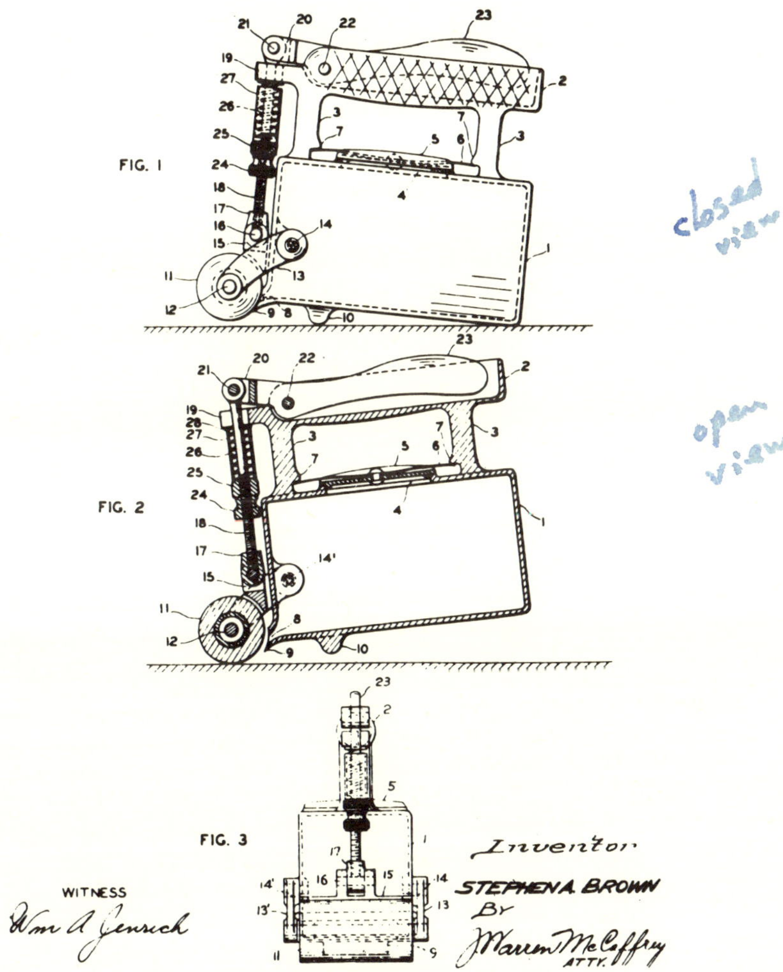

PROBLEM

Write three claims of varying scope.

Case 5

PREPARING APPARATUS CLAIMS GIVEN ONLY A DRAWING

SAMPLE CLAIMS—GLUE APPLICATOR

1. A liquid applicator which comprises:

a container for the liquid, said container having a discharge opening extending along a lower frontal edge thereof;

a rotatable, liquid-applying roller;

means for mounting said roller to said container for movement from a first position closing the discharge opening to a second position uncovering said discharge opening to receive liquid issuing from said uncovered discharge opening; and

an actuator connected to said mounting means for selectively moving said roller between said first and second positions.

further restricts

2. An applicator in accordance with claim 1, wherein said mounting means comprises:

an arm hingedly connected to said container for pivotally moving said roller between said first and second position.

adding new element

3. An applicator in accordance with claim 2, further comprising:

a spring connected to said roller mounting means for resiliently urging said roller into said first position to close said discharge opening.

COMMENTS

This is from an old Agent's Exam. No description was given, and it is impossible or nearly so to figure out all the structural details. One must claim what he can understand or guess at. Rarely if ever would the main features of novelty be in structural details such as the springs and levers in the actuating mechanism. It is better to focus on the main functions performed, with some structural detail, in this type of case.

Note, it is not necessary to make the claim preamble "liquid applicator" conform to the title of the patent "glue applicator." The claim preamble can be broader whenever one wishes, but of course must be consistent with the title.

Case 6

PREPARING APPARATUS CLAIMS GIVEN ONLY A DRAWING

July 12, 1955 **S. W. CHAMBERS** **2,712,689**

ELECTRICALLY OPERATED AUTOMATIC CAN OPENER

Filed Sept. 28, 1954

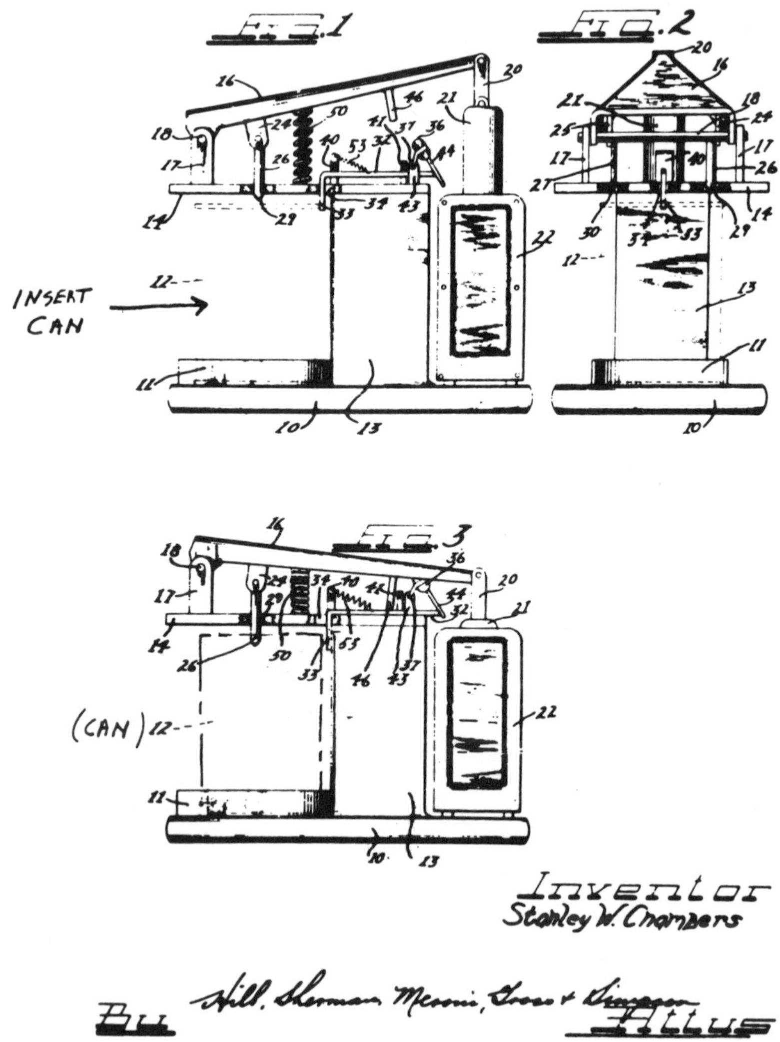

PROBLEM

Write three claims of varying scope and label them "Broadest," "Intermediate" and "Narrowest."

Case 6

PREPARING APPARATUS CLAIMS GIVEN ONLY A DRAWING

BROADEST: SAMPLE CLAIMS—CAN OPENER

1. A can-opener, which comprises:

a frame having a can-receiving space;
a can punch;
means for mounting the punch on the frame above the can-receiving space for movement into and out of engagement with the top of a can positioned in said space;
a can-sensing member movably mounted on the frame and having a portion thereof normally projecting into said space for engagement and movement by a can inserted in the space; and
means, responsive to the engagement and movement of said can-sensing member by a can positioned in said can-receiving space, for moving the punch into engagement with the can top for perforation thereof.

INTERMEDIATE:

2. A can-opener as defined in claim 1, wherein said mounting means comprises:

a lever pivotally mounted on the frame, the punch being pivotally mounted on the lever and depending toward said can-receiving space.

NARROWEST:

3. A can opener as defined in claim 2, wherein said moving means comprises:

a solenoid for pivoting said lever; and

a switch, operated by a predetermined movement of the can sensing member, for energizing the solenoid.

COMMENTS

From the August 1966 Exam. This one is very difficult, as the drawing is poor, many would not know what some of the parts are in any event (solenoid 22, mercury switch 36, etc.). Also, the title may be misleading in can "opener," rather than punch.

But, if one had to try to claim this without any description, he would have to look for the main functions performed and omit the structural details of how it works. The solenoid and switch actuating mechanism are probably conventional anyway.

In this kind of case, where you are not sure exactly what is going on, study the drawings carefully (colored pencils help, to locate the same element by number in different views). Comparing the before and after pictures of FIGS. 1 and 3, it should be apparent, or almost so, that the can 12 goes in a space at the left, above a base or frame 11. Since the title says "electrically operated automatic," the can must hit or actuate something (tip 33 of arm 32, note how it has moved to the right in FIG. 3 from FIG. 1), to turn on the electrical gadget 22. This is a good time for "means responsive to insertion of a can . . . for moving the punching [or opening] means . . . ," since the details of what 22 is and how the switch works probably are not important, at least to claim 1.

It should be clear, in any case, that rod 20 moves down to pivot lever 16 down, thus lowering punch 29 into the can top. There are actually two punches 29, 30 as seen with difficulty in FIG. 2, but this is not important.

Sample claim 1 is a fairly broad claim to the main functional elements, which seems appropriate here: some sort of frame or support to locate the can; a punch, or punching means; something to mount the punch for movement into and out of the can top; something to sense the can ("automatic"); and something to operate or actuate the punch after (*"in response to"*) sensing.

Since there is a combination of several cooperating means functions here, there would be no problem with a claim of all means elements, since no one of them would by itself constitute "means plus function at the point of novelty" (Section 31), assuming that were improper or dangerous. However, to play safe and not include all means clauses, it costs nothing to specify a frame, a can punch, and a sensing *member*. These expressions are just as broad as "punching means" or "sensing means."

Case 7

PREPARING APPARATUS CLAIMS GIVEN ONLY A DRAWING

SOWING DEVICE

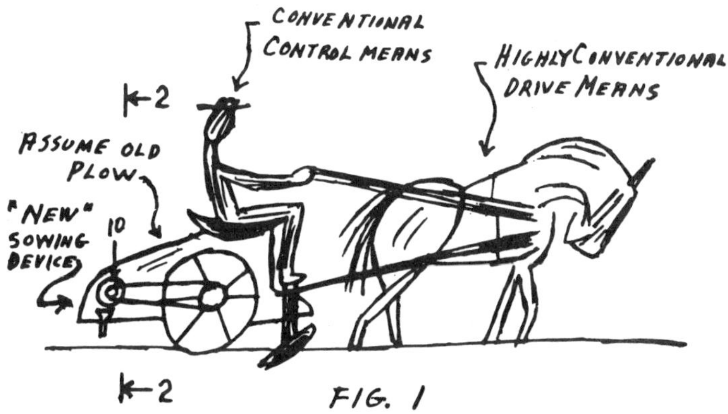

FIG. 1

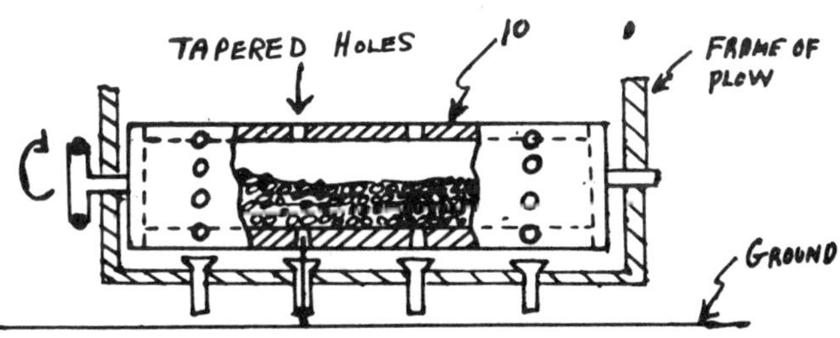

FIG. 2

PROBLEM

Object is to sow seeds behind plow blade. Holes are spaced to sow optimum numbers of seeds per acre. Draft three claims of varying scope.

Case 7

PREPARING APPARATUS CLAIMS GIVEN ONLY A DRAWING

SAMPLE CLAIMS—SOWING DEVICE

1. Apparatus for sowing seeds, which comprises:

a movable frame;

a hollow cylinder, having closed ends, in which the seeds to be sown are placed, the cylinder having a plurality of holes through its walls slightly larger than the seeds to be sown;

means for mounting the cylinder rotatably on the frame and in a horizontal position with its longitutinal axis perpendicular to the direction of movement of the frame; and

means for rotating the cylinder in timed relation to movement of the frame so that, as the cylinder rotates, the seeds drop individually to the ground through the holes in the cylinder.

2. A sowing apparatus as recited in claim 1, in which the holes are tapered, larger on the outside of the cylinder than on the inside, to prevent the holes from clogging with seeds.

3. A sowing device as recited in claim 1, in which a plurality of funnels are mounted on the frame below the cylinder and in alignment with the holes to collect the seeds as they are dropped from the cylinder and conduct them to the ground.

COMMENTS

This invention was by George Washington.

The problem stated three claims of "varying scope," thus it is permissible to make claims 2 and 3 both dependent from claim 1.

A subcombination claim (Section 56) would also be in order:

1A. In combination with a wheeled plow, a device for sowing seeds into the freshly plowed ground, which comprises:

[here recite claim 1, with "frame" changed to ". . . plow . . ."]

Claim 1 illustrates claiming holes (Section 23), and a "means for doing something so that . . ." clause (Section 31).

Claim 2 illustrates a dependent claim adding details of an element of the main claim.

Claim 3 adds a new element to the main combination (Section 53 on dependent claims).

Case 8

PREPARING APPARATUS CLAIMS GIVEN ONLY A DRAWING

May 30, 1961 — L. D. WENSTRAND — 2,986,261

APPARATUS FOR TRANSFERRING ARTICLES FROM AN ARTICLE-FEEDING DEVICE TO AN ARTICLE-RECEIVING DEVICE

Filed Dec. 21, 1959 — 4 Sheets-Sheet 1

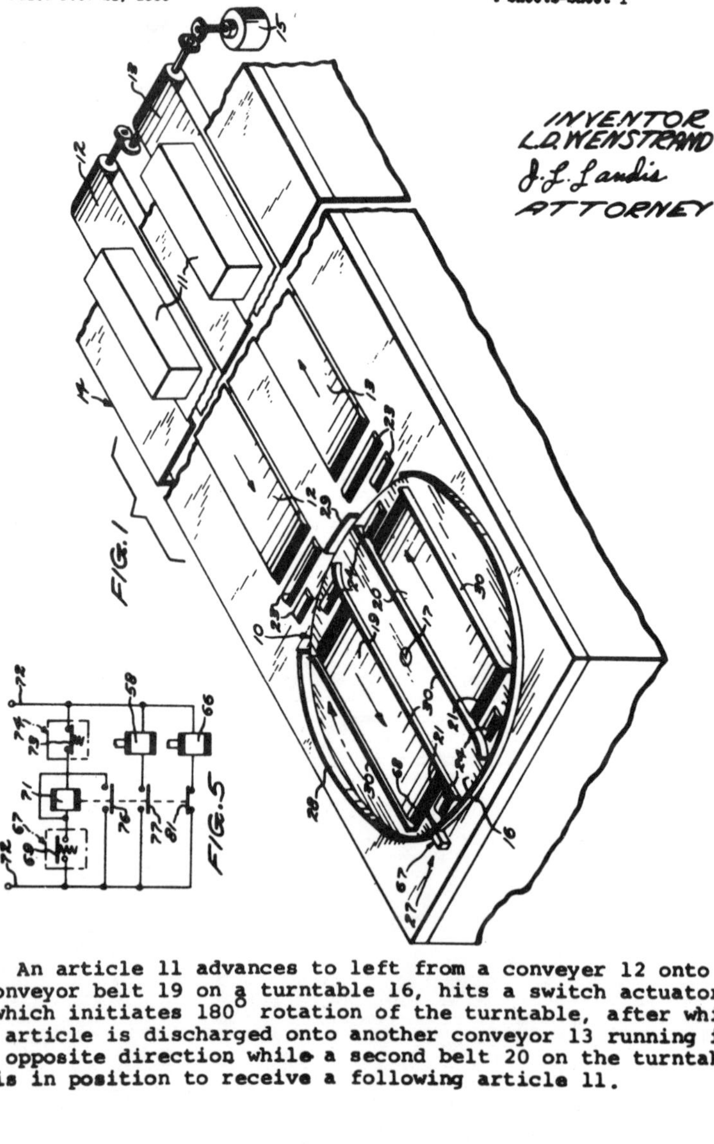

An article 11 advances to left from a conveyer 12 onto a conveyor belt 19 on a turntable 16, hits a switch actuator 68 which initiates 180° rotation of the turntable, after which the article is discharged onto another conveyor 13 running in the opposite direction while a second belt 20 on the turntable 16 is in position to receive a following article 11.

PROBLEM

Draft an apparatus claim.

Case 8

PREPARING APPARATUS CLAIMS GIVEN ONLY A DRAWING

SAMPLE CLAIM — APPARATUS FOR TRANSFERRING ARTICLES

Apparatus for transferring an article from an article-feeding device to an article-receiving device, which comprises:

a turntable mounted adjacent to the receiving device and to a discharge end of the feeding device;

a conveyor mounted on the turntable for selective alignment with the feeding device or the receiving device, depending on the position of the turntable;

means for positioning the turntable initially to align the conveyor with the feeding device to receive an article therefrom;

means, responsive to the presence of an article on the conveyor, for rotating the turntable from the initial position to a discharge position in which the conveyor aligns with the receiving device; and

means for actuating the conveyor to transfer the article from the conveyor to the article-receiving device after the turntable has been rotated to the discharge position.

COMMENTS

This claim covers what are believed to be the essential elements of the invention: the turntable, one conveyor and drive, and means responsive to the article on the conveyor to rotate the turntable. The responsive means could have been a photocell, weight sensor or the like; one conveyor on the turntable is all that is absolutely essential; and the main conveyors 12 and 13 could be any feeding and receiving devices.

This was not an Agent's Exam question.

Case 9

PREPARING APPARATUS CLAIMS GIVEN THE SPECIFICATION

T. KOKEISL PATENT 3,125,256

APPARATUS FOR STORING AND DELIVERING GRANULAR OR LIKE FLOWABLE MATERIALS

Fig.1

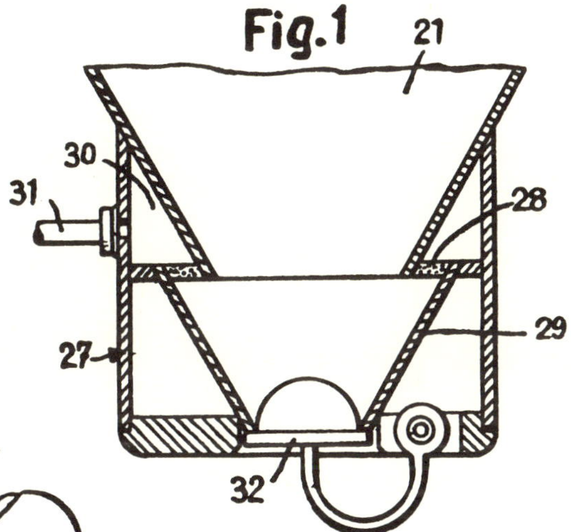

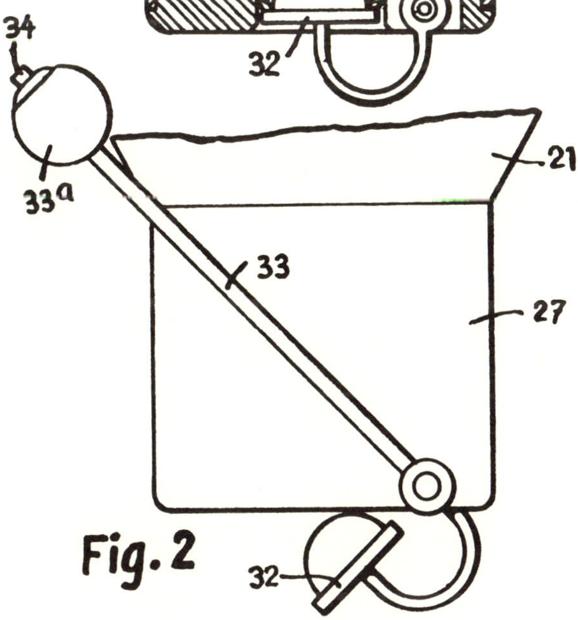

Fig.2

APPARATUS FOR STORING AND DELIVERING GRANULAR OR LIKE FLOWABLE MATERIALS

This invention relates to an apparatus with at least one container for storing and delivering measured quantities of granular or like flowable bulk materials and, more particularly, foods in powder form, such as flour, caster sugar, etc., the container having a funnel-shaped bottom part with a discharge device, a locking member and a porous filter element for introducing a gaseous medium into the container for loosening the granular material and preventing arch formations therein.

In embodiments of the type known heretofore, the inner wall of the funnel-shaped bottom part of the container is lined with porous filter elements which are at a distance from the inner wall to form an interspace, through which compressed air is supplied; this air penetrates through the porous elements into the granular material to loosen the same. Now such a construction is particularly disadvantageous because the granular material must flow out along the porous elements and its movement is hindered by the comparatively high coefficient of friction of the surface of these filter elements. In order that the material can move over the filter elements with as little frictional engagement as possible, the gaseous medium must be blown in at a correspondingly high pressure which, however, results in a relatively large part of the air escaping through the funnel throat with formation of eddy currents, whereby not inconsiderable quantities of the material are carried along, thereby leading not only to loss of material but also to the formation of dust and contamination of the environment. The amount of material blown out of the container in this manner reaches unacceptable proportions if the filter elements, as is usually the case in prior art embodiments, extend into the range of the funnel throat. Said shortcomings are naturally not only encountered in embodiments in which the air is blown in through filter elements carrying the granular material, but in all constructions, in which the inlets of the air supply open into the slide way of the material, whereby the associated air slots and air holes as such offer a high resistance to the flow of the material so that a particularly high air pressure is necessary.

The primary object of the invention is to obviate the drawbacks mentioned and to create the possibility of taking from the container or its funnel-shaped bottom part any desired quantity of material, down to the very smallest measure, without any appreciable amount of dust being formed thereby. According to the invention this is achieved in that the funnel-shaped bottom part of the container has a cross-sectional enlargement in at least one location between the inlet and outlet of the funnel, and that the porous filter element for the inflow of the gaseous medium is arranged outside the slide way of the granular material. The porous filter disk can thus have no influence upon the flow of the granular material. Since, moreover, the filter element, lying outside the slide way of the granular material, is preferably disposed in the range of the cross-sectional enlargement situated between the inlet and outlet of the funnel, hence at a point located some distance from the outlet of the funnel, the air cannot escape directly through the funnel outlet and thereby blow out any part of the material. The air flowing out through the porous filter element, thereby not only penetrates into the material to loosen the same, but, moreover, pushes the goods and acts in aiding relationship with, the action of gravity to force the bulk material through the funnel part beneath the filter element towards the throat of the funnel, so that minimum pressure is required to ensure proper outflow of the material. Preferably the funnel-shaped bottom part, at the location of said cross-sectional enlargement, may exhibit an annular gap having the filter element set therein and coextensive therewith, the gap communicating with an annual distribution chamber for the gaseous medium, which chamber, at the location of said enlargement, surrounds the funnel-shaped part of the container.

The accompanying drawing shows, by way of example, one embodiment of the invention; in the drawing.

FIG. 1 is a vertical cross-sectional view of the funnel-shaped bottom part of the container of the apparatus, with the outlet closed, and

FIG. 2 is an elevational view of the apparatus with the funnel outlet open.

Referring to the drawing, the funnel-shaped bottom part 21, 29 of the surmounted storage container (not shown) has, at a location between the inlet and outlet of the funnel, a cross-sectional enlargement receiving porous filter body 28 for the inflow of the gaseous medium; this body being located out of the slide way of the granular material, so that the same upon discharging of the container, does not pass over the filter element 28. The arrangement according to the invention is such that the funnel-shaped bottom part, at the location of the cross-sectional enlargement, has an annular gap filled with the filter element 28, which communicates with an annular distribution chamber 30 for the gaseous medium, said chamber at said enlargement extending round the funnel-shaped bottom part or feed means of the container. The chamber 30 may be connected through a pipe 31 to an air compressor (not shown) that supplies conditioned compressed air to the apparatus. The outlet of the funnel-shaped chute means 21, 29 is closable by a locking member designed as a swivably mounted plug 32 which, by means of a lever 33, can be pivoted into either the closed or open position. The lever 33 at one end is provided with a spherical headpiece 33*a* having mounted therein a push-button switch 34 adapted to close a circuit to start the driving motor of the air compressor. Thereby the funnel-shaped bottom part is surrounded by a casing 27, whose top part laterally defines the annular distribution chamber 30, and whose lower part has the lever 33 pivoted thereon.

If it is required to take material from the container, the lever 33 is swung in a sense opening the outlet of the funnel-shaped bottom part 21, 29, after the push-button 34 has previously been pressed down to switch on the air compressor motor. The compressed gaseous medium is pressed through the filter element 28, whereby the material will be loosened and, at the same time, be pushed towards the outlet of the bottom part; it does not slide over the filter element which, as being porous, has a correspondingly rough surface, but over the smooth wall of the funnel part 29, whereby a relatively low pressure ensures continuous emptying without the formation of any appreciable amount of dust.

PROBLEM

Draft three claims of substantially varying scope covering the apparatus for storing and delivering granular or like flowable materials described in the following specifications. Claims in dependent form may be used. The claims should not distinguish from each other by merely immaterial limitations and should distinguish over any prior art described in the specifications.

Case 9

PREPARING APPARATUS CLAIMS GIVEN THE SPECIFICATION

SAMPLE CLAIMS—KOKEISL PATENT 3,125,256

1. An improved apparatus for storing and delivering flowable bulk material, the apparatus being of the type having a vertically disposed funnel-shaped member with an inlet opening at the top for receiving the material and an outlet opening at the bottom for delivering the same, a closure member for selectively opening and closing the outlet opening, and a porous filter element for introducing a gaseous medium under pressure into the funnel-shaped member to loosen the material and assist in discharging it, the improvement wherein:

the funnel-shaped member is formed with a cross-sectional enlargement between the inlet and the outlet openings thereof; and

the filter element is mounted at the cross-sectional enlargement outside of the slide way of the material, to deliver the gaseous medium into the funnel-shaped member in the direction of the outlet opening.

2. An improved apparatus for storing and delivering bulk material as recited in claim 1, wherein:

the funnel-shaped member comprises two similar conically tapered funnels mounted one above the other so as to define an annular gap between the lower end of the upper funnel and the upper end of the lower funnel; and

the filter element is mounted in and fills the annular gap, so that the gaseous medium may be delivered generally downward through the filter element into the upper portion of the lower funnel.

3. An improved apparatus for storing and delivering bulk material as recited in claim 2, wherein:

a generally cylindrical casing is provided for mounting the funnels and the closure member, the casing defining in conjunction with a portion of the outer wall of the upper funnel an annular distribution chamber for the gaseous medium which is closed except for the space occupied by the filter element; and

means are provided for selectively admitting the gaseous medium under pressure into the annular chamber.

COMMENTS

This patent was used on the February 1968 Exam in the form reproduced here. As sometimes is done, a choice was given between writing claims to this patent and a chemical process, Crowell patent 2,308,588 on purifying maleic anhydride (Appendix B, Case 20).

The specification states, paragraphs 1 and 2, that the general combination of a funnel, a closure and a filter element is old for the same general purpose. In paragraph 3, it states that the main point of novelty consists in (1) providing a cross-sectional enlargement, and (2) in locating the filter element in a particular stated fashion. Thus, claim 1 should focus primarily on these factors. Statements in the specification such as "preferably the funnel-shaped bottom part . . . may exhibit an annular gap . . ." (p. 2, lines 3-10) indicate preferred but not critical features. Things such as this are good to include in claims 2 or 3, but should not be in claim 1.

Sample claim 1 indicates one approach to this structure, using the Jepson form to put the elements stated to be old in the preamble. This is probably not necessary for this case, but should be helpful both to better point out the invention and avoid a possible "old combination" rejection. (See Sections 54 and 60.) Various other approaches are possible, the main points being to limit details of description of the admittedly old elements and concentrate on the portions stated to be new.

As usual, the additional claims should be devoted primarily to the new features and not merely add elements or features stated to be old in the art. See Section 58, citing MPEP 706.03(k); ". . . it is possible to reject one claim on an allowed claim if they differ only by subject matter old in the art . . ." Although this "rule" may be questionable and is probably little used, it indicates Patent Office policy on the subject.

In addition, items such as the shape of the closure member 32, while not expressly stated to be old, have no real bearing on the subject invention and would be best not to describe in detail.

Also, note that since the container from which the granules come and the source of compressed air are not shown, they should not be positively recited in the claim (Rule 83).

Since the question said to write three claims of *substantially varying scope,* claim 3 need not be dependent from 2. The choice would depend on whether you were adding in claim 3 items closely related to those added in claim 2 (in series) or items related to the elements of claim 1 and not particularly important to the additions of claim 2 (in parallel).

Case 10

PREPARING APPARATUS CLAIMS AFLOAT

June 21, 1960 J. W. McBRIDE **2,941,494**

POWER PROPELLED WATER CRAFT

Filed Feb. 23, 1954 3 Sheets-Sheet 1

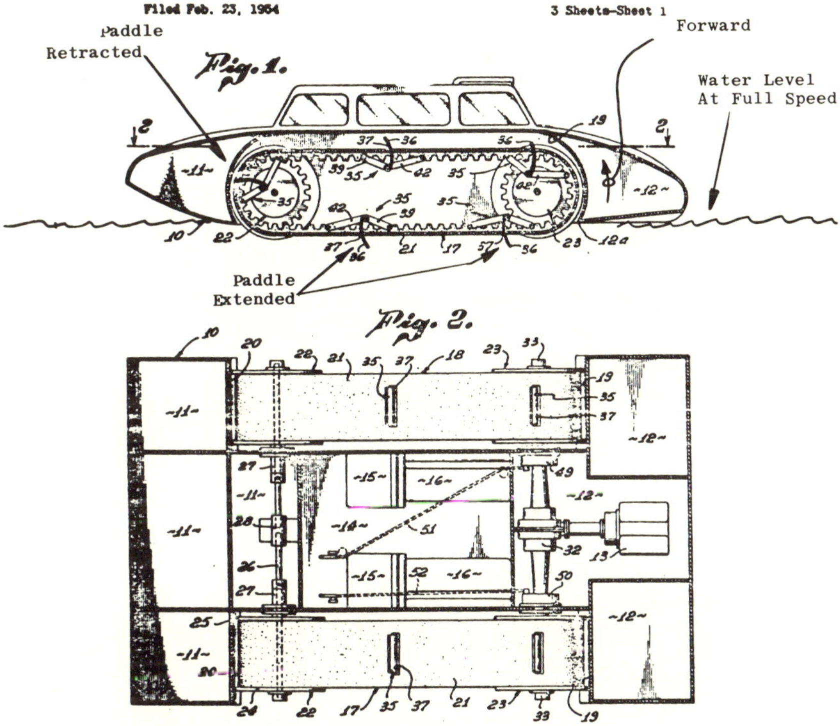

Paddles 36 are mounted to pivoted links 42 of a yoke 35 which is carried by toothed endless belts 21-21. The belts pass around sprocket wheels 22-23. As the links travel around the sprocket wheels, they pivot to retract the paddles inward through slots 37 in the belts. The object is to eliminate turbulance as the paddles enter and leave the water, by retracting the paddles.

INVENTOR.
JOHN W. McBRIDE,

June 21, 1960 J. W. McBRIDE 2,941,494

POWER PROPELLED WATER CRAFT

Filed Feb. 23, 1954 3 Sheets-Sheet 2

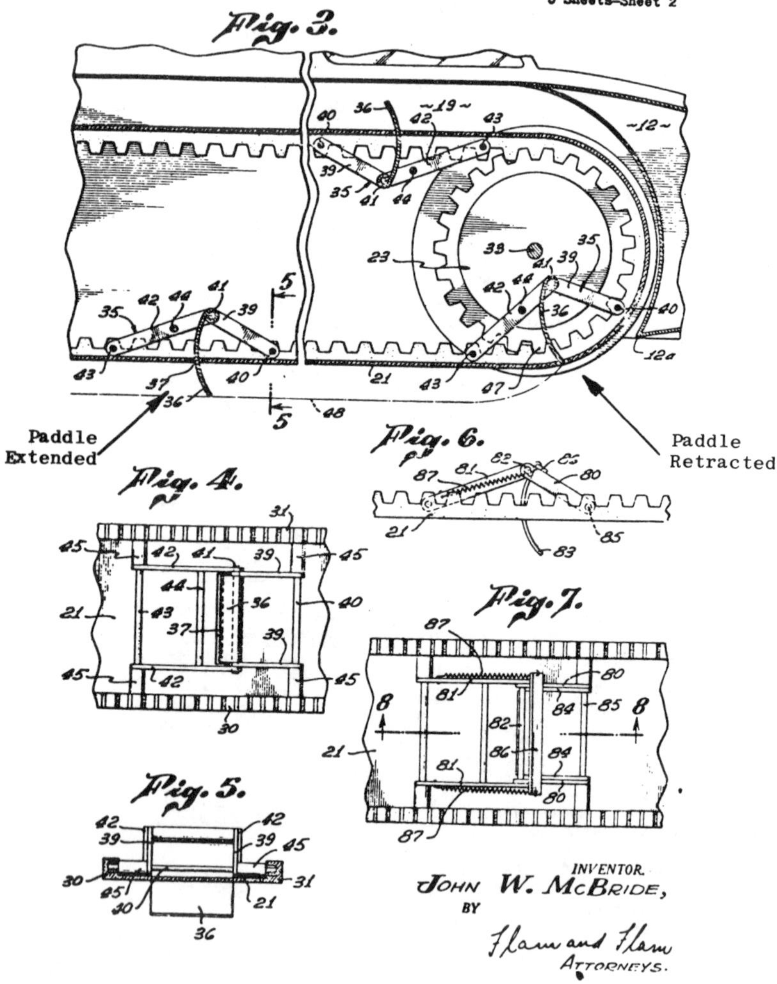

PROBLEM

Draft two claims of varying scope, assuming paddle boats are old, including ones with two sets of paddles mounted to conveyor belts on opposite sides of the boat.

Case 10

PREPARING APPARATUS CLAIMS AFLOAT

SAMPLE CLAIMS—McBRIDE PATENT 2,941,494

FAIRLY BROAD CLAIM

1. A propelling mechanism for a water craft, which comprises:

(a) an endless belt carried by the craft with a lower run thereof extending substantially horizontally beneath the craft, the belt having a plurality of transverse slots therethrough at intervals along the length thereof;

(b) means for driving the belt;

(c) a plurality of paddles movably mounted to the belt at intervals along the length thereof for movement therewith; and

(d) means for governing the position of each paddle with respect to the belt so that (1) each paddle extends outward beneath the belt into the water to propel the craft when the paddle is traveling with the lower run of the belt, and (2) each paddle is retracted with respect to the belt before the paddle breaks water at the end of the lower run of the belt.

COMMENTS

This rather broad claim covers what are believed to be the main elements of the invention: the belt, drive, paddles and position-governing means. Various other means could be employed to extend and retract the paddles, the essential thing being that a means be provided. On the "means + function so that . . ." clause, note *In re Chandler*, 117 USPQ 361, 364 (CCPA 1958), discussed in Section 31.

ANOTHER CLAIM

2. In a drive for propelling a boat:

a hull on the boat which always will float;
a wheel at the bow and one at the stern,
and a belt 'round the wheels which moves with a turn;
and for driving a wheel, a motor in tote;

a set of strong oars from a tree,
extending in slots through the belt to the sea;
on the belt, for each oar, in pivot a yoke,
for retracting these oars at the end of each stroke
to stop any splash and to set the oars free.

COMMENTS

This claim covers the main elements in somewhat different order. It may be too broad in the last two lines, in that "a yoke for" performing the function might not be considered as entitling one to the same breadth as a statutory "means for" clause as in claim 1. (See Section 31.) With relatively broad, functional clauses such as this it is probably safer to use the exact statutory language "means for," for example "Yoke means mounted pivotally on said belt. . . ."

YET ANOTHER CLAIM

3. A craft used on sea or on sand, having:

(a) Wheels supporting
(i) A band with
(ii) A scissor-like link dips
(b) Some oars in the drink
(c) Then retracts them to forestall the craft's becoming becalmed in the medium on which it rests.*

---

*Incomplete claim (JDK), to be completed in time for the third edition.

Case 11

PREPARING ELECTRICAL CIRCUIT CLAIMS

OPTICAL SOUND REPRODUCTION

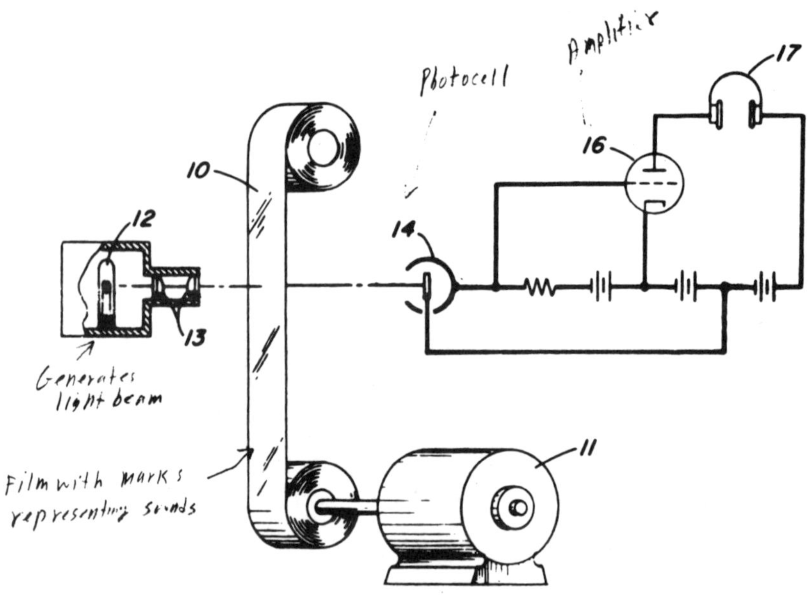

PROBLEM

Sound movie patent—draft a claim to the system.

Case 11

PREPARING ELECTRICAL CIRCUIT CLAIMS

SAMPLE CLAIM—OPTICAL SOUND PRODUCTION

?

A system for producing audible sounds in accordance with a varying visual pattern formed on a transparent film, which system comprises:

means for projecting a beam of light;

a photoelectric detector means for receiving said beam of light and for generating an output signal which varies as the amount of said light received by said detector;

means for advancing said film between said projecting means and said detector to vary the amount of light received by said detector in accordance with the variations in said visual pattern; and

means responsive to variations in said output signal for producing audible sounds.

COMMENTS

Note, this claim is a mixture of electrical, optical and mechanical elements, which is OK. "Means for" clauses are very common in circuit claims, since the specific circuit components are rarely critical in combination claims.

Case 12

PREPARING ELECTRICAL CIRCUIT CLAIMS

UNIJUNCTION PULSE GENERATOR

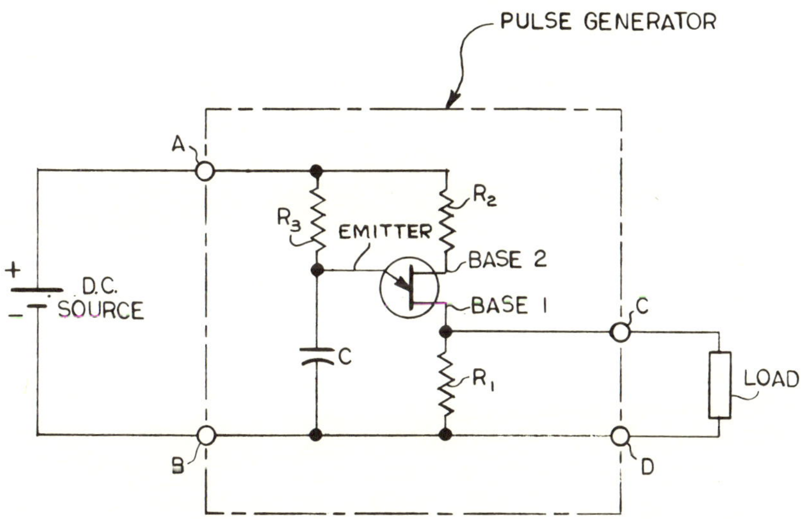

DRAFT A SPECIFIC CLAIM TO THIS CIRCUIT

PROBLEM

Draft a specific claim to this circuit.

Case 12

PREPARING ELECTRICAL CIRCUIT CLAIMS

SAMPLE CLAIM—UNIJUNCTION PULSE GENERATOR

A pulse generator for generating voltage pulses across an external load, which comprises:

a unijunction transistor having an emitter and first and second bases;

a first resistor;

means for connecting said first resistor between said first base and the negative terminal of an external d.c. voltage source;

a second resistor;

means for connecting said second resistor between said second base and the positive terminal of said d.c. voltage source;

a third resistor;

means for connecting said third resistor between said emitter and said positive terminal;

a capacitor;

means for connecting said capacitor between said emitter and said negative terminal; and

means for connecting the external load for said generator between the first base and the negative terminal of said d.c. voltage source;

said transistor, resistors and capacitor having parameters selected so that, when the source and load are connected to the pulse generator by the connecting means, said capacitor repetitively charges from the d.c. source through said third resistor until the voltage across said capacitor reaches a valve that causes said unijunction transistor to conduct, and then discharges through said transistor, and the parallel paths of said first resistor and the external load, whereby each discharge of said capacitor generates a voltage pulse across the external load.

COMMENTS

This claim further illustrates practice in composing detailed circuit claims (Section 32); listing the elements and parts, and connecting them together both structurally (Section 26) and operationally (Section 27).

Note that the power source and load are not made elements of the claim, as the pulse generator would normally be sold including only the components in the phantom-line box, up to terminals or connectors A, B, C, D. The purchaser or user would usually add the battery and load. The clauses such as "means for connecting said first resistor between said first base and the negative terminal of *an* external d.c. source" illustrate one way to claim the subcombination (pulse generator) as it is connect*able* to operate, without expressly claiming the battery. The "means for connecting" would always include a terminal (clip or post) such as B; thus the claim covers the circuit in the phantom box as a subcombination (Section 56). The claim also covers the complete unit connected as shown in the drawing, in which case the "means for" clause also includes the lead or wire connecting terminal B to the battery.

The operational clause (Section 27) was placed at the end of the claim (Section 30) since it requires the presence of all of the recited circuit components connected in the stated manner. This was made a separate clause since it relates to the operation of all of the elements, not just the last named one (means for connecting the capacitor). Note the "whereby clause" (Section 29) is proper since the pulse-generation function necessarily follows from the previously recited structure. If the structure had novelty, the clause about selecting parameters (R_s, C, and turn-ON voltage of the transistor) would clearly not be unduly functional under the cases cited in Section 28. Given some novelty, any "man skilled in the art" would know how to select the components to generate the desired pulse.

In all probability, if the circuit had novelty and was not obvious in the connection of the components in the stated manner, the last clause of the claim, telling how the circuit works, would not be necessary and could be omitted. Circuit claims are frequently patented with only statements of physical connection. Whether a final clause telling how it works should be included is largely up to the judgment of the claim writer, and to some extent the Examiner. Such a clause may help make the claim more definite and help convince the Examiner it is novel and unobvious, and may avoid an "accidental anticipation"—type rejection on a circuit that looks structurally similar but works entirely differently.

Case 13

PREPARING METHOD CLAIMS
MARKUSH CLAIMS—GENERIC AND SPECIES CLAIMS

April 7, 1959 **R. E. GUNDERMAN ET AL** **2,880,466**

PROCESS FOR PREPARING FILMS FROM POLYMER LATEXES

Filed Jan. 14, 1957

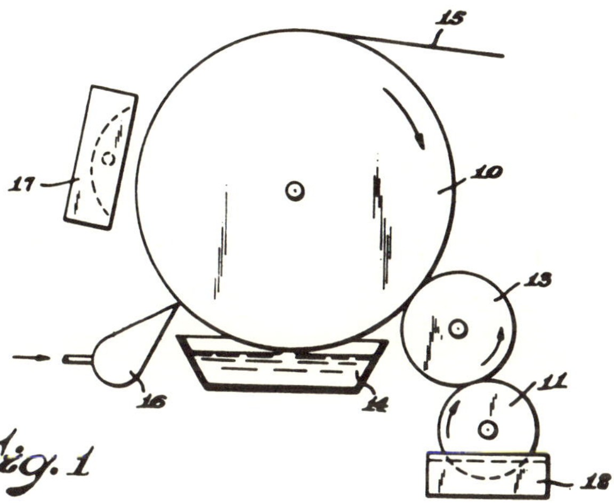

Fig. 1

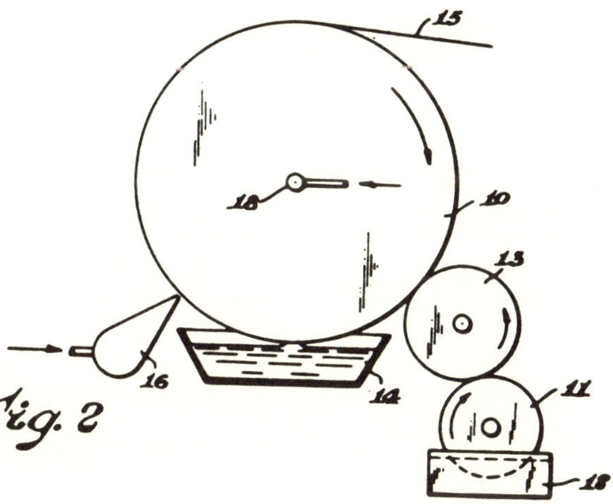

Fig. 2

2,880,466
PROCESS FOR PREPARING FILMS FROM POLYMER LATEXES

Roland E. Gunderman, Clare, and Max E. Elder, Midland, Mich., assignors to The Dow Chemical Company, Midland, Mich., a corporation of Delaware

Application January 14, 1957, Serial No. 634,125
7 Claims. (Cl. 18–57)

This invention relates to an improved process for preparing thermoplastic films from polymer latexes. More particularly it relates to such a process involving the continuous localized coagulation of the latexes.

Polymer latexes are particularly useful forms from which to prepare continuous articles, such as films, tapes, and filaments. The number of procedural steps required to convert a latext into a continuous article is at a minimum, the steps are operationally simple, the capital investment in film forming equipment is low, the equipment is easy to clean and maintain and is fairly versatile in being useful for many different latexes without major modification. In preparing such articles the latex may be cast into the approximate shape desired on a supporting surface by suing a transfer roll, doctor blade, air knife, or the like. The cast wet shape may be then dried and fused either sequentially or simulanteously. That method or technique, however, is limited to a relatively few latexes which are capable of film formation by air drying. More recently a technique was developed whereby a film forming latex was cast on a supporting surface wetted with an electrolyte coagulant solution to form a porous coagulum which was then washed, dried, and fused. Although the latter technique increased the number of useful latexes which could be formed into continuous coherent articles, there was still a large family of polymers and copolymers with which the porous coagulum was so incoherent and weak as to make further processing extremely difficult and in many cases impossible. Included among those difficulty processable latexes are the polymers and copolymers of cinyl chloride and of vinylidene chloride with each other or with other monoethylenically unsaturated comonomers, such as the alkyl acrylates. It would be desirable if an improved process could be found for fabricating these difficulty processable latexes into continuous coherent articles, and it is the principal object of this invention to provide such an improved process.

It is a further object to provide such a process which is readily adaptable to existing equipment.

The above and related objects are realized with a process wherein an electrolyte-coagulable polymer latex is cast and electrolyte coagulated into approximately the desired shape as a continuous, coherent, porous coagulum which is washed to remove substantially all of the electrolyte coagulant, the excess water removed without destroying the porosity of the coagulum, and the coagulum then dried and fused. The improvement in the above process which is contemplated by this invention is the subjecting of the freshly cast porous coagulum to relatively mild beating prior to washing. By the use of this improvement polymer latexes which could not be fashioned by prior procedures into continuous coherent articles are capable of such fabricaton.

Although any film-forming electrolyte-coagulable, polymer latex may be used in the process of this invention, it has been found to be especially useful and necessary with the latexes of the polymers and copolymers of vinyl chloride and vinylidene chloride with each other or with other monoethyenically unsaturated comonomers, such as the alkyl acrylates, and acrylonitrile. Within this family of difficultly processable polymer latexes it has been found that those latexes of the normally crystalline vinylidene chloride copolymers are particularly troublesome and such latexes accordingly represent preferred materials for use in the process. The useful latexes must be electrolyte coagulable into a continuous, coherent coagulum. It is not essential that the continuous, coherent coagulum be self-supporting, impermeable, transparent, or commercially useful by air drying, but it is necessary that the coagulum be a unitary integral article, however weak it may be. It is known that some latexes require minor treatment to aid their inherent film forming characteristics, their casting ability, or their coagulability. For example it is frequently advantageous to add a very small amount of a hydrophilic, colloidal thickener, such as the water-soluble cellulose ethers, and to adjust the pH of the latex prior to casting. Such techniques which enhance the film formability of the latex are intended to be within the scope of the invention.

The latexes may be prepared by any of the known procedures for polymerization in aqueous emulsion. Typically the monomer or monomers are dispersed in an aqueous solution of from about 0.05 to 5 percent polymerization catalyst, such as potassium persulfate or hydrogen peroxide, and from about 0.05 percent of a surface active agent as an emulsifies.

Polymerization is initiated by heating the emulsified mixture usually between 35 degrees C. and 100 degrees C. and continued by maintaining the polymerizing emulsion at the selected temperature. After the polymerization has reached the desired conversion of monomer to polymer, the latex is filtered to remove any precoagulum and stabilized to storage by the addition of a small amount of a surface active agent.

Latexes which are to be used in forming continuous coherent articles, such as films, should preferably contain from about 30 to about 50 percent by weight of non-volatile solids. When less than about 30 percent of weight of non-volatile solids are present in the latex, no useful, continuous coherent articles can be produced by simple deposition of the latex. Latexes having appreciably more than 50 percent by weight of non-volatile solids are difficult to prepare and are extremely sensitive to mechanical shear and to storage and may coagulate prematurely.

It is also known that the quality of continuous coherent articles prepared by the deposition of a latex is dependent upon the latex particle size. The particle size is a function of the kind and concentration of emulsifier, the temperature of polymerization, and the rate of agitation used in forming the initial dispersion. Most latexes will generally not form films by simple deposition unless substantially all of the particles are under 3000 angstrom units in diameter. Most desirable results are obtained when the majority of the dispersed particles have diameters between 400 and 2000 angstrom units. Means for makin latexes whose particles are of those dimensions are known.

The coagulents useful for coagulating polymer latexes are well-known. Typically they consist of aqueous solutions of bi- and polyvalent inorganic salts, such as calcium chloride, magnesium chloride, and aluminum sulfate. It has been found that a solution of from about 5 to about 20 percent concentration provides the best coagulating characteristics. The greater the concentration that is used, the more extensive will the washing step have to be to remove residual electrolyte. Such electrolytes frequently have a deleterious effect on the stability of the polymer. It has also been found to be desirable to add a small amount of surface active agent to the aqueous coagulant solution to improve the wetting qualities of the solution.

The operation and advantages of this process will be more apparent from the following description and annexed drawings which represent schematically a preferred and illustrative apparatus for carrying out the steps of the process.

In the drawing:

Figure 1 represents a schematic elevation of an apparatus employing external heating means, and

Figure 2 represents a schematic elevation of an apparatus employing internal heating means.

In the embodiment illustrated in Figure 1 a large rotatably driven, smooth-surfaced drum 10 is used as a casting surface. The surface 10 of the drum is first wetted with aqueous electrolyte coagulant solution. The wetting is conveniently accomplished using a transfer roll technique wherein a pickup roll 11 rotating partially in a coagulant bath 12 is in contact with a transfer roll 13 which in turn is in contact with the drum 10. The transfer roll technique assures a constant wetting of the drum surface 10. As the drum 10 rotates further the wetted surface dips into or touches a latex bath 14 forming a wet latexcoagulant film 15. Excess water and latex is removed from the wet film by a planiform air blast, sometimes called an air knife 16, which is directed at a slight angle to the surface of the wet film 15. The rotating drum surface 10 next passes under a radiant heating means 17 such as a quartz bar heater, which strengthens and conditions the film 15 without destroying its porosity. It is only necessary that the temperature of the wet film 15 be raised to about 35 to 70 degrees C. to achieve the desirable result. If the film 15 is not raised to at least 35 degrees C., there is little improvement noticed in the coagulum characteristics. If temperatures of much over 70 degrees C. are used, there is a danger that much of the porosity will be lost, and the other processing steps made more difficult. It should be apparent that the actual temperature to be used to give optimum results will depend upon the polymer composition, the latex characteristics, the thickness of th wet film and other variables. An investigator will be able to make a judicious choice of temperature by examining the coagulum following the beating step.

Following the warming step the continuous, coherent, porous coagulum is stripped from the drum surface, washed, dried, and fused.

In the embodiment represented in Figure 2 the apparatus consists of the same elements in the same relative positions except that the external radiant heating means 17 is omitted. In this embodiment the axis of drum 10 is fitted with a conventional rotary union 13 and heat transfer fluids circulated therethrough to maintain the drum surface at a temperature of from 35 to about 70 degrees C.

The drum or other supporting

surface should be contacted with the latex as soon as possible after wetting with coagulant to avoid drying of the coagulant on the drum surface. This is particularly important when a heated drum or supporting surface is employed as in the embodiment of Figure 2 since that heat increases the drying problem. Dried coagulant does not provide good continuous localized coagulation characteristics.

Plasticizers, stabilizers, dilers, pigments, and the other additives commonly incorporated into polymer components may be employed in this process by water blending them into the latex prior to casting or by passing the wet washed coagulum through a solution of the additive prior to fusion.

The thickness of the continuous, coherent article is easily controlled by the setting of the air knife, doctor blade, or other device, by the time of contact of the drum with the latex, by the concentration of the coagulant, and by the latex compositions. The process operates best when the article has a thickness of from 0.001 to 0.003 inch. When it is attempted to prepart articles of much greater thickness than 0.003 inch by the continuous localized coagulation of a latex, it is found that it is difficult to achieve uniform coagulation, the coagulant is difficult to wash away, and the wet article is difficult to dry and fuse.

In a specific example an aqueous latex prepared by the emulsion polymerization of 91 percent by weight of vinylidene chloride and 9 percent by weight of acrylonitrile and having 40 percent solids was formulated by stirring in 5 percent by weight based on the weight of nonvolatile solids of ethyl phthalyl ethyl glycolate as a plasticizer. One percent of the dioctyl ester of sodium sulfosuccinic acid was added to reduce the surface tension of the latex to 38.8 dynes. An 8 inch steel drum having a Heresite surface was wetted with a 10 percent aqueous calcium chloride solution containing 0.4 of a nonionic wetting agent. The wet drum surface was then rotated through a bath of the formulated latex and then through the blast of an air knife. The drum was maintained at a temperature of 60 degrees C. by circulating hot water therethrough. Also the drum was rotated to give a peripheral speed of 20 feet per minute. The coagulum formed on the roll was continuous and coherent, could be stripped from the roll and passed through a water bath, then air dried, and finally fused at 170 degrees C.

By way of contrast when the process was repeated omitting the heating of the drum, the coagulum could not be stripped from the drum without breakage.

In a further example a latex prepared by the emulsion polymerization of 30 percent by weight of vinylidene chloride and 70 percent by weight of vinyl chloride and containing 47.4 percent by weight of non-volatile solids was formulated with 1 percent of the dioctyl ester of sodium sulfosuccinic acid and 10 percent plasticizer. The drum, without any fluid circulating therethrough, was wetted with 10 percent aqueous calcium chloride solution then passed through the latex bath, finally subjected to the air knife blast. The west drum surface was passed under a 1000 watt quartz bar heater placed 2 inches from the drum at a speed of 14 feet per minute. The porous coagulum was stripped from the drum, washed, then dried and fused into a continuous coherent film.

Similar results are observed when latexs of copolymers of vinylidene chloride and ethyl acrylate are processed in this manner.

The process of this invention allows the preparation of films, filaments, and other continuous, moherent articles from latexes which heretofore could not be used in the continuous, localized coagulation technique because of the inherent weakness of the coagulum.

We claim:

? ? ? ?

PROBLEM

Part I—Write three method claims of varying scope, based on the specification as written.

Part II—Write a Markush claim covering the specific coagulants mentioned at the start of the ninth paragraph of the specification.

Part III—Write two method species claims to the two ways of heating described.

Case 13

PREPARING METHOD CLAIMS
MARKUSH CLAIMS—GENERIC AND SPECIES CLAIMS

SAMPLE CLAIMS—
PROCESS FOR PREPARING FILMS

PART I

1. In a process for preparing a continuous coherent article from a film-forming, electrolyte-coagulable polymer latex, the process being of the type including the steps of

(a) wetting a moving supporting surface with an electrolyte coagulant solution,
(b) casting a film of the polymer latex on the wet surface to form a continuous, coherent, porous coagulum of the polymer and coagulant solution,
(c) washing the coagulum so formed to remove the electrolyte, and
(d) drying and fusing the washed coagulum into a continuous coherent article;

the improvement which comprises:

(e) heating the coagulum prior to step (c) to a temperature sufficient to strengthen and condition the coagulum without destroying its porosity, and below the fusion temperature of the coagulum.

2. A process as recited in claim 1, wherein the polymer latex is selected from the group consisting of the polymers and copolymers of vinyl chloride and vinylidine chloride with each other and with other monoethylenically unsaturated comonomers.
3. A process as recited in claim 2, wherein the coagulum is heated to a temperature of about 35 to 70°C. in step (e).

PART II

4. A process as recited in claim 2, wherein the coagulant solution is an aqueous solution of an inorganic salt selected from the group consisting of calcium chloride, magnesium chloride, and aluminum sulfate.

PART III

A–First Species–FIG. 1:

5. A process as recited in claim 3, wherein the heating step is accomplished by localized radiant heating of the outer surface of the coagulum after step (b).

B–Second Species–FIG. 2:

6. A process as recited in claim 3, wherein the heating step is accomplished by uniformly heating the supporting surface.

COMMENTS

In preparing method claims from a specification, there should be no problem in understanding the method or in naming the parts or steps. Usually, the names given in the specification will suffice, such as "wetting," "casting," etc. A problem might be in figuring out what is most fundamental to the method for inclusion in claim 1, and what details should be left for other claims. Since the specific question asked in Part I was to write three claims of "varying scope," it is not necessary (but would not hurt) to make each claim include all of the limitations of the preceding claim.

In this case, the specification states very clearly (especially Col. 1, lines 34-43 and 55-67) that the "Invention" in this case involves an improvement in a prior known process which is *otherwise unchanged.* Specifically, the "Invention" involves adding a single step, heating (e of sample claim 1), to the several conventional steps (a thru d) of the prior process.

This factual situation should point the way toward using a "Jepson," or improvement-type, claim, one form of which is employed in sample claim 1. (See Section 54.) Note on this subject the amendment to the Rules of Practice, effective January 1, 1967. New rule 75(e) reads as follows:

> "Where the nature of the case admits, as in the case of an improvement, any independent claim should contain in the following order, (1) a preamble comprising a general description of all the elements or steps of the claimed combination which are conventional or known, (2) a phrase such as 'wherein the improvement comprises,' and (3) those elements, steps and/or relationships which constitute that portion of the claimed combination which the applicant considers as the new or improved portion."

From the use of the word "should," it would appear that the Office would like to force or at least strongly urge the use of Jepson claims for improvement inventions. It is not quite certain what "should" means, when "may" is used in some rules and "must" in others.

As to the format for a Jepson claim, Section 54 gives several alternatives, the exact choice of which is not critical. However, for the transition between the preamble and the body of the claim, it might be advisable to use the exact language of new rule 75(e) —"wherein the improvement comprises."

As to the scope of claim 1, a question is presented as to whether the specific temperature range (35-70°C.) should be recited. From the way this is discussed in Column 3, lines 31-45, it appears that the precise temperature is noncritical, and will vary for different latexes to give optimum results. Therefore, it would appear satisfactory to define the amount of heating functionally, in terms of the result effected, even though the heating step per se is the "heart of the invention." Of interest, claim 1 of the patent did issue in functional terms in this respect, as follows:

> In a process for preparing . . . (etc.) . . . , the improvement consisting of subjecting said coagulum to heating below the fusion temperature . . . prior to said washing step . . .

Note that sample claim 1 tried to be a little more specific, without reciting a temperature range, by telling everything about the heating step mentioned in the specification.

Whether to recite specific latexes is another problem. The way the specification is written, one would not think this necessary since the class of resins is said to be known as is the basic process of preparing such coagula. However, claim 1 of the patent does recite a class of resins.

Sample claims 2 and 3 add what appear to be important subfeatures of the invention. If one or both of these items were included in claim 1, subclaims could be drafted to specify the way or ways of heating, the type of coagulants, the "air knife" step, etc. If the "moving" supporting surface were omitted from claim 1, this could also be added.

One caution is to avoid submethod claims which add *only* mechanical structure such as:

> The method as recited in claim X, wherein the supporting surface is a rotary drum.

Subordinate method claims should add method steps, tell more about previously recited steps, or add details of the materials being worked on, such as the composition of the latex, etc. In general, avoid structure insofar as reasonably possible in writing method claims (see Part IV.) Of course, there is no objection to describing the article or materials being worked on in whatever detail is necessary to the method being claimed.

Part II was intended to familiarize the student with "Markush" language. (See Section 47.)

Part III was intended to test knowledge of genus and species expressions. (See Section 55.) On some exams, the examinees have been asked to prepare genus and species claims on the examination. When this disclosure was used on the November 1965 examination, genus and species claims were requested. Presumably, species would have been acceptable directed either to the two methods of heating, as in Part III, or to two specific latexes.

The most important point to remember about species claims is that they must define two or more alternative and mutually exclusive variations on an element of the generic claim.

Case 14

PREPARING METHOD CLAIMS

Feb. 15, 1938. F. J. BICKEL **2,108,742**

BRUSH

Filed July 13, 1936

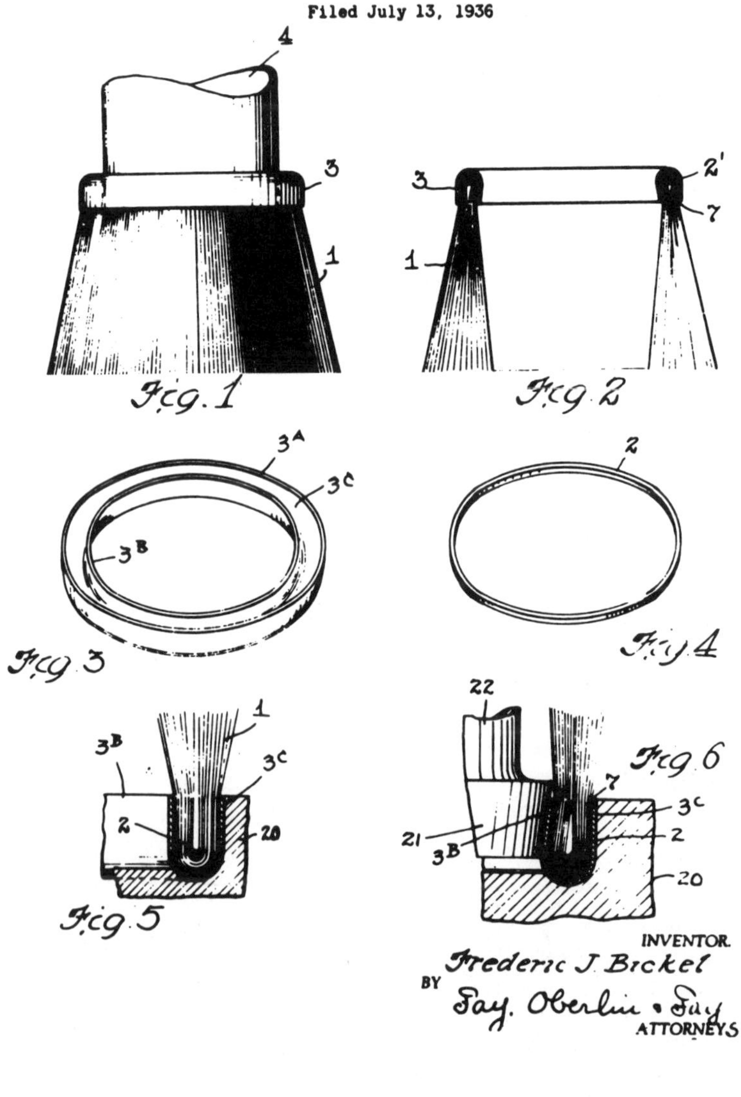

1,108,742
BRUSH
Frederic J. Bickel, Cleveland, Ohio, assignor to The Osborn Manufacturing Company, Cleveland, Ohio, a corporation of Ohio
Application July 13, 1936, Serial No. 90,306
6 Claims. (Cl. 300–21)

This invention pertains to the brush art and particularly aims to improve the manufacture and construction of hollow center end brushes.

Among the aims and purposes are: the production of brushes which present certain advantages particularly for use as elements of vacuum cleaning tools; absence of rough projections or irregular junctions, edges, points and so on, which would cause difficulty in placing the bristles during manufacture or cause injury to furniture, draperies, household ornaments and the like, by catching, pulling or scratching; firm gripping of the bristles without damage thereto; simplification of the manufacture of such brushes: adaptability to manufacture with economical materials and methods of construction.

To the accomplishment of the foregoing and related ends, said invention, then consists of the means hereinafter fully described and particularly pointed out in the claims.

Thc annexed drawing and the following description set forth in detail certain means and one mode of carrying out the invention, such disclosed means and mode illustrating, however, but one of various ways in which the principle of the invention may be used.

In the accompanying drawing:

Fig. 1 is a side elevation of my brush on the end of a vacuum cleaner attachment;

Fig. 2 is a median section through the brush on an axial plane;

Fig. 3 is a perspective of the brush channel;

Fig. 4 is a perspective of a preferred form of retaining ring;

Fig. 5 is a cross section through
The brush, as completed, com-
o fassembly; and

Fig. 6 is a cross section through the brush, showing the final assembly step.

The brush, as completed, comprises a filling of bristlcs 1, looped about a ring 2 or 2′ and secured in an annular channel 3, which is of slightly modified U-shape when seen in cross section in its final form, and which has its opening pointed endwise, that is, in such a direction that the bristles 1 form a cylinder instead of a disc. In use the brush is mounted on or secured to suitable holder means, the principal intended purpose being to use it on a tube such as

4 which represents part of a vacuum cleaner attachment. The inner surface of the channel 3 is placed on the tube by a sliding forced fit, or otherwise, as may be most suitable. As best shown in Figs. 2 and 6 the rim channel is somewhat narrowed at the open end to constrict the bristles at 7 and thus firmly anchor the bristles and the retaining ring against withdrawal.

In the manufacture of this brush I have found it preferable to use an annular channel in the shape 3A, having straight inner and outer sides 3B and 3C respectively, Figs. 3 and 5. This channel is designated by the reference character 3 when the brush is in its completed form.

A preferred method of constructing the brush is to fit the channel 3A with the wall of the bristles 1 looped upon the retaining ring 2 or 2′. In the manufacture of the brush a die 20, Figs. 5 and 6, shaped to support the bottom and the outer wall 3C, is used. The filled channel A3 is placed therein, or the empty channel may be placed therein and the die also used to serve the purpose of a holder during the filling of the channel.

Fig. 5 shows, in a partly sectional fragment, the channel in the die, there filled, ready for the next step, shown in Fig. 6. A central expanding tool, such as 21, Fig. 6, conically sided with an outward upward taper, is moved down by a suitably guided and driven actuating plunger 22 to expand the inner wall 3B of the channel 3A, thus contricting the channel top at 7. My preference is to leave the wall 3C straight both for the reason that this makes a simpler manufacturing operation, and also that it avoids excessive narrowing of the top of the channel and danger of damage to or wear upon the bristles at the portion 7. The completion of construction by the forming tool 21 is shown in Fig. 6.

It will be observed that the retaining ring, as shown in Figs. 4, 5 and 6, is of rectangular cross section, the specific showing being square. I do not confine myself to this shape of retaining ring, but may use a ring of ordinary wire as at 2′, Fig. 2. My preference for the ring of rectangular cross section is that it may be more cheaply made than a wire ring, by cutting off successive ends of a seamless tube of proper diameter and wall thickness. The use of square cut sections of a seamless tube has been found in practice not to be injurious to the bristles, and is more economical than making rings of round section.

From the foregoing it will be seen that I have invented a brush of simple and durable construction, free from rough or projecting parts, junctions or seams, wherein the bristles are held firmly, but without injurious pressure at the point of construction, and have likewise invented a method of making such a brush which is simple, economical and quick and in some measure permits utilization of less expensive material than has heretofore been deemed necessary, but without lowering the quality of the product.

PROBLEM

Part I—Write three method claims of varying scope, based on the specification as written.

Part II—Assume that specification disclosed that, for some applications, it was desirable to bend the inner and outer walls 3B and 3C equally toward the center of the channel. With this in mind, prepare a generic claim and two species method claims (using claims from Part I where possible).

Case 14

PREPARING METHOD CLAIMS

SAMPLE CLAIMS—BRUSH MAKING

PART I:

1. A method of making a brush, which comprises:

assembling a plurality of bristles with a core member and a channel having a U-shaped cross section so that the core member is received in the channel and the bristles are lopped about the core member with the ends of the bristles projecting from the open end of the channel; and

partially closing the open end of the channel to secure the bristles and the core member in the channel.

2. A method as recited in claim 1, for making a hollow cylindrical brush, wherein the assembling step comprises:

looping a plurality of the bristles about a ring-shaped core member; and

inserting the core member and bristles into an annular channel having a U-shaped cross section of such size as to receive the core member and bristles therein.

3. A method as recited in claim 2, wherein the channel is partially closed by bending the edge of the inner wall of the channel toward the outer wall while maintaining the outer wall fixed.

PART II:

Claims 1 and 2 are generic. Claim 3 is directed to the first species, that disclosed in the specification. The following claim covers the second species:

4. A method as recited in claim 2, wherein the channel is partially closed by bending the edges of the inner and outer walls of the channel toward each other.

COMMENTS

This disclosure was used on the November 1956 Agent's Exam. As is customary for the method claims, the entire specification (minus claims) was given. In some instances in the past, not this one, the student has been requested to compose genus and species method claims.

In preparing method claims from a specification, there is usually no problem in understanding the method or in naming the parts or steps. Usually, the names given in the specification will suffice, such as "looping," "annular channel," etc. A problem is in figuring out what is most fundamental to the method for inclusion in claim 1, and what details should be left for other claims. Since the specific question asked in this case was to write three claims of "varying scope," it is not necessary (but would not hurt) to make each claim include all of the limitations of the preceding claim.

Claim 1 covers what appear to be the most important steps—assembling the elements and closing the channel. This claim covers other possible methods of assembling the core, bristles and channel, such as laying the bristles in the channel first and then inserting the core. In this case, some details must be left out of claim 1 because the method is so simple that there would otherwise be a problem in preparing three claims of *materially* different scope.

Another approach to claim 1 would be to claim the looping and inserting steps separately perhaps along the following lines:

". . . looping a plurality of bristles about a core member; inserting the core member and bristles into a channel. . . ."

Probably the most important thing in writing method claims

is to make certain that the "elements" of the claim are manipulative steps or acts (looping, inserting, closing, bending, etc.). Apparatus used in carrying out the method should not be mentioned insofar as it is possible to avoid it; thus, in this case, there is no need to recite the die 20 or the expanding tool 21. Of course, there is no problem in describing as much of the *article* being worked on as is essential to the method being described, such as the core member, channel and bristles.

On the species claims 3 and 4, see Section 55.

Case 15

PREPARING METHOD CLAIMS

Sept. 7, 1943. G. S. HIERS 2,328,904

METHOD OF ATTACHING AND STRAIGHTENING FLOCK

Filed April 2, 1941

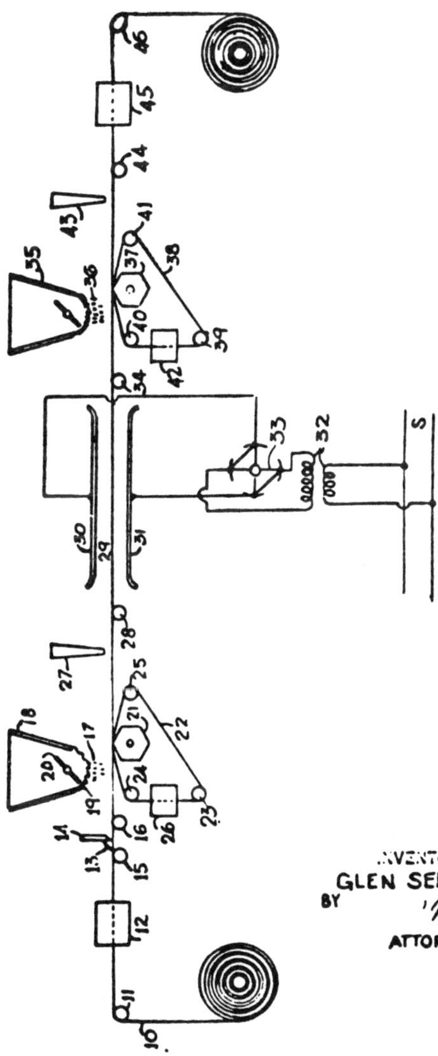

INVENTOR
GLEN SEFTON HIERS.
BY
ATTORNEY

G. S. HIERS PATENT 2,328,904
SPECIFICATION

This invention relates to a method of and apparatus for producing flocked pile fabrics.

High voltage electrostatic methods have heretofore been used in the production of flocked pile fabrics, but fabrics so produced, while having a great number of pile fibers per unit area and hence sufficient density of face coverage as well as excellent erectness of pile, have been characterized by deficient anchorage of the fibers to the adhesive with the result that the durability of the fabric has been unsatisfactory. In addition, the great number of pile flock fibers per unit area is undesirable for many purposes, as too great density of the pile face, particularly with straight fibers of equal length, causes stiffness which interferes with the draping properties of the fabric. As it is exceedingly difficult to control the regular deposition of pile forming flock when less than an excess of the amount actually secured to the base fabric is introduced into the electrostatic field or positioned on portions of the base fabric, as by sifting, prior to those portions of the base fabric entering the electrostatic field, prior flocked fabrics were produced which were relatively costly because of the amount of flock used and yet undesirable because of their lack of desired draping quality and softness of appearance.

Beater methods have also been employed in the production of flocked pile fabrics, but in fabrics so produced, while the anchorage of the fiber to the adhesive is good, the erectness of pile and density of coverage is not all that is desired for some uses.

According to my improvements, I overcome these prior difficulties and deficiencies and produce a flocked pile fabric having a desired erectness of pile, density of coverage and excellence of anchorage of fiber to adhesive and hence a fabric which is superior to fabrics produced by either the beater or the high potential electrostatic methods alone or prior combinations of these methods. It will be understood, of course, that wool fibers which are cured or crescent shaped, will not have the erectness of the straighter fibers, but the wool fibers will be oriented to the extent permitted by their shape.

I accomplish the above desirable result by subjecting the adhesively coated fabric successively to a rapid beater operation and to high potential electrostatic forces. The successive steps of first rapidly beating or otherwise vibrating the fabric upon which fibers have been or are being deposited and then positioning the flocked fabric within a high potential electrostatic field may be repeated as often as and to the extent that is necessary to produce the desired result. During the rapid beating step a low potential electrostatic field may be generated by frictional engagement of the beating means with a material other than the base fabric and/or with the base fabric itself, although beating alone will form a pile face.

The generation of the low potential electrostatic field is not essential to the broad concept of the present improvements and the particular methods will be the subject matter of separate applications. The rapid beating alone will cause the pile forming flock to stand on end in a known manner, although the erectness and density of pile is less than exists in fabrics produced by high potential methods. The beating step, aside from embedding the end of the flock in the adhesive, also uniformly distributes it over the face of the base fabric. The adhesive is not yet set and the pile fibers are adjustable therein, as will be explained. In cases where the adhesive has set it may be treated with a solvent to soften it to tackiness. This latter step is not essential to the continuous process. The loose or excess fibers resulting from the beating step may be removed by a vacuum device or other convenient means.

In the initial operation flock fibers are dropped upon the adhesively coated surface of a cotton or other base fabric which is vibrated rapidly preferably under the beats of a rapidly rotating polygonal bar or bars which may be in actual contact with the back of the base fabric or which may be in engagement with a flexible apron interposed between the beater and the base fabric and in contact with both.

Following the rapid beating and excess flock removal operations or a softening operation, the flocked fabric is placed within a high potential electrostatic field to cause the deposited fibers to assume a more erect position in the adhesive and to thereby create openings into which additional flock may subsequently be dropped. I prefer that the high potential field be used solely for straightening the position of fibers previously applied without additional flock being deposited while the fabric is within the high potential field. Additional flock may, however, be introduced within the field if desired.

Upon removal from the high potential electrostatic field, the flocked fabric is brought into contact with a beating means which may be similar to or somewhat different from that used in the initial step, and during the second beating operation additional flock of the same or different kind and/or length is dropped upon the rapidly vibrating fabric. Following this operating, the fabric may again be placed within a high potential electrostatic field and this sequence of steps may be continued until the desired result is obtained. Ordinarily, two applications of flock will suffice.

It is an object of this invention to provide a method of and apparatus for producing a flocked pile fabric having good anchorage of fiber to base, erectness of pile and sufficient density of face coverage.

Another object is to provide a means of controlling the amount and uniformity of an application of pile flock fibers before their entrance to a high potential electrostatic field.

Another object is to provide a method of producing flocked pile fabrics which includes the steps in sequence of depositing flock fibers upon an adhesively coated base fabric by a beater method, and then by means of a high potential electrostatic force causing the deposited fibers to assume a more erect position in the adhesive.

Another object is to anchor flock fibers in the adhesively coated surface of a base fabric by heating and to thereafter subject the flocked fabric to a high potential electrostatic force to cause the anchored fibers to assume a more erect position and thereby create openings in the face of the fabric, and then to anchor additional fibers by a subsequent beating operation.

Another object is to subject an adhesively coated base fabric to a plurality of flocking operations by beater methods and interpose between the flocking operation the step or steps of pulling the deposited fibers to more erect position in the adhesive.

A further object is to deposit upon an adhesively coated base fabric as much flock as can be secured by a single beating operation, and then by high potential electrostatic methods to cause the fibers to assume a more erect position and thereby create openings into which additional flock may be dropped and anchored by a subsequent beating operation.

These and other objects of invention will clearly appear from the following description of a preferred embodiment, in which:

The figure depicts schematically apparatus suitable for flocking a base fabric in accordance with my improvements.

Referring to the drawing, reference numeral 10 depicts a base fabric of cotton or other suitable material which is carried over guide roll 11 to drier 12, in which moisture may be removed from the fabric to the point of bone dryness if desired, after which an adhesive 13 of rubber cement, pyroxylin, or other composition, may be applied to the face side of the fabric as by doctor blade 14 positioned between guide rolls 15 and 16. Flock fibers 17 of wool, mohair, cotton, viscose, casein, acetate, or other textile material, and of desired length may be deposited upon the adhesively coated surface as from hopper 18, having screen bottom 19 and rotating blade 20 for forcing the flock through the screen.

Polygonal beater bar 21, positioned beneath the fabric and apron 22 at a point preferably just beyond that at which the fibers are dropped upon the fabric, may be rotated by conventional means (not shown) at a speed sufficient to cause rapid vibration of the base fabric.

The apron 22 may be supported as by rollers 23, 24 and 25 and may be dried as by can drier 26 if desired. The beating bar 21 may be of all metal or metal with a surface covering of lucite, Bakelite, hard rubber, or other good dielectric material, and should be rotated at a speed which will produce at least three thousand beats per minute.

Fibers dropped upon the rapidly vibrating base fabric are forced into the adhesive in somewhat erect position by the mechanical forces alone or together with the electrostatic forces present the degree of erectness being dependent somewhat upon the intensity of the electrostatic field. The fabric so flocked is then passed beneath suction tube 27 which extends across the fabric to remove the excess flock, after which the fabric supported by guide roller 28 passes into high voltage electrostatic field 29, established between electrodes 30 and 31 by the impression thereupon of voltages on the order of from 20 to 100 k. v. The high potential field may be of alternating polarity if desired, but is preferably unidirectional and its energy may be supplied from low voltage alternating current line supply S through step-up transformer 32 and mechanical rectifier 33. One of the electrodes is preferably grounded.

Within the high potential field the previously deposited fibers are caused to assume a more erect position in the still soft adhesive thereby creating openings which are more or less uniformly distributed over the face of the fabric and which may be later filled by the deposit of additional flock. Such additional flock may if desired be applied while the fabric is still within the high potential field, but I prefer that the high potential field be used solely for fiber straightening purposes.

Upon leaving the high potential field, the flocked fabric is passed over guide roller 34 and beneath hopper 35 containing additional fibers 36 of the same or different kinds and/or lengths as those initially applied and which may be sifted upon the fabric while it is being rapidly vibrated by rapidly rotating polygonal bar 37. As in the first beating operation, apron 38 of wool may be interposed between the bar 37 and the base fabric. The apron may be supported as by rollers 39, 40 and 41 and may be dried as in can drier 42 if desired.

The fibers deposited in this second beating step will fill the openings created when the fibers were straightened up in the high potential field. Following the second application of flock, the excess may be removed as by suction tube 43, or by other conventional means.

If for any reason further straightening of deposited fibers and application of additional flock is desirable, the fabric may be passed through a second high potential field similar to the first and then to another flocking and beating operation. These steps may, of course, be continued until the desired result is attained. Ordinarily, two flockings interposed by a single straightening operation will be sufficient.

After the final flocking and/or straightening operation, the fabric may be passed over guide roller 44 to drier 45 where the adhesive is set and thence over roller 46 to the roll up of the finished fabric.

I have found that fabrics made in accordance with my improvements have excellent anchorange of fiber to base, erectness of pile and density of face coverage.

My invention also contemplates the application of flock of different kinds, colors, and/or lengths, whereby pleasing effects may be attained.

PROBLEM

Write three method claims of varying scope, given the specifications.

Case 15

PREPARING METHOD CLAIMS

SAMPLE CLAIMS—METHOD OF ATTACHING AND STRAIGHTENING FLOCK

1. A method of attaching and straightening flock fibers on a base material, which comprises the steps of:

depositing flock fibers upon an adhesively-coated base while the adhesive is soft,

vibrating the base to attach an end of some of the flock fibers to the still soft adhesive,

removing unattached flock fibers, and then

electrostatically *attracting* the attached fibers into erect positions on the still soft adhesive.

2. The method according to claim 1, including the additional steps of:

depositing additional flock fibers upon the still soft adhesive,

vibrating the base material to attach the ends of some of the additional flock fibers to the still soft adhesive to fill any openings on the face thereof, and

removing unattached flock fibers.

3. The method according to claim 2, including the additional steps of:

electrostatically *attracting* the attached fibers into erect positions on the still soft adhesive, and

setting the adhesive to fix the fibers to the base material in their erect positions.

COMMENTS

Action words have been italicized for illustration (only). Instead of "depositing," there could be recited two steps, *viz.*,

(a) *coating* the base with an adhesive, and
(b) *depositing* . . .

The written description states that the additional "depositing" and "vibrating" steps of claim 2 may be repeated until a desired density of flocking is achieved. Thus, an additional claim could take the form of:

> 2A. The method according to claim 2 wherein the steps thereof are continuously repeated in sequence until a predetermined density of the flock fibers is achieved.

Note how the main claim, 1, can often be lifted from the "Summary of the invention" (rule 73) given in the specification prior to the detailed description. In this case, the "summary" appears in the first full paragraph on page 2 of the specification, where the patentee tells what he thinks his invention is, in a relatively broad sense. These summaries are required by rule 73, but cannot always be relied on in practice to define the scope of the invention accurately. But in claim-drafting practice, this is usually the best guideline one has.

Case 16

PREPARING METHOD CLAIMS

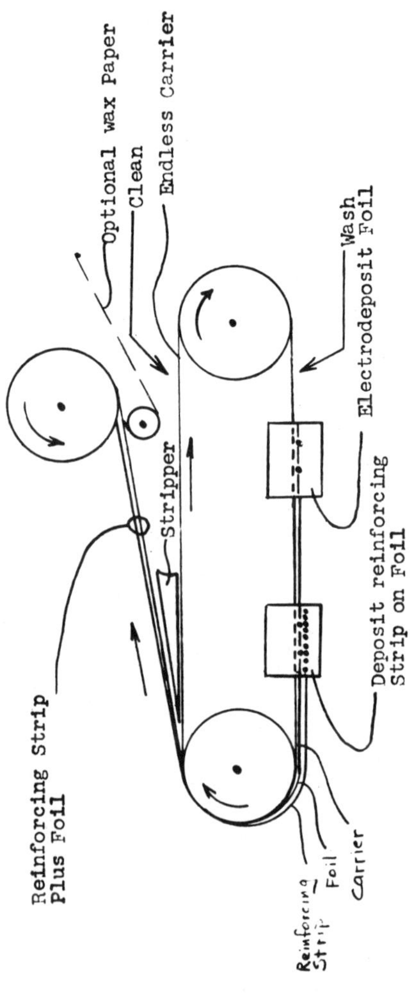

METHOD OF MAKING FOIL

PROBLEM

Write three claims of varying scope on the depicted process. Prepare a fourth claim covering zinc, tin or aluminum as the material of the foil.

Case 16

PREPARING METHOD CLAIMS

SAMPLE CLAIMS—METHOD OF MAKING FOIL

1. A method of making a continuous strip of metal foil, which comprises:

advancing an endless carrier through a metal-deposition chamber;
depositing a layer of metal foil on the carrier as it passes through the chamber;
stripping the layer of foil from the advancing carrier; and then returning the stripped carrier to the metal-deposition chamber.

2. A method as recited in claim 1, for making a continuous composite strip of the metal foil having a backing sheet, which further comprises:

depositing a continuous adherent backing sheet on the layer of foil prior to stripping the foil from the carrier.

3. A method as recited in claim 2, further comprising:

winding the composite strip of foil and the adherent backing sheet into a coil with the layer of foil exposed; and
inserting a protective layer of wax paper between the convolutions of the coil as it is wound.

4. A method as recited in claim 1, wherein the foil metal is selected from the group consisting of zinc, tin and aluminum.

COMMENTS

Claim 1 covers the endless feature without defining the reinforcing strip, which is one approach. Another equally good approach would be to cover the step of adding the reinforcing strip, in which case the endless feature could be omitted from claim 1.

Claim 2 is a dependent claim varying the preamble of the parent claim.

Claim 3 adds preferred details, and claim 4 illustrates Markush practice (Sec. 47).

Case 17
PREPARING METHOD CLAIMS

Oct. 11, 1955 A. LIPPMAN, JR **2,720,106**

METHOD FOR DETERMINATION OF ADHESION OF ICE

Filed June 9, 1953

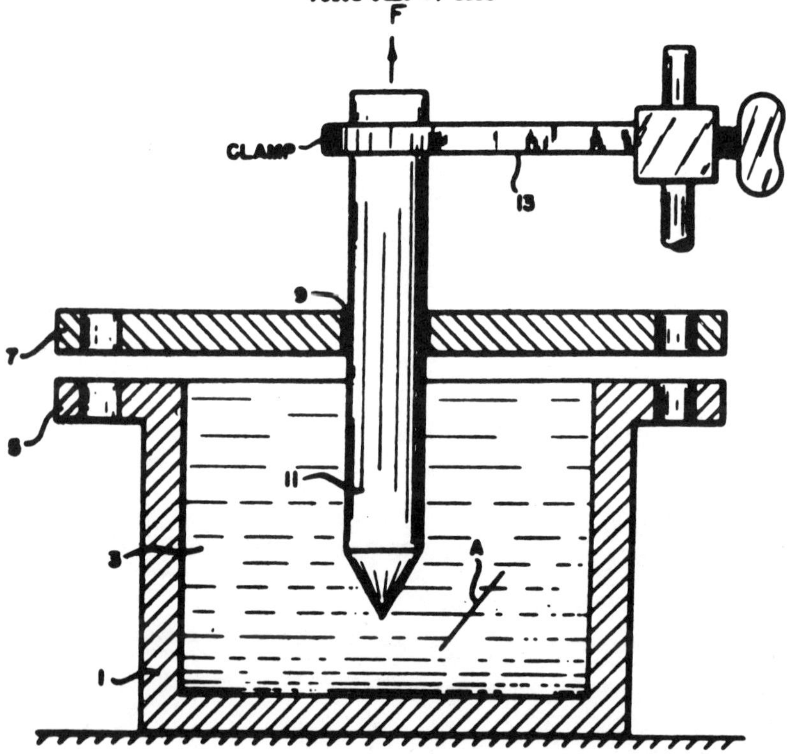

PROBLEM

Draft three method claims of varying scope, given the drawing and the following:

1) First, the container 1 is filled with a solidifiable liquid, preferably water.

2) Next, the sliver 11 is inserted through the opening 9 in the cover 7, and the sliver 11 is placed in the liquid.

3) Then, the liquid is solidified as at 3, preferably from the bottom up, so that no unsolidified liquid is trapped within the solid during freezing and to minimize the formation of faults or cleavage points, as at A, during solidification.

4) The solidified body 3 is confined within the cover 7 via clamp 13.

5) The sliver 11 is pulled up with a force F, and the pulling force is measured at the time when the sliver 11 is pulled from the solidified, confined body 3.

6) The difficulty with the prior art was that it did not use the cover 7, with the result that the solified body 3 would fracture at the fault A, giving a false reading. The object of the method is to get an accurate reading as to when the adhesion between the sliver 11 and the body 3 is broken by the force F.

Case 17

PREPARING METHOD CLAIMS

SAMPLE CLAIMS—TESTING ADHESION

1. A method of determining the adhesion of one solid material to another solid material, which comprises the steps of:

a) inserting a member formed of one of the materials into a liquid mass of the other material, the member being inserted into the mass with a portion thereof extending therefrom;
b) solidifying the mass;
c) confining the entire external surface of the solidfied mass;
d) applying a gradually increasing, separative force to both the solidified mass and the member; and
e) measuring the force at which separation is effected to determine the adhesion of the one solid material to the other.

2. A method as recited in claim 1, wherein the member is a metal and the solidified mass is ice.

3. A method as recited in claim 2, wherein the mass is solidified by freezing it in stages from the bottom thereof to the top thereof.

Case 18

PREPARING METHOD CLAIMS

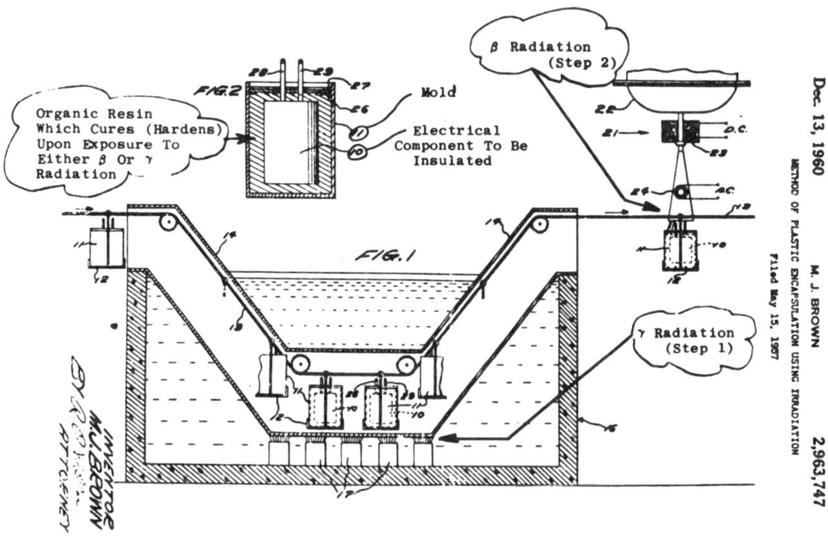

PROBLEM

The object is to encapsulate the component in a soft body of plastic having a hard outer shell. The gamma radiation cures the plastic only to the soft state and is then stopped. The beta radiation is much less penetrating, and hardens only the outer surface of the resin, so that the interior remains soft and gelatinous.

Draft a claim to this method. Assume both gamma and beta radiation, per se, are known to cure such resins for encapsulation purposes.

Case 18

PREPARING METHOD CLAIMS

SAMPLE CLAIM—ENCAPSULATION METHOD

A method of encapsulating an article, which comprises:

positioning the article in a body of liquid resin of a type that cures gradually upon exposure to both gamma and to beta radiation;

irradiating the body of resin with gamma radiation until the body has been partially cured to form a gelatinous body surrounding the article; and

irradiating the gelatinous body with beta radiation so that an outer layer thereof is cured to form a hard protective shell of the resin on the surface of the gelatinous body.

COMMENTS

Structural (apparatus) elements, such as the mold, are not needed in a method claim (Section 38), and should be omitted insofar as possible. The main method steps are "irradiating" and then "irradiating" in the prescribed sequence.

Note the phraseology "irradiating . . . until . . . cured. . . ." As discussed in Section 34, this follows the format "performing an act [irradiating] to accomplish a step or function [curing]." This could equally well have been phrased "partially curing . . . by irradiating" or "by exposing," etc. This is the form of reciting the overall step performed by the act.

The first and second steps could be combined: "irradiating *a* body of a liquid resin . . . having the article positioned therein. . . ."

Case 19

PREPARING METHOD CLAIMS

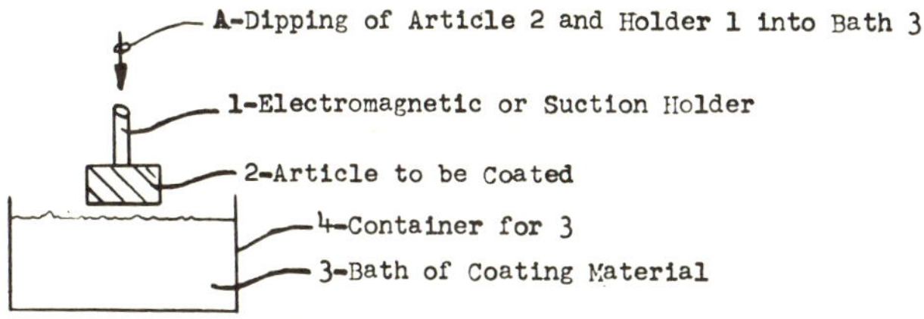

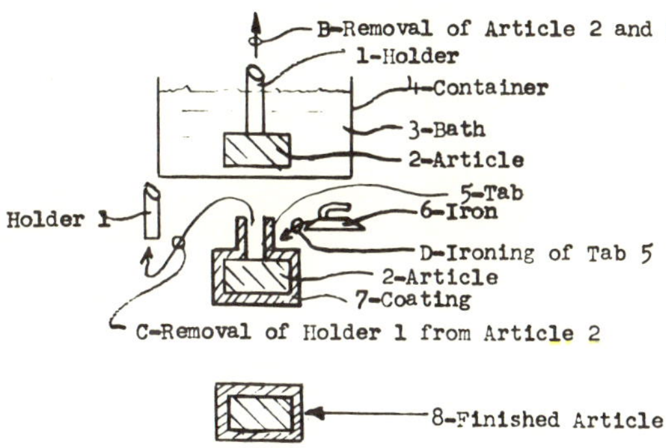

STEPS

(1) Support Article 2 by holder 1.
(2) Dip article 2 and lower end of holder 1 into bath 3, as shown at A.
(3) Remove article 2 from Bath 3, as shown at B.
(4) Remove holder 1 from Article 2, as shown at C, leaving resulting tab 5.
(5) As shown at D, iron 6 is used to flatten tab 5 to produce finished article 8 having coating 7 thereon.

NOTE- This is about the form that many informal disclosures from engineers and other technical personnel take when presented to the patent attorney or agent. Nothing fancy-- just enough to draft initial, fairly good claims.

PROBLEM

Part I—Draft one generic and two species method claims to the method shown.

Part II—Would it be proper to present claims to the coating apparatus or the finished article? Assume there are no restriction requirement problems.

Case 19

PREPARING METHOD CLAIMS

SAMPLE CLAIMS—COATING METHOD

Part I–*Generic and Species Claims*

1. A method of coating an article with a thermoplastic material, which comprises:

supporting the article with a holder;

coating the article and adjacent portions of the holder with the thermoplastic material in liquid form, and allowing the coating material to solidify;

withdrawing the holder from the article so as to leave a tab of soldified coating material projecting from the article at the portions formerly engaging the holder; and

heating and forming the tab so as to coat the portion of the article formerly engaging the holder.

2. A coating method as recited in claim 1, wherein the supporting step includes applying a partial vacuum between the holder and portions of the article, and wherein the partial vacuum is released prior to the withdrawing step.

3. A coating method as recited in claim 1, for use with a paramagnetic article, wherein the supporting step includes applying an electromagnetic force to the holder to support the article, and wherein the electromagnetic force is released prior to the withdrawing step.

COMMENTS

Step 2, "coating . . . and allowing to solidify," is a perfectly proper *step*, allowing something to happen—that is, just sitting there doing nothing. Also, the coating and allowing steps are clearly related, and can be put in the same subparagraph of the claim. They could equally well have been separated. The "allowing" concept could also have been put into the following clause instead: "withdrawing . . . after the coating has solidified." In clause 4, the "heating and forming" steps are done together and can be combined.

Part II—*Query*

1. Apparatus claims are not proper, because there is nothing new in the magnetic or vacuum holder. The sole novelty is in the manipulation (new use) of such old equipment as part of a novel coating process. New uses for old devices may be claimed only as methods. (See Section 52.)

2. Article claims are not proper, because the coated article is the same as that produced in any other manner. It has no distinguishing characteristics based on the novel method of manufacture. Also, a product-by-process claim is proper only if the article cannot be defined any other way, which is not the case here. (See Section 43.)

Case 20

PREPARING CHEMICAL PROCESS CLAIMS

MALEIC ANHYDRIDE PURIFICATION CROWELL PATENT 2,308,588

This invention relates to purification of maleic anhydride and particularly to a method for refining maleic anhydride produced by catalytic vapor phase oxidation and containing colored and/or color-forming impurities.

In the catalytic vapor phase partial oxidation of organic compounds, such as, for example, benzene, methyl-naphthalene, phenol, cresol, benzophenone, furane, diphenyl, toluene, butene, furfural, and naphthalene, to produce maleic anhydride, various methods for recovering maleic anhydride from the gaseous reaction mixtures resulting from such processes have been employed; for example, the gases have been subjected to controlled preliminary cooling to effect a partial condensation therefrom of maleic anhydride before further treatment of the gases to effect removal of remaining condensible vapors; or the gases have been conducted through an organic solvent to absorb maleic anhydride and the anhydride then has been recovered from the resulting solvent solution, as described in United States Patent 2,140,140; or the gases have been conducted into water to form an aqueous solution of maleic acid from which the acid has been recovered and converted to maleic anhydride by a dehydration process such as that described in United States Patent 1,066,853 or that described in United States Patent 2,205,402. Maleic anhydride recovered by some methods is very dark; that recovered by others is less so; but an attribute common to all such products is the presence therein of colored and/or color-forming impurities.

Hereinafter, in the specification and in the claims, maleic anhydride which contains colored or color-forming impurities to be removed will be termed "crude maleic anhydride," and colored and color-forming impurities will be designated genetically by the term "chromogenic impurities."

While it might be presumed that processes applicable to the removal of chromogenic impurities which are present in crude phthalic anhydride obtained from the catalytic vapor phase partial oxidation of organic compounds, e.g., napthalene, should be suitable also for the purification of crude maleic anhydride, such has not been found to be the case. Thus, while a treatment with sulfuric acid at high temperature followed by distillation to recover the purified product has been employed successfully to produce colorless phthalic anhydride products which are surprisingly stable, and remain colorless for long periods of time, the same process when applied to crude maleic anhydride has been found to produce products which are only temporarily colorless.

In my United States Patent 2,129,166 of September 6, 1938, I have described and claimed a process for purifying maleic anhydride by maintaining the anhydride at an elevated temperature for a sufficient time to convert chromogenic impurities to products differing greatly in volatility from the anhydride, and separating the anhydride and reaction products by volatilization. This "aging" process accomplishes as effective purification, but when a product characterized by a commercially acceptable standard of color is required from a not particularly good grade of crude maleic anhydride, it entails heating for so many hours that the process becomes an excessive burden to maintenance of low production costs.

The present invention is in the nature of an improvement over and upon the hot-aging process of my United States Patent 2,129,166.

Objects of the present invention are to provide a more rapid method of purifying crude maleic anhydride than methods hitherto available, and to effect more complete purification of crude maleic anhydride and thereby produce a purified maleic anhydride product distinguished by its unusual stability to the development of color.

In accordance with the present invention, crude maleic anhydride is subjected to a hot-aging in liquid phase in contact with an oxide of boron, or a hydrated oxide of boron, to convert the chromogenic impurities contained in the crude maleic anhydride to products which are relatively nonvolatile compared with maleic anhydride, and maleic anhydride is separated from such products by fractional distillation.

The process of the present invention accomplishes the purification of even refractory types of crude maleic anhydride rapidly and at relatively low temperatures, and produces from highly impure and highly colored grades of crude maleic anhydride excellent yields of purified maleic anhydride characterized by excellent color and stability to development of color during storage.

The crude maleic anhydride may be treated either alone in molten condition or in the form of a solution in an organic solvent which is inert to the maleic anhydride and to the reagent employed. As examples of solutions may be mentioned solvent naphtha solutions or chlornaphthalene solutions containing from 50% to 70% by weight of maleic anhydride.

Pressure, aside from its effect upon the boiling point of maleic anhydride, is substantially without effect on the present treatment, and the process may be carried out under superatmospheric, normal, or reduced pressure under otherwise like conditions with substantially identical results.

The mixture of maleic anhydride and purifying reagent may be maintained at the selected treatment temperature until the mixture or a sample thereof brought to its refluxing temperature under the pressure at which the distillation is to be effected, produces a distillate or reflux condensate, the color of which is equal to or better than a desired color standard. The mass then may be subjected to distillation to obtain a very high yield of purified maleic anhydride of the desired color standard. However, the stability of the product towards development of color may be further improved by prolonging the hot-aging period beyond the minimum time required to attain the desired color of distillate. Hence the hot-aging may be regulated to provide the desired degree of stability.

I have found that with otherwise like conditions, to effect a particular degree of purification in a particular mixture of molten maleic anhydride and a purifying described, the necessary period of reagent of the type hereinbefore treatment diminishes as the temperature of treatment is increased.

In general, with other conditions equal, an increase in the amount of the reagent employed permits a reduction in the time required to effect a commensurate purification. On the other hand, with the addition of an amount of solid reagent such as B_2O_3 greater than 30% of the crude maleic anhydride, it has been found difficult to maintain the mixture as a homogeneous mass; and when such a mixture is distilled, this lack of homogeneity appears to cause an impairment of heat transfer which results in excessive decomposition and loss of yield of refined maleic anhydride.

It is preferable to employ an amount of purifying agent not exceeding about 10% by weight of the crude maleic anhydride.

Examples of guitable compounds for effecting the purification are boric oxide and metaboric and orthoboric acids, which are hydrated boric oxide.

When the crude maleic anhydride to be treated contains free water or maleic acid, the crude product is preferably dehydrated by rectification prior to applying the purification treatment.

The purification treatment of a crude maleic anhydride which contains only a small proportion of chromogenic impurities may be effected by mixing the molten maleic anhydride with the purifying reagent, agitating the mixture for a short time, for example 10 minutes, at a temperature above the melting point of the maleic anhydride, and thereupon distilling the mixture.

However, when the crude maleic anhydride is contaminated by a relatively large content of chromogenic impurities, a short treatment with the purifying reagent may be insufficient to produce more than a small recovery of maleic anhydride exhibiting a commercially acceptable standard of color or stability towards development of color during storage. In such cases, the first part of the distillate may contain excessive proportions of chromogenic impurities, while as the distillation proceeds and thus prolongs the duration of action of the purifying agent on the crude maleic anhydride, more extensive purification takes place and the distillate becomes progressively lighter and in general has a decreasing tendency to develop color during storage. Thus, a late portion of the distillate may be actually satisfactory in color and stability to development of color on standing, but the yield of acceptable maleic anhydride so obtained may be comparatively small. Hence in the treatment of such refractory crude maleic anhydride products the crude is heated in the presence of the purifying reagent for at least three hours and usually considerably longer prior to distillation of maleic anhydride.

A good grade of crude maleic anhydride which is intermingled with a limited quantity of boron oxide can be purified to produce a distillate of a commercial standard of "whiteness" by maintaining the mixture before distillation at a suitable temperature, for example, at 150° C., for substantially less than the time necessary to effect the same degree of decolorization employing an aging treatment in the absence of the boron oxide at the same temperature; and, in general, stability against development of color during storage of the purified maleic anhydride obtained with the aid of the treatment with boron oxide is greater than that of the maleic anhydride purified by the aging treatment without the aid of the boron oxide.

Preferably the aging treatment is conducted at temperatures between 140° C. and 200° C.

The following examples further illustrate the purification process of the present invention. In these examples, deviation from colorlessness of the shade of the purified maleic anhydride in the molten state is expressed in terms of a scale of color standards wherein each color standard bears a number which is synonymous with the shade of a specific dilution of a stock aqueous solution of potassium chlorplatinate and cobalt chloride. The stock solution is prepared by adding 100 cc. of concentrated hydrochloric acid to a solution of 1.246 grams of potassium chlorplatinate (K_2PtCl_3), corresponding at 0.50 gram of platinum, and 1.00 gram of cobalt chloride hexahydrate ($CoCl_2.6H_2O$), corresponding to 0.25 gram of cobalt, in distilled water, and diluting the resulting solution with distilled water to a volume of one liter. The stock solution thus prepared is given a color number of 500 and the remaining color numbers of the scale are ascribed to solutions obtained by specific degrees of dilution of the stock solution as follows:

Color number	Dilution (parts by volume of distilled water per part of stock solution)
10	48
20	24
40	11.50
60	7.30
80	5.25
100	4.00
150	2.30
200	1.30
300	0.67
400	0.25
500	0.00

To determine the color number of a purified maelic anhydride, a molten sample of the latter is compared, under substantially identical conditions, with standard solutions which correspond to these identified by the numbers in the foregoing color scale; the number of the solution whose color is most closely approximated by the color of the molten anhydride is said to be the color number of the latter.

In the following examples "parts" signifies parts by weight.

Example 1

In the catalytic vapor phase oxidation of benzene by means of air, a crude maleic anhydride product may be obtained by contacting the reaction gases with solvent naphtha. The resulting solvent naphtha solution of maleic anhydride may be fractionally distilled to expel the solvent naphtha and yield a crude maleic anhydride.

To 100 parts of such a crude product 6 parts of boric acid were added and the mixture was heated. The boric acid dissolved and when a temperature of about 135° C. was reached, water vapor came off from the hot mixture; the maleic anhydride began to boil at a temperature between 160° and 170° C. and water was gradually expelled until the boiling point of maleic anhydride was reached. Maleic anhydride was thereupon distilled from the mixture and collected as a substantially colorless product.

A second portion of the sam crude maleic anhydride, treated by the same procedure except for omission of boric acid, yielded a deep orange-colored distillate.

Example 2

To 100 parts of crude maleic anhydride obtained in the same manner as the anhydride employed in the preceding example, 10 parts of boric anhydride (B_2O_3) were added. The mass was refluxed at atmospheric pressure for 30 minutes and then distilled. A substantially colorless distillate was obtained.

By subjecting another portion of the same crude anhydride to the same treatment except for omission of boric anhydride an orange distillate was obtained.

Example 3

Crude maleic anhydride obtained by direct partial condensation in the absence of solvents from the hot reaction gases produced by catalytic air oxidation of benzene was refluxed in a glass still fitted with a reflux condenser until no further water distilled off from the product.

100 parts by weight of the dehydrated crude anhydride were mixed with 1 part by weight of metaboric acid. The mixture was agitated in a glass vessel at 150° to 160° C. at atmospheric pressure for about four hours and then was transferred to a glass distillation flask and fractionally distilled at an absolute pressure of 60 mm. to 70 mm. of mercury. A distillate comprising 75% by weight of the still charge and a distillation residue comprising 25% thereof were obtained. The color of the distillate immediately after

distillation and after standing 20 and 50 days was 40, 100, and 100+, respectively.

A control run was conducted using the same type of dehydrated crude anhydride alone but under otherwise like conditions and fractionally distilling the product as described for the metaboric-acid-treated anhydride. The control distillate comprising about 83% by weight of the still charge had a color of 100 which darkened to 300 after only 20 days of standing.

Example 4

Boric acid (H_3Bo_3) is an amount equal to 10% by weight of the dissolved maleic anhydride, is added to a solution of maleic anhydride in solvent naphtha. The mass is refluxed at a temperature between about 120° C. and 130° C. for 30 minutes, during which time any water vapors in the reflux vapors are not condensed but allowed to escape. The mixture is then distilled. The distillate has a color equal to about 3.5 on the Barrett scale. (The Barrett scale consists of a series of fifteen standard color solutions. It is described in the Journal of Industrial and Engineering Chemistry, 1918, vol. 10, page 1008. The color number as obtained above is that of the standard color solution most nearly approximating the color of a sample of the distillate when both distillate and color solution are observed under the same conditions.)

A distillate possessing a color equal to 6.5 (Barrett scale) is produced if the addition of boric acid is omitted.

PROBLEM

Draft three claims of substantially varying scope covering the method described in the specification. Claims in dependent form may be used. The claims should not distinguish from each other by merely immaterial limitations and should distinguish over any prior art described in the specification.

Case 20

PREPARING CHEMICAL PROCESS CLAIMS

SAMPLE CLAIMS — MALEIC ANHYDRIDE PURIFICATION

1. An improved process of purifying crude maleic anhydride containing chromogenic impurities, wherein crude maleic anhydride is subjected to a hot-aging process in liquid phase, wherein the improvement comprises:

conducting the hot-aging process in the presence of a compound selected from the group consisting of the oxides and hydrated oxides of boron to convert the chromogenic impurities to products which are relatively nonvolatile compared to maleic anhydride; and then

separating the maleic anhydride from such products by fractional distillation.

2. A process as recited in claim 1, wherein the hot-aging process is carried out at a temperature between about 140° C. and 200° C.

3. A process as recited in claim 2, wherein:

the compound is selected from the group consisting of boric oxide, metaboric acid and orthoboric acid, in an amount not exceeding 10% by weight of the crude maleic anhydride.

COMMENTS

This patent was used on the February 1968 Exam. A choice was given between this patent and a mechanical structure on apparatus for delivering granular materials, Kokeisl patent 3,125,256 (Appendix B, Case 9).

Note the specification, first five paragraphs, describes the prior art, particularly the patentee's own "hot-aging" process. In paragraphs six to eight (the "summary of the invention," required by Rule 73), he tells one exactly what the invention is in a broad sense. In preparing claim 1, it is best to abstract this summary in claim language, as was done for example claim 1.

The Jepson form (Section 54) "*should*" be used for claim 1 in this case (Rule 75-e) because it is pellucid from paragraphs 5 and 6 of the specification that this "invention is in the nature of an improvement over . . . the hot-aging process of my . . . [prior] patent. . . ." Thus, this is a very clearcut "improvement" invention, so that the Jepson form should be used, with the elements of the old process set out in the preamble. (See Sections 54 and 60 (on "old combination")).

Note how phrases such as "crude maleic anhydride," "chromogenic impurities," and "hot-aging," which are defined in the specification, can and should be lifted out of the specification and used in the claim without further definition. (See Section 15 on "Support in the specification" for words used in the claims, and Section 16, that applicant can be his own lexicographer, define the words as he choses so long as he is not using a meaning repugnant to the customary meaning of the word.)

One should not attempt to claim any broader than the patentee says the invention is in the summary, nor much narrower. Note that process details such as "preferably, the aging treatment is conducted at temperatures between 140° C. and 200° C." should be left for subordinate claims. These the patentee says are important but not critical.

In chemical process claims, useful things to add in dependent claims are temperatures, pressures, times, proportions, specific materials, etc.

Case 21

PREPARING CHEMICAL PROCESS CLAIMS

PURIFICATION OF PHENOL

This invention relates to a novel process for the purification of phenol prepared by decomposition of cumene hydroperoxide.

Phenol is prepared by the partial oxidation of cumene and subsequent decomposition of the resulting cumene hydroperoxide. The decomposition reaction mixture comprises phenol, acetone, and unreacted cumene. The phenol, recovered from the cumene hydroperoxide decomposition reaction mixture by distillation methods, contains acetone condensation products, principally mesityl oxide as well as other carbonyl compounds. Although present in only minute quantities, the carbonyl compounds have color-forming tendencies which render the phenol product commercially unacceptable in many instances.

It is therefore an object of this invention to present a novel process for the purification of phenol containing carbonyl compounds as impurities therein.

In one of its broad aspects, this invention embodies a process which comprises contacting the carbonyl compound contaminated phenol with a nitrogen compound hereinafter described, forming reaction products of the said carbonyl compounds and the said nitrogen compounds and thereafter separating phenol from the said reaction products, the aforesaid nitrogen compound being represented by the formula

$$R_1-\overset{\displaystyle H}{\overset{|}{N}}-R_2$$

wherein R_1 and R_2 are selected from the group consisting of hydrogen, alkyl, cycloalkyl, aryl, alkaryl, aralkyl, hydroxyalkyl and polymethylene radicals, said polymethylene radicals together forming a heterocyclic ring in combination with the nitrogen atom to which they are attached.

Other objects and embodiments of this invention will become apparent in the following detailed specification.

In accordance with the process of this invention, the carbonyl compound-containing phenol is contacted with a nitrogen compound of the formula:

$$\begin{array}{c} H \\ | \\ R_1\text{—}N\text{—}R_2 \end{array}$$

R_1 and R_2 can be polymethylene radicals which in combination, and together with the nitrogen atom through which they are attached, form a heterocyclic ring. Also, R_1 and R_2 may be independently selected from the group consisting of hydrogen, alkyl, cycloalkyl, aryl, alkaryl, aralkyl and hydroxyalkyl.

Thus it will be seen that the nitrogen compound can be ammonia, and one of the more specific embodiments of this invention relates to a process for the purification of phenol containing carbonyl compounds as impurities, which process comprises contacting the phenol with ammonia, forming reaction products of the said carbonyl compounds and ammonia, and separating phenol from the said reaction products.

Nitrogen compounds with which the phenol can be contacted pursuant to the process of this invention further include alkyl primary amines like methylamine, ethylamine, propylamine, isopropylamine, n-butylamine, secbutylamine, beta-ethylbutylamine, amylamine, isoamylamine, alpha-methylamylamine, n-hexylamine, isohexylamine, n-heptylamine, heptadecylamine, etc., and also dialkyl secondary amines, for example, dimethylamine, diethylamine, ethylmethylamine, diisopropylamine, di - n - butylamine, di-sec-butylamine, bis(beta-ethylbutyl)amine, morpholine, and the like. One of the embodiments of this invention relates to a process for the purification of phenol containing carbonyl compound as impurities, which process comprises contacting the phenol with an alkyl primary amine, preferably methylamine, and forming reaction products of the said carbonyl compounds and the said amine and thereafter separating phenol from the said reaction products. In another embodiment, a dialkyl secondary amine, preferably diethylamine, is utilized.

Still another embodiment of this invention concerns a process for the purification of phenol containing carbonyl compounds as impurities wherein the nitrogen compound is an alkanolamine, preferably ethanolamine. Other suitable alkanolamines include 3-hydroxy-n - propylamine, 2 - hydroxy - n - propylamine, 4 - hydroxy - butylamine, 3 - hydroxy - n - butylamine, and the like, and also dialkanol amines such as diethanolamine, etc.

In still another embodiment, the nitrogen compound is benzylamine. Other such aralkyl amines like beta - phenylethylamine, alpha-phenylethylamine, beta-phenylethylamine, alpha-phenylethylamine, beta-phenylpropylamine, etc., and also diaralkylamines like di-beta-phenylethylamine and the like, are also operable.

Other nitrogen compounds of the described formula

$$R_1-\underset{}{\overset{H}{\overset{|}{N}}}-R_2$$

which can be utilized include cycloalkyl amines like cycyopentylamine, cyclohexylamine, etc., and also dicycloalkylamines such as dicyclopentylamine, dicyclohexylamine, and the like. Arylamines like aniline, 1-naphthylamine, 2-naphthylamine, N-methylaniline, N-ethylaniline, etc., as well as diarylamines including diphenylamine, di-2-naphthylamine and the like, and also alkarylamines, for example, toluidine, xylidine, o-ethylaniline, etc., are also operable. Piperidine, pyrrolidine, and other like compounds of the formula

$$R_1-\overset{H}{\overset{|}{N}}-R_2$$

wherein R_1 and R_2 are polymethylene radicals which, together with the nitrogen atoms to which they are attached, form a heterocyclic ring, can also be utilized.

The required amount of any particular nitrogen compound herein described is dependent on the concentration of the carbonyl compound impurities in the phenol product to be treated. In the usual case, from about .02% to about 0.2%, based on the weight of the phenol to be treated, is adequate although larger amounts can be utilized. The optimum amount in any particular case is in part dependent on the nitrogen compound being utilized and in part on the concentration of carbonyl compounds, the latter being readily determined by routine experimentation. The reaction products of the nitrogen compound and the carbonyl compounds, as well as any excess nitrogen compound utilized, can be separated from the phenol by acid extraction methods, distillation methods, or other suitable means. When the phenol is recovered by distillation methods, any excess of ammonia or other nitrogen compound may distill over with the phenol. This can be obviated by including only the required amount of nitrogen compound in the phenol, which amount may be readily determined by experiment. Alternatively, the excess nitrogen compound as well as the reaction products of the nitrogen compound and carbonyl compounds can be retained in the distillation bottoms by treatment with an equivalent amount of an acid, for example sulfuric acid. However, since the addition of any excess acid tends to decompose the nitrogen compound-carbonyl compound reaction products, it is preferred to avoid the use of an acid altogether and to utilize instead a higher boiling nitrogen compound, for example diethanolamine (B.P. 270° C.), to achieve the same effect.

The phenol is preferably contacted with the nitrogen compound at liquid phase reaction conditions. While this can be accomplished at normal room temperature of about 25° C., for example in the case where phenol and ammonia are contacted in aqueous solution, it may be desirable to utilize an elevated temperature within the melting and the boiling point range of phenol, i.e. from about 41° C. to about 182° C. Although the temperature is not a critical aspect of this invention, reaction rates are accelerated at higher temperatures and the necessary contact time between phenol and the nitrogen compound is thereby minimized.

The following examples are presented in illustration of the process of this invention and are not intended as an undue limitation on the generally broad scope thereof.

Example I

104 grams of phenol prepared by decomposition of cumene hydroperoxide was analyzed by gas-liquid chromatography methods and found to contain 0.16 wt. percent mesityl oxide and 0.17 wt. percent of a carbonyl compound described as an acetone trimer, as well as 0.02 wt. percent of unknown impurity. The phenol was therefore 99.65% pure. About 5 grams of ammonia in dilute aqueous solution was added to the phenol and the resulting solution was thoroughly mixed at room temperature. Thereafter, phenol was separated from the ammonia and the impurity products by distillation. Gas-liquid chromatography analysis of the recovered phenol indicated a product purity of 99.91%. There was no evidence of "acetone trimer" and mesityl oxide had been reduced to about 0.02 wt. percent.

Example II

150 grams of a phenol sample prepared by decomposition of cumene hydroperoxide was analyzed by gas-liquid chromatography methods and found to contain 0.11 wt. percent acetone, 0.13 wt. percent mesityl oxide, 0.08 wt. percent acetophenone and 0.34 wt. percent of undetermined impurity. The phenol sample was

therefore 99.34% pure. About 1.5 grams of ammonia in dilute aqueous solution was added to the phenol and the resulting solution was heated at 70° C. with stirring. Thereafter, the phenol was separated from the ammonia and the impurity products by distillation. Gas-liquid chromatography analysis indicated a product purity of 99.93%. The melting point of the product was 40.89° C.

Example III

In the purification of phenol containing carbonyl substances as impurities, the phenol is heated in mixture with about 0.2% ethanol amine, based on the weight of the phenol, at reflux conditions for a period of about 4 minutes. Thereafter, a phenol fraction substantially free of carbonyl impurities is separated from the impurity products by distillation.

Example IV

Phenol, prepared by decomposition of cumene hydroperoxide and containing carbonyl compounds as impuriities, is mixed with .02% ethylamine, based on the weight of the phenol, in aqueous solution. The solution is thoroughly mixed for about 2 hours at room temperature. Thereafter, the impurity products are extracted from the solution with dilute hydrochloric acid. The phenol is recovered substantially free of carbonyl substances.

Example V

In the purification of phenol containing carbonyl impurities, about .02% dimethylamine, based on the weight of the phenol, is prepared in aqueous solution and admixed with the phenol. After about 1 hour of mixing at room temperature, the impurity products are extracted with dilute hydrochloric acid and phenol is recovered substantially free of carbonyl impurities.

Example VI

In the purification of phenol containing carbonyl impurities, the phenol is heated in mixture with about 0.2% benzylamine, based on the weight of the phenol, at a temperature of about 70° C. for a period of about 5 minutes. Thereafter, the impurity products are extracted with dilute hydrochloric acid and phenol is recovered substantially free of carbonyl substances.

PROBLEM

Draft three claims of substantially varying scope covering the process described in the disclosure. The *three* claims should be in *independent* form. The claims should not distinguish from each other by merely immaterial limitations and should distinguish over any prior art described in the disclosure.

Case 21
PREPARING CHEMICAL PROCESS CLAIMS
SAMPLE CLAIMS—PURIFICATION OF PHENOL

1. A method of purifying phenol in a mixture containing phenol and carbonyl-compound impurities, this method comprising contacting said mixture with a nitrogen compound of the formula R_1-NH-R_2 wherein R_1 and R_2 are selected from the group consisting of hydrogen, alkyl, cycloalkyl, aryl, alkaryl, aralkyl, hydroxyalkyl, and a polymethylene radical which taken together with the nitrogen atom forms a heterocyclic ring, with the carbonyl compounds, and separating the phenol from the resulting reaction products.

2. A method of purifying phenol in a mixture containing phenol and carbonyl-compound impurities, this method comprising contacting said mixture *in the liquid phase* with a nitrogen compound of the formula R_1-NH-R_2, wherein R_1 and R_2 are selected from the group consisting of hydrogen, alkyl, cycloalkyl, aryl, alkaryl, aralkyl, hydroxyalkyl, and a polymethylene radical which taken together with the nitrogen atom forms a heterocyclic ring, the amount of the nitrogen compound being *from about 0.02 to about 0.2* percent by weight of the weight of the phenol present in the mixture, to thereby react the nitrogen compound with the carbonyl compounds, and separating the phenol from the resulting reaction products.

3. A method of purifying phenol in a mixture containing phenol and carbonyl-compound impurities, this method comprising contacting said mixture with *ammonia at a temperature from about 41° to 182° C*, the amount of ammonia being from about 0.02 to about 0.2 percent by weight of the weight of the phenol present in the mixture, to thereby react the ammonia with the carbonyl compounds, and separating the phenol from the resulting reaction products by *distillation*.

COMMENTS

The question asked for three independent claims; otherwise dependent claims would be more suitable here. Since claims of varying scope were requested, claim 3 need not include everything in claims 1 and 2, but this would not hurt either. Italicization in claims 2 and 3 is solely to show what was added.

Case 22

PREPARING ARTICLE OF MANUFACTURE CLAIMS

Sept. 18, 1962 **L. MORRIS** **3,054,212**

SOAP DISH

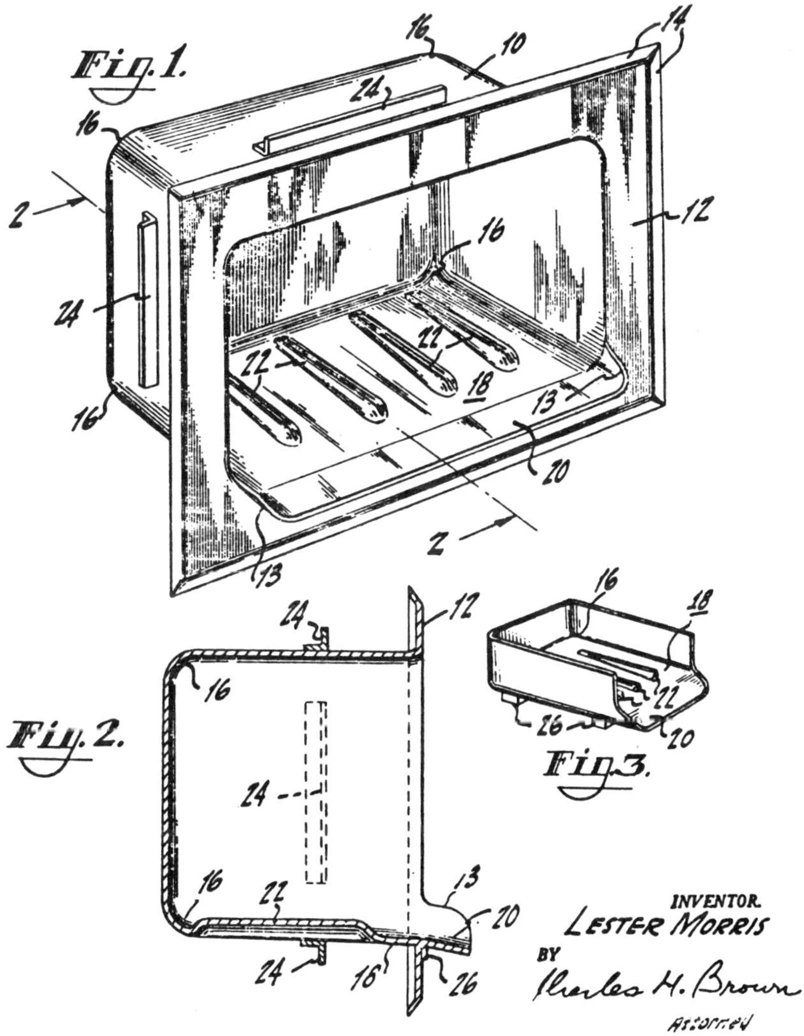

PROBLEM

Draft three claims of varying scope. Label them "broad," "intermediate" and "narrow."

Case 22

PREPARING ARTICLE OF MANUFACTURE CLAIMS

SAMPLE CLAIMS—SOAP DISH

BROAD:

1. A soap dish, which comprises:

a housing having a bottom wall and a frontal opening, the bottom wall being slanted downward from the back toward the frontal opening; and

a plurality of spaced projections extending upward from the bottom wall, the upper surfaces of the projections defining a generally horizontal surface for supporting a cake of soap out of contact with the bottom wall, the projections being spaced to define channels therebetween such that water on a cake of soap placed on the projections drains downward between the projections and then along the slanted bottom wall out the frontal opening.

INTERMEDIATE:

2. A soap dish as recited in claim 1, wherein the projections comprise spaced parallel ribs running from the back toward the front of the housing.

NARROW:

3. A soap dish as recited in claim 2, for mounting into a recess in a wall, wherein:

the housing also includes three side walls and a rear wall, all shaped to fit in the recess with the frontal opening substantially flush with the wall; and

the housing further includes means for mounting the housing

in the recess, and a downwardly turned lip forming a continuation of the bottom wall and projecting forward beyond the frontal opening to permit water to drain out of the dish and away from the wall.

COMMENTS

Claim 1 illustrates typical technique in preparing article of manufacture claims. The procedure is essentially the same as for machine claims, but usually much simpler:

(1) Select a preamble—"soap dish"—pretty easy.

(2) Find and name what you think are the essential elements (A) "housing," or base, support, frame, etc.; (B) "projections," or ribs, etc. (see Sec. 16 on "naming"). Best to make projections separate element, as they would not have to be integral with housing.

(3) Select essential features of elements (Sec. 22). Slanted bottom wall and opening (Sec. 23 on claiming holes) for base (the side walls and wall mounting are not vital to operation); and horizontal surface, with channels, formed by projections.

(4) Connect elements together (Sec. 25-26) and with workpiece (soap), "extending upward from the bottom wall," "for supporting a cake of soap."

(5) Preferably, tell what elements do and how, as in last three lines of claim 1.

Claim 2 further defines the "projections" as "ribs," which hopefully is fairly significant. See Section 57 on claims of varying scope, and Section 53 on dependent claims.

Claim 3 is a dependent claim adding one element and also further defining one element of a parent claim. Claim 3 also contains a revised preamble, adding further details of the setting for the dish (See Sec. 53). Note the wall into a recess of which the wish is placed should *not* be an element of the claim. See Sections 12, and 13. Put the workpiece or background in the preamble; and try to claim the combination in the form in which it would be sold (Sec. 32), not as it would be used (wherever possible).

Case 23

PREPARING ARTICLE OF MANUFACTURE CLAIMS

March 16, 1954 E. HASLETT **2,672,250**

COASTER

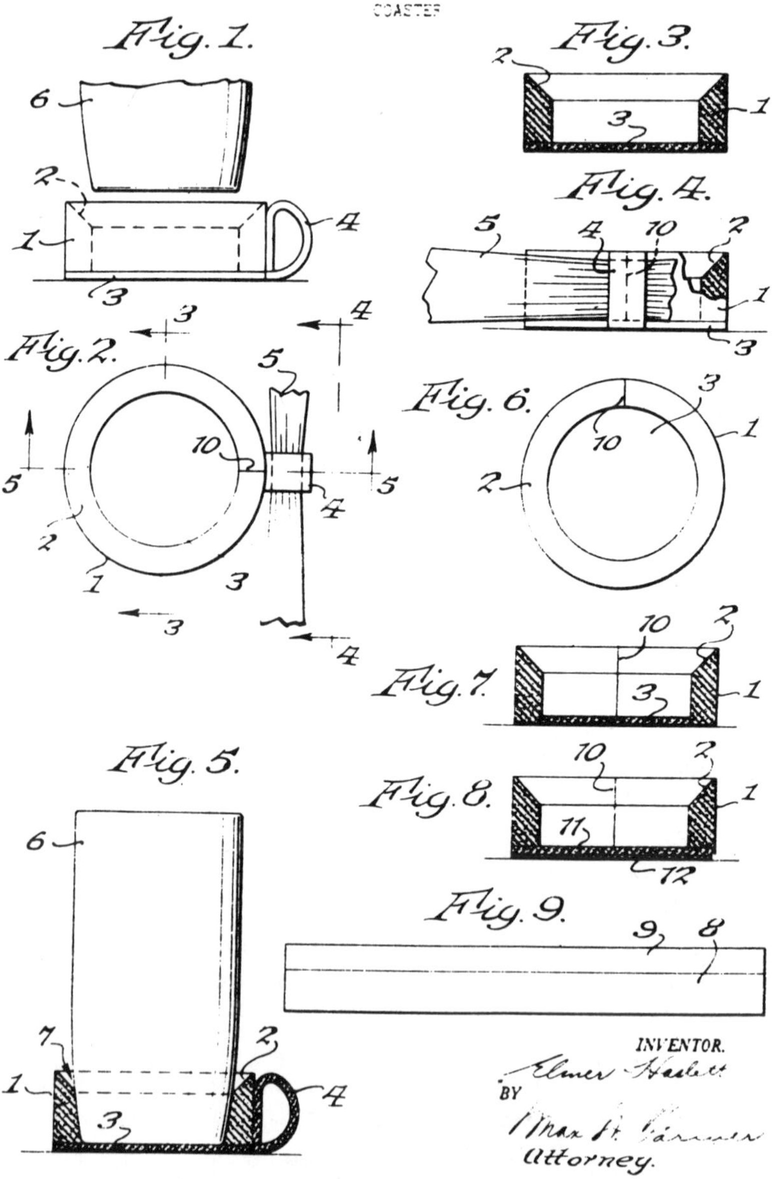

PROBLEM

Draft three claims of varying scope to the coaster shown in the drawings. Following are some of the disclosed features and characteristics of the coaster:

1) **It will remain attached to the bottom of a glass even when picked up.**
2) **It fits glasses of different sizes.**
3) **It is light in weight.**
4) **It absorbs condensate that runs down the side of the glass.**
5) **Its outside surface will not mar a surface on which it is placed.**
6) **The annular ring 1 and the disc-like bottom 3 are made of a cellular, elastic material.**
7) **The upper end of the annular ring 1 is bevelled as at 3.**
8) **The loop 4 may hold a napkin 5.**
9) **The ring 1 and the bottom 3 may be molded as a unit, or may be separate items which are adhesively attached.**
10) **The bottom 3 may also be made of an elastic material such as rubber, but in any event its outer surface is liquid impervious.**
11) **The cellular, elastic material of the ring 1 and the bottom 3 is liquid absorbent.**
12) **The basic shape is old.**

Case 23

PREPARING ARTICLE OF MANUFACTURE CLAIMS

SAMPLE CLAIMS—COASTER

1. A coaster for a glass, which comprises:

a cup-shaped glass-receiving member having a flat bottom of liquid-impervious, elastic material, and an upstanding side wall of an elastic, liquid-absorbent material.

2. A coaster as recited in claim 1, wherein the interior rim of the side wall is so bevelled inwardly that as the glass container is inserted into the coaster, the bottom edge of the glass engages the rim and expands the side wall outwardly, allowing entry of the container into the coaster.

3. A coaster as recited in claim 2, further comprising a handle formed integrally with the bottom and attached to the exterior of the side wall.

COMMENTS

Similar to the previous problem, this rather easy-to-write claim involves selecting a preamble and essential elements, here a "glass-receiving member" which includes a "bottom" and a "side wall." Note that while the shape of the 'member" is per se old (see item 12 above) the characteristics of the bottom ("liquid-impervious" and "elastic") and the side wall ("elastic" and "liquid-absorbent") result in a novel coaster. The glass (workpiece) is set forth in the preamble. Claim 2 adds mechanical detail about the side wall and claim 3 adds a new element ("handle") both in independent fashion.

Case 24

PREPARING COMPOSITION OF MATTER, CHEMICAL PROCESS AND METHOD OF USE CLAIMS

PARABANIC ACID DERIVATIVES

ABSTRACT OF THE DISCLOSURE

Compound of the formula

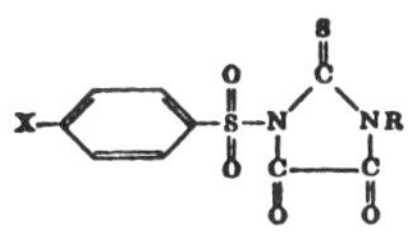

wherein X is selected from the class consisting of amino, nitro and alykyl of not more than 4 carbon atoms, and R is selected from the class consisting of hydrogen, alkyl and alkenyl of not more than 12 carbon atoms are useful as phytotoxicants.

This invention relates to parabanic acid derivatives which are useful as biological toxicants, particularly phytotoxicants.

The parabanic acid derivatives of this invention can be represented by the formula

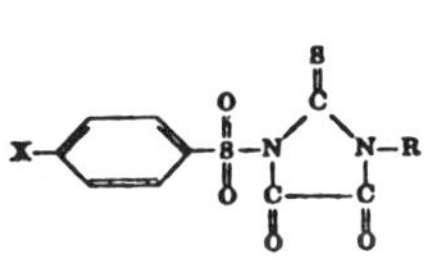

wherein X is selected from the group consisting of nitro, alkyl of not more than 4 carbon atoms and amino, and R is selected from the group consisting of hydrogen, alkyl of not more than 12 carbon atoms and alkenyl of not more than 12 carbon atoms.

The parabanic acid derivatives of this invention can be prepared by reacting axolyl chloride with para - substituted benzenesulfonyl thioureas having the R substituent. The substituted thioureas can be prepared by reacting para-substituted benzenesulfonyl isothiocyanate with a primary amine or a secondary amine having the R substituent. Many of the thioureas which are reacted with oxalyl chloride in accordance with this invention can be prepared by processes disclosed in Martin et al. U.S. Patent No. 2,411,661.

The reaction is usually carried out at temperatures from about 40° C. to about 150° C. in the presence of an aromatic hydrocarbon medium. Suitable aromatic hydrocarbon media include benzene, toluene, xylene and the like. The reaction is preferably carried out by slowly adding oxalyl chloride to an admixture of para-substituted benzenesulfonyl thiourea and aromatic organic media, and heating the reaction mixture at reflux until the emulsion of hydrogen chloride substantially ceases.

The desired product can be separated from the reaction mixture by conventional means for example distillation, extraction and the like.

The following examples will illustrate the invention. In these examples, as well as in the specification and appended claims, parts and percent are by weight unless otherwise indicated.

EXAMPLE 1

About one mole of oxalyl chloride is added dropwise to about one mole of p-nitrobenzenesulfonyl thiourea in benzene at about 25° C. Upon evolution of hydrogen chloride, the reaction mixture is heated at reflux for about two hours. The product is 1 - (p-nitrobenzenesulfonyl) thioparabanic acid.

EXAMPLE 2

A solution of 1 - (p-aminobenzenesulfonyl) - 3 - ethyl thiourea in ethylene dichloride is treated by dropwise addition of oxalyl chloride and the mixture heated to reflux. After the evolution of hydrogen chloride has substantially ceased, the following crystalline product is recovered from the reaction mixture:

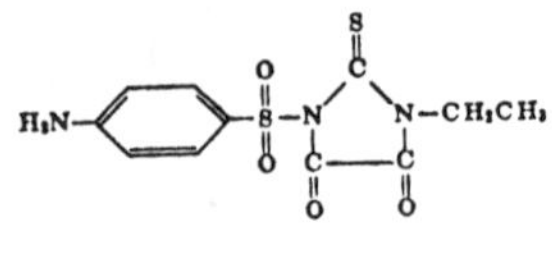

[1-(p-aminobenzenesulfonyl)-3-ethylthioparabanic acid]

EXAMPLE 3

The procedure of Example 1 is repeated using 1-(p-methylbenzenesulfonyl) - 3 - (2-ethylhexyl) thiourea in place of p-nitrobenbenesulfonyl thiourea to form 1 (p-methylbenzenesulfonyl) - 3 - (2-ethylhexyl)thioparabanic acid.

Following substantially the same procedure as in the foregoing examples, the following compounds of this invention are prepared:

1-(p-aminobenzenesulfonyl)-3-n-butylthioparabanic acid
1-(p-ethylbenzenesulfonyl)-3-ethylthioparabanic acid
1-(p-n-butylbenzenesulfonyl)-3-methylthioparabanic acid
1-(p-aminobenzenesulfonyl)-3-allylthioparabanic acid
1-(p-nitrobenzenesulfonyl)-3-dodecylthioparabanic acid
1-(p-nitrobenzenesulfonyl)-3-(2-pentenyl)thioparabanic acid

The parabanic acid derivatives of this invention are useful for controlling or modifying the growth of plants. They are effective as general phytotoxicants including postemergent phytotoxicants and preemergent phytotoxicants, but their most outstanding utility is as preemergent phytotoxicants. Furthermore, these compounds are characterized by a broad spectrum of herbicidal or phytotoxic activity, i.e., they modify the growth of a wide variety of plant systems including both monocotyledonous and dicotyledonous plants. For the sake of brevity and simplicity the term "active ingredient" will be used hereinafter in this specification to describe the parabanic acid derivatives of the above formula.

When operating in accordance with the present invention, effective amounts of the active ingredients are dispersed in soil or plant growth media and applied to plant systems in any convenient fashion. Application to the soil or growth media can be carried out by simply mixing with the media, by applying to the surface of the soil and thereafter dragging or discing into the soil to the desired depth, or by employing a liquid carrier to accomplish the penetration and impregnation. The application of liquid and particulate solid phytotoxic compositions to the surface of soil or to plant systems can be carried out by conventional methods, e.g., power dusters, boom and hand sprayers and spray dusters. The compositions can also be applied from airplanes as a dust or a spray because of their effectiveness at low dosages. In a further method, the distribution of the active ingredients in soil can be carried out by admixture with the water employed to irrigate the soil. In such procedures, the amount of water can be varied with the porosity and water holding capacity of the soil to obtain the desired depth of distribution of the phytotoxicants.

The exact amount of active ingredient to be employed is dependent upon the response desired in the plant as well as such other factors as the plant species and stage of development thereof, the specific soil and depth at which the active ingredients are distributed in the soil and the amount of rainfall as well as the specific active ingredient used. In foliat treatment for the control or modification of vegetative growth, the active ingredients are supplied in amounts from about 1 to about 50 or more pounds per acre. In applications to soil for the control or modification of the growth of germinant seeds, emerging seedlings and established vegetation, the active ingredients are applied in amounts from about 0.01 to about 25 or more pounds per acre. In such soil applications, it is desirable that the active ingredients be distributed to a depth of at least 0.2 inch and preferably in amounts from about 0.01 to about 5 pounds per acre.

The active ingredients can be uesd alone or in combination with a material referred to in the art as a phytotoxic adjuvant in liquid or solid form. The phytotoxic compositions are prepared by admixing the active ingredient with an adjuvant including diluents, extenders, carriers and conditioning agents to provide compositions in the form of finely divided particulate solids, granules, pellets, solutions and aqueous dispersions or emulsions. Thus thc active ingredient can be used with an adjuvant such as finely divided particulate solid, a liquid or organic origin, water, a wetting agent, dispersing agent, an emulsifying agent or any suitable combination of these.

Typical finely divided solid carriers and extenders which can be used in the phytotoxic compositions include for example, the talcs, clays, pumice, silica, diatomaceous earth, quartz, fuller's earth, salt, sulfur, powdered cork, powdered wood, walnut flour, chalk, tobacco dust, charcoals, volcanic ash, and the like. Typical liquid diluents include for example water, kerosene, Stoddard solvent, hexane, benzene, toluene, acetone, ethylene dichloride, xylene, alcohols, Diesel oil, glycols and the like.

The phytotoxic compositions, particularly liquids and wettable particles, usually contain as a conditioning agent one or more surface-active agents in amounts sufficient to render a given composition readily dispersible in water or in oil. By the term "surface-active agent" it is understood that wetting-agents, dispersing agents, suspending agents, emulsifying agents and the like are included therein.

Surface-active agents which can be used in the phytotoxic compositions of this invention are set out, for example, in Searle U.S. Patent 2,426,417, Todd U.S. Patent 2,655,447, Jones U.S. Patent 2,412,-510, and Lenher U.S. Patent 2,-139,276. A detailed list of such agents, is also set forth by J. W. McCutcheon in "Soap and Chemical Specialties," November 1947, page 8011 et seq., entitled "Synthetic Detergents"; "Detergents and Emulsifiers—Up to Date" (1960), by J. W. McCutcheon, Inc., and Bulletin E-607 of the Bureau of Entomology and Plant Quarantine of the U.S.D.A. In general, less than 15 parts by weight of the surface active agent is present per 100 parts by weight of phytotoxic composition.

Although the invention is described with respect to specific modifications, the details thereof are not to be construed as limitations except to the extent indicated in the following claims.

The embodiments of the invention in which an exclusive property or privilege is claimed are defined as follows.

PROBLEM

Draft three claims in *independent* form which distinguish over any prior art described in the specification. Claim 1 should cover broadly the parabanic acid derivatives of the invention. Claim 2 should cover broadly the method of making parabanic acid derivatives of Examples 1 and 2. Claim 3 should cover a method of using the compound of Example 2.

Case 24

PREPARING COMPOSITION OF MATTER, CHEMICAL PROCESS AND METHOD OF USE CLAIMS

SAMPLE CLAIMS— PARABANIC ACID DERIVATIVES

1. A compound having the formula:

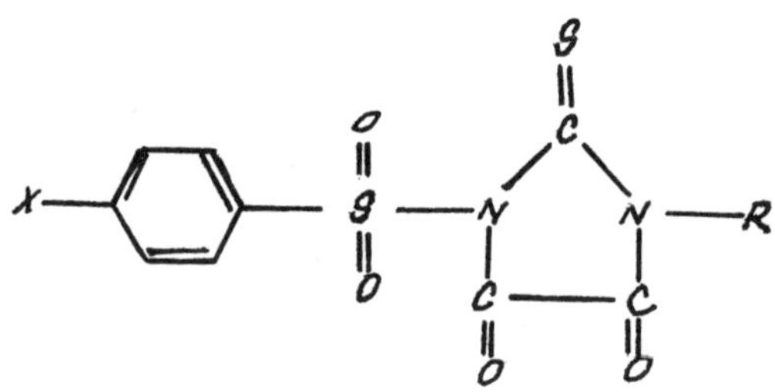

wherein X is selected from the group consisting of nitro, amino, and alkyl of not more than four carbon atoms, and

wherein R is selected from the group consisting of hydrogen, alkyl of not more than 12 carbon atoms, and alkenyl of not more than 12 carbon atoms.

2. A method of preparing a compound selected from the group consisting of 1-(p-nitrobenzenesulfonyl) thioparabanic acid and 1-(p-aminobenzenesulfonyl)-3-ethylthioparabanic acid, which comprises:

(a) reacting oxalyl chloride with a material selected from the group consisting of p-nitrobenzenesulfonyl thiourea and 1-(p-aminobenzenesulfonyl)-3-ethyl thiourea, at a temperature sufficient to form the corresponding compound and to drive off hydrogen chloride; and

(b) recovering said compound from the mixture.

3. A method of modifying plant growth, comprising dispersing

in plant growth media an amount of 1-(p-aminobenzenesulfonyl)-3-ethylthioparabanic acid effective to modify the plant growth.

COMMENTS

From the September 1970 Agent's Exam. Claim 1 must be "a broad claim" to the derivatives of the invention. This should be very simple, given the specification. In fact, one can practically copy the "summary of the invention," column 1, lines 35-48. Note—do not claim any broader than the specification clearly states, such as by imagining that X could just as well be pentyl (5 carbons) or benzene.

Claim 1 follows the general form in the book, Section 46, and various modifications of form are possible. However, "a compound having the formula" or "of the formula" is a very common, standard form for claims to new compounds, or molecules. One could equally well claim "parabanic acid derivatives having the formula. . . ." Avoid any statement of use in a "pure compound" claim, such as "phytoxicants having the formula. . . ." There is no need to state the preferred use in a compound claim. In this problem, as given, the compounds are presumably novel; this, claim 1 should cover the compounds per se, for any use.

Note the classic Markush phraseology, "wherein R is selected from the group consisting of. . . ." (See Section 47.) It is now equally correct to use the "alternative" phraseology provided in MPEP 706.03(y): "wherein X is nitro, amino, or alkyl. . . ."; and "wherein R is hydrogen, alykyl of . . . , or alkenyl of. . . ." Note that this use of the alternative is limited by the Notice to materials "so related as to constitute a proper Markush group," as in this problem.

Of interest, this claim covers 150 individual compounds (not counting isomers), 25 R substituents with any of six X substituents. Note also, that it is not necessary to know what parabanic acid is, or "nitrobenzene sulfonyl. . . . ," etc. to write this claim. One can safely copy the pertinent language in the specification, where the patentee is supposed to state what the claimed invention is as well as giving examples, etc.

CLAIM 2

This requires more care, as one wants a *broad* method (as to the steps performed) for making the two specific compounds of Examples 1 and 2. Thus, the preamble should be limited to the method of preparing the two named compounds (not a broad Markush group), and preferably using the named reactants, oxalyl chloride and the particular thiourea precursors. The student could not conceivably know what if any other precursors or chlorides could be substituted, and would be very ill advised to guess.

As to the process steps, these should be phrased fairly broadly since a broad method claim was requested. The common steps of examples 1 and 2 appear to be mixing (or adding, treating, reacting), heating (or refluxing), and recovering. These can be combined into two or even one step the choice is optional so long as the scope is correct.

A single step process could be phrased as "reacting [A] with [B] at a temperature sufficient to form [C]." There would be no problem in including the broad temperature ranges (40-150° C) from column 1, lines 59-60, but most preferred process details should be omitted since this is to be a broad claim to the process, and it does not appear from the specification that process parameters are critical to success.

Note, on the law (not part of *this* question), that a process for making a novel compound, such as in claim 2, is not necessarily patentable (nonobvious) merely because the compound is patentable. (See Section 36.) The CCPA has held (over vigorous dissent and with much adverse criticism by the bar) that a so-called "obbious method" of making a new compound or product of any kind is not patentable merely because the compound or product is patentable.

CLAIM 3

This claim is to cover a method of using the specific compound of Example 2, which should be specifically named in claim 3. The preamble could be "controlling" or "modifying" plan growth (not both in the alternative), as indicated in column 2, line 44. The only possible step can be "dispersing" (col. 2, lines 57-58) or contacting, treating, etc. This claim typifies the relatively rare case of a single-step method (Section 33), which is perfectly permissible.

Note that this method of using claim is a "new use" claim (Section 52), and that such claims can be patentable for new uses for new compounds as well as for old compounds. If the compounds turned out to be old for other purposes, the "use claims" such as claim 3 could still be patentable if the use was unobvious. This happened in the DDT case (*Ex parte Müller*) cited in the book, Section 52.

Note that claim 3 specifies "an amount . . . effective to . . ." The more recent cases hold that the recitation ". . . an effective amount . . ." is *not* indefinite. This is particularly true in this case, where the specification defines the term "effective amount" (col. 2, lines 56, etc.) and gives many examples of effective amounts. Obviously, in the present case, the invention as to use of the compounds resides in discovering that the parabanic acid derivatives *are* plant growth modifiers (inhibitors or poisons), rather than in the determination of particular amounts needed to effect such modification. As stated in the specification, the amount can vary quite widely based on particular plants, soils, even rainfall, for a particular one of the compounds.

Note that this question asked for all claims in *independent form*, as sometimes is requested. Make certain to follow directions! In this case, because of the specific nature of the claims requested, including varying statements of the compounds involved in each successive claim, it would be difficult and highly cumbersome to use a dependent claim anyway. If this question were stated otherwise, there would be nothing wrong with dependent claims "crossing statutory classes" (process, compound), such as "A method of preparing the compounds recited in claim 1 . . . ," or "A method of modifying . . . comprising dispersing . . . a compound as recited in claim 1. . . ."

For those interested in the chemical details, parabanic acid is:

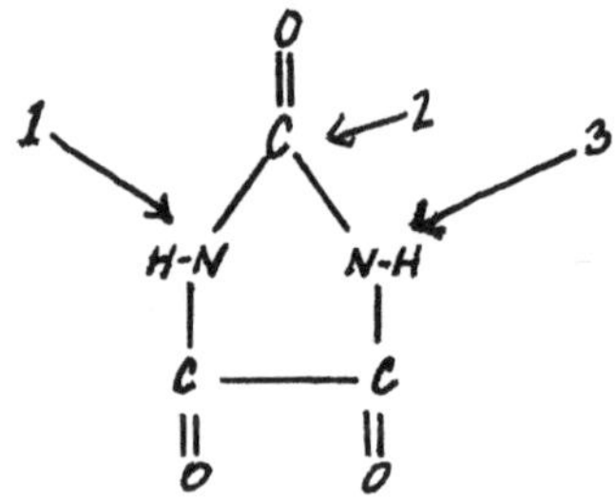

This is a cyclic diacid formed by oxidation of uric acid. *Thio* parabanic acid substitutes = S for the = 0 in the 2 position. The thiourea radical is:

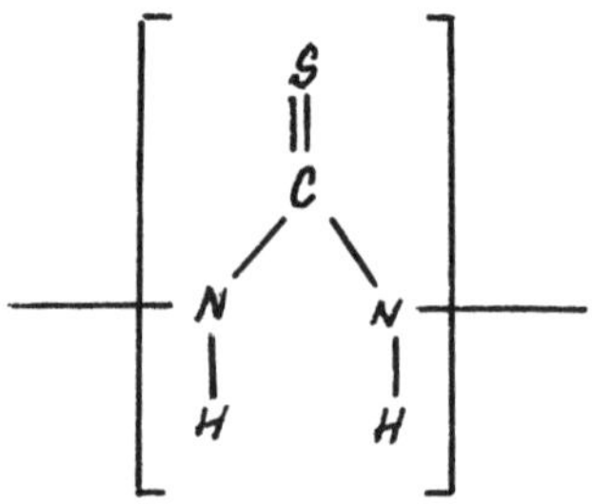

Oxalyl chloride is:

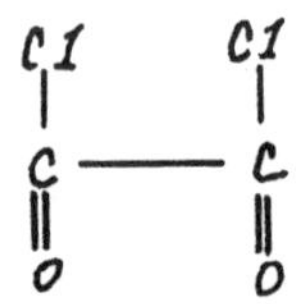

Thus, with HCl driven off, the amine nitrogens of the thiourea bond to the carbons of the oxalyl radical to form the parabanic ring.

PART II — Criticizing "Sloppy Claims"

The following examples are from Agents' Exams given between August 1966 and September 1970, where the student was given a specification and a set of claims, and asked to comment on errors or possible errors in those claims.

This required a detailed knowledge of the law, rules and Patent Office practices on many points of claim-drafting law practice.

Case 25
CRITICIZING "SLOPPY CLAIMS"
(Suction Cleaner)

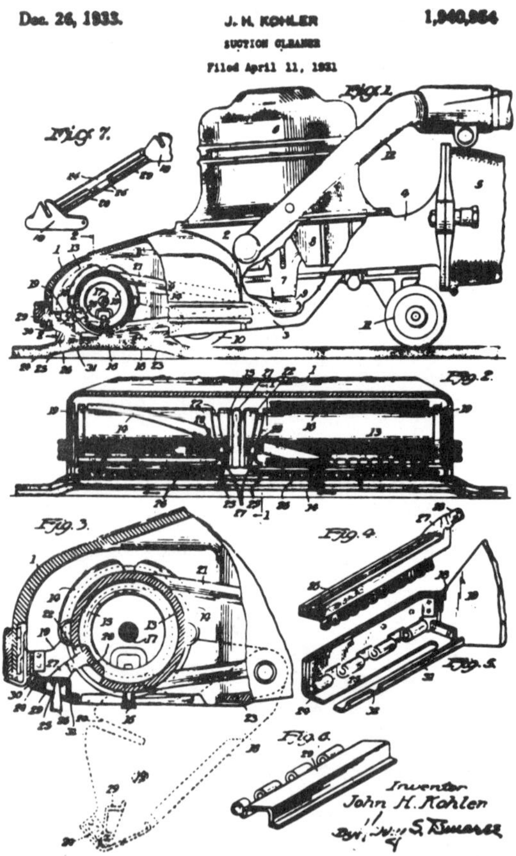

SPECIFICATION

The present invention relates to suction cleaners and particularly to new and improved agitating means in suction cleaners. More specifically the invention comprises the provision, in a suction cleaner, of the combination of a rotary agitator, embodying both positive beating and brushing means, with a reciprocating brush whose direction of movement is parallel to the axis of the rotary agitator.

It is an object of the present invention to provide a new and improved suction cleaner. It is a further object to provide new and improved surface-agitating means in a motor-driven suction cleaner. A still further object is the provision, in a suction cleaner, of combined rotary and reciprocating agitating means. Still another object is the provision of a suction cleaner in which rotary agitating means are provided in the suction cleaner nozzle from which a reciprocating brush is driven. A still further object is the provision, in a motor driven suction cleaner, of a rotary agitator embodying positive agitating means and brushing means, and a horizontally reciprocating agitator comprising a brush. These and other objects will appear upon reading the following specification and claims and upon considering in connection therewith the attached drawing to which they relate.

In the drawing in which a preferred embodiment of the present invention is disclosed:

> Fig. 1 discloses a side view of a modern suction cleaner, with certain parts broken away, with the present invention embodied therein;
>
> Fig. 2 is a section upon the line 2-2 of Fig. 1;
>
> Fig. 3 is an enlarged section thru the cleaner similar to that shown in Fig. 1 showing, in dotted lines, the supporting frame of the rotary and reciprocating agitators pivoted downwardly from the nozzle mouth;
>
> Fig. 4 is a view in perspective of a reciprocating brush element;
>
> Fig. 5 is a partial view in perspective of the agitator-supporting frame showing the reciprocating brush seat;
>
> Fig. 6 is a view in perspective of the pivoted luatch or retaining cover of the brush seat;
>
> Fig. 7 is a view in perspective of the pivoted brush supporting frame.

The present invention is disclosed embodied in a modern suction cleaner which comprises a main casting or casing including a nozzle 1, a fan chamber 2, which is interiorly connected to the nozzle 1 by means of the air passageway 3, and an exhaust outlet 4 to which is detachably connected a dust bag 5. A motor casing 6 is positioned upon the main casing immediately above the fan chamber 2 and houses a suitable driving motor, which is not shown but the shaft 7 of which extends downwardly thru the fan chamber 2 where the fan 3 is mounted thereon. The shaft 7 extends into the rear end of the air passageway 3 where it carries a suitable pulley 9. The cleaner is movably supported by means of front wheels, of which one is shown resting upon a supporting surface being indicated by reference character 10, and by means of a rear wheel 11. A pivoted handle 12 is mounted on the casing of the cleaner and provides means by which the operator can propel the machine over the surface covering undergoing cleaning.

Within the nozzle 1 of the cleaner and extending thereacross is a rotary agitator which, in its general appearance, differs but slightly from a common and well known type. This agitator comprises a large diameter cylindrical body 13 on the surface of which are mounted helically-extending rigid beater elements 14, 14 which extend substantially the length of the agitator, with the exception of a small central portion which is reduced in diameter to form a pulley 15. Carried by the cylindrical body 13 of the agitator and seated within the periphery thereof are longitudinally-extending brushes 16, 16 which are of a common and well-known type and which are removably secured in their seats in any suitable manner. Upon the surface body 13 of the agitator, immediately adjacent the sides of the pulley 15, which is connected to the driving pulley 9 on the motor shaft 7 by a suitable belt 21, are encircling cam races positioned below the periphery of the body. These cam races are designated by the reference characters 22, 22 and have a function which will be apparent from the following description. A shaft 17, which extends thru the agitator with each of its ends resting in a seat 20 in the side member 19 of the frame 18, rotatably supports the agitator.

Between the side members 19, 19 of the frame 18, which is pivoted within the nozzle 1 at a point somewhat in the rear of the rear nozzle lip 23, is a front cross member 24 which extends closely adjacent and parallel to the front wall of the nozzel 1, being secured thereto, and holding the frame 18 within the nozzle, by ordinary and suitable means which form no part of the present invention. This cross member 24 slopes downwardly from the lower end of the front wall of the nozzle 1 and forms the front lip of the nozzle thereby cooperating with the rear nozzle lip 23 in defining the nozzle mouth. The lip 24, however, differs from the usual nozzle lip thru being provided with two transversely-extending openings or apertures 25, 25, each of which extends parallel to the axis of the rotary agitator and has a length substantially equal to half the length of the agitator. Seated upon the lip 24 with their bristles projecting downwardly thru the apertures 25, 25 are brush elements 26, 26 which comprise rigid backs having the flexible brush bristles mounted therein. The length of each brush element 26 is slightly less than the length of the aperture 25 in the nozzle lip 24 thru which the bristles extend, thereby permitting the brush a limited range of movement transversely of the agitator mouth, that is, parallel to the longitudinal axis of the agitator itself. To make use of this permissible movement of the brushes 26, 26 in order to obtain the maximum agitation of the surface covering undergoing cleaning, each brush element 26, 26 is provided at its inner end, with an upstanding lug 27 on which is mounted a roller or head 28 of such size that with the brush seated upon the front lip 24 the roller 28 extends within the adjacent cam race 22 in the cylindrical body 13 of the rotary agitator, with the result that upon the rotation of that body the brush 26 will be reciprocated back and forth as the roller 28 is moved by the cam. To insure the permanent positioning and the correct alinement of each brush 26 with the aperture 25, relative to which it must slide, a pivoted cover element 29 is provided which is pivotally mounted upon a pin 30 carried by the side of the transverse member or lip 24. The cover member 29 is adapted to closely enclose the sides and top of the brush 26 to hold it in contact with the upper surface of the lip 24. To prevent the unintentional displacement of the cover relative to the lip the forward edge of the lip is curved upwardly, as at 31, and is adapted to resiliently clamp the forward edge of the cover which extends against it in the closed position.

In the operation of a suction cleaner constructed in accordance with the present invention, the suction-creating fan within the fan chamber is rotated by the driving motor resulting in a decrease in the pressure existing within the nozzle thereby effecting the lifting of the surface, covering undergoing cleaning against the nozzle lips, as is clearly indicated in Figure 1. With the surface covering suspended against the nozzle lips the rotary agitator is rotated at high speed by the driving belt 21 which is connected, as aforedescribed, between the pulleys

15 and 9, the latter carried by the motor shaft. The beating elements 14, 14 upon the agitator function to violently vibrate the surface covering to dislodge the embedded foreign matter which is positioned therein. The longitudinally-extending brushes 16, 16 upon the agitator surface cooperate with the rigid beating elements 14, 14 and assist in the removal of the light dirt. As the agitator is revolved the brushes 26, 26, which are carried by the front nozzle lip 24 of the cleaner, are reciprocated transversely or parallel to the longitutinal axis of the rotating agitator and, thru extending below the nozzle lip, contact the surface covering which is positioned adjacent thereto and function to deflect, bend and agitate the pile of that covering in a direction at right angles to the direction of vibration and bending effected by the beating elements 14, 14 and the brush elements 16, 16 carried by the rotary agitator.

To effect the removal of the agitators constructed in accordance with the present invention from the nozzle, it is only necessary to pivot the supporting frame 18 downwardly to the position shown in dotted lines in Figure 3. With the frame so positioned the rotary agitator may be lifted therefrom, the supporting shaft 17 sliding outwardly from its open ended seat 20 in each end plate 19 of the frame. With the rotary agitator removed it is then possible to pivot each brush-holding cover 29 on its supporting pin 30, a recess 32 being conveniently provided in the forward edge of the nozzle lip into which an instrument such as a screw driver may be inserted to wedge the cover free from the retaining forward edge of the lip. With the cover pivoted back it is then possible to remove the brush 26 by merely lifting it from the lip and withdrawing the bristles thru the aperture 25 thru which they were extended, there being two brush elements, the same operation is necessary to release the other element.

If desired, a single brush element extending across the full width of the nozzle may be used instead of two brush elements.

PROBLEM

Part I—Given the specification and drawings, comment on the "Problem Claims" following.

Part II—Assuming you were asked to write three claims of varying scope, and indicate "broadest," "intermediate" and "narrowest." Write *only* the first such claim ("broadest"), and indicate what features you might include in the other two claims.

PART I—PROBLEM CLAIMS

Below is the statement of the question from the April 1967 Exam:

> This part of the examination consists of three claims drawn to a suction cleaner apparatus proposed to be added to an application having the accompanying specification and drawings. Certain words and phrases in the claims have been italicized and numerically designated. *Most, but not all,* of the italicized portions represent instances where in the claims fail to comply with United States patent law or accepted claim writing practice. In addition to the 10 numbered items in the claims, there are two additional instances involving deficiencies in the claims in substance or form. These instances should be listed as items 11 and 12 in your answer. For each number in each claim and for items 11 and 12, make a short statement as to why the underlined portion does represent a defect, if such is the case.

NOTE: For this exercise, try to find *four* more major errors (11), (12), (13), 14) and discuss.

Case 25

CRITICIZING "SLOPPY CLAIMS"
(Suction Cleaner)

SAMPLE CLAIMS TO BE CRITICIZED

6. A suction cleaner comprising a body supported by wheels, a drive motor mounted on said body forward of *the rear pair of wheels* (1), *the nozzle* (2), formed on the front portion of the body having a lip, *a flexible* (3) agitator roll mounted in said nozzle, and drive means connecting said motor and agitator to cause it to rotate. Said nozzle being further provided with a rear lip, a supporting frame for the agitator pivotally mounted adjacent *said lip* (4), a single brush agitator mounted on said other lip and extending across the full width of said nozzle, *adapted to reciprocate* upon rotation of said rotary *agitator* (5), drive means for said reciprocating agitator including *a cam race* (6), on said rotary agitator.

7. The suction cleaner of this invention *includes* (7) a motor, a suction creating means, a rotary agitator, and an additional brush agitator mounted to reciprocate relative to the surface being cleaned.

8. A suction cleaner according to *claims 6 or 7* (8) in which the nozzle has mounted therein forward of the rotary agitator *two reciprocating agitators* (9) having brush elements made of *nylon* to ensure long *wear* (10).

COMMENTS ON PART I—PROBLEM CLAIMS

1(a). There is *no antecedent* in the claim for the "rear pair" of wheels. The claim has previously stated only that there are wheels.[1*]

---

1. These notes are not part of the suggested typical answers, but rather further comments and suggestions for students. *See* Section 20.

*See notes—Case 25, following these comments.

1(b). Also, there is *no support in the disclosure* for the rear "pair" of wheels. The specification discloses "*a* rear wheel 11." A claim may not be contrary to, or inconsistent with, the specific example(s) disclosed.[2]

2. There is *no antecedent* in the claim for "*the* nozzle."[3]

3. There is no support in the disclosure for a "flexible" agitator roll. The agitator 14 is shown as a solid member.[4]

4. "Said lip" is indefinite because two different lips have previously been recited.[5]

5. "Adapted to reciprocate . . ." was stated by the Patent Office to be improper "functional language without supporting structure." The "adapted to" phrase attempts to imply the mounting of the brush element (26) and its driving connection to the rotary agitator (13).[6]

6. "A cam race" was considered "OK."[7]

---

2. See rule 75(d) and Section 15:

   > "The . . . claims must conform to the invention as set forth in the remainder of the specification and the terms and phrases used in the claims must find clear support or antecedent basis in the description. . . . "

   In these problem claims, when the specification is given, watch very carefully for discrepancies between the specification and the problem claims. It would help to find the place in the specification where each term in the claim is described and underline, so as to locate ambiguities and misdescriptions. Even though the number of wheels probably is not important, it would not be *improper* to claim a pair if supported by the description.

3. *See* Section 20. This should have been "*a* nozzle."

4. *See* note 2, *supra*.

5. *See* Section 20.

6. *See* Section 28. This may be a debatable point, as "adapted to" phrases are used fairly often in practice, but quite obviously such usage should be avoided on the Agent's Exam. Make certain that sufficient structure is included to support functional statements.

7. The drive means does *include* a cam race (22), as well as other elements. There is nothing wrong with claiming *a* cam race when two are shown, if the invention can work with one. *See* Section 17. Also, this is not an attempt to claim "a hole" positively (Section 23), since the *race* can be considered a structural unit including the walls of the groove, which actually do the guiding.

7. The wrong verb form, "includes," is used. The claim must form a *complete sentence*, being the direct object of the (understood) phrase "I claim. . . ."[8]

8. "Or 7" is improper. A dependent claim must refer back to and further restrict a single preceding claim.[9]

9. "Two reciprocating agitators" is improper. If this claim is dependent from claim 6, the recitation of *two* agitators is *inconsistent* with "a *single* brush agitator" in the parent claim. A dependent claim may not add statements inconsistent with the structure of the parent claim.[10] If claim 7 is the parent claim, "an additional brush agitator" is already an element of the parent claim, so that it would be improper to add two more, apparently as new elements. This would be *double inclusion* of elements.[11]

10. There is no support in the disclosure for "nylon."[12] The specification does not state of what material the brushes are made.[13]

OTHER ERRORS

11. Claim 7 is directed to a catalog of elements. There is no connection or cooperation whatever between the elements.[14]

12. Claim 6 is composed of two sentences, and is thus improper under Patent Office practice.[15]

---

8. This should read "including" rather than "includes." "Which includes" would be a satisfactory alternative. There is nothing wrong with the transitional phrase "including" rather than "comprising," although the latter is much more common, and is almost conventional for mechanical cases. *See* Section 7. Note: watch for little things (Section 4), capital letters, periods, punctuation, verb tenses.
9. Rule 75(c). *See* Section 53.
10. *See* Section 7.
11. *See* Section 18.
12. *See* note 2, *supra.*
13. This would probably be immaterial to the invention, but it is not improper in this context to claim too narrowly.
14. *See* Section 25.
15. *See* Section 4.

13. There is no antecedent in claim 6 for "said *other* lip." Nothing in the claim would tell which of the lips referred to is meant by "other."

14. In claim 6, "a *single* brush agitator" is not illustrated in the drawings.[16] Every feature of the invention specified in the claims must be shown in the drawings.[17]

The foregoing were the four other specific errors identified by the Patent Office. There may be other errors of a lesser or more technical nature. For example:

15. Claim 6 does not have sufficient elements or cooperation between elements to make the complete combination stated in the preamble. Specifically, the combination claimed is a "*suction cleaner*," but nothing is recited in the claim to produce suction.[18]

16. "Of this invention" in claim 1 appears to be surplusage. The same could be said of "to insure long wear" in claim 8.[19]

SOME GENERAL NOTES ON ANSWERING SLOPPY CLAIMS QUESTIONS

Be quite specific as to the error; don't just say "no antecedent" or "indefinite," etc. For example (1) item (3) "*flexible* agitator," point out that the description does not state that the agitator is flexible and, if you noted it, that the agitator is illustrated as being solid. If you remembered that the rules of practice provide that all terms in the claims must find clear support or antecedent basis in the description, you could mention this. There is no need to cite rule number[20] or the exact language so long as the substance is correct.

---

16. Although it is described in the last paragraph of the description as an alternative.
17. Rule 83. *See* Section 15.
18. Even though the suction elements are *per se* conventional, either they should be included or, preferably, the claim should be in Jepson form. *See* Section 54.
19. *See* Section 9.
20. Rule 75(d).

At the other extreme, there is no need for a long essay or any discussion of philosophy or policy. Up to two or three short sentences along the lines of the suggested answers are sufficient.

Normally, do not volunteer how you would do it correctly. This can hardly gain, and might lose if you are wrong.

Where you think there are two things wrong, mention both in the order you think most important. For example, if you thought (as many do) that "nylon" (item 10) is a trademark and might be improper for that reason,[21] mention also that there is no support in the description (since nylon is not a trademark and you might get most of the credit for having the right answer, as well as an incorrect statement).

PART II—SAMPLE CLAIMS AND COMMENTS SUCTION CLEANER

From the specification, it is quite clear that the general arrangement of the suction cleaner, including the motor, fan (8), rotary agitator (13), beaters (14) and rotary brushes (16) is conventional. The invention is stated to relate to adding the transversely reciprocating brushes 26 to this old structure. Thus, an improvement or Jepson-type claim should be suggested.

Such a claim follows, of fairly broad scope:

> 1. An improved suction cleaner of the type including a movable casing, a rotary agitator mounted in the casing for rotation about an axis transverse to the direction of movement of the cleaner, and drive means for rotating the agitator and producing suction within the casing; wherein the improvement comprises:
>
> (a) a brush element mounted in the casing for reciprocating movement parallel to the axis of rotation of the agitator; and
> (b) means for reciprocating the brush element in timed relation to the rotation of the agitator.

---

21. Section 48.

Note Section 54, and new rule 75(e) with respect to Jepson-type claims. It would probably not be necessary in claim 1 to specify the mechanical details of the cam-type drive linkage between the agitator and the reciprocating brushes. This per se is generally conventional. The main point of novelty, so the specification states, is in adding the transverse brushes. This should be claimable fairly broadly, within the general combination of the suction cleaner.

Claims 2 and 3 could add details of the cam drive, and the specific mounting and positioning of the reciprocating brushes with respect to the agitator.

It would be best not to use dependent claims adding *only* matters that the specification (or any instructions given with the problem) says are old. Thus, such things as the helical beater (15) structure would not be appropriate to add via a dependent claim since it is part of the old structure *and* does not coact in any new way with the new structure.

Case 26
CRITICIZING "SLOPPY CLAIMS"
(Steam and Dry Iron)

Jan. 5, 1954 J. D. VOSKRESENSKI 2,664,653

STEAM AND DRY IRON

Filed Aug. 17, 1951

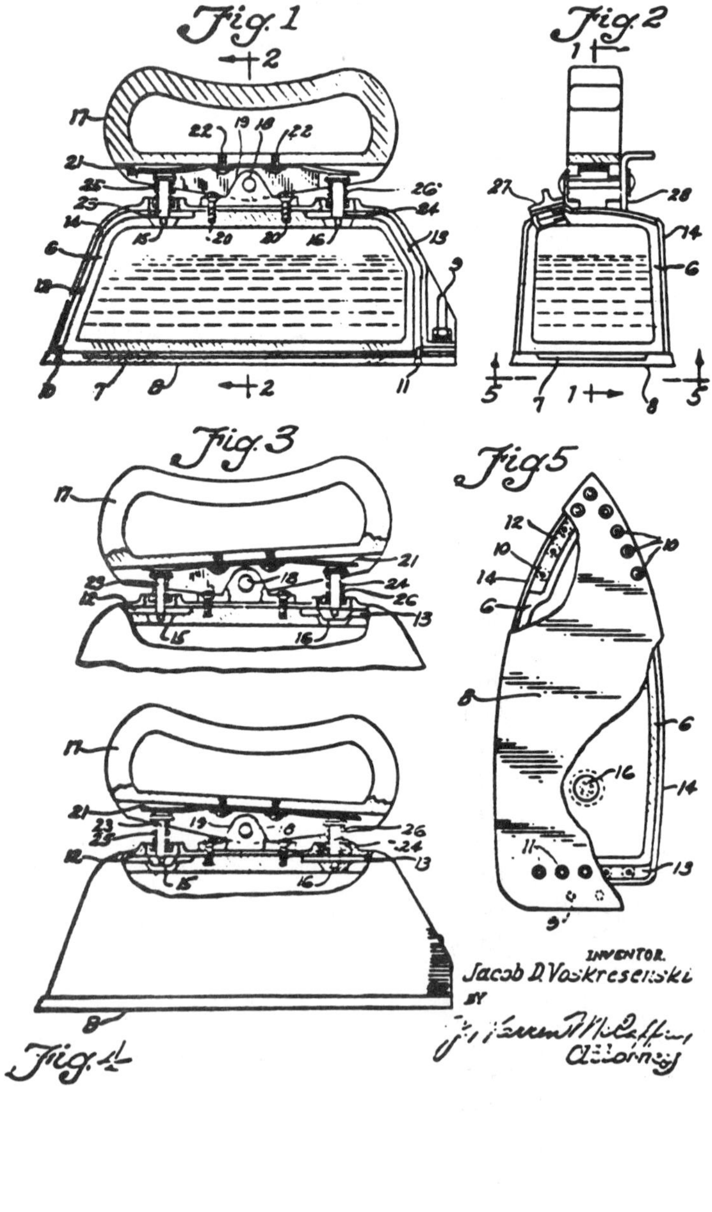

Excerpts From Specification

. . . . .

The feature of this invention is the supplying of steam to the article being ironed in advance of, and while moving the iron across the article whether in a frontward or backward direction.

However, if the operator desires to iron dry, he may shut off the supply of steam and use the device of this invention as a dry iron.

An equally important feature of this invention is the controlling of the supply of steam through either the front or rear ports of the iron to the article being ironed as desired. The operation of the means for controlling the supply of steam is simple and coincides with the normal movement by hand of any iron over an article to be ironed.

. . . . .

The water chamber of the steam iron is indicated as 6 and the upper section of the chamber becomes a steam dome when the water is heated sufficiently by electrical element 7. The heating element is encased in the bottom of the iron by a flat ironing surface 8 and connection between usual electric cords and the heating element 7 is made by wiring not shown to the electrical terminals 9.

A plurality of steam ports represented by 10 are located in the flat ironing surface 8 around the front end of the iron and a similar plurality of ports 11 are located in the flat surface 8 around or across the back end of the iron. The front ports 10 lead to the forward steam chamber 12 while the rear ports 11 connect with the rear steam chamber 13. The front steam chamber 12 may encircle the forward part of the iron and back along the sides of the iron as far as desired. Similarly the back steam chamber 13 may extend across the back as shown and also extend back along the sides of the iron as desired. However, in order to accomplish one of the features of the iron of this invention the front and rear steam chambers cannot be connected. The chambers are formed between the wall of the combination water and steam chamber 6 and the outside casing 14 of the iron. In areas of the side walls beyond the limits of front steam chamber 12 and rear steam chamber 13 the casing 14 and wall 6 of the combined steam and water chamber are contiguous as seen in Figures 2 and 5 of the accompanying drawing.

A steam valve 15 controls the passage of steam from the steam and water chamber 6 to the front steam chamber 12 and a similar valve 16 controls passage of steam into the rear chamber 13. In Figure 1 the two steam valves 15 and 16 are shown in closed positions. In Figure 4 valve 15 is open and 16 is closed which would be their relative positions when the iron is being moved forward. In Figure 3 front valve 15 is closed while rear valve 16 is open which would be their relative positions when the iron is being moved backward. The operation of these steam valves 15 and 16 is accomplished by handle 17 which is free to rock on pin 18 in trunnion 19 which is bolted by means 20, or in any other way connected to casing 14.

A strip of spring steel 21 is fastened to the underside of handle 17 by any means, such as bolts 22, and is preformed so that its two end sections bear down on the heads of valve stems 23 and 24 so as to keep steam valves 15 and 16 closed as shown in Figure 1.

. . . . .

When the operator of the steam iron decides to move it forward, he naturally presses on the rear of the handle so that the front of the iron will slide over the article being pressed. Thus in the normal operation of the iron he inclines the handle down in the rear and it rocks on pin 18 so that the forward part of the handle is up. This movement of the handle causes steam valve 15 to open up whereas steam valve 16 is firmly shut as shown in Figure 4.

Similarly if the operator decides to pull the iron backwards across the article being ironed, he bears down on the forward end of the handle, and thus on the front of the iron, thereby releasing pressure on the back end of the rockable handle and the back of the iron, so that the iron will slide backward over the article being ironed. This manipulation of the handle in turn closes steam valve 15 tight and allows steam valve 16 to open as shown in Figure 3.

The obvious reason for so operating the handle of the steam iron is to simultaneously operate the steam valves and thus supply moist steam through ports 10 when moving the iron forward while ironing, and through ports 11 when moving the iron backward. Thus supplying moist-steam to the article being ironed eliminates otherwise sprinkling or wetting the article before ironing.

. . . . .

PROBLEM

Given the drawing and excerpts from the specification, criticize errors in the folowing "sample" claims 1-7.

SAMPLE CLAIMS TO BE CRITICIZED

1. A combination steam and dry iron, comprising a body having a water chamber therein and front and rear steam chambers. The iron includes a bottom member, a first plurality of openings formed in the forward portion of the bottom plate and communicating with the front steam chamber, a second plurality of openings formed in the rear section of the bottom plate, and a toggle member connected to alternately activate the valve means whereby the iron may be operated either forwardly or backwardly to iron clothes more effectively than heretofore.

2. An iron including push-pull valve means for automatically spraying steam ahead of the iron when moving forwardly and behind the iron when moving backwardly.

3. Apparatus as recited in claims 1 or 2, wherein the water chamber is omitted and steam is supplied directly to the iron from a central steam boiler through a flexible hose.

4. A base 8, a heater 7, a plurality of valves 15-16, a selective actuator 21 for the valves selected from the group consisting of springs, weights and levers, a plurality of steam ports 10-11, and a handle 17.

5. A method as recited in claim 4, further comprising the step of moving the iron alternately forward and back to iron the clothes.

6. A method as recited in claim 5, further comprising a pair of leaf springs for actuating the valves when the handle is pivoted.

7. Any and all novel features described, referred to, exemplified or shown.

Case 26

CRITICIZING "SLOPPY CLAIMS"
(Steam and Dry Iron)

COMMENTS

This specification was given on the August 1966 Exam, and the examinees were asked to criticize defective claims, rather than to prepare claims to a structure as had been customary in the past. The "sample claims to be criticized" used here are similar to those used on the Exam, but not identical.

The following list covers errors and debatable points which were intentionally made in the "sample" claims. There may be other errors.

Claim 1, in general. As an overall criticism, this claim does not set forth all of the elements necessary to "the invention," as defined in the specification. In particular, there is no specific description of the main point of the invention, which has to do with supplying steam selectively through front and rear ports as the iron is moved forward and back, by manipulating the handle to actuate valves. Thus, the claim is "incomplete" (See Section 63) and "inconsistent with the disclosure" (Section 15).

Claim 1, line 3, the claim consists of two sentences rather than one. (See Section 4.)

Lines 3 and 5, "plurality of openings" are made "elements" of the claim. (See Section 23.) Holes must not be positively recited. This should read, for example, "a bottom member having a plurality of openings . . . [etc.]."

Lines 4 and 6, "bottom *plate*" is "indefinite" (Section 20). This should read bottom "member," as in line 3. One must use consistent terminology for the same element throughout the claim.

Lines 4 and 6, no antecedent for "*the* forward portion" or "*the* rear section." It is at least debatable whether or not "bottom members" inherently have forward or rear sections. (See Section

16 and Section 12.) Better practice is, for example, "a bottom plate having a forward portion . . . etc."

Line 6, no connection of the second plurality of openings with the rear steam chamber. Also, no connection between the water chamber and the steam chamber, and nothing about heating the water. Thus, the claim is drawn, in part, to a "catalog of elements." (Section 25.)

Line 7, "toggle member." Mechanically this is not a "toggle member" but even if the student did not know this, the word "toggle" does not appear anywhere in the specification. Terms and phrases used in the claims must find clear support or antecedent basis in the specification. (Rule 75(d) and Section 15.) If this type of question is given, read the specification fairly closely and watch for inconsistencies in terminology.

Line 7, "connected to." It is doubtful whether this phrase sets forth enough structural cooperation with the other elements. (See Section 27.) There is insufficient structure recited to support the functional statement.

Lines 7 and 8, "*the valve means.*" No antecedent. This should have been made an element of the claim. (See Section 20.)

Lines 8 and 9, "whereby." The function immediately following "whereby" has nothing to do with the claimed structure in that all ordinary irons may be operated either forwardly or backwardly. The statement about ironing more effectively does necessarily follow from the previously recited structure. (See Section 29.)

Also, laudatory expressions of this type ("more effectively than heretofore") are not permitted. This is "surplusage." (Section 9.)

Claim 2, line 1. It seems unclear whether "*push-pull* valve means" has any meaning, and this language is not used in the specification. This clause is vague and indefinite. (Section 64.)

Line 1, this iron does not work "automatically." Thus, the claim is "misdescriptive" and "inconsistent with the specification."

Line 1, the claim is a "single means" claim. (See Section 31.) The statute (35 U.S.C. § 112) sanctions "means plus function" clauses only in claims to *combinations*. Also, the claim may be objectionable as being too broad, in that the broad means plus function language comes at the point of novelty. (Sections 31 and 28.)

Line 1, the transition "including" is acceptable. (Section 7.) However, "comprising" is preferred.

Claim 3, line 1, "claims 1 *or* 2." Rule 75(c) states that dependent claims must further restrict a *single* preceding claim. (See Section 53.)

Line 2, *omitting* the water chamber. See above, a dependent claim must *further restrict* the preceding claim. Thus elements cannot be subtracted, because this is a broadening of the claims.

Line 2 and 3, steam boiler and water hose. This runs afoul of rule 83, that the drawing must show every feature of the invention specified in the claims. (Section 15.) Also, this is not described in the excerpts from the specification which were given (although it was described in the full specification as a conventional technique for commercial establishments).

Line 2, "steam *is supplied*." This sounds like a method limitation, and would be better defined (if included at all) in such terms as ". . . further comprising a central steam boiler, and a flexible hose . . . etc."

Claim 4, line 1, no preamble. Claims normally have some form of preamble, and it may be improper to omit it altogether. (See Sections 6 and 12.)

Lines 1-4, reference numerals. There is no objection to the use of reference characters in claims, but this is done very rarely. However, when used, the characters should be enclosed in parenthesis. This is provided on an optional basis in a notice "Guidelines for Drafting a Model Patent Application under the Revised Rules," 832 O.G. 5 (November 1, 1966). (Section 19.)

Lines 1-4. The claim is merely a "catalog" of elements, with no structural or operational cooperation set forth. (See Section 25.) The claim must be drawn to an assembled, operable combination. This type of claim is often called an "aggregation," meaning as claimed. (Section 61.)

Lines 2 and 3, "*selected from the group* . . ." This is an attempt to use Markush language (Section 47) for mechanical elements, which has been held improper in decided cases. The Markush type of alternative phraseology is limited to chemical cases where no generic expression is available. Also, the complete expression is alternative, which is improper. (See Section 21.) Note also that weights and levers are not disclosed or shown, which is improper, as noted earlier, because it lacks "support in the description."

Line 4, the steam "ports" (holes) are claimed positively.

Claim 5, line 1, the "*preceding* claim (4) is not a method claim. It is an improper dependent claim because it is "inconsistent" with its parent claim.

Lines 2 and 3. The step added by the subclaim is only the overall step of moving the iron in the conventional manner. It is probably objectionable, or at least poor practice, to add dependent claims which add only highly conventional steps. (Section 58.)

Claim 6. This is a dependent *method* claim adding *only* further details of *structure,* which is improper. Dependent method claims should add method steps or further define method steps. Also, apparatus limitations should be avoided as far as possible in method claims. (See Sections 53 and 38.)

Line 2. There is no antecedent for "when the handle is pivoted," *in either Claim 6 or "parent" Claims* 5 or 4.

Claim 7. This is a so-called "omnibus" claim, which is improper under 35 USC 112. Such claims have been held not "to particularly point out and distinctly claim" the invention. (Section 2.)

GENERAL APPROACH TO "SLOPPY CLAIMS" QUESTIONS OF THIS TYPE

Given the first drawing, specification and sloppy claims, skim the claims first to see what they cover, generally, and mark obvious or trivial errors. (Here, unlike the previous case, the possible errors were not underlined). Then read the specification fairly carefully against the claims. You must understand the main points of the invention fairly well to find some of the more sophisticated errors (incomplete, omits essential elements, reads on admitted prior art, etc.).

Underline the main elements (from the claims) in the specification, and make sure all are described in the same or consistent terminology. Make sure that everything in the claims is described, and that all structure claimed is shown in the drawings.

Then, of course, all of the formal, grammatical, and language errors described in the book must be found and identified, and answers written along the lines suggested in the previous problem.

One had approximately one and one-half hours to answer this type of question.

Case 27

CRITICIZING "SLOPPY CLAIMS"
(Bomb-Proof Coating)

PROTECTION DEVICE AGAINST AERIAL AND OTHER BOMBARDMENT

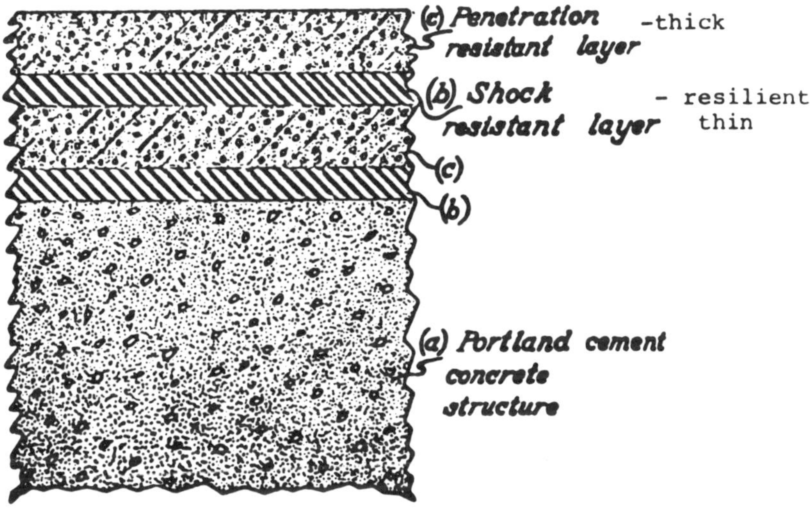

This invention relates to the safeguarding of structures and various objects of importance from the destructive effects of aerial or other bombardment. The invention also relates to the composition of materials which are used, and the way in which the materials are integrated to give the best protection.

One of the important factors in defense is the safety of many of the structures which are essential to the continuance of economic life, during was as well as peace. Among structures which represent great engineering feats, the preservation of which would be a necessity in waging a defensive war, there might be mentioned the Panama Canal locks and numerous dams, such as Boulder Dam. Unfortunately, these edifices were built without anticipating the effectiveness of aerial bombardment, and must now be considered with reference to their vulnerability to attack.

An object of the present invention, therefore, is to provide a method whereby not only structures already completed may be rapidly safeguarded, but also the protection of structures yet to be completed, such as forts, etc., of the new defense bases along the coasts of the United States and at various points in the Caribbean and Hawaiian Islands.

A further object of my invention is to provide protection of other than stationary objects, since protection against the shattering effects of bombs on the steel decks of battleships, for instance, may be obtained by using a material having a high degree of protection with reference to its specific gravity.

The effects of bombardment are essentially twofold:

(1) The penetrating effect due to the kinetic energy possessed by the projectiles, and

(2) The shattering effect caused by the rapid expansion and production of gases from the explosive contained in the shell.

The importance of the penetration factor varies, being dependent on the speed of the shell, and whether the shell is equipped with a delayed timing detonator. A deeply imbedded shell is, of course, much more effective than one which explodes on the surface. In constructing any protection against bombardment, therefore, one must consider primarily the two effects enumerated above.

My invention resides in the utilization of a covering material composed of layers, each layer being characterized by either its shock-absorbing powers or its resistence to penetration. Such a structure would include comparatively thin layers of shock resistent material while the penetration resistant layer would be comparatively thick. As shown in the drawing: *a* is a portion of a concrete dam or fortification, *b* is composed of a resilient material, while *c* is penetration resistant material. The number of layers need not be restricted, as shown.

Furthermore, the shock absorbent layer *b* may be continuous, or it may be honeycombed with air spaces to give a waffle-like structure, as long as there is sufficient material to act as a support for the upper layer. This form has shock absorbent powers not realized in the solid continuous form, since air is an ideal shock absorber. Again, this structure has the advantage of being capable of diffusing the shock waves so that their destructive effect is minimized.

As examples of shock absorbent materials which are resistant to shattering and spalling I wish to list particularly bituminous materials of all kinds, including air-blown, steam blown and filled asphalts; mixtures of asphalt with rock, sand and dust which have a high proporton of asphalt, and bituminous saturated roofing felt. However, besides bituminous materials I may use rubber and rubber compounds, cork and, in fact, any similar material which has a minimum capacity of transmitting shock waves. The materials need not necessarily be resilient, since a shattering or spalling resistance may even be obtained by including a layer of Cellophane between layers of cement, the desired effect here not being due to the Cellophane, but to its producing a discontinuity in the concrete structure, which in turn interrupts the shock waves. A preferred asphalt which has maximum shock absorbing qualities and yet has sufficient supporting strength is one with a melting point of 225° F.-325° F. and a penetration of 77° F. (100 g.—5 sec.) of 0.-20. The invention need not be limited to the examples of compositions just enumerated, since the essence of the invention is in the use of the two materials having the herein described characteristics and their use in conjunction with one another.

In general, a first layer of a resilient shock absorbing substance, such as air-blown asphalt of a high melting point, or mineral rubber. Cellophane, felt containing asphalt, etc., is placed next to the structure to be protected using some suitable thickness which has been determined to suit the properties of the materials used in each of the layers. The second, or penetration resistant layer *e*, is then applied. As example of penetration resistant materials which may be used in this layer are Portland cement concrete, steel, brick, sand, rock, hard asphalting concrete and the like, although I prefer to use hard asphaltic concrete, which comprises a mixture of steam blown or air-blown asphalt with a suitable quantity of graded sand and/or rock dust.

The advantage of using asphalt compositions in preference to Portland cement mixtures in protection for fortifications and the like, is evident because of several outstanding reasons. One of these is that asphalt mastic mixtures reach their final condition of maximum strength as soon as they have cooled, while the average Portland cement concrete requires a twenty-eight day period before approaching its maximum strength. This is important especially in picking possible effective emergency repairs. Freshly poured asphaltic mixtures bond perfectly to old asphaltic mixtures, thus if a portion of the structure is partially destroyed, it can be repaired quickly by merely filling the crater and cracks with a fresh asphaltic mixture. On the other hand, it is not feasible to obtain a good bond between cured and fresh Portland cement concrete. A damaging shrapnel effect following explosions is avoided, since an asphalt mixture of good strength can be made without using large proportions of relatively coarse rock. Asphaltic mixtures do not split out large fragments on the surface when a direct hit is made and, furthermore, when an indirect hit is made the cushioning effect of the rubbery plastic binder in the asphalt mastic is of benefit because the asphalt resists shock relatively well. Besides these characteristics, certain types of asphaltic mastic compositions resist penetration of high impact missiles to about the same extent as well-cured Portland cement concrete.

In order to test materials for shock absorbent power, the following method can be employed:

A piece of material to be tested is placed on a smooth surface of a lead block and a half stick of dynamite is then placed on the test material. The depth of the impression produced by detonation of the dynamite serves as a measure of the shock absorbent power of the material. Table I gives the materials used as absorbers and the corresponding impression made on lead by the explosion.

Table I

Material description	*Thickness, inches*	*Depth of impression, inches*
Air	*	*
Pine		
Mineral rubber—300 M. P. oxidized asphalt		
Asphalt mortar—9% steam blown—penetration (at 100 g. and 5 sec.)— 150-200, remainder sand		
Saturated felt—6 plys of 1/18″ felt, saturated with asphalt		
Tile		

The penetration resistance of various compositions is conveniently tested by simply firing rifle bullets at the test substance perpendicular to the surface of this material. The Springfield 30-06 rifle bullet fired point blank at fifty feet using different compositions penetrates as indicated below in Table II.

Table II

Material	*Thickness of specimen, in.*	*Penetration, in.* *	*Spall crater area, sq. in.*	*Spall crater depth, in.*
Asphaltic concrete	*		*	*
Portland cement concrete				
Steel				
Sand				
Oak				

*[Ed. Note: The copy of the specifications from which this material was set was insufficiently clear to complete the tables. The textual disclosure suffices for the problem.]

The asphaltic concrete 2½ inches thick was composed of 43 parts 10-28 mesh gravel, 62 parts 33-80 mesh sand, 4 parts rock dust finer than 80 mesh, 10 parts rock larger than 10 mesh, and 29 parts asphalt having a penetration of 80-80 at 77° F. (100 g.-5 sec.). The 8 inches thick sample of asphaltic concrete was prepared using 17.1 parts asphalt and 120 parts allicious concrete sand. The asphalt had a penetration value of 150-200 (100 g.—5 sec.) at 77° F., while the sand used had the following characteristics: passed 200 mesh—1.4 parts; 80 to 200 mesh—2.4 parts; 28 to 80 mesh—52 parts; 10 to 28 mesh—48 parts; retained on 10 mesh—10.3 parts; diatomaceous earth—6.3 parts. All quantities given are parts by weight.

The Portland cement concrete was a mix containing 1 part of Portland cement, 2 parts sand (10-80 mesh) and 4 parts rock (retained on 10 mesh).

The asphaltic mixture compositions may be further improved to give them more resistivity to penetration, mainly by varying the type of filler used. In the case of the Portland cement concrete, the spall crater was very large or about 5-10 times greater in diameter than that produced in the asphalt composition having the penetration resistance given in the examples described herein. As the resistance to penetration is increased in the asphaltic concrete, i.e., up to a value equal to that characteristic of a Portland cement concrete, the brittleness increases and the spalls from a rifle bullet shot being thrown several feet. These two opposed qualities of low spalling and low penetration resistance may be compromised by varying the composition at will. The compositions may be varied considerably by using asphalts having wide ranges of properties and by using different kinds of sand and rock. For instance, the shock resistant layer may contain 8-25% asphalt having a "normal" penetration at 77° F. (100 g. at 5 sec.) of 10-300 and the penetration resistant layer may contain 3-15% asphalt having approximately the same specifications.

Tests were also carried out to demonstrate the greatly improved resistance of a Portland cement concrete structure to explosives when it is protected using the method herein described.

Two blocks, each 5 ft. x 5 ft. x 3½ ft. were employed in the test. One block was not protected in any way, while the second one was covered with asphalt saturated paper followed by a 12 inch layer of 9% asphalt concrete. The asphalt concrete was composed of about four parts 10-50 mesh decomposed granite, four parts less than No. 10 mesh decomposed granite, one part greater than 80 mesh decomposed granite and limestone dust, and ½ part asphalt. This asphalt had the specification: Melting point of 95-105° F.; penetration at 77° F. (100 g.—5 sec.) of 150-200.

To simulate a hit by an aerial bomb, the blocks were subjected to repeated blastings using three sticks of Hercules straight 60% nitroglycerin dynamite at a time. The sticks weighed 6 ounces apiece, and the bundle was placed each time in the crater produced by the preceding explosion. After five charges, no shattering of the asphalt block had occurred, while after four charges, long cracks were produced in the Portland cement concrete block. After seven blastings the Portland cement block was seriously cracked all over the top and down the sides, the top foot of the block having no supporting value at all. Al though seven blasts finally had split the asphalt covering into four segments, the Portland cement concrete block beneath was undamaged.

This experiment also presented an opportunity to show clearly the reduced spalling which occurs in the asphalt mastics as compared to the Portland cement concrete. At the end of the sixth blasting, the crater in the Portland cement concrete block measured 34 x 29 inches at the surface of the block and was 9¾ inches deep, while the crater in the protective covering of asphalt mastic at the end of the sixth blasting measured only 13 x 13 inches at the surface and was 9¼ inches deep. The reduction in spalling of the asphalt compositions in comparison to the Portland cement mixture is shown in Table II, where rifle fire was the method of testing employed.

It is understood that the above description is merely illustrative of preferred embodiments of my invention of which many variations may be made within the scope of the following claims without departing from the spirit thereof.

PROBLEM*

READ INSTRUCTIONS CAREFULLY

This part of the examination requires analysis of 5 claims proposed to be added to an application having the accompanying specification and drawing. Certain words and phrases in the claims have been underlined and numerically designated. *Most, but not all,* of the underlined portions represent instances wherein the claims fail to comply with United States patent law or accepted claim writing practices. In addition to the 10 numbered items in the claims, there are 2 additional instances involving deficiencies in the claims in substance or form. These instances should be listed as items 11 and 12 in your answer. For each number in each claim and for items 11 and 12, make a short statement as to why the underlined portion does represent a defect, if such is the case.

6. (1) *A bombardment-resistant coating for structures* which comprises an (2) *inner layer of shock resistant material and a thick external layer* formed of (3) *asphaltic concrete containing mineral fibers.*

7. (4) *A structure having thereon a coating* comprising layers of material (5) *such as* (6) *mineral rubber* combined with layers of penetration resistant materials selected from (7) *the group consisting of steel, cement concrete, and asphalt concrete.*

8. (8) *A new process for rendering a structure resistant to penetration and shattering by bombardment* which comprises covering the externally exposed surfaces of said structure with an inner layer $\frac{1}{16}$-$\frac{1}{2}$ inch thick of (9) *paper saturated with asphalt or felt saturated with asphalt,* and applying to said inner layer a layer at least six inches thick of penetration-resistant hard asphalt concrete.

9. A structure having thereon (10) *a coating essentially as described in the drawing.*

10. A bombardment-resistant structure consisting of the product of the method set forth in claim 8.

---

*Reprinted as given on the Feb. 13, 1968, Exam.

(THIS PAGE IS INTENTIONALLY BLANK)

Case 27

CRITICIZING "SLOPPY CLAIMS" (Bomb-Proof Coating)

COMMENTS

(Quoted from Patent Office Approved Answers)*

(1) (a) Claiming a coating without claiming the combination with the base material

(b) No antecedent basis in specification for "bombardment-resistant coating".

(c) O.K.

(2) Indefinite—unbased comparative "thick."

(3) No disclosure of "concrete containing mineral fibers."

(4) O.K.

(5) Indefinite or alternative.

(6) O.K.

(7) The members are not properly grouped in Markush form, because they are not chemicals of a recognized genus.

(8) The term "new" in the claim is unnecessary and surplusage.

(9) Indefinite because alternative.

(10) Claim may not refer to the drawing and is indefinite as defining structure only by reference to the drawing.

Answers for 11 and 12 (unnumbered deficiencies).

(a) Claim 10 obviously nonstatutory because the structure can be defined other than by reference to the method.

(b) Claim 8 drawn to an obvious method.

(c) Claim 8—the range ($\frac{1}{16}$"-½") lacks antecedent support in the specification.

(d) Improper location of claim 10.**

---

*Note: there are fewer errors here than in the previous two problems, but they are more sophisticated. Also, many more require knowledge of the law.

**This would now be proper under the new rule on the placement of dependent claims described in Section 53. (At the time of this Exam, dependent claims could not be separated from their parent by an independent claim.)

Case 28
CRITICIZING "SLOPPY CLAIMS"
(Self-Priming Pump)

SELF-PRIMING SYSTEM FOR HORIZONTAL PUMPS

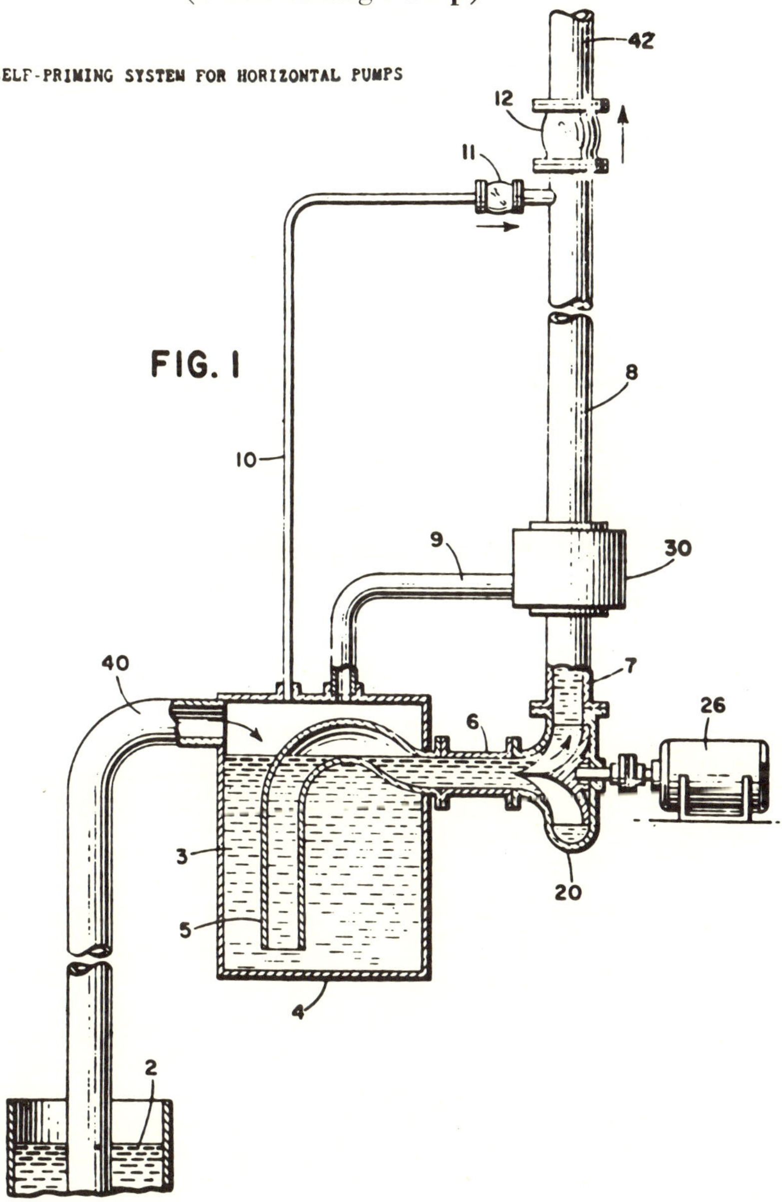

FIG. 1

FIG. 2

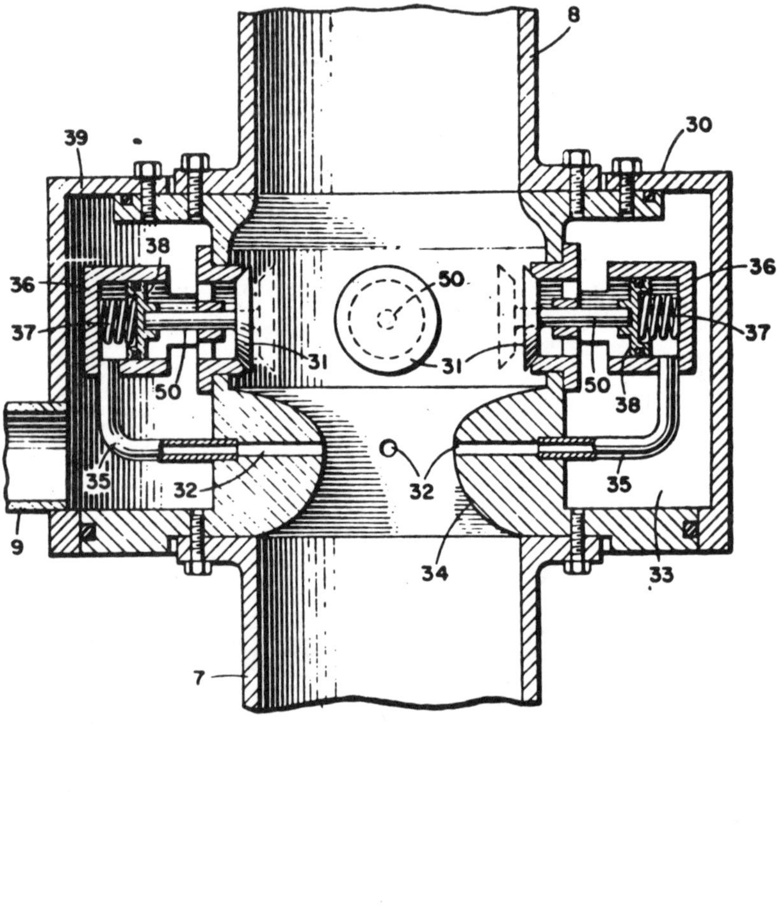

SELF-PRIMINC SYSTEM FOR HORIZONTAL PUMPS

ABSTRACT OF THE DISCLOSURE

During repriming of a horizontal pump by recycling liquid from the discharge conduit of the pump to the suction well for the pump, air is displaced from the suction well through an air vent. Air may also be bled from the impeller casing of the pump, preferably by a conduit leading to the upper portion of the suction well.

Background of the invention

The present invention relates to a self-priming pumping system. In the past, there have been many different devices developed to automatically prime a liquid pump when the pump runs dry due to an insufficient amount of liquid being present at the pump inlet and to prevent air from being introduced to the suction side of the pump. These devices are essential to the efficient operation of a pumping system, since, as is well known, once air is admitted to the suction passage in sufficient quantities to allow the pump to exhaust the supply of liquid in the suction well, the pump no longer is able to maintain suction to pump the liquid. Consequently, the pumping operation would be stopped and the attention of an operator would be required if no automatic means for repriming the system is provided.

Summary of the invention

In accordance with the present invention, a horizontal pump is primed by liquid from a suction well or reservoir located at the pump inlet. The suction well is normally supplied with liquid to be pumped by a suction line communicating with the liquid source of pumpage. A repriming valve is located in the pump discharge column to allow automatic recycling of liquid from the discharge line to the suction well when the pump has lost suction. A one-way check value is positioned downstream from the repriming valve and allows fluid movement only in the downstream direction, and thus limits the quantity of liquid which may be recycled to that in the system between the repriming valve and the check valve. An air relief line with a one-way check valve connects the top of the suction well to the discharge column intermediate the first mentioned check valve and the repriming valve. Air is displaced from the suction well through the air relief line by the liquid which is recycled from the discharge column through the repriming valve to the suction well. When a portion of the recycled liquid flows from the suction well into the pump inlet, the liquid will be pumped into the discharge column causing the repriming valve to close. If the pump is not fully reprimed, the repriming valve will thereafter again allow the same liquid to be recycled to the suction well. This recycling will continue in this fashion until the normal pumping cycle is restored.

The present invention is designed for automatically repriming single or multi-stage pumps employing any reasonable length suction line. In the event of loss of suction head due to the pump running dry, there is no danger of pump damage since the system will continue to reprime itself.

According to a further feature of the invention, an air relief line may vent air from the impeller inlet casing. It has been found that when liquid in the suction well is exhausted and air is sucked into the pump, an air lock may be formed between the inlet of the pump intake line and the impeller. This entrapped air may keep liquid from reaching that point in the impeller section of the pump where sufficient velocity can be imparted to it to force the liquid and the entrapped air into the discharge column. By the use of an air relief line extending through the casing of the pump impeller chamber, a path is provided for venting such entrapped air when the repriming fluid flows into the pump inlet.

It is a principal object of the present invention to provide novel apparatus for automatically repriming a pumping system which is fed by a suction intake line.

Another object of the present invention is to provide a self-priming pumping system for a horizontal pump capable of developing a suction head by recycling its priming fluid.

Another object is to provide a self-priming pumping system capable of repeatedly developing a suction head to draw liquid up through a relatively long suction line.

A further object of the invention is to provide a self-priming pumping system wherein the component parts, including the pump, can be conveniently located to facilitate replacement or servicing, if necessary.

A still further object of the invention is to provide a self-priming pumping system that is rugged, positive in operation, and capable of pumping any sort of pumpage without becoming clogged or jammed.

An even further object of the present invention is to provide a self-priming pumping system for a horizontal pump that is compact, contains a minimum of moving parts, and is economical to manufacture.

The above and still further objects, features, and advantages of the present invention will become more apparent as this description proceeds.

Brief description of the drawing

FIGURE 1 is a side elevational view, partially in section, illustrating one embodiment of the present invention.

FIGURE 2 is a vertical sectional view of the repriming valve employed as part of the present invention.

Description of the preferred embodiments

Referring to FIGURE 1, reference numeral 4 designates a suction well or casing which acts as a reservoir for priming liquid 3. In normal operation, liquid 3 is supplied to the suction well through a suction line 40 which has its other end immersed in pumpage 2. A suction skirt 5 is positioned with its lower end adjacent the bottom of suction well 4, and is connected at its other end to an inlet 6 of a horizontal pump 20 which is driven by a motor 26. In the illustrated embodiment, suction skirt 5 has a curved upper portion, the lower inner surface of which is approximately level with the upper inner surface of the eye of the impeller, i.e., the horizontal inlet 6. A small aperture may be provided in the curved upper portion of the skirt 5 to function as an air bleed between this portion of the skirt and the top of the suction well 4. It is also possible to connect the vertically extending portion of skirt 5 to the pump inlet without elevating the upper portion of the skirt above the pump inlet 6, for example, by means of a 90° pipe elbow.

Pump 20 pumps fluid through an outlet 7, and a repriming valve assembly 30 to be described hereinafter into a discharge column 8. A one-way check valve 12 is positioned at the upper end of the discharge column 8 and connects the discharge column to a discharge line 42. A drain pipe 9 leads from valve 30 to the top of the suction well 4 so that liquid may be recycled in a manner to be described hereinafter to reprime the pump 20. The liquid in discharge column 8 and the quantity of liquid in repriming valve 30 above the level of drain pipe 9 are available to reprime the pump. Therefore, the discharge column 8 and the above mentioned portion of repriming valve 30 effectively function as a reservoir for repriming liquid. The volumetric capacity of this reservoir is at least sufficient to ensure that the quantity of liquid available to reprime the pump is sufficient to fill the pump inlet, inlet 6, skirt 5 and suction well 4 to a level corresponding to the level of the eye of the pump impeller.

An air relief conduit 10 leads from the top of the enclosed suction well 4 to the upper end of the discharge column 8 upstream from the check valve 12. A one-way check valve 11 in conduit 10 allows fluid movement only in a direction towards discharge column 8 to prevent liquid in column 8 from returning to the suction well via conduit 10.

FIGURE 2 illustrates a presently preferred repriming valve assembly 30. Valve assembly 30 basically comprises an inner casing 34 which has a lower portion in the shape of a venturi. The upper portion of the casing part of the reservoir section for the repriming liquid forms a cage structure for a plurality of peripherally spaced poppet valves 31 and the associated valve seats. A tube 35 is connected from each of four openings 32 in the throat of the venturi to a chamber formed by a cylinder 36 and a cooperating piston 38 which is connected to a valve 31 by a valve stem 50. A spring 37 between the head of each cylinder 36 and the associated piston 38 functions to normally bias each poppet valve 31 towards its open position which is shown by dashed lines in FIGURE 2. A jacket 39 surrounds the valve assembly and together with casing 34 forms an enclosed space 33 which is in communication with the drain pipe 9.

When liquid is being pumped during normal operation, the poppet valves 31 are maintained in their closed position by a pressure differential between the liquid in the upper portion of casing 34 and the liquid in cylinders 36, which pressure differential is of sufficient magnitude to overcome the bias of the springs 37. This pressure differential is established by the venturi in the lower section of casing 34 and control tubes 35 leading from openings 32 in the venturi to the cylinders 36. Since the tubes 35 communicate with the venturi, the static pressure in the venturi is present in the tubes, and in the cylinders 36. Due to the magnitude of the dynamic pressure factor flowing through the venturi which is proportional to the square of the velocity of the liquid, the static pressure in the venturi and hence in cylinders 36 is less than the static pressure acting upon the poppet valves 31 in the enlarged upper portion of casing 34. It is evident that the velocity of the liquid in the venturi is greater than the ambient velocity in the upper portion of casing 34 and therefore the pressure in conduits 35 is lower than the ambient pressure in the upper portion of the casing 34. Thus, a drop in pressure is created in cylinder 36 which permits pressure against valves 31 to force the valves 31 against their valve seats in opposition to the bias of springs 37. When the velocity of liquid flowing through the repriming valve reaches a predetermined low value, for example, when air is introduced into the system, and the pressure differential is sufficiently reduced in magnitude, the bias of springs 37 is effective to open the poppet valves 31. When the poppet valves open, liquid may flow through the valve ports into the space 33 and then into drain pipe 9.

The operation of the FIGURE 1 embodiment will now be described. With the suction well 4 filled with liquid to a level above the pump inlet 6, liquid pumped into discharge column 8 by pump 20 creates a suction which draws more liquid into the suction well from suction line 40. As long as liquid flow continues, repriming valve 30 and check valve 11 remain closed.

However, if air or other gas enters the suction well and suction is lost, the pumping action stops when the liquid in the suction well is depleted. When the liquid flow from the outlet 7 of the pump stops, the pressure differential holding the poppet valves 31 in their closed positions is reduced, and the valves are opened by springs 37. Liquid now flows out of valve assembly 30 and discharge column 8 through the ports associated with poppet valves 31, into space 33, and through drain pipe 9 back to the suction well 4. As the repriming liquid enters the suction well, air is displaced through air relief conduit 10 and check valve 11 into the now empty upper end of discharge column 8. When the repriming fluid from the suction well passes through the suction skirt 5 into the pump inlet 6, the pump 20 then draws the repriming liquid out of the suction well and pumps it into the discharge column 8. The flow of the repriming liquid from the pump outlet reestablishes the pressure differential which causes the poppet valves 31 to move to the closed position. Check valve 11 closes as the liquid enters the discharge column 8, and the air which has entered the discharge column is now forced through check valve 12 into discharge line 42. The removal of liquid from the suction well 4 reduces the pressure at the opening of suction line 40 so that liquid is drawn upward therein. When the repriming liquid is depleted, the cycle is repeated until suction is reestablished for the pump 20. Factors such as the length in diameter of the suction line 40 will determine how many times the pump will be reprimed before full pumpage flow is reestablished.

In one of the embodiments tested, a suction line 22 feet long and 14 inches in diameter achived full discharge after three repriming cycles which took place in less than a minute.

PROBLEM*

This part of the examination requires analysis of the four following claims proposed to be added to an application having the accompanying specification and drawings. The claims all would be subject to rejection.

Identify the portions or attributes of each claim that afford grounds for rejection and make a short statement for each as to why rejection is in order.

5. A self-priming pump system comprising a pump, an inlet for said pump, an outlet therefor, and means automatically supplying liquid to prime said pump when insufficient liquid is present at the pump inlet, said means including a suction well and an automatic valve regulating the flow of repriming liquid to said well.

6. A self-priming pump system comprising a pumpage supply (2), a suction casing (4), a pump (20), a drive motor (26), an automatic valve (30), and a drain pipe (9) communicating with the said valve.

*Reprinted as given on the Nov. 19, 1968, Exam.

7. A self-priming pump system comprising a pump having a horizontal inlet and an outlet, a suction well having a cavity which is partially below said inlet, the suction line opening into the suction well at a level above said inlet to supply liquid to the cavity, a suction skirt having a lower end positioned in said cavity below said inlet and having an upper end connected to said inlet. A portion of said upper end is elevated above said inlet, reservoir means for repriming liquid having an upstream end connected to said outlet of said pump, a repriming valve connected to said pump outlet, a drain conduit connecting said valve to said suction well, means in the inlet of said valve for detecting a drop in liquid velocity, a valve device within the repriming valve biased to closed position, a discharge column leading from said valve, and an air relief conduit extending from said discharge column to a point upstream of said inlet.

8. A self-priming pump system as described in claim 7 in which said upper end of said suction skirt extends up to but not above the pump inlet and in which the said fluid responsive detecting means includes a Venturi passage.

Case 28

CRITICIZING "SLOPPY CLAIMS"
(Self-Priming Pump)

COMMENTS

(Quoted from Patent Office Approved Answers)*

(Claim 5). Failure to point out novel combination in view of admitted prior art (under "Background of the Invention"). Also full credit for recognition of lack of structural relationship of suction well and automatic valve to remaining elements of claim.

(Claim 6). Mere catalog of elements, claim is incomplete in not setting forth relationship between elements. Use of reference numerals is not a defect. Section 608.01(m).

(Claim 7).

(a) no antecedent for suction line.

(b) use of period improper.

(c) use of verb "is" is improper, should be a clause, not a sentence.

(d) not supported by disclosure, inaccurate.

(e) double inclusion, the valve casing and discharge pipe serve as the reservoir previously claimed.

(f) indefinite as to which valve is antecedent.

(g) indefinite as to which inlet is antecedent.

(Claim 8). Improper dependent claim is not including all elements of base claim, i.e. dependent claim is inconsistent with base claim. No proper antecedent for "said fluid responsive detecting means" since original claim called only for detecting means.

*Note: some of these errors required careful study of the specifications and a good knowledge of how the device works.

Case 29

CRITICIZING "SLOPPY CLAIMS"
(Coated Pipe)

FIG. 1.

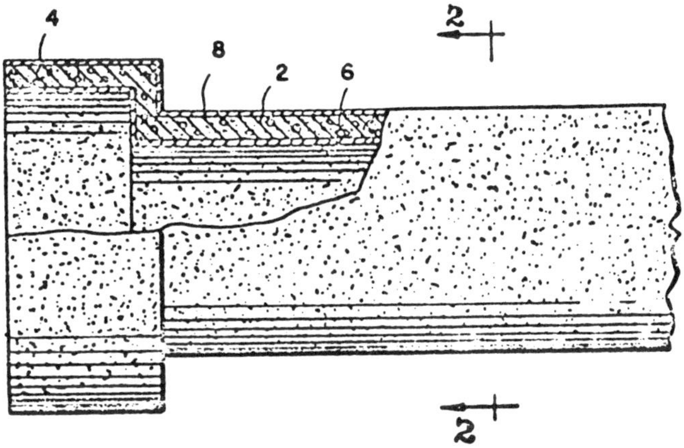

FIG. 2.

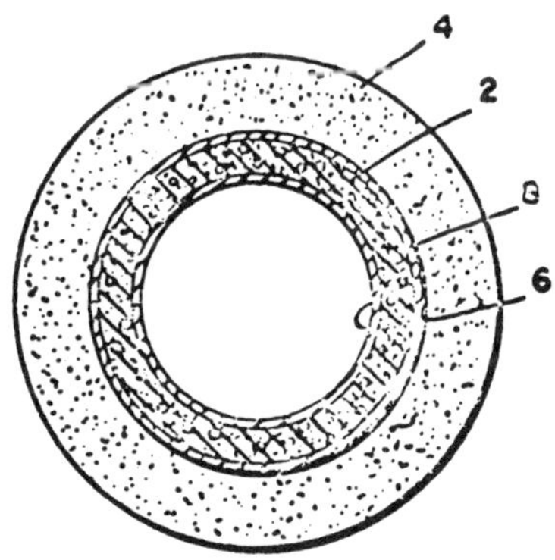

PIPE AND METHOD OF MAKING SAME

This invention relates to the coating of concrete pipe.

It is an object of the present invention to increase the wear resistance of concrete pipe.

A further object is to increase the chemical resistance of concrete pipe.

Yet another object to to provide concrete pipe with a smooth surface having low frictional loss as well as low cleavage.

It has been found that these and other objects of the invention which will be apparent as the description proceeds can be attained by coating concrete pipe with a composition comprising an ethylenically unsaturated alkyd resin and a polymerizable vinyl monomer together with sand as a filler.

It is important to use sand as satisfactory results are not obtained when other fillers, such as calcium carbonate for example, are used to replace the sand.

In the following specification and claims all parts and percentages are by weight unless otherwise indicated.

For convenience the mixture of an ethylenically unsaturated alkyd resin and polymerizable vinyl monomer will hereinafter alternatively be called a polyester resin.

The coating composition of the polyester resin and sand should contain 50-90% of sand and 10-50% of resin. Preferably, the sand and resin are used in a ratio of 3.8 parts of sand to one part of resin.

The concrete pipe employed is of the conventional type and can be either reinforced or unreinforced. When reinforced pipe is employed, the reinforcing agent is a steel mesh, as is understood in the art. The concrete can be a 1:2.5:5 mix (cement to sand to aggregate), although any conventional concrete that is used to make concrete pipe can also be used. The present invention is applicable to all standard sizes of concrete pipe, e.g., from 4 inches to 12½ feet inside diameter and lengths up to 16 feet or longer.

The pipe can be coated either on the outside or on the inside or both. The advantages obtained by coating the pipe on the inside are that there is a marked increase in the wear resistance of the pipe, and the very smooth surfaces formed result in low frictional loss and also result in low cleavage, i.e., there is prevented the adherence to the pipe of salts and other materials which come out of the liquids which are transmitted through the pipe. Additionally, the polyester and sand coating imparts high chemical resistance to the inside surface of the pipe.

The primary purpose of applying an outside coating of the resin-sand coating composition is to impart high chemical resistance. Without such a coating the concrete pipe is completely unsuitable, for example, to be buried in soils of high acid content. Where there is no problem of chemical attack, however, the outside coating of polyester resin-sand can be omitted. Similarly, where the only problem is attack of the external environment of the pipe, then the internal polyester resin-sand coating can be omitted.

The polyester resin-sand coating can be applied externally by means of a spray gun or paint brush or by trowelling. An internal coating can be applied by the same methods or by extruding the resin-sand composition on the internal surface of the pipe while at the same time imparting a rotation to the pipe. In this latter case, the rotation speed is slow until the resin-sand composition has been inserted and then the speed is increased to uniformly spread the resin-sand coating.

In the drawings:

Figure 1 is a vertical section of a concrete pipe having both an internal and an external coating of the polyester resin-sand composition; and

Figure 2 is a section along the line 2–2 of Figure 1.

Referring more specifically to the drawings, there is shown a concrete pipe 2 having a conventional flange 4 at one end. The pipe throughout its length has an internal coating 6 of polyester resin-sand and an external coating 3 of the same polyester resin-sand composition.

The polyester resin-sand composition normally is applied internally to a thickness of 1/16 to 1/4 inch, and externally to the same thickness. Larger thicknesses can be imparted although they are not normally necessary and have the disadvantage of unduly increasing the cost of the finished product.

The polyester resins are a class of resins with which the resin chemist is familiar. The preferred resins of this class for employment in the coating compositions of the invention are the polymetric ester reaction products of one or more dicarboxylic acids and one or more polyhydric alcohols. Desirably one or more of these reactants shall contain a reactive double bond or ethylenic linkage. Among the dicarboxylic acids which may be used are phthalic, malic, maleic, fumaric, adipic, pimelic, suberic, sebacic, itaconic, citraconic, and succinic acids and their anhydrides. It is essential that some of the dicarboxylic acid component of the polyester resin contain an unsaturated ethylenic linkage. For this reason, maleic and fumaric acids are most desirable. Among the polyhydric alcohols which may be used are ethylene glycol, diethylene glycol and propylene glycol. A mixture of propylene glycol and dipropylene glycol is the most satisfactory polyhydric alcohol. One may use an unsaturated monohydric alcohol in place of part of the polyhydric alcohol. A typical example of such an alcohol is allyl alcohol which produces an allyl ester of the dicarboxylic acid. The polyester resins may be suitably modified or plasticized by the incorporation of alcohols, fatty acids, etc., to modify the chemical and physical characteristics as desired. The polyesters should comprise upward from about 15 or 30% and preferably 50% to 85% by weight of the resin and resin forming component, e.g., styrene, of the coating composition.

The resin component of the coating composition should also contain a non-volatile, monomeric, crosslinking solvent for the polyester resin. The function of this solvent is to make the polyester resin more fluid and also to crosslink the polyester resin at the time of curing to produce a crosslinked, or three dimensional resin with the polyester resin which is thermosetting in character. This monomeric solvent is an important member of the resin component, for it provides the necessary fluidity to the resin component, imparts thermosetting characteristics to the cured resin and is consumed during the curing of the resin without forming volatile materials. This freedom from volatility is highly important for otherwise the release of volatile matter would produce bubbles, voids or pinholes on the surface and throughout the finished coating of the pipe. The lack of volatile matter permits curing when under pressure without requiring provision for vents, etc., in the molds. Also, escaping combustible, volatile matter may produce explosions, or fire hazards.

Among the monomeric polymerizable solvents which may be used are the hydrocarbons: styrene, vinyl toluene, e.g., o-vinyl toluene, p-vinyl toluene, and m-vinyl toluene, cyclo-pentadiene; vinyl acetate; diallyl esters, e.g., diallyl phthalate and triallyl cyanurate, as well as alpha methyl styrene. Styrene has produced the most satisfactory results thus far.

When produced commercially, these resin compositions also contain a small amount of a polymerization inhibitor so as to prevent gelation during storage prior to usage. Such inhibitors include the well known antioxidants; hydroquinone, t-butyl catechol, quinone, etc.

Polyester resins of the character contemplated for use in the present invention are sold in the trade and identified as "Paraplex" or "Vibrin" resins. In general, these resins are unsaturated high molecular weight polymers made by reacting one or more acids or a blend of acids, such as maleic or fumaric acid, with a dihydroxy alcohol, such as ethylene glycol. The specific properties of these resins vary depending largely upon the type and amount of each constituent in the combination. For best results, I prefer to employ a mixture of two different types of such resins. Certain of these resins form masses upon curing that are very rigid or inflexible, while others form more flexible rubbery masses. For the coating composition of my invention, I prefer to use a mixture of the rigid and flexible resins, and have found that with resins commercially available about 2 to 5 parts of rigid resin and 1 part of flexible resin produce excellent results. These proportions may, of course, be varied within wide limits depending upon the particular properties desired for the cured coating layer and the properties of the resins that are mixed.

I mix the resin and monomeric polymerizable solvent, such as styrene or other othylenically unsaturated monomer, e.g., vinyl acetate or vinyl toluene, with the finely divided sand filler to form a coating composition having the consistency of a thick slurry. The monomer is used in an amount of 15-85% or occasionally slightly more of the total of resin solids and monomer. Preferably, the monomer is employed in an amount of 50-85% of this resin solids-monomer liquid mix. About 40% resin solids and 60% styrene has been found to give a good workable consistency when employed with the sand, especially when the ratio of sand to polyester resin is about 3.8 to 1. The sand filler is finely divided silica which can be obtained from any source as silica. While sand is the preferred filler because of its chemical inertness and hardness, it is also possible to use other finely divided acid-resistant crushed rock as fillers, e.g., gravel.

The sand increases the hardness and strength of the coated surface. While it is possible to employ irregularly shaped particles of sand, it is preferable to use rounded particles of the sand filler.

While the sand can be of uniform particle size, e.g., between 30 and 200 mesh (U.S. Standard Sieve Series), it is preferable to employ sand having a gradation of particle size. When there is a gradation of particle size of the sand filler, there preferably is a gradual diminution in the quantity of material (by weight) corresponding to each sieve size as one goes from larger to smaller

Standard Sieve sizer.

In practice, satisfactory results may be obtained by using particles having at least two general particle size classifications, one of which may be said to be of large size (in the order of 30-70 mesh) and another of small size (in the order of 100-325 mesh). It has been found desirable to employ a major proportion, and preferably 60% or more, by weight, of the large size particles. One particularly successful gradation has been one in which about 65% by weight of the filler is of sand of approximately 40-70 mesh and 35% is of 70-140 mesh size. I have found also that a gradation of 80% of the former mesh size and 20% of the latter is equally satisfactory.

In addition to using a gradation of particle size of filler material, I prefer to use some filler of extremely small particle size, in the order of 325-mesh or smaller. Such material is sold under the designation "silica flour" or "Surfex." I prefer to add this material to the liquid resin component of the coating composition.

If desired, it is possible to add pigments and dyes for decorative purposes, but normally there is no need to utilize such materials. Either just prior to or just subsequent to mixing the polyester resin with the filler, a suitable polymerization catalyst should be added. The mixture of polyester resin, sand and catalyst is then applied to the pipe in one of the manners previously set forth. The resin is cured on the pipe at a temperature from room temperature up to about 350° F. To obtain a quick cure, temperatures in the upper range, e.g., 325-350° F., are preferable. Where time is not of the essence, lower temperatures can be satisfactorily employed.

As the catalysts there can be utilized numerous oxidizing catalysts, such as cumene hydroperoxide, dicumyl peroxide, benzoyl peroxide, and methyl ethyl ketone peroxide. The catalyst is usually employed in an amount of 0.4-4% of the polyester resin. Preferably, there is utilized with the catalyst a metallic drier such as manganese or cobalt naphthenate, for example. A typical example of a satisfactory catalyst-drier combination is 2% benzoyl peroxide, .75% manganese naphthenate and .75% cobalt naphthenate based on the polyester resin when using a cure in the upper end of the temperature range previously set forth.

On occasion it has been found advantageous to incorporate into the coating slurry a small percent, e.g. 1½-2% by weight of the total slurry of a cation modified clay, such as those disclosed in Hauser Patent 2,531,427. A preferred material of this class is dimethyldioctadecylammonium bentonite which is sold under the name "Bentone 34."

Typical examples of polyester resin-sand compositions which may be employed in forming the inside or the outside coating on the pipe are given below.

Example 1

A coating composition was prepared by stirring in a mixing vessel just prior to the coating operation an initial mixture having the following composition:

A mixture of about 27% by weight of polyester resins made up of 3 parts of rigid type polyester resin (Paraplex P43, believed to be a condensation product of propylene glycol and dipropylene glycol in the ratio of 1 to 3 with phthalic anhydride and maleic anhydride in ratio of 3 to 2) and 1 part of flexible type polyester resin (Paraplex P13, believed to be a condensation product of ethylene glycol and diethylene glycol with phthalic anhydride, maleic anhydride and adipic acid), 23% by weight of styrene monomer, 5% by weight of titanium dioxide as a pigment, and about 45% by weight of #325-mesh asbestine	lbs.	25.5

To this initial mixture were added the following:

Styrene monomer (solvent)	lbs.	6.5
Bentone 34 (dimethyldioctadecylammonium bentonite)	lbs.	0.5
Methyl ethyl ketone peroxide (catalyst)	cc.	250
Manganese naphthenate (catalyst)	lbs.	0.4

The resulting mix was agitated and to it was added promptly the following fillers:

86 lbs. crystal silica sand having the following approximate sieve analysis—

Sieve sizes:	Approx. percentages
No. 40	38.0
No. 50	41.0
No. 70	14.0
No. 100	1.0

22 lbs. banding sand having the following approximate sieve analysis—

Sieve sizes:	Approx. percentages
No. 50	0.9
No. 70	20.0
No. 100	48.2
No. 140	20.9
No. 200	7.0
No. 270	2.5

Example 2

	Parts by weight
Rigid type polyester resin (Paraplex P43)	45
Flexible type polyester resin (Paraplex P13)	15
Methyl ethyl ketone peroxide (catalyst) ....)	2
Manganese naphthenate (catalyst)	2
Titanium dioxide (pigment)	12
Resin coated calcium carbonate (Surfex, believed to be calcium carbonate coated with polydimethyl siloxane resin) (filler)	19
Bentono 34 (dimethyldioctadecylammonium bentonite)	2
Monomeric styrene (solvent)	3
Total	100

To this mixture was added about 2 parts of silica sand to 1 part of the mixture. This silica sand was composed of about 65% by weight of particles of about 40 to 50 sieve size and 35% of about 100 sieve size.

Example 3

A solid polyester resin was prepared from 1266 pounds phthalic anhydride, 636 pounds maleic anhydride, 501 pounds dipropylene glycol and 855 pounds of propylene glycol. This resin which possessed an acid number of 35, was admixed with 1.32 pounds of hydroquinone as an inhibitor. This mixture of resin and inhibitor was diluted with 1284 pounds of styrene.

To 52 pounds of this resin, inhibitor and styrene mixture, there were added 1.5 pounds of benzoyl peroxide and 1.5 pounds of methyl ethyl ketone peroxide as well as 1.5 pounds of manganese naphthenate, 0.5 pound of cobalt naphthenate, 4.5 pounds of titanium dioxide (pigment), 1.5 pounds of Bentone 34, 5 pounds of antimony trioxide, 10 pounds of solid chlorinated paraffin and 18 pounds of styrene.

To one pound of the above composition, there is added 3.8 pounds of graded silica sand (of the same composition as in Example 1).

Example 4

The coating composition prepared in Example 1 was applied to the interior of the reinforced concrete pipe of 6 feet internal diameter by employing a spray gun. The coating was smoothed out by applying a sheet of cellophane over the coating and allowing the cellophane to remain until the coating composition had cured at room temperature. This took about 24 hours. The cellophane was then removed and the resulting coating on the interior of the pipe had a smooth surface.

The same procedure was employed to coat the exterior of the pipe with the composition of Example 1 and in similar fashion the coating was made smooth by the use of a cellophane covering which was subsequently removed after the resin had cured.

The finished product after removal of the cellophane is illustrated in Figure 1.

Example 5

A reinforced concrete pipe of 12 feet internal diameter and 2 feet in length was placed on rollers which were suitably connected to a variable speed motor. The resin-sand composition prepared in Example 3 was introduced to the interior of the pipe through a flexible hose. The hose was attached to a piston which was actuated by a cylinder containing compressed air. The piston was of sufficient length that the hose could travel from one end of the pipe to the other. The variable speed motor was started so that the pipe rotated at a speed of about ⅓ of a revolution per minute, and the resin was allowed to drip into the pipe through the hose. Simultaneously, the piston was actuated so that the resin composition was supplied throughout the length of the pipe. After three minutes, the resin had been supplied to the entire pipe and the piston and hose were removed from the interior of the pipe. The variable speed motor was then adjusted so that the pipe rotated at about 80 r.p.m. and this speed of rotation was continued for about three minutes in order to make the coating uniform throughout the pipe. The motor was then shut off.

Next, there were inserted into the pipe 2 split hemispherical steel molds which were kept apart by a jack. These molds were covered with cellophane as a parting agent and the jack was raised so that the cellophane coating on the split mold contacted the coating composition. The coating composition was then allowed to cure for about 24 hours at room temperature and the jack released so that the mold could be removed. The resulting coating on the interior of the pipe was smooth. In this example the split mold could be made of wood, metal or other material, and the parting agent could be a polytetrafluoroethylene coating or a silicon, e.g., a polymeric dimethylsiloxane coating.

Example 6

Example 5 was repeated but the curing time was reduced to 30 minutes by placing the entire assembly of pipe and split molds in an oven heated to 325° F.

Example 7

An unreinforced concrete pipe of 6 inch internal diameter and 3 feet in length was coated on the outside with the composition of Example 2 by the brush method. A cellophane film was applied over the coating to smooth out the same and the pipe was then placed in an oven at 350° F. for 30 minutes in order to cure the resin. After removal from the oven, the cellophane film was taken off. The resulting pipe had a smooth, hard coating of the polyester resin-sand composition.

PROBLEM*

This part of the examination requires analysis of 6 claims proposed to be added to an application having the accompanying specification and drawing. Certain words and phrases in the claims have been underlined, and designated by a number in parenthesis. *Most, but not all* of the underlined portions represent instances wherein the claims fail to comply with United States patent law or accepted claim writing practice. For each number before an underlined section, make a short statement as to why the underlined portion does represent one or more defects, if such is the case.

7. (1) *a pipe having chemical and heat resistant properties* comprising a base pipe material and (2) *a coating applied on the exterior, on the interior, or on both the exterior and interior of the concrete base,* said coating being formed from a composition consisting of a polyester resin, (3) *a granular filler material,* a polymerization catalyst, and (4) *a polymerization inhibitor selected from the group comprising hydroquinone, t-butyl catechol, or quinone.*

8. A pipe as defined in claim 7 in which the granular filler material (5) *is sand.*

9. A method of treating a concrete pipe to impart wear resistance which comprises (6) *the steps of coating the inner surface of the pipe with a composition comprising an unsaturated polyester resin, styrene monomer, and* (7) *a catalyst selected from the group consisting of dicumyl peroxide and benzoyl peroxide, applying sand of 40-140 mesh size to the coating on the pipe, and curing the coating at 325°F.*

10. (8) *A pipe as defined in claim 8 in which the sand is used in a ratio of 3.8 parts to one part of resin.*

11. A pipe as described in claim 7 in which the composition includes (9) *a pigment to impart a desired color to the pipe.*

12. (10) *A novel pipe comprising concrete, and a composition of polyester resin, sand, and a catalyst curing agent.*

*Reprinted as given on Aug. 26, 1969, Exam.

Case 29

CRITICIZING "SLOPPY CLAIMS"
(Coated Pipe)

COMMENTS

(Quoted from Patent Office Approved Answers)

(1) (a) Lower case "a" improper as first word.
(b) No support for "heat resistant."
(2) (a) alternative expression is indefinite.
(b) No antecedent for "concrete."
(3) "granular material" is too broad since specification indicates that only certain materials (e.g. sand, gravel) will yield satisfactory results.
(4) improper Markush claiming by reason of (a) "comprising" and (b) "or."
(5) no error involved.
(6) sequence of steps not supported by disclosure—sand is incorporated in composition prior to application to pipe.
(7) no error—proper Markush group.
(8) claim 10 is an improper dependent claim because it is separated from a previous dependent claim. MPEP 608.01(n).
(9) addition of pigment renders the claim inconsistent with parent claim in which the composition is limited ("consisting of") to certain stated components.
(10) (a) "novel" is surplusage.
(b) mere catalog of elements—does not set forth structural relationship of concrete and composition.

Case 30

CRITICIZING "SLOPPY CLAIMS"

(Golf Ball Cleaner)

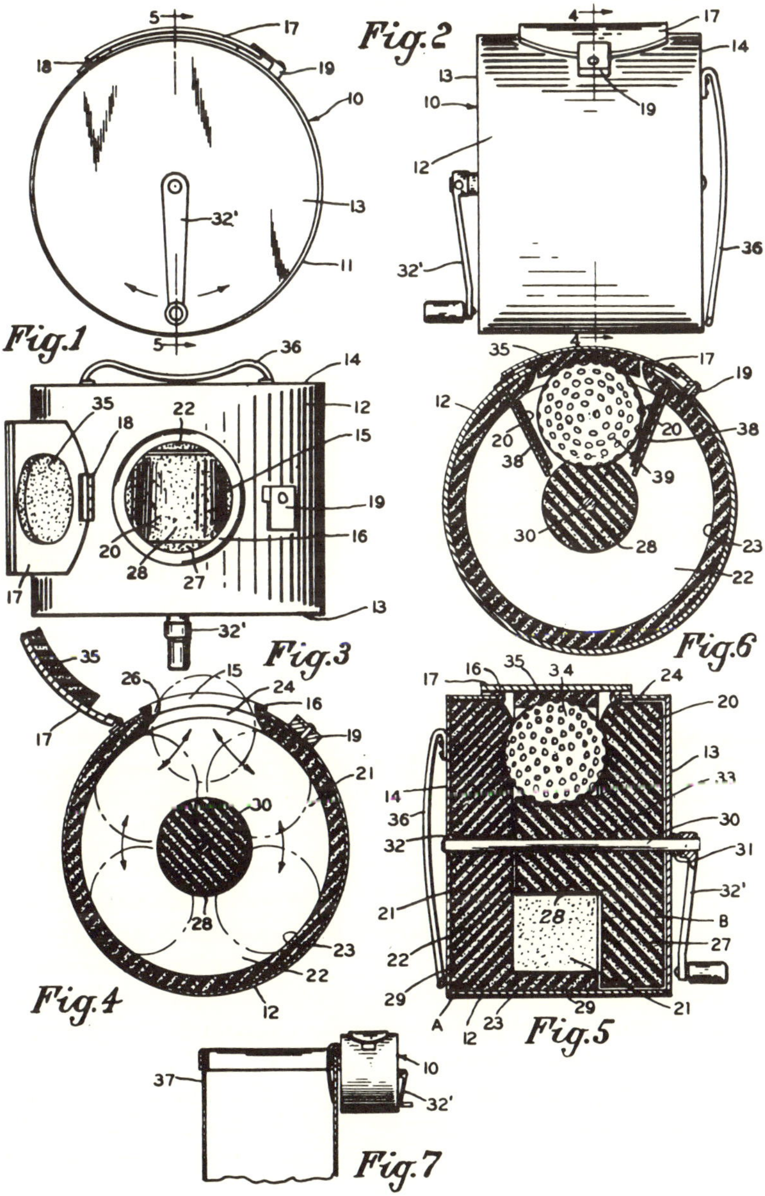

BALL WASHING APPARATUS

Our present invention relates to ball washing apparatus and more particularly and specifically to a portable golf ball washer which may be conveniently attached to a golf bag, wheeled caddy or the like in a readily available position for use by a golfer during play, and a washer which may be easily and conveniently stored in a pocket of the golf bag during periods of non-use.

Generally, certain golf ball washing apparatus constructions have been used heretofore for the purposes of cleaning dirt, grass stains and the like from the covers of golf balls. However, such prior apparatus as has been heretofore provided has had numerous disadvantages both from the standpoint of construction as well as from the standpoint of function and availability of use.

Certain of these prior golf ball washer constructions include a container provided with a pair of spaced brushes fixed in the container and a paddle like golf ball holder reciprocably supported between the brushes for the purpose of moving a golf ball back and forth in contact with the brush surfaces for cleaning the same.

In these prior constructions, the cleaning of golf balls is accomplished by the brushing action on the ball covers accompanied by the application to the balls of a liquid detergent solution which is carried in the container to a depth of approximately one-half the height of the brushes therein.

In the use of such prior constructions as those above noted, it has been discovered that during the hot days normal to the golfing season the detergent solution contained in the washers will evaporate rapidly thus necessitating constant refilling of the washers by golf course personnel in order to maintain the washers in satisfactorily operable condition. Unfortunately, the time and labor requirements necessary to maintain a program of refilling for washers of this type has resulted in a great laxity toward that end, thereby leaving such ball washers unattended and as such substantially useless to golfers.

Certain other types of prior constructions have been tried, but all of such constructions have required the maintenance of a liquid detergent level therein at all times in order to render the construction operative. Thus all prior constructions have the inherent disadvantages common to those above denoted relative to the evaporation of the cleaning solutions.

Another disadvantage in the use of prior constructions is inherent in the fact that such constructions are bulky and thus require stationary foundations for placement at intervals about a golf course where they are available to golfers. However, it has been the practice because of the costs involved in the provision of such washers as well as in the necessity that their placement be at points of normal congregation of all golfers to restrict the placement of such prior apparatus to points adjacent tees or greens about the course. Further, it has been an unfortunate practice for golf courses of the unusual management to space stationary washers of the type above noted at intervals of every other or every third tee about the course because of the requirements noted as well as the initial costs of installation.

Thus, the average golfer is confronted with a lack of facility to properly wash or clean dirty golf balls at points about the course other than those widely spaced stationary washers of the type above noted.

It is a general object of the present invention to provide a golf ball washer which substantially eliminates those disadvantages inherent in both the construction, use and availability of prior known apparatus.

Another object of the present invention lies in the provision of a portable golf ball washer which may be carried by each individual golfer in his golf bag with a minimum requirement of storage space, and a washer which may be quickly and easily attached to the golf bag or on a wheeled caddy in a position of ready availability for use at any time and at any point in his travels about a course.

Still another object of the present invention resides in the provision of a portable golf ball washer which eliminates the necessity of maintaining free liquid in the washer for washing purposes thus avoiding the spilling of detergent solutions in or on the golf bag of the user, and a washer which will remain in operable washing condition for long periods of time without the necessity of reconditioning the same by the addition of washing solutions.

Still a further object is to provide a golf ball washer which may be removably attached to a golf bag, a wheeled caddy or the like in such a position as to make it readily available for use by either right or left handed persons at any time.

Still another important object of the present invention is to provide a portable golf ball washer which is of substantially simple and inexpensive design and manufacture and which is highly efficient and easily operable in use for the purpose of cleaning those dirty substances from golf balls which are normally incurred with the use of the same.

These and other objects are accomplished by the parts, constructions, arrangements, combinations and subcombinations comprising the present invention, the nature of which is set forth in the following general statement, and preferred embodiments of which—illustrative of the best modes in which applicants have contemplated applying the principles—are set forth in the following description and illustrated in the accompanying drawings, and which are particularly and distinctly pointed out and set forth in the appended claims forming a part hereof.

The nature of the present invention may be stated in general terms as including a cylindrical container taking the form of a housing, a pair of members of a spongy, liquid absorbent material substantially filling the housing, an arcuate passage formed in said spongy material between said members, said passage being of slightly lesser breadth than the diameter of a golf ball, an opening in said housing communicating with said passage to permit the insertion of a golf ball into said passage and its removal therefrom, a portion of said spongy material defining said passage being mounted for rotation relative to said container and said golf ball, whereupon a golf ball inserted in said passage will be resiliently abraded by those areas of the spongy material defining the passage, a hand crank means on said container having operable engagement with said movable portion of said spongy material, closure means on said container for said opening, and clip means on said container for removably securing the container to a golf bag, wheeled caddy or the like.

In the accompanying drawings in which like numerals designate similar parts throughout the several views:

Figure 1 is a side elevation of the washer;

Fig. 2 is an end view of the washer;

Fig. 3 is a plan view of the washer with the closure member in open condition;

Fig. 4 is a vertical section on line 4–4, Fig. 2 with the closure member in open condition;

Fig. 5 is a vertical section on line 5–5, Fig. 1 looking in the direction indicated;

Fig. 6 is a vertical section similar to Fig. 4 illustrating a modified construction of the washer; and

Fig. 7 is a pictorial illustration of the washer attached to a golf bag.

Referring now in particular to the accompanying drawings, the ball washer constituting the present invention is generally indicated at 10 and includes a cylindrical container 11 forming a housing having a continuous cylindrical wall 12 closed at each end by end walls 13 and 14. The cylindrical wall 12 is provided with a substantially circular access opening 15 therein which opening is of a slightly greater diameter than the diameter of a golf ball. The peripheral edges of the opening 15 are finished off with a circular rubber grommet 16 which is of general U-shaped configuration in cross section and which is applied as an edging strip to the container edges defining the opening. A curved or arcuate cover plate 17 is hinged as at 18 to the continuous cylindrical wall of the housing to form a closure member for the access opening 15. A suitable releasable catch member 19 is secured to the housing in such a manner as to selectively engage that edge of the cover plate opposite its hinged connection to lock the cover plate in closed condition over the access opening.

Interiorly the housing is provided with separate, complementary portions of a spongy, liquid absorbent material 20, which portions are so arranged within the container so as to define generally between them an annular passage 21 which is located within the container concentrically of the cylindrical wall thereof and which is centered substantially equidistant between the end walls of the container, as is best seen in Fig. 5.

Referring to Fig. 5, one of those portions A of the spongy, liquid absorbent material 20 located in the washer housing takes the form of a circular cup 21 having a circular body portion 22 provided with a perpendicular ring flange or rim 23 extending outwardly about the entire circumference of the body portion except where it is broken off to provide a channel 24 therethrough, having tapered edges 26, (Fig. 4) to coincide with the peripheral edges of the access opening 15 in the container. A second portion B of the spongy liquid absorbent material takes the form of a circular disc 27 provided with a circular hub 28 extending outwardly centrally from one face of the disc 27, said circular hub extending outwardly from the disc a distance substantially equal to the depth of the peripheral rim flange 23 of the cup member 21.

The cup member 21 is disposed with the base portion thereof against the inner face of the end wall 14 of the housing to which it is secured by suitable adhesive means 29 and which disposition places the outer face of the rim flange 23 thereof in juxtaposition with the inner face of the cylindrical wall 12 of the housing substantially centrally between the ends thereof with the channel 26 in the rim flange coinciding with the access opening 15 in the container as is best seen in Fig. 4. The outer face of the rim flange 23 is also connected as at 29 to the inner face of the cylindrical wall 12.

A shaft 30 is extended through said container on the longitudinal axis thereof and is journaled in bearings 31 and 32 carried by the end walls 13 and 14 of the container respectively. Externally of the container wall 13, and beyond the bearing 31, the shaft 30 is provided with a crank handle 32′ for manual rotation of the shaft 30 in the bearing.

The second portion B of the spongy material is mounted on the shaft 30 with the shaft extending centrally through the hub portion 28. The mounting of sponge portion B on shaft 30 positions hub 28 centrally within the cup-shaped member 21. The disc 27 and hub member 28 constituting the second spongy portion B are cemented as at 33 to the shaft 30 to space the extended end of the hub portion at a slight clearance from the base portion of the circular cup member 21, and to cause rotation of the disc and hub with the shaft. The aforedescribed complementary assembly of the first sponge portion A and the second sponge portion B provides for the formation of the annular passage 21 defined in cross section between the base portion and the rim flange of the sponge portion A and the disc portion and extended hub of the sponge portion B.

The cross sectional area of the annular passage 21 is such that when a golf bag 34 is placed downwardly through the access opening 15 of the container into the passage through the channel 26 in the rim flange 23 of the first sponge portion A, limited areas of the ball cover will resiliently embed themselves in the spongy material in the portions A and B as is best seen in Fig. 5.

A section of spongy, liquid absorbent material of general circular configuration is applied as at 35 to the inner face of the cover plate 17 so that when said cover plate is closed this section of spongy material will complete the continuity of the circular rim flange 23 on the sponge portion A by filling in the channel 26 therein.

Thus, when a ball is inserted into the annular passage 21 and the cover is closed, those portions of the golf ball immediately surrounding the intersecting perpendicular axes of the ball will be impressed into the spongy material and will be subject to resilient abrasion upon relative movement of the ball and portions of said spongy material.

To complete the construction of the ball washer as described heretofore, a resilient, substantially U-shaped clip 36 is secured to the outer face of the end wall 14 of the housing for the purposes of permitting detachable connection of the washer housing to a golf bag by any one of several possible modes of connection, one of such modes being illustrated in Fig. 7 where the clip is inserted downwardly over the top edge of a golf bag 37 adjacent the inner face of the bag with the washer 10 disposed adjacent the outer face of the bag with the access opening 15 therein disposed upwardly for the convenient insection of a ball thereinto, and with the handle 32′ disposed outwardly away from the bag to facilitate rotation of the shaft 30 and rotation of the sponge portion B and the golf ball 34.

To condition the ball washer for use, a liquid detergent solution is introduced into the container wherein the spongy material portions A and B absorb a substantial portion of such detergent solution for retention therein.

After completely wetting the spongy portions within the container, all free liquid remaining in the container is emptied out and the cover is closed and secured thus permitting the easy storage and transportation of the ball washer. The closure plate 17 also substantially seals the housing preventing loss of the detergent solution through evaporation.

When the washer is attached to a golf bag, as shown in Fig. 7, the cover plate 17 may be opened and one or more golf balls 34 inserted into the annular passage 21 in the container through the access opening 15. These golf balls will be moved through the annular passage 21 in either a clockwise or counterclockwise direction, as indicated by arrows in Fig. 4, dependent upon the direction of operation of the crank handle 32′ by the resilient, frictional movement of the disc 27 and the hub 28 in engagement with the ball 34. When such ball or balls return to a position immediately beneath the access opening 15 the resilience of the central hub portion 28 will cause the balls to spring upwardly to positions partially clear of the access opening 15 permitting their ready removal from the washer.

During movement of the golf balls 34 through the annular passage, the balls will be oscillated and rotated without any uniform pattern by reason of the frictional braking action applied to the ball by the stationary cup member 21 and the frictional impelling action of the disc 27 and hub 28 whereby all surface areas of the ball cover will be resiliently abraded or rubbed by the detergent solution bearing spongy material thereby cleaning all foreign substances from the cover of the ball.

Referring to Fig. 6, a modification of the present ball washer is shown wherein the construction of the container and the spongy portions therein are identical with those aforedescribed. In this modified construction, a pair of stop members or gates 38 are secured to the inner face of the container at spaced positions on either side of the access opening 15 in the general direction of the annular passage. The stop members 38 are faced with spongy material 20. These stops extend substantially radially inwardly into the annular passage 21 to restrict movement of a golf ball 39 positioned in said passage and to maintain the ball within a fixed region immediately below the access opening 15 in the container. In this modified construction, a ball positioned in the annular passage 21 between the stop members or gates 38 will, when the cover plate 17 is closed and locked, have portions thereof embedded on all sides in spongy material 20, as aforedescribed relative to the previously disclosed construction, and rotation of the sponge portion B will cause oscillation, twisting and rotation of the ball in contact with the spongy material thereby cleaning all foreign substances from the cover of the ball. Upon opening of the cover plate 17 there will be a resilient projection of the ball by hub 28 upwardly and outwardly of the access opening 15 for its removal from the container.

While in the instant disclosures the annular passage 21 is shown with a rectangular cross section, since such a configuration constitutes the most economical construction, it is fully contemplated that the sponge portions defining the annular passage could be so shaped as to provide an annular passage of round or oval cross-sectional configuration without departing from the spirit and secope of this invention.

It is further contemplated that any wet retaining material such as sponge rubber, neoprene or the like could be utilized as the abrading detergent holding means within the container of the washer construction shown and described.

Accordingly, a portable golf ball washer is provided which has inherently all those attributes, objects and advantages set forth above, and which provides an extremely new and useful article of manufacture of a type and function unique in the light of prior constructions.

In the foregoing description,

certain terms have been used for brevity, clearness and understanding, but no unnecessary limitations are to be implied therefrom beyond the requirements of the prior art, because such words are used for descriptive purposes herein and are intended to be broadly construed.

Moreover, the embodiments of the improved construction illustrated and described herein are by way of example, and the scope of the invention is not limited to the exact details of construction.

Having now described the invention, the construction, the operation and use of preferred embodiments thereof, and the advantageous new and useful results obtained thereby; the new and useful construction, and reasonable mechanical equivalents thereof obvious to those skilled in the art, are set forth in the appended claims.

PROBLEM*

This part of the examination requires analysis of 5 claims proposed to be added to an application having the accompanying specification and drawing. Certain phrases in the claims have been *underlined* and designated by a number in parenthesis. Most, but not all of the underlined portions represent instances wherein the claims fail to comply with United States patent law or accepted claim writing practice. For each number before an underlined section, make a short statement as to why the underlined portion does represent a defect, if such is the case.

3. A golf ball washer comprising (1) *a first housing,* said housing having (2) *at least one access opening* therethrough, means for selectively closing said opening, a first body of absorbent material fixed to a portion of said housing (3) *by adhesively securing* said first body to said housing on the inside thereof, a second body of

absorbent material within (4) *said cylindrical housing,* means including a shaft mounting (5) *one of said first and second bodies for rotation* relative to said housing, said bodies defining an annular chamber therebetween, and means attached to said shaft for manually rotating said rotatable body; (6) *a detergent solution is contained within the absorbent material of said first and second bodies.*

4. A washer as set forth in claim 3 wherein (7) *the first and second bodies cooperate with one another to form an annular chamber.*

5. A washer as defined in claim 3 wherein (8) *the means for rotating said rotatable body is omitted.*

6. A washer as recited in claim 3 in which the absorbent material of both said first and second bodies is (9) *selected from the group consisting of neoprene and sponge rubber.*

7. A washer as defined in claim 3 wherein said means for rotating said rotatable body includes a crank attached to said shaft and (10) *means for rotating said crank.*

---

*Reprinted as given on March 31, 1970, Exam.

Case 30

CRITICIZING "SLOPPY CLAIMS"
(Golf Ball Cleaner)

COMMENTS

(Quoted from Patent Office Approved Answers)

(1) "first" is surplusage.

(2) "at least one" is improper since there is no support in the disclosure for more than one.

(3) Improper method limitation.

(4) "cylindrical" does not have antecedent basis in the claim.

(5) The recitation is inaccurate and inconsistent with the preceding recitations in the claim, since the first body has previously been defined as being fixed; accordingly, only the second body may rotate.

(6) The recitation is improper, since a claim must be the object of a single sentence starting with "I (or We) claim" (or the equivalent).

(7) The recitation is a double inclusion of the previously recited element in Claim 3.

(8) A dependent claim is not proper if it expressly omits a previously recited element since an essential characteristic of a proper dependent claim is that it shall include every limitation of the claim from which it depends.

(Full credit was given for alternate answer drawn to claim 5 being incomplete because it omits an essential element of the invention).

(9) No error; proper Markush group.

(10) The recitation is unsupported in the specification because there is no disclosure of structural means for rotating the crank. The specification only discloses the operator's hand for rotating the crank which cannot be claimed.

Case 31

CRITICIZING "SLOPPY CLAIMS" (Foam Breaking)

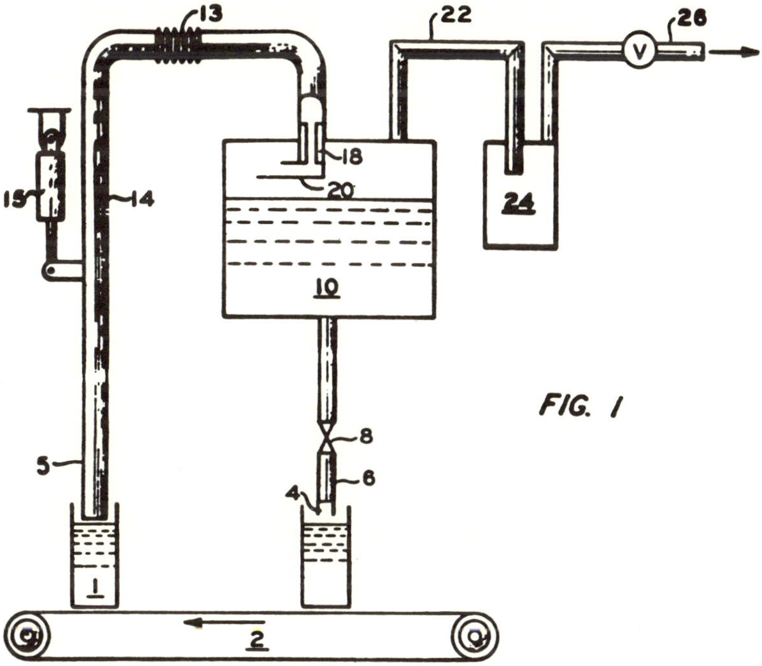

FIG. 1

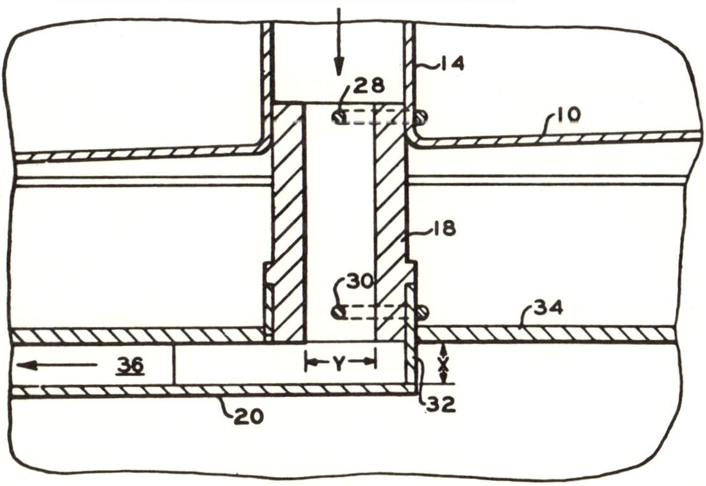

FIG. 2

FOAM BREAKING

ABSTRACT OF THE DISCLOSURE

Foam is passed through a cylindrical constriction and directed against a solid plate surface positioned substantially perpendicularly to the line of flow of the impinging foam, at a velocity sufficiently great to break down the foam. The ratio of the distance between the effluent end of the constriction and the solid plate surface to the diameter of the constriction is in the range of 0.25 to 1.

This invention relates to foam breaking. In one of its aspects, it relates to a method and apparatus for converting foam to a liquid by impinging the foam on a surface at such a force that the foam is thereby substantially destroyed and converted to liquid.

A milk filling apparatus for filling paper milk cartons uses one or more sets of piston and valve arrangements to pump a metered volume of milk into the cartons. This method and apparatus create foam on top of the liquid, which foam must be removed prior to the closing of the top of the cartons.

Many methods of breaking foam have been devised. Naucler 2,184,195 discloses a method of breaking foam in which foam is taken from a tank and passed through a pump to increase the pressure thereon and the foam is then sprayed back into the tank through a nozzle which emits the foam in a conical spray so that the individual froth bubbles travel in diverse directions to stretch the froth layer until the bubbles burst. This apparatus, due to the pump, subjects the foam material to contamination and is expensive. Further it is relatively inefficient.

One system for removing foam from the top of milk cartons is to direct a blast of live steam into the carton or in the filler bowl to eliminate rather than remove the foam. This method adequately eliminates the foam but is undesirable because live steam is dangerous. Further, there is some degree of water dilution to the milk, milk particles become cooked and give milk an off-flavor, and this method is expensive to incorporate into a commercial operation.

It was thought that the problem of foam formation in the top of the milk cartons could be overcome by drawing off the foam and returning it to the filler tank. However, the foam builds up in the tank to the point that it discharges from the blower used to draw the foam into the tank and must be trapped in a can. Using this method, about 100 to 200 gallons of milk per day will be trapped; however, this milk cannot be used as premium grade milk but must be reprocessed and used as a by-product.

I have now discovered that milk foam can be broken without loss of quality of material and with a minimum of equipment by impinging the foam against a solid surface at such a velocity that the foam is thereby broken.

By various aspects of this invention one or more of the following or other objects can be obtained.

It is an object of this invention to provide a novel process and apparatus for breaking foam.

It is a further object of this invention to provide a novel process and apparatus for recovering milk foam resulting from the filling of milk cartons.

It is a still further object of this invention to provide an economical process and apparatus for recovering milk foam from a filling operation without loss of quality of the removed product.

Other aspects, objects, and the several advantages of this invention are apparent to one skilled in the art from a study of this disclosure, the drawings, and the appended claims.

According to the invention, a foamed liquid is converted back into the liquid state by impinging the liquid against a surface at such a velocity that the foam is thereby broken. This process is advantageously employed in breaking milk foam which results from filling of milk cartons.

In one embodiment the foam is drawn through a constriction prior to being impinged on the surface. In another embodiment the surface is perpendicular to the direction of flow of the foam at the surface.

The invention will now be described with reference to the accompanying drawings in which FIGURE 1 schematically shows an embodiment of the invention and FIGURE 2 is a detailed view of a portion of the apparatus schematically shown in FIGURE 1.

Referring now to the drawings, a plurality of cartons 1 traveling on conveyor 2 are systematically filled by filling spout 4 which has supplied to it milk which passes through line 6 from tank 10. A valve 8 is advantageously provided in line 6 to stop the flow of milk into the cartons at fixed periods of time or after a predetermined quantity of milk has been discharged. Milk is maintained in tank 10 at a predetermined level schematically shown in FIGURE 1. After the cartons have been filled and some foam remains on top, valve 8 is closed. The filled carton is then conveyed to a foam removal station and foam removal nozzle 5 is lowered into the carton by means 15 such as an air cylinder and a vacuum source 26 draws foam from carton 1 through nozzle 5, line 14, flexible connection 13 through restriction 18 in line 14, and impinges the foam against surface 20. The impingement of foam against surface 20 is at such a velocity that the foam will be converted to milk and fall back down into the tank. A suitable draw-off conduit 22 with trap-out tank 24 it provided for vacuum source 26.

Referring now to FIGURE 2 wherein a detailed version of the restriction means 18 and plate 20 is seen. As can be seen from the drawing, the restriction means 18 comprises a cylindrical tube through which the foam passes. This restriction increases the velocity of the foam through line 14. Restriction 18 has pin 28 which extends through line 14 to hold restriction 18 in line 14. Another pin 30 attaches to member 32, which is in turn attached to plate 20, and to restriction 18. Member 32, the bottom portion of which is U-shaped, has an outlet at 36. As can be seen from the figure the plate 20 is substantially perpendicular to the line of flow of the foam at plate 20. Other supporting means such as a baffle 34 can be employed to maintain restriction 18 and member 32 in place.

The distance between plate 20 and the end of restriction 18 is designated by the letter X, The diameter of the constriction is designated by Y. The ratio of X to Y can be important in breaking the foam. As is understood by one skilled in the art there is a minimum velocity of the foam which is required, however. This velocity is achieved by the suction means 26. Generally, the suction means must be less than 5, preferably in the range of 8 to 10 inches of Hg below atmospheric pressure. For a suction within the tank below the minimum value and within the preferred range, the ratio of X to Y will advantageously be in the range of .25 to 1, preferably .50 to .60.

Although the invention has been described with relation to impinging the foam against a surface which is perpendicular to the direction of flow at the surface, it is obvious that the surface could be slightly inclined as long as the flow is impinged against the surface at such velocity that the foam is thereby broken. Of course, it is preferred that the surface be perpendicular to the flow of foam so that a minimum velocity will be required.

It has been found that milk foam from milk cartons has been broken very effectively using an apparatus such as that hereinbefore described with the use of an American Blower Company, Size D, centrifugal fan with a 14 inch fan and a 3 inch pipe operating at a speed of 3600 r.p.m. Under these conditions the vacuum pulled in the tank 10 was in the range of 8 to 10 inches of Hg below atmospheric pressure and the velocity of the foam was estimated to be between 40 to 80 feet per second, probably about 60 feet per second.

Whereas the invention has been described with relation to having the impinging surface within the tank, it is obvious that the surface can be without the tank and a conduit can be used to drain the liquid into tank 10 from the surface.

Whereas the invention has been described with relation to breaking milk foam, it is obvious that other types of foams can be broken by the use of the invention. Other foams include beer, soap and the like.

*Excerpted from instructions given on Sept. 15, 1970, Exam.

PROBLEM*

This part of the examination requires analysis of claims proposed to be added to an application already on file in the United States Patent Office from which claims 1-9 have been cancelled and having the [accompanying] specification and drawings directed to "Foam Breaking."

Certain words and phrases in the claims have been underlined and designated by number in parenthesis.

Some, but not all, of the underlined portions represent instances wherein the claims fail to comply with United States Patent Law or accepted claim writing practice.

. . . [S]tate whether each items (1) through (12) is "proper" or "improper" and if "improper" why so.

10. An apparatus for converting foam to a liquid comprising a tank means to hold a quantity of liquid, (1) *outlet means or equivalent means* at the bottom of said tank means to pass liquid from said tank, saidoutlet means adapted to fill a container and (2) *draw liquid therefrom,* conduit means to remove foam from (3) *said filled containers,* said conduit means leading to said tank means, a solid plate having a surface thereof positioned substantially perpendicularly to the line of flow of said conduit means, (4) *means to draw said foam* through said conduit means at such a velocity that said

foam impinges on said surface and will thereby be converted to (5) *fluid,* a constriction provided within said conduit means adjacent the outlet end thereof and adjacent said surface, the ratio of the distance from the end of said constriction to said surface to the diameter of said constriction being in the range of 0.25 to 1.

11. (6) *An apparatus for converting foam to a liquid comprising a tank means to hold a quantity of liquid, outlet means at the bottom of said tank means to pass liquid from said tank means, said outlet means adapted to fill a milk carton, conduit means to remove foam from milk carton, said conduit leading to said tank, and means to draw said foam through said conduit.*

12. A method of converting (7) *liquid to a foam* which comprises passing said foam through a substantially cylindrical constriction to increase the velocity of the foam passing therethrough and impinging the effluent from said constriction against a solid plate positioned substantially perpendicular to the line of flow of the impinging foam, at a velocity sufficiently great to break down the foam, (8) *the ratio of the distance between the effluent end of said constriction and said solid plate surface to the diameter of said constriction being in the range of 0.2 to 1.*

13. (9) *The product produced by the process of claim 12.*

14. The method of claim 11 wherein (10) *said ratio is in the range of 0.4 to 0.6.*

Case 31

CRITICIZING "SLOPPY CLAIMS"
(Foam Breaking)

COMMENTS

(Quoted from Patent Office Approved Answers)

1. The recitation is improper because of the inclusion therein of "or equivalent means." Such inclusion is improper because (i) the expression is thus rendered alternative, MPEP 706.03(d), or (ii) the meaning of "equivalents thereof" is not necessary to cover the invention. (2 points.)

2. The phrase is improper because it is vague and indefinite, MPEP 706.03(d), or no antecedent for "outlet means" (2 points).

3. The phrase is improper because there is no antecedent basis therefor or because the scope is vague and indefinite. MPEP 706.03(d). (2 points.)

4. The phrase is considered proper. (2 points.)

5. The phrase is improper. The term "fluid" is broader than the written disclosure. The term should be "liquid" because fluid includes gases. Also, no antecedent basis for "fluid" exists. (2 points).

6. This phrase is improper because (i) it reads on the prior art described in the specification or (ii) it omits material limitations or (iii) it is misdescriptive (4 points).

7. The phrase is improper because the process described in the specification converts a foam to a liquid and not a liquid to a foam. (2 points.)

8. The phrase is considered proper. (2 points.)

9. The phrase is improper (i) because it is drawn to an improper product by process, MPEP 706.03(e) or (ii) is so broad that it reads on the prior since it covers nothing more than a carton of liquid, such as milk. (4 points.)

10. The phrase is improper because it contains new matter 35 USC Section 132, last sentence. The limitation "0.4" is not found in the specification and therefore cannot appear in the claims. MPEP 706.03(o). (2 points.) In addition full credit was given if it was noted that claim 11 was not a method claim or there is no antecedent basis in claim 11 for the underlined portion.

REVIEW AND CATALOG OF "SLOPPY CLAIMS" ERRORS

The following chart lists the type of claim errors, or problems that were not errors, including the seven prior Agents Exam questions given in the preceding examples, (Appendix B cases 25-31). Also listed are a few additional types of errors not included in the Exam questions. The chart keys the errors to the pertinent sections of this book, and to each case 25 to 31 where the error or possible error appeared.

TYPE OF ERROR		APPENDIX B–CASES						
		25	26	27	28	29	30	31
	Book Section	Suction Cleaner	Steam and Dry Iron	Bomb-Proof Coating	Self-Priming Pump	Coated Pipe	Golf Ball Cleaner	Foam Breaking
1. Claim in two sentences	4, 10	✓	✓		✓		✓	
2. Wrong verb form ("A suction cleaner includes. . . .") or improper punctuation	4, 7, 10	✓			✓			
3. Nonstatutory claim:	1		✓	✓				
a. Omnibus claim ("The invention as shown and described.")	2		✓					
b. Referring to drawing where unnecessary ("A ___ as shown in the drawing.")	2, and see 51			✓				
4. Lack of antecedent and/or support in claim		✓	✓		✓	✓		✓
a. Inferential—adding limitations not previously introduced (". . . rear pair of wheels. . . ." where number not previously recited)	17, 20	✓	✓		✓		✓	✓
b. Inferential—adding element not previously introduced (". . . connected to said gear. . . ." where gear not previously introduced)	20	✓	✓		✓	✓		
5. Indefinite	64	✓	✓	✓	✓	✓		✓
a. Unclear which of two previous elements reference is being made to ("front and rear wheels" previously introduced; reference is to "said wheel")	20	✓	✓		✓			
b. Alternative expressions ("such as")	21		✓	✓		✓		✓
c. Different names for same elements	16, 20		✓					

TYPE OF ERROR	Book Section	25 Suction Cleaner	26 Steam and Dry Iron	27 Bomb-Proof Coating	28 Self-Priming Pump	29 Coated Pipe	30 Golf Ball Cleaner	31 Foam Breaking
		APPENDIX B—CASES						
d. Referring to previously introduced element as though it were a new element ("a handle" previously recited; later on, claim recites "a handle" again—unclear if same or new handle)	20		✓					
e. Basically not clear								✓
f. Unbased comparative ("thick")	22			✓				
6. Lack of antecedent and/or support in specification	15, 16	✓	✓	✓	✓			✓
a. Not described at all	15, 16	✓	✓	✓		✓		✓
b. Inconsistent with specification	15, 16	✓			✓	✓	✓	✓
c. Misdescriptive	15, 16		✓			✓	✓	✓
d. Omits material limitations								✓
7. Lack of antecedent and/or support in drawings	15	✓	✓					
8. Catalog or elements—Lack of cooperation	25-30, 61	✓	✓		✓			
a. Whole claim is mere catalogue	25	✓	✓		✓	✓		
b. Only some elements not connected (especially in dependent claims)	25	✓	✓		✓			
9. Functional—too broad	27, 28	✓	✓		✓			
a. No structure to support function ("adapted to be reciprocated")	27, 28	✓	✓					
b. Single "means" claim	31		✓					
c. Claiming result only	28							
d. "Whereby" clause which does not necessarily follow from rest of claims	29		✓					

TYPE OF ERROR	Book Section	APPENDIX B—CASES 25 Suction Cleaner	26 Steam and Dry Iron	27 Bomb-Proof Coating	28 Self-Priming Pump	29 Coated Pipe	30 Golf Ball Cleaner	31 Foam Breaking
e. Failure to distinguish over prior art set forth in specification		✓			✓			✓
10. Double inclusion of elements (especially in dependent claims—claim previously recites "reservoir," then recites "casing" and "pipe," which are "the reservoir")	18, 31, 53	✓	✓		✓		✓	
11. Surplusage (laudatory statements, *i.e.*, "new," "better," etc.)	9		✓	✓		✓	✓	✓
12. Improper Markush	47		✓	✓		✓		
a. Mechanical group	47		✓					
b. Chemicals not in art-recognized class	47			✓				
13. Improper product-by-process (product can be described otherwise)	43			✓				✓
14. Obvious method of making product (*i.e.*, novelty only in product)	36			✓				
15. Trademark and proprietary material	48							
16. Positively reciting workpiece	13							
17. Positively reciting holes, grooves, etc.	23		✓					
18. Dependent claim errors	53							
a. Inconsistent with parent	53	✓	✓				✓	✓
b. Alternative (*i.e.*, depends on more than one independent claim)	53	✓	✓					
c. Incorrect statutory class-adding method limitation to apparatus claim and vice versa	53		✓					
d. Improper location (not sufficiently close to parent claim)	5			✓		✓		
e. Refers to element absent in parent (see 4.b., *supra*)	20, 53		✓					✓

TYPE OF ERROR		APPENDIX B—CASES						
		25	26	27	28	29	30	31
	Book Section	Suction Cleaner	Steam and Dry Iron	Bomb-Proof Coating	Self-Priming Pump	Coated Pipe	Golf Ball Cleaner	Foam Breaking
f. Deletes element from parent							✓	
19. Incomplete claim—claim lacks an element the specification and/or preamble require to yield proper combination. Omits element specification says is "essential." See 8 and 9, *supra.*	25-30, 63							✓
20. Negative limitations—may be O.K.	14							
21. Reference numerals in claim —O.K., if parenthesized	19							
22. Unnecessary apparatus limitation in method claim—questionable in view of elimination of "method functional of the apparatus" rejection	37-38							
23. Mental steps—may be O.K. if proper apparatus required to effect the steps	41							
24. Design claim in terms of structure instead of formalistic (See 3, *supra.*)	44							
25. Old combination	60							
26. Duplicate claiming—two claims differ only trivially or by very old matter	58							
27. Old material claimed per se, instead of in method (*i.e.,* "new use")	52							
28. Attempting to expand Markush grouping, esp. in dependent claim (Markush group: "A, B, and C"; dependent claim says element may also be "D")	8, 47					✓		
29. Unnecessary method limitation in apparatus claim.							✓	

APPENDIX C

THE ART OF DESCRIBING STRUCTURES IN PATENT DRAWINGS INCLUDING A GLOSSARY OF MECHANICAL TERMS

By Louis B. Applebaum*

(Edited by John D. Kaufmann)

The effective communication of facts and ideas is the essence of the role of the patent attorney or agent. As amanuensis ("the hand of another") of the inventor, the patent attorney must select from the vast wealth that constitutes the words and phrases of the language, to convey the precise meaning that is appropriate to the application at hand, in the light of the prior art of record.

Three "languages"—three stylized forms of communication—are prescribed by the Rules of Practice: The specification must fully, clearly and concisely describe the invention (rule 71) and thus constitutes our primary language. The claims must particularly point out and distinctly claim what the *applicant* (not someone else) regards as his invention (rule 75), thus being a precis of the salient portions of the specification. And, third, the drawing must show every feature of the invention claimed (rule 83), depicting what is essential in the specification and claims. It thus becomes necessary for patent students to acquire facility in each of these three "languages," and to be able to translate from one to another.

---

*Reprinted with permission from material prepared for the Practising Law Institute's Patent Agent's Examination Review Course. Mr. Applebaum is Patent Counsel, United States Navy Applied Science Laboratory.

No one of the three "languages" is a logical starting point for the translation process. However, since the pictorial is a fundamental base, we can ideally commence with a drawing and translate the invention shown therein to the language of claims. The development will, however, be limited to the translation from drawings to a detailed description (or specification) to avoid premature and incomplete treatment of the substantive and procedural complexities of claim drafting, which are discussed in this book.

This process of translating from drawings to words involves the understanding of the elements of patent drawings (as distinguished from other drawing formats), the understanding of the elements of mechanics, and the establishment or reinforcement of a basic and minimal vocabulary. With this learned, the words can be put together to provide a coherent and clear description.

First, it *must* be noted that patent drawings are stylized, simple and generally pictorial: Extracting pertinent phrases from the Rules of Practice, the drawing

> . . . must show every feature of the invention.
>
> . . . when the invention is an improvement, the drawing must show the invention disconnected from the old structure, and in another view must show so much only of the old structure as will suffice to show the connection of the invention with what is old.
>
> . . . surface shading should be open.
>
> . . . sectional shading is by oblique parallel lines.
>
> . . . solid black should not be used for sectional or surface shading.
>
> . . . drawings should have the fewest lines possible consistent with clearness.
>
> . . . the plane on which a sectional view is taken should be indicated on the general view by a broken or dotted line, designated by numerals corresponding to the number of the sectional view.
>
> . . . heavy lines on the shade side of objects should be used; light comes at 45° from the upper left hand corner.

. . . the same numeral is a reference to the same part.
. . . certain symbols, illustrated at pages 139-142 in the Rules of Practice are accepted as conventional (these should be known).

A description of structure, in the language we call a "specification," is a grouping of words and phrases (each word or phrase being identifiable as an *element* or "island"), at times qualified by modifying appendage words and phrases (sub-elements or "peninsulas" of the island) AND LINKING WORDS AND PHRASES, COUPLING OR PROVIDING A BRIDGE FROM ONE ISLAND TO AT LEAST ONE OTHER ISLAND. Without this coupling or bridging, an "island" is left floating, and is not a proper part of the description: merely listing the "islands" *without including the coupling bridges,* results in a fatally defective description, in that it is no more than a listing or cataloging. (For example, do *not* say ". . . a motor, a rotary cam and a cam follower. . . ." Instead, say ". . . a motor, a rotary cam driven by the motor, and a cam follower engaging the cam. . . ." Note especially the terms below under the heading "Placement (relation)." One may find the following useful in successfully erecting and coupling together an integral empire of islands, peninsulas and bridges:

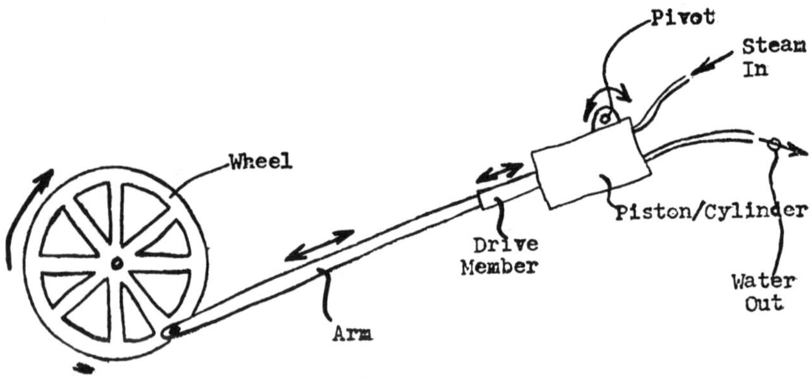
Pivot
Steam
In
Wheel
Piston/Cylinder
Drive
Member
Water
Out
Arm

FOUR QUESTIONS

1. What is it? What is the element's name?

   EXAMPLE: "*An arm. . . .*"

2. Where is it located?

   EXAMPLE: "An arm . . . *having one end . . . mounted on . . . said flywheel and the other end . . . mounted . . . on said drive member. . . .*"

3. What does it do?

   EXAMPLE: "An arm . . . having one end . . . mounted on . . . said flywheel and the other end . . . mounted . . . on said drive member, *for rotating said flywheel upon reciprocation of said drive member. . . .*"

4. How does it do what it does?

   EXAMPLE: "An arm *freely reciprocable* having one end *pivotally* mounted on *the periphery of* said flywheel and the other end *fixedly* mounted *for reciprocation therewith* on said drive member, for rotating said flywheel upon reciprocation of said drive member. . . ."

NOTE: The "arm" as described is really a "pitman" or connecting rod as it operates, *e.g.*, on a steam locomotive. Similar descriptive language for the wheel and drive member must have preceded the description of the arm.

To build this description of structure from the drawings, the writer must have a vocabulary of general and "mechanical" words to constitute his translation of the elements and connectives or "bridges" he sees in the drawing. The following terms, grouped loosely by function, are probably a fairly comprehensive vocabulary of many terms used in the mechanical arts and patents.

GENERAL AND MECHANICAL TERMS

The following terms are grouped loosely by function. The list is illustrative rather than comprehensive.

Structure
- arm
- bail
- band
- base
- beam
  - cantilever
  - simple
- belt
- blade
- blower
- body
- boom
- branch
- carriage
- case
- chute
- column
- container
- conveyor
- cover
- device
- die
- drum
- enclosure
- finger
- frame
- gauges
- handle
- head
- housing
- jacket
- jaw
- leg
- member
- neck
- object
- particle
- partition
- platform
- plug
- rib
- ring
- rod
- shell
- shoe
- shoulder
- sleeve
- step
- strut
- track
- truss
- upright
- wall

Mounting Method
- attach
- bolt
- couple
- demountably
- engage
- fix
- hold
- lock
- mount
- secure
- set
- weld

Fastener
- bolt
- cable
- clamp
- connection
- coupling
- dowel
- hold down
- hook
- joint
  - universal
- keeper
- key
- latch
- lock
- lug
- nail
- nut
- pin
- rivet
- screw
- seam

Bearing
- antifriction
  - ball
  - needle
  - roller
    - tapered
- bushing
- fulcrum
- guide
- journal
- pivot
- radial

seal
seat
sliding
support
thrust

Spring
air
bias
element
coil
helical
compression
tension
leaf
torsional

Numbers
multiplicity
plurality

Placement (relation)
adjacent
aligned
attached
axial
complementary
concentric
eccentric
contiguous
distal-proximate
divided
engaged
extended
integral
intermediate
interposed
juxtaposed
located
mating
meshing
offset
opposed
overlapping
perpendicular
parallel
positioned
projecting
removable
resting
retractable
spacer
staggered
superposed
supported
surrounding
symmetrical

Voids (having a void)
aperture
bore
cavity
chamber
duct
groove
hole
hollow
notch
opening
orifice
passage
slit
slot

Shape
A-. . . Z-(etc.)
("a C-shaped member")
annular
arch
arcuate
barrel
bucket
channel
circular
concave-convex
conical
corrugated
cup
cylinder
depression
disc
dome
elliptical
fin
flange
fold
fork
helical
hook
notch
oblong
oval
parabolic
plane
rectangular
round
sheet
shelf
sinusoidal
spherical
square
taper
triangular
trough
tubular
twist
web
wedge

Material properties
- dense
- elastic
- enlarged
- flexible
- foraminous
- insulation
- opaque
- porous
- resilient
- rigid
- translucent
- transparent

Optical
- bezel
- bulb
  - fluorescent
  - incondescent
- lamp
- light
  - beam
  - ray
- reflection
- refraction
- transmission
- window

Fluid Flow
- accumulator
- aspirator
- bellows
- conduit
- connector
- convection
- cylinder
  - piston
    - rod
- dashpot
- diaphragm
- discharge
- dispenser
- filter
- fitting
- flue
- gasket
- hose
- hydraulic
- medium
- nozzle
- outlet
- pipe
- plunger
- port
  - inlet
  - outlet
- pump
  - centrifugal
  - gear
  - piston
  - vane
- reservoir
- seal
- siphon
- tank
- tube
- valve
  - ball-check
  - control
  - gate
  - shut-off

Position
- angle
  - oblique
  - obtuse
- bottom-top
- close-open
- crest
- edge
- external-internal
- face
- film
- horizontal-vertical
- layer
- lower-upper
- normal to-parallel
- rim
- section
- slant
- surface
- tilt

Materials
- adhesive
- concrete
- cork
- fabric
- fibre
- insulation
- liquid
- metal
- plastic
- refractory
- rubber
- sand
- screen
- wood

Electrical
- contact
- electrode
- electromagnet
- filament
- insulator
- lead
- line cord
- motor
- power supply
- resistance
- socket
- solenoid
- switch
- transformer
- wire

Rotation to translation
- bell crank
- cam
- connecting rod
- crank arm
- jack
- radius bar
- screw
- winch
- yoke

Translation to translation
- inclined plane
- lever
- linkage
  - parallel
- straight line
  - motion
- toggle
- wedge

Sequence
- alternate
- cyclic
- interval
- lag-lead

Movement
- compression
- downward-upward
- drag
- eccentric
- emergent
- extensible
- extrude
- grinding
- impact
- inertia
- longitudinal
- meeting
- pressing
- propelling
- pulverize
- sagging
- severing
- slidable
- terminating
- torque
- transverse
- traversing
- vibrating

Rotation to rotation
- brake
  - band
  - disc
  - shoe
- chain
- clutch
  - centrifugal
  - sprag
  - toothed
  - one-way
- drive
  - belt
    - pulley
    - sheave
    - toothed
- friction
- gear
  - bevel
  - crown
  - internal
  - non-circular
  - pinion
  - right angle
  - spur
  - worm and wheel
- intermittent
  - escapement
  - geneva
  - pawl and
    - ratchet
    - pendulum
- journal
- variable speed
- flexible coupling
- sprocket

If one knew all of these terms and what they meant, he would be well put to write the vast majority of mechanical patent claims; *i.e.*, to translate these key words and phrases for naming the elements (Section 16) and their connectives and interrelationships (Sections 25-27) into good mechanical *combination* claims.

No two writers need generate descriptions from drawings in the same manner. But these procedural steps may be useful in writing mechanical claims.

1. Start with a title. Name or define generically the thing to be described (Sections 6 and 12).

2. List the elements and the subelements of the thing (Section 13). This list can be tabular, or can be marked on the drawing, with lead lines to the part or the coupling element defined.

3. Note particularly how the elements are combined or associated with each other (Sections 25-27). This is a vital step. The description must include the structure that establishes how the elements function and cooperate with each other. Otherwise, it is a mere catalog of elements (Sections 25 and 61).

4. Numerate where numeration is significant: "One, two, etc."; "a pair"; "a plurality"; "at least two"; a "first—" and later a "second—" etc. are very useful descriptions (Section 17). " . . ." when any number, one or more, will do.

Finally, and most important: Recite the elements and their connectives in a logical order, rather than at random (Section 24). There are many possible logical orders: Recite from the base up, as the thing might be erected. Recite in the probable sequence of assembly of the thing. Recite elements and their connectives in the order of their operation. Or recite the main body element, followed by a systematic description of the appendage elements—making certain to include the connective elements. And, usually, try to avoid describing the thing when it is in motion—try to describe it when it is at a rest point.

Of course, avoid all of the negative caveats as best you can: alternatives (Section 21); negative limitations except for emergencies (Section 14); "unduly functional" expressions (Section 28); "vague and indefinite" expressions, including ambiguous words or "unbased comparatives" such as "large" (Sections 20 and 64); the twin evils of incompleteness (Section 63) and unnecessary, superfluous, needless, redundant prolixity (Section 65); and all the other evils described in the book.

In gaining skill in translating drawings to descriptions, there is no substitute for practice. Write—and then critically review your writing. Write—and critically review the writing of another as he reviews your description. The reward will be improved skill in the most vital of our efforts, which fundamentally comes down to the communication of intelligence.

APPENDIX D

Part I

TITLE 35 UNITED STATES CODE

(Selected sections of the patent statute concerning claims and related items discussed in this book)

§6. Duties of Commissioner

The Commissioner, under the direction of the Secretary of Commerce, shall superintend or perform all duties required by law respecting the granting and issuing of patents and the registration of trade-marks; and he shall have charge of property belonging to the Patent Office. He may, subject to the approval of the Secretary of Commerce, establish regulations, not inconsistent with law, for the conduct of proceedings in the Patent Office.

§41. Patent fees

(a) The Commissioner shall charge the following fees:

1. On filing each application for an original patent, except in design cases, $65; in addition, on filing or on presentation at any other time, $10 for each claim in independent form which is in excess of one, and $2 for each claim whether independent or dependent which is in excess of ten. Errors in payment of the additional fees may be rectified in accordance with regulations of the Commissioner.

2. For issuing each original or reissue patent, except in design cases, $100; in addition, $10 for each page (or portion thereof) of specification as printed, and $2 for each sheet of drawing.

3. In design cases:

a. On filing each design application, $20.

b. On issuing each design patent: For three years and six months, $10; for seven years, $20; and for fourteen years, $30.

§100. Definitions

When used in this title unless the context otherwise indicates—

(a) The term "invention" means invention or discovery.

(b) The term "process" means process, art or method, and includes a new use of a known process, machine, manufacture, composition of matter, or material.

§101. Inventions patentable

Whoever invents or discovers any new and useful process, machine, manufacture, or composition of matter, or any new and useful improvement thereof, may obtain a patent therefor, subject to the conditions and requirements of this title.

§102. Conditions for patentability; novelty and loss of right to patent

A person shall be entitled to a patent unless—

(a) the invention was known or used by others in this country, or patented or described in a printed publication in this or a foreign country, before the invention thereof by the applicant for patent, or

(b) the invention was patented or described in a printed publication in this or a foreign country or in public use or on sale in this country, more than one year prior to the date of the application for patent in the United States, or

(c) he has abandoned the invention, or

(d)* the invention was first patented or caused to be patented *or was the subject of an inventor's certificate* by the applicant or his legal representatives or assigns in a foreign country prior to the date of the application for patent in this country on an application *for patent or inventor's certificate* filed more than twelve months before the filing of the application in the United States, or

(e) the invention was described in a patent granted on an application for patent by another filed in the United States before the invention thereof by the applicant for patent, or

(f) he did not himself invent the subject matter sought to be patented, or

(g) before the applicant's invention thereof the invention was made in this country by another who had not abandoned, suppressed, or concealed it. In determining priority of invention there shall be considered not only the respective dates of conception and reduction to practice of the invention, but also the reasonable diligence of one who was first to conceive and last to reduce to practice, from a time prior to conception by the other.

§103. Conditions for patentability; non-obvious subject matter

A patent may not be obtained though the invention is not identically disclosed or described as set forth in section 102 of this title, if the differences between the subject matter sought to be patented and the prior art are such that the subject matter as a whole would have been obvious at the time the invention was made to a

---

*Amended, effective six months after Articles 1-12 of the Paris Convention of 1883, as revised in Stockholm on July 14, 1967, come into force in the United States, to add the italicized portions. Pub. L. 92-538 (July 28, 1972).

person having ordinary skill in the art to which said subject matter pertains. Patentability shall not be negatived by the manner in which the invention was made.

§112. Specification

The specification shall contain a written description of the invention, and of the manner and process of making and using it, in such full, clear, concise, and exact terms as to enable any person skilled in the art to which it pertains, or with which it is most nearly connected, to make and use the same, and shall set forth the best mode contemplated by the inventor of carrying out his invention.

The specification shall conclude with one or more claims particularly pointing out and distinctly claiming the subject matter which the applicant regards as his invention. A claim may be written in independent or dependent form, and if in dependent form, it shall be construed to include all the limitations of the claim incorporated by reference into the dependent claims.

An element in a claim for a combination may be expressed as a means or step for performing a specified function without the recital of structure, material, or acts in support thereof, and such claim shall be construed to cover the corresponding structure, material, or acts described in the specification and equivalents thereof. (Amended July 24, 1965, Public Law 89-93, sec. 9, 79 Stat. 261.)

§113. Drawings

When the nature of the case admits, the applicant shall furnish a drawing.

§121. Divisional applications

If two or more independent and distinct inventions are claimed in one application, the Commissioner may require the application to be restricted to one of the inventions. If the other invention is made the subject of a divisional application which complies with the requirements of section 120 of this title it shall be entitled to the benefit of the filing date of the original application. A patent issuing on an application with respect to which a requirement for restriction under this section has been made, or on an application filed as a result of such a requirement, shall not be used as a reference either in the Patent Office or in the courts against a divisional application or against the original application or any patent issued on either of them, if the divisional application is filed before the issuance of the patent on the other application. If a divisional application is directed solely to subject matter described and claimed in the original application as filed, the Commissioner may dispense with signing and execution by the inventor. The validity of a patent shall not be questioned for failure of the Commissioner to require the application to be restricted to one invention.

§134. Appeal to the Board of Appeals

An applicant for a patent, any of whose claims has been twice rejected, may appeal from the decision of the primary examiner to the Board of Appeals, having once paid the fee for such appeal.

§161. Patents for plants

Whoever invents or discovers and asexually reproduces any distinct and new variety of plant, including cultivated sports, mutants, hybrids, and newly found seedlings, other than a tuber propagated plant or a plant found in an uncultivated state, may obtain a patent therefor, subject to the conditions and requirements of this title. (Amended September 3, 1954, 68 Stat. 1190.)

The provisions of this title relating to patents for inventions shall apply to patents for plants, except as otherwise provided.

§162. Description, claim

No plant patent shall be declared invalid for noncompliance with section 112 of this title if the description is as complete as is reasonably possible.

The claim in the specification shall be in formal terms to the plant shown and described.

§171. Patents for designs

Whoever invents any new, original and ornamental design for an article of manufacture may obtain a patent therefor, subject to the conditions and requirements of this title.

The provisions of this title relating to patents for inventions shall apply to patents for designs, except as otherwise provided.

§251. Reissue of defective patents

Whenever any patent is, through error without any deceptive intention, deemed wholly or partly inoperative or invalid, by reason of a defective specification or drawing, or by reason of the patentee claiming more or less than he had a right to claim in the patent, the Commissioner shall, on the surrender of such patent and the payment of the fee required by law, reissue the patent for the invention disclosed in the original patent, and in accordance with a new and amended application, for the unexpired part of the term of the original patent. No new matter shall be introduced into the application for reissue.

The Commissioner may issue several reissued patents for distinct and separate parts of the thing patented, upon demand of the applicant, and upon payment of the required fee for a reissue for each of such reissued patents.

The provisions of this title relating to applications for patent shall be applicable to applications for reissue of a patent, except that application for reissue may be made and sworn to by the assignee of the entire interest if the application does not seek to enlarge the scope of the claims of the original patent.

No reissued patent shall be granted enlarging the scope of the claims of the original patent unless applied for within two years from the grant of the original patent.

§252. Effect of reissue

The surrender of the original patent shall take effect upon the issue of the reissued patent, and every reissued patent shall have the same effect and operation in law, on the trial of actions for causes thereafter arising, as if the same had been originally granted in such amended form, but in so far as the claims of the original and reissued patents are identical, such surrender shall not affect any action then pending nor abate any cause of action then existing, and the reissued patent, to the extent that its claims are identical with the original patent, shall constitute a continuation thereof and have effect continuously from the date of the original patent.

No reissued patent shall abridge or affect the right of any person or his successors in business who made, purchased or used prior to the grant of a reissue anything patented by the reissued patent, to continue the use of, or to sell to others to be used or sold, the specific thing so made, purchased or used, unless the making, using or selling of such thing infringes a valid claim of the reissued patent which was in the original patent. The court before which such matter is in question may provide for the continued manufacture, use or sale of the thing made, purchased or used as specified, or for the manufacture, use or sale of which substantial preparation was made before the grant of the reissue, and it may also provide for the continued practice of any process patented by the reissue, practiced, or for the practice of which substantial preparation was made, prior to the grant of the reissue, to the extent and under such terms as the court deems equivable for the protection of investments made or business commenced before the grant of the reissue.

§271. Infringement of patent

(a) Except as otherwise provided in this title, whoever without authority makes, uses or sells any patented invention, within the United States during the term of the patent therefor, infringes the patent.

(b) Whoever actively induces infringement of a patent shall be liable as an infringer.

(c) Whoever sells a component of a patented machine, manufacture, combination or composition, or a material or apparatus for use in practicing a patented process, constituting a material part of the invention, knowing the same to be especially made or especially adapted for use in an infringement of such patent, and not a staple article or commodity of commerce suitable for substantial noninfringing use, shall be liable as a contributory infringer.

* * *

§281. Remedy for infringement of patent

A patentee shall have remedy by civil action for infringement of his patent.

* * *

§282. Presumption of validity; defenses

A patent shall be presumed valid. Each claim of a patent (whether in independent or dependent form) shall be presumed valid independently of the validity of other claims; dependent claims shall be presumed valid even though dependent upon an invalid claim. The burden of establishing invalidity of a parent or any claim thereof shall rest on the party asserting it.

The following shall be defenses in any action involving the validity or infringement of a patent and shall be pleaded:

(1) Noninfringement, absence of liability for infringement, or unenforceability.

(2) Invalidity of the patent or any claim in suit on any ground specified in part II of this title as a condition for patentability,

(3) Invalidity of the patent or any claim in suit for failure to comply with any requirement of sections 112 or 251 of this title,

(4) Any other fact or act made a defense by this title.

* * *

APPENDIX D

Part II

RULES OF PRACTICE

(Selections from the Patent Office Rules of Practice)

58. Chemical and mathematical formulas and tables. (a) The specification, including the claims, may contain chemical and mathematical formulas, but shall not contain drawings or flow diagrams. The description portion of the specification may contain tables; claims may contain tables only if necessary to conform to 35 U.S.C. 112.

* * *

[Detailed regulations follow on size and type of paper, etc.]

71. Detailed description and specification of the invention. (a) The specification must include a written description of the invention or discovery and of the manner and process of making and using the same, and is required to be in such full, clear, concise, and exact terms as to enable any person skilled in the art or science to which the invention or discovery appertains, or with which it is most nearly connected, to make and use the same.

(b) The specification must set forth the precise invention for which a patent is solicited, in such manner as to distinguish it from other inventions and from what is old. It must describe completely a specific embodiment of the process, machine, manufacture, composition of matter or improvement invented, and must explain the mode of operation or principle whenever applicable. The best mode contemplated by the inventor of carrying out his invention must be set forth.

(c) In the case of an improvement, the specification must particularly point out the part or parts of the process, machine, manufacture, or composition of matter to which the improvement relates, and the description should be confined to the specific improvement and to such parts as necessarily cooperate with it or as may be necessary to a complete understanding or description of it.

75. Claim(s). The specification must conclude with a claim particularly pointing out and distinctly claiming the subject matter which the applicant regards as his invention or discovery.

(b) More than one claim may be presented provided they differ substantially from each other and are not unduly multiplied.

(c) When more than one claim is presented, they may be placed in dependent form in which a claim may refer back to and further restrict a single preceding claim. Claims in dependent form shall be construed to include all the limitations of the claim incorporated by reference into the dependent claim.

(d) (1) The claim or claims must conform to the invention as set forth in the remainder of the specification and the terms and phrases used in the claims must find clear support or antecedent basis in the description so that the meaning of the terms in the claims may be ascertainable by reference to the description.

(2) See rules 141 to 146 as to claiming different inventions in one application.

(e) Where the nature of the case admits, as in the case of an improvement, any independent claim should contain in the following order, (1) a preamble comprising a general description of all the elements or steps of the claimed combination which are conventional or known, (2) a phrase such as "wherein the improvement comprises, and (3) those elements, steps and/or relationships which constitute that portion of the claimed combination which the applicant considers as the new or improved portion.

81. Drawings required. The applicant for patent is required by statute to furnish a drawing of his invention whenever the nature of the case admits of it; this drawing must be filed with the application. Illustrations facilitating an understanding of the invention (for example, flow sheets in cases of processes, and diagrammatic views) may also be furnished in the same manner as drawing, and may be required by the Office when considered necessary or desirable.

83. Content of drawing. (a) The drawing must show every feature of the invention specified in the claims. However, conventional features disclosed in the description and claims, where their detailed illustration is not essential for a proper understanding of the invention, should be illustrated in the drawing in the form of a graphical drawing symbol or a labeled representation (e.g. a labeled rectangular box).

(b) When the invention consists of an improvement on an old machine the drawing must when possible exhibit, in one or more views, the improved portion itself, disconnected from the old structure, and also in another view, so much only of the old structure as will suffice to show the connection of the invention therewith.

105. Completeness of examiner's action. The examiner's action will be complete as to all matters, except that in appropriate circumstances, such as misjoinder of invention, fundamental defects in the application, and the like, the action of the examiner may be limited to such matters before further action is made. However, matters of form need not be raised by the examiner until a claim is found allowable.

126. Numbering of claims. The original numbering of the claims must be preserved throughout the prosecution. When claims are canceled, the remaining claims must not be renumbered. When claims are added, except when presented in accordance with rule 121(b), they must be numbered by the applicant consecutively beginning with the number next following the highest numbered claim previously presented (whether entered or not). When the application is ready for allowance, the examiner, if necessary, will renumber the claims consecutively in the order in which they appear or in such order as may have been requested by the applicant.

141. Different inventions in one application. Two or more independent and distinct inventions may not be claimed in one application, except that more than one species of an invention, not to exceed five, may be specifically claimed in different claims in one application, provided the application also includes an allowable claim generic to all the claimed species and all the claims to each species in excess of one are written in dependent form (rule 75) or otherwise include all the limitations of the generic claim.

142. Requirement for restriction. (a) If two or more independent and distinct inventions are claimed in a single application, the examiner in his action shall require the applicant in his response to that action to elect that invention to which his claims shall be restricted, this official action being called a requirement for restriction (also known as a requirement for division). If the distinctness and independence of the inventions be clear, such requirement will be made before any action on the merits; however, it may be made at any time before final action in the case, at the discretion of the examiner.

(b) Claims to the invention or inventions not elected, if not canceled, are nevertheless withdrawn from further consideration by the examiner by the election, subject however to reinstatement in the event the requirement for restriction is withdrawn or overruled.

146. Election of species. In the first action on an application containing a generic claim and claims restricted separately to each of more than one species embraced thereby, the examiner, if of the opinion after a complete search on the generic claims that no generic claim presented is allowable, shall require the applicant in his response to that action to elect that species of his invention to which his claims shall be restricted if no generic claim is finally held allowable. However, if such application contains claims directed to more than five species, the examiner may require restriction of the claims to not more than five species before taking any further action in the case.

152. Drawing. [For design patents] The design must be represented by a drawing made in conformity with the rules laid down for drawings of mechanical inventions and must contain a sufficient number of views to constitute a complete disclosure of the appearance of the article. Appropriate surface shading must be used to show the character or contour of the surfaces represented.

153. Title, description and claim, oath or declaration. (a) The title of the design must designate the particular article. No description, other than a reference to the drawing, is ordinarily required. The claim shall be in formal terms to the ornamental design for the article (specifying name) as shown, or as shown and described. More than one claim is neither required nor permitted.

(b) The oath or declaration required of the applicant must comply with rule 65 except that the period of twelve months specified therein with respect to foreign applications is six months in the case of designs.

164. Claim. The claim shall be in formal terms to the new and distinct variety of the specified plant as described and illustrated, and may also recite the principal distinguishing characteristics. More than one claim is not permitted.

181. Petition to the Commissioner. (a) Petition may be taken to the Commissioner (1) from any action or requirement of any examiner in the ex parte prosecution of an application which is not subject to appeal to the Board of Appeals or to the court; (2) in cases in which a statute or the rules specify that the matter is to be determined directly by or reviewed by the Commissioner; and (3) to invoke the supervisory authority of the Commissioner in appropriate circumstances.

* * *

205. Interference with a patent; copying claims from patent. (a) Before an interference will be declared with a patent, the applicant must present in his application, copies of all the claims of the patent which also define his invention and such claims must be patentable in the application. However, an interference may be declared after copying the claims excluding an immaterial limitation or variation if such immaterial limitation or variation is not clearly supported in the application or if the applicant otherwise makes a satisfactory showing in justification thereof.

* * *

APPENDIX D

Part III

MANUAL OF PATENT EXAMINING PROCEDURE*

(Selected sections pertinent to claims
and related topics discussed in this book)

608.01 (j) Numbering of Claims

Rule 126. Numbering of claims.

* * *

In a single claim case, the claim is not numbered.

608.01 (k) Statutory Requirement of Claims [R-22]†

35 U.S.C. 112 requires that the applicant shall particularly point out and distinctly claim the subject matter which he regards as his invention. The portion of the application in which he does this forms the claim or claims. This is an important part of the application, as it is the definition of that for which protection is granted.

---

*The *Manual* is revised quite often, and one must subscribe to the revision sheets as they issue, and make sure that he always has the latest "R" number for a section in question. Appendix D contains the latest text of the sections quoted through R-38, dated October 1973.

†Where a designation such as "R-22" appears in brackets, it indicates "Revision 22" of the *Manual*, which bears a particular date and on which the section in question was amended.

608.01 (l) Original Claims

In establishing a disclosure, applicant may rely not only on the specification and drawing as filed but also on the original claims if their content justifies it.

Where subject matter not shown in the drawing or described in the specification is claimed in the case as filed, and such original claim itself constitutes a clear disclosure of this subject matter, then the claim should be treated on its merits, and requirement made to amend the drawing and specification to show this subject matter. The claim should not be attacked either by objection or rejection because this subject matter is lacking in the drawing and specification. It is the drawing and specification that are defective; not the claim.

It is of course to be understood that this disclosure in the claim must be sufficiently specific and detailed to support the necessary amendment of the drawing and specification.

608.01 (m) Form of Claims [R-22]

While there is no set statutory form for claims, the present Office practice is to insist that each claim must be the object of a sentence starting with "I (or we) claim" (or the equivalent). If, at the time of allowance, the quoted terminology is not present, it is inserted by the Clerk. Each claim begins with a capital letter and ends with a period. Periods may not be used elsewhere in the claims except for abbreviations. A claim may be typed with the various elements subdivided in paragraph form.

There may be plural indentations to further segregate subcombinations or related steps. In general, the printed patent copies will follow the format used but printing difficulties or expense may prevent the duplication of unduly complex claim formats.

Reference characters corresponding to elements recited in the detailed description and the drawings may be used in conjunction with the recitation of the same element or group of elements in the claims. The reference characters, however, should be enclosed within parentheses so as to avoid confusion with other numbers or characters which may appear in the claims. The use of reference characters is to be considered as having no effect on the scope of the claims.

Many of the difficulties encountered in the prosecution of patent applications after final rejection may be alleviated if each applicant includes, at the time of filing or no later than the first response, claims varying from the broadest to which he believes he is entitled to the most detailed that he is willing to accept.

Claims should preferably be arranged in order of scope so that the first claim presented is the broadest. Where separate species are claimed, the claims of like species should be grouped together where possible and physically separated by drawing a line between claims or group of claims. (Both of these provisions may not be practical or possible where several species claims depend from the same generic claim.) Similarly, product and process claims should be separately grouped. Such arrangements are for the purpose of facilitating classification and examination.

The form of claim required in Rule 75(e) is particularly adapted for the description of improvement type inventions. It is to be considered a combination claim. The preamble of this form of claim is considered to positively and clearly include all the elements or steps recited therein as a part of the claimed combination.

See Rejections not based on Prior Art § 706.03.

608.01(n) Dependent Claims [R-22]

Rule 75(c), reads as follows:

* * *

For applications filed on or after October 25, 1965, the initial determination, for fee purposes, as to whether a claim is dependent must be made by persons other than Examiners; it is necessary, at that time, to accept as dependent virtually every claim which refers to another claim, without determining whether there is actually a true dependent relationship. Such acceptance does not, however, preclude a subsequent holding by the Examiner that a claim is not a proper dependent claim. Any claim which is in dependent form but which is so worked that it, in fact is not, as for example it does not include every limitation of the claim on which it depends, will be required to be canceled as not being a proper dependent claim; and cancellation of any further claim depending on such a dependent claim will be similarly required. The applicant may thereupon amend the claims to place them in proper dependent form, or may redraft them as independent claims, upon payment of any necessary additional fee.

An essential characteristic of a proper dependent claim is that it shall include every limitation of the claim from which it depends (35 U.S.C. 112) or in other words that it shall not conceivably be infringed by anything which would not also infringe the basic claim. Thus, for example, if claim 1 recites the combination of elements *a*, *b*, *c* and *d*, a claim reciting the structure of claim 1 in which *d* was omitted or replaced by *e* would not be a proper dependent claim, even though it placed further limitations on the remaining elements or added still other elements.

The fact that a dependent claim which is otherwise proper might require a separate search or be separately classified from the claim on which it depends would not render it an improper dependent claim, although it might result in a requirement for restriction.

The fact that the independent and dependent claims are in different statutory classes does not, in itself, render the latter improper. Thus, if claim 1 recites a specific product, a claim for the method of making the product of claim 1 in a particular manner would be a proper dependent claim since is could not be infringed without infringing claim 1. Similarly, if claim 1 recites a method of making a product, a claim for a product made by the method of claim 1 could be a proper dependent claim. On the other hand, if claim 1 recites a method of making a specified product, a claim to the product set forth in claim 1 would not be a proper dependent claim if the product might be made in other ways. Note, that since Rule 75(c) requires the dependent claim to "further restrict" the preceding claim, this Rule does not apply to product-by-process claims.

CLAIM FORM AND ARRANGEMENT

A dependent claim 2 could read as follows:

2. The product of claim 1 in which . . .

A dependent claim cannot directly refer back to two or more preceding claims. For example, a claim reading as follows:

7. A machine as specified in claims 5 or 6 (or, 5 and 6) in which . . .

is not permitted. Such a claim disguises the true number of claims, since it is in reality two claims. It is also alternative.

However, a series of dependent claims is permissible in which a dependent claim refers to a preceding claim which, in turn, refers to another preceding claim.

A claim which depends from a *dependent* claim should not be separated therefrom by any claim which does not also depend from said "dependent" claim. It should be kept in mind that a dependent claim may refer back to *any* preceding *independent* claim. These are the only restrictions with respect to the sequence of claims and, in general, applicant's sequence should not be changed. See § 608.01(j).

REJECTION AND OBJECTION

If the base claim has been cancelled, a claim which is directly or indirectly dependent thereon should be rejected as incomplete. If the case claim is rejected, the dependent claim should be *objected to* rather than rejected, if it is otherwise allowable.

Examiners are reminded that a dependent claim is directed to a combination including everything recited in the base claim *and* what is recited in the dependent claim. It is this combination that must be compared with the prior art, exactly as if it were presented as one independent claim.

Dependent claims should be carefully checked when claims are renumbered (Rule 126).

608.01(o) Basis for Claim Terminology in Description [R-22]

The meaning of every term used in any of the claims should be apparent from the descriptive portion of the specification with clear disclosure as to its import, and in mechanical cases it should be identified in the descriptive portion of the specification by reference to the drawing, designating the part or parts therein to which the term applies. A term used in the claims may be given a special meaning in the description. No term may be given a meaning repugnant to the usual meaning of the term.

Usually the terminology of the original claims follows the nomenclature of the specification, but sometimes in amending the claims or in adding new claims, new terms are introduced that do not appear in the specification. The use of a confusing variety of terms for the same thing should not be permitted.

New claims and amendments to the claims already in the case should be scrutinized not only for new matter but also for new terminology. While an applicant is not limited to the nomenclature used in the application as filed, yet whenever by amendment of his claims, he departs therefrom, he should make appropriate amendment of his specification so as to have therein clear support or antecedent basis for the new terms appearing in the claims. This is necessary in order to insure certainty in construing the claims in the light of the specification. Ex parte Kotler 1901 C.D. 62; 95 O.G. 2684. See Rule 75, sections 608.01(i) and 1302.01.

608.01(v) Trademarks and Names Used in Trade [R-26]

The expressions "trademarks" and "names used in trade" as used below have the following meanings:

Trademark: a word, letter, symbol or device adopted by one manufacturer or merchant and used to identify and distinguish his product from those of others. It is a proprietary word pointing distinctly to the product of one producer.

Names Used in Trade: a nonproprietary name by which an article or product is known and called among traders or workers in the art, although it may not be so known by the public generally. Names used in trade do not point to the product of one producer, but they identify a single article or product irrespective of producer.

Names used in trade are permissible in patent applications if:

(1) Their meanings are established by an accompanying definition which is sufficiently precise and definite to be made a part of a claim, or

(2) In this country, their meanings are well known and satisfactorily defined in the literature.

Condition (1) or (2) must be met at the time of filing of the complete application.

TRADEMARKS

The relationship between a trademark and the product it identifies is sometimes indefinite, uncertain and arbitrary. The formula or characteristics of the product may change from time to time and yet it may continue to be sold under the same trademark. In patent specifications, every element or ingredient of the product should be set forth in positive, exact, intelligible language, so that there will be no uncertainty as to what is meant. Arbitrary trademarks which are liable to mean different things at the pleasure of manufacturers do not constitute such language.

However, if the product to which the trademark refers is otherwise set forth in such language that its identity is clear, the examiners are authorized to permit the use of the trademark if it is distinguished from common descriptive nouns by capitalization. If the trademark has a fixed and definite meaning it constitutes sufficient identification unless some physical or chemical characteristic of the article or material is involved in the invention. In that event as also in those cases where the trademark has no fixed and definite meaning, identification by scientific or other explanatory language is necessary.

The matter of sufficiency of disclosure must be decided on an individual case by case basis. In re Metcalfe and Lowe, 161 USPQ 789; 869 O.G. 691.

Where the identification of a trademark is introduced by amendment it must be restricted to the characteristics of the product known at the time the application was filed to avoid any question of new matter.

If proper identification of the product sold under a trademark, or a product referred to only by a name used in trade, is omitted from the specification and such identification is deemed necessary under the principles set forth above, the examiner should hold the disclosure insufficient and reject on the ground of insufficient disclosure any claims based on the identification of the product merely by trademark or by the name used in trade. If the product cannot be otherwise defined, an amendment defining the process of its manufacture may be permitted. Such amendments must be supported by satisfactory showings establishing that the specific nature or process of manufacture of the product as set forth in the amendment was known at the time of filing of the application.

Although the use of trademarks having definite meanings is permissible in patent applications, the proprietary nature of the marks should be respected and every effort made to prevent their use in any manner which might adversely affect their validity as trademarks. The examiner should not permit the use of language such as "the product X (a descriptive name) commonly known as Y (trademark)" since such language does not bring out the fact that the latter is a trademark. Language such as "the product X (a descriptive name) sold under the trademark Y" is permissible.

The use of a trademark in the title of an application should be avoided as well as the use of a trademark coupled with the word "type"; i.e., "Band-Aid type bandage."

The owner of a trademark may be identified in the specification.

Examiners should reply to all trademark misuse complaint letters and forward a copy to the editor of this manual.

See appendix [I], following, for a partial listing of trademarks and the particular goods to which they apply.

APPENDIX [I]

Partial List of Trademarks [R-36]

The following is a partial list of trademarks which may appear from time-to-time in patent applications. Proper usage of trademarks requires that they be capitalized at all times. See section 608.01(v).

Any question as to whether an apparent trademark is in fact a registered trademark or not, and to what particular goods it applies, should be referred to the Trademark Classification and Search Division (ext. 73281) for determination.

Trademark	*Particular goods on or in connection with which the trademark is used*
Adrenalin	Blood-pressure raising and stimulating preparations
Aerosol	Wetting agents
Alemite	Automotive lubricants, additives and equipment
Alpha	Protein
Al-Si-Mag	Antacid and absorbent preparations
Alumel	Alloys containing nickel and aluminum
Alundum	Abrasive, polishing and heat refractory materials
Amberlite	Ion exchange resins, jewelry, insulation, resinous materials
Ameripol	Rubber-like materials
Anchor	Fence
Aquadag	Colloidal graphited water

Trademark	*Particular goods on or in connection with which the trademark is used*
Aqua Pik	Oral hygiene appliance
Areskap	Wetting, spreading and related materials
Aresket	Wetting, spreading and related materials
Aresklene	Wetting, spreading and related materials
Atraumatic	Surgical and dental needles
Bactratycin	Pharmaceutical ointment
Bakelite	Plastics, adhesives, varnishes, etc.
Banbury	Mixers, upholstery material, scotch whisky, tableware
Band-Aid	Bandages and spray antiseptic
Bathinette	Infant furniture
Benzedrine	Medicinal preparation
Betalight	Self-powered light sources
Bitumastic	Paints and joint compounds
Black Leaf 40	Tobacco extracts
Blue Rock	Clay pigeon targets
Bobbie	Bobby pins, combs, cigars
Calgon	Water softening chemicals, cleaning agents
Calrod	Electric heating units
Camoquin	Antimalarial preparation
Carbitol	Solvents
Carbofrax	Furnaces, refractory materials, etc.
Carborundum	Abrasives, refractory materials, related equipment
Carousel	Photographic projectors, organs and other items
Catalin	Synthetic resins
Caterpillar	Tractors, engines, treads, etc.
Celanese	Compositions, threads, fabrics, clothing
Celastic	Fabrics, softeners
Cello-Solve	Solvents
Cellucotton	Surgical dressing
Celotex	Wallboard and other building materials
Chevron	Machinery packing, petroleum products and other items
Chlorex	Solvents

Trademark	*Particular goods on or in connection with which the trademark is used*
Chloromycetin	Anti-biotic preparations and sensitivity dics
Chromax	Low conductivity wire, lacquers, castings and other items
Chromel	Alloy
Coca-Cola	Beverages
Coke	Beverages
Corex	Glass paints, sets, tops and other items
Cumar	Resin
Cyclone	Fencing, aircraft engines, seeders and other items
DAA	Diacetone acrylamide
Dacron	Synthetic fibers
Danforth	Anchors, marine hardware and devices
Debeaker	Machine for trimming the beak of a fowl
Decalin	Decahydronaphthalene
Deepfreeze	Home freezers, water heaters and ranges
De-Ion	Electrical equipment
Di-Phenolic Acid	Chemical intermediate
Dry Ice	Solid carbon dioxide, containers and sportswear
Dual-Seal	Covers, strips and insulated glass
Dulux	Resins, paints and other items
Duraloy	Metal alloys
Duraplex	Synthetic alloys
Eidophor	Electrical apparatus
Electronic Secretary	Telephone answering apparatus
Electro-Silicon	Cleaning and polishing preparations
Elon	Rayon textile fabric, photographic developer, sunwear
Emulphor	Emulsifying agent
Erector	Toys
Evapor-Ion	Vacuum pumps
Fascinator	Spectacles
Fathometer	Depth measuring apparatus
Fiberglas	Glass fibers and products made therefrom

Trademark	Particular goods on or in connection with which the trademark is used
Flexowriter	Power-operated typewriters, tape and ribbons
Flexwood	Fabric backed wood veneer
Fluorophene	Bactericide and fungicide chemicals
Foamite	Fire extinguishing devices and compositions and cups
Footlets	Socks and hosiery
Formica	Flakeboard, adhesives, wall tile, and other items
Freon	Fluorinated hydrocarbons
Gantrisin	Chemo-therapeutic agent
Geon	Polyvinyl resins and automobile parts
Glyptal	Synthetic resins and paints
Go Kart	Miniature automobiles
Gyropilot	Automatic steering mechanism
Gyrosyn	Compass equipment
Helanca	Yarns and threads and clothing made therefrom
Hercolyn	Ester of rosin
Hipersil	Magnetic metal alloys
Hovercraft	Vehicles and platforms supported on a gaseous cushion
Humantin	Antibiotic preparation
Hydrafrac	Hydraulically fracturing oil-producing formations
Hydroseal	Plastic cement and other items
Igepon	Washing and scouring agent
Inductosyn	Electrical apparatus
Jeep	Automobiles, valves, and other items
Jet Line	Hardwear, compressed gas equipment and other items
Kaltron	Pharmaceutical preparations and fertilizer
Kodak	Photographic and related equipment and other items

Trademark	Particular goods on or in connection with which the trademark is used
Kodapak	Solvents, sheets and film cartridges
Koroseal	Various plastic items
Kovar	Alloyed metal
Laminac	Synthetic resins
Lastex	Yarns
Laundromat	Renting of washers in self service laundries
Lavite	Electrical insulation
Leatherette	Fabric, gloves and various paper items
Lexide	Sheet material made of fabric and rubber
Link	Pilot training equipment, computers, servo-mechanisms
Linotype	Machines for producing type bars
Liquid lead	Ink
Lucite	Plastics and paints
Lux	Aircraft flotation, fire extinguishers and other items
Masonite	Fiberboard and plastics
Methocel	Methyl cellulose
Micarta	Various molded products
Microballoon(s)	Hollow synthetic resin particles
Micro-data	Microfilm equipment
Modutrol	Medicinal preparations and electric motor controls
Monel	Alloys
Monotype	Type casting equipment and insulated wire
Mycalex	Electrical insulating material
Mylar	Plastic film
Nekal	Solvents, wetting agents and other items
Nichrome	Resistance wire, alloys, metal castings
Nico-fume	Insecticide and fumigants
Ni-Rist	Ferrous castings
Nitralloy	Alloy steel
Nonex	Glass lantern and lamp globes and chimneys
O	Silicate of soda

Trademark	*Particular goods on or in connection with which the trademark is used*
Oilgear	Valves, pumps and hydraulic devices
Orlon	Synthetic fibers
Paraplex	Synthetic chemical compositions
Perbunan	Rubber and rubber substitute materials
Perf-a-tape	Joint tape for wallboard
Permutit	Water purifying materials
Phospor bronze	Alloy
Photostat	Cameras and photographic devolping equipment
Photronic	Light sensitive cells
Phytin	Pharmaceutical product
Ping-pong	Game apparatus
Pitocin	Pharmaceutical preparation
Plasmatron	Electrical plasma-flame or plasma-jet apparatus
Plastacele	Thermoplastic materials
Plexiglas	Synthetic resin materials
Pliofilm	Rubber derivative films, sheets or strips
Pliolite	Latex, resinous materials and paints
Pliowax	Resinous material for use in paints
Pluronic	Polyoxyalkylene ether
Polane	Chemical addition agents for fuels
Polaroid	Photographic equipment and other items
Polyfoam	Polyurethane foam sheets and electrical lines
Polymerin	Paints, varnishes, and paint enamels
Polynosic	Synthetic textile fibers
Pop	Rivets and rivet tools, chemicals and other items
Porocel	Absorbent materials
Primacord	Detonating fuse
Priscoline	Preparation having an action on blood circulation
Push-Back	Theatre chairs
Pusher	Polymeric compositions and fresh grapes
Pyralin	Pyroxylin enamels, paints, adhesives and other items
Pyrex	Glass, cooking ware, lenses and other items

Trademark	*Particular goods on or in connection with which the trademark is used*
Ram	Electronic equipment, tools, presses and other items
Refinite	Pool equipment, water softening equipment
Resinox	Synthetic resins
Revertex	Rubber and rubber substitutes
Rice Krispies	Cereal breakfast food
Ripple	Soles, colognes, knives, wines and other items
Rocklath	Plaster board
Rockwell	Hardness tester, tools and other items
Roll-Bond	Heat exchangers and refrigerator exaporators
Roots	Blowers, pumps and meters
Roquefort	Cheese
Rotary Union	Rotary joints
Santomerse	Chemical compounds
Scintillometer	Gamma ray spectrometers
Scotch	Pressure sentitive tape, paper, films and other items
Shakeproof	Electrical terminals, screws, screwdrivers, and gears
Sheetrock	Plaster wall board, plaster and other items
Snap-on	Wrenches, dental polishers and other items
Solid Circuit	Integrated semiconductor networks
Solvesso	Hydrocarbon solvents
Sonar	Fish lures, insecticides and hairdressing
Speed-Nut	Fasteners
Steel-Flex	Sectional air bags
Stellite	Metal alloys, textile machine parts and machinery
Stenograph	Shorthand machines and ribbons, paper tapes, tripods and instruction materials
Steri-Pad	Surgical dressing
Stiflex	Fiber reforced rubber compositions
Storm Choke	Subsurface safety valves
Staddle Truck	Vehicles adapted to move piled lumber
Styrofoam	Expanded synthetic resinous material
Sylphon	Heat regulators
Sylphrap	Sheets made of regenerated cellulose

Trademark	*Particular goods on or in connection with which the trademark is used*
Synchrotester	Photographic flash synchronization testers
Synpor	Storage battery separators and retainers
Syntron	Rectifiers, infra-red heaters, tools and other items
Tagalong	Trailers and perfume dispensers
Talon	Fasteners, threads and yarns, tents and other items
Tapper	Keg-like containers and shoe soles
Technicolor	Motion picture films and other items
Teflon	Synthetic resin polymers and products
Teletype	Printing-telegraph apparatus
Teletypesetter	Typesetting and type-casting apparatus
Tenderay	Meat and meat products
Tetralin	Tetrahydronaphthalene
Tetronic	Nonionic polymerized alkylene oxide compound
Textolite	Nonmetallic sheet material
Thenfadil	Antihistaminic preparation
Thermit	Metal compounds for welding
Thermos	Vacuum bottles, camp stoves, tents and other items
Thiokol	Sulfur-containing plastics, rocket motors and other items
Transite	Asbestos cement pipe and other items
Triton	Synthetic organic compounds and other items
Trombone	Sprayers
Twist-Lock	Torch tips and electrical wiring apparatus
Uformite	Synthetic resins
Urotropin	Hexamethylenetetramine or hexamethethylenamine
Vacumatic	Fountain pens, pencils and desk sets
Varsol	Hydrocarbon solvents and oils
Vaseline	Petroleum jelly, medicinal preparations and other items

Trademark	*Particular goods on or in connection with which the trademark is used*
Velcro	Synthetic materials which adhere when pressed together
Verichrome	Photographic film
Victrola	Records, talking machines, radios and other items
Vinylite	Resins and paints
Vistac	Synthetic hydrocarbon polymers and oils
Vistanex	Compounding agents, adhesives and other items
Votator	Machines for processing fluid, plastic or other materials
Vultex	Rubber latex, bricks and bowling pins
Vycor	Glassware and seal rings
Water Pik	Oral hygiene appliance
Weather-Ometer	Apparatus for testing the effect of weather on objects
Wig-Jig	Frame for holding wigs
Zip	Ball point pens, jewelry, vending machines and other items
Zipper	Electrical plugs, fresh vegetables, belting, cigarettes and undergarments

706.03 Rejections Not Based on Prior Art [R-31]

The primary object of the examination of an application is to determine whether or not the claims define a patentable advance over the prior art. This consideration should not be relegated to a secondary position while undue emphasis is given to non-prior art or "technical" rejections. Effort in examining should be concentrated on truly essential matters, minimizing or eliminating effort on technical rejections which are not really critical. Where a major technical rejection is proper (e.g., lack of proper disclosure, undue breadth, utility, etc.) such rejection should be stated with a full development of the reasons rather than by a mere conclusion coupled with some stereotyped expression.

Rejections not based on prior art are explained in §§ 706.03(a) to 706.03(z). IF THE ITALICIZED LANGUAGE IN THESE SECTIONS IS INCORPORATED IN THE REJECTION, THERE WILL BE LESS CHANCE OF A MISUNDERSTANDING AS TO THE GROUNDS OF REJECTION.

706.03(a) Nonstatutory Subject Matter [R-34]

Patents are not granted for all new and useful inventions and discoveries. The subject matter of the invention or discovery must come within the boundaries set forth by 35 U.S.C. 101, which permits patents to be granted only for "any new and useful process, machine, manufacture, or composition of matter, or any new and useful improvement thereof."

The term "process" as defined in 35 U.S.C. 100, means process, art or method, and includes a new use of a known process, machine, manufacture, composition of matter, or material.

Decisions have determined the limits of the statutory classes. Examples of subject matter not patentable under the Statute follow:

PRINTED MATTER

For example, a mere arrangement of printed matter, though seemingly a "manufacture," is rejected as *not being within the statutory classes.* See In re Miller, 164 USPQ 46, 57 CCPA 809 (1969); Ex parte Gwinn, 112 USPQ 439 (Bd. App. 1955); and In re Jones, 153 USPQ 77, 54 CCPA 1218 (1967).

NATURALLY OCCURRING ARTICLE

Similarly, a thing occurring in nature, which is substantially unaltered, is not a "manufacture." A shrimp with the head and digestive tract removed is an example. Ex parte Grayson, 51 USPQ 413.

METHOD OF DOING BUSINESS

Though seemingly within the category of a process or method, a method of doing business can be rejected as not being within the statutory classes. See Hotel Security Checking Co. v. Lorraine Co., 160 Fed. 467 and In re Wait, 24 USPQ 88, 22 CCPA 822 (1934).

SCIENTIFIC PRINCIPLE

A scientific principle, divorced from any tangible structure, can be rejected as not within the statutory classes. O'Reilly v. Morse, 15 Howard 62.

This subject matter is further limited by the Atomic Energy Act explained in § 706.03(b).

706.03(b) Barred by Atomic Energy Act [R-18]

A limitation on what can be patented is imposed by the Atomic Energy Act of 1954. Section 151(a) (42 U.S.C. 2181a) thereof reads in part as follows:

> No patent shall hereafter be granted for any invention or discovery which is useful solely in the utilization of special nuclear material or atomic energy in an atomic weapon.

The terms "atomic energy" and "special nuclear material" are defined in Section 11 of the Act (42 U.S.C. 2014).

Sections 151(c) and 151(d) (42 U.S.C. 2181c and d) set up categories of pending applications relating to atomic energy that must be brought to the attention of the U.S. Atomic Energy Commission. Under rule 14(c), applications for patents which disclose or which appear to disclose, or which purport to disclose, inventions or discoveries relating to atomic energy are reported to the Atomic Energy Commission and the Commission will be given access to such applications, but such reporting does not constitute a determination that the subject matter of each application so reported is in fact useful or an invention or discovery or that such application in fact discloses subject matter in categories specified by the Atomic Energy Act.

All applications received in the Patent Office are sent to Licensing and Review for screening by Group 220 personnel, under rule 14(c), in order for the Commissioner to fulfill his responsibilities under section 151(d) (42 U.S.C. 2181d) of the Atomic Energy Act. Papers subsequently added must be inspected promptly by the examiner when received to determine whether the application has been amended to relate to atomic energy and those so related must be promptly forwarded to Licensing and Review.

All rejections based upon sections 151(a) (42 U.S.C. 2181a), 152 (42 U.S.C. 2182), and 155 (42 U.S.C. 2185) of the Atomic Energy Act must be made only by Group 220 personnel.

706.03(c) Functional [R-34]

See Ex parte Ball, et al., 1953 C.D. 4; 675 O.G. 5: In re Arbeit et al., 1953 C.D. 409; 677 O.G. 843 and Ex parte Stanley, 121 USPQ 621.

35 U.S.C. 112. Specification. The specification shall contain a written description of the invention, and of the manner and process of making and using it, in such full, clear, concise, and exact terms as to enable any person skilled in the art to which it pertains, or with which it is most nearly connected, to make and use the same, and shall set forth the best mode contemplated by the inventor of carrying out his invention.

The specification shall conclude with one or more claims particularly pointing out and distinctly claiming the subject matter which the applicant regards as his invention. A claim may be written in independent or dependent form, and if in dependent form, it shall be construed to include all the limitations of the claim incorporated by reference into the dependent claim.

An element in a claim for a combination may be expressed as

a means or step for performing a specified function without the recital of structure, material, or acts in support thereof, and such claims shall be construed to cover the corresponding structure, material, or acts described in the specification and equivalents thereof.

Paragraph 3 of 35 U.S.C. 112 has the effect of prohibiting the rejection of a claim for a combination of elements (or steps) on the ground that the claim distinguishes from the prior art solely in an element (or step) defined as a "means" (or "step") coupled with a statement of function. However this provision of paragraph 3 must always be considered as subordinate to the provision of paragraph 2 that the claim particularly point out and distinctly claim the subject matter. If a claim be found to contain language approved by paragraph 3 such claim should always be tested additionally for compliance with paragraph 2 and if it fails to comply with the requirements of paragraph 2, the claim should be so rejected and the reasons fully stated.

Paragraph 3 of 35 U.S.C. 112 makes no change in the established practice of rejecting claims as *functional* in situations such as the following:

1. A claim which contains functional language not supported by recitation in the claim of sufficient structure to warrant the presence of the functional language in the claim. An example of a claim of this character may be found in In re Fuller, 1929 C.D. 172; 388 O.G. 279. The claim reads:

> A woolen cloth having a tendency to wear rough rather than smooth.

2. A claim which recites only a single means and thus encompasses all possible means for performing a desired function. For an example, see the following claim in Ex parte Bullock, 1907 C.D. 93; 127 O.G. 1580:

> In a device of the class described, means for transferring clothes-carrying rods from one position and depositing them on a suitable support.

Note the following cases:

1. In re Hutchinson, 69 USPQ 138, 33 CCPA 879 (1946), the terms "adapted for use in" and "adapted to be adhered to" were held not to constitute a limitation in any patentable sense.

2. In re Mason, 114 USPQ 127, 44 CCPA 937 (1957), the functional "whereby" statement was held not to define any structure and accordingly could not serve to distinguish.

3. In re Boller, 141 USPQ 740, 51 CCPA 1484 (1964), the term "volatile neutralizing agent" was held to be patentably effective and commensurate with the breadth of the disclosed invention.

4. In re Land and Rogers, 151 USPQ 621 (1966), the expression "adapted to be rendered diffusible in said liquid composition only after at least substantial development" was given weight.

5. In re Halleck, 164 USPQ 647, 57 CCPA 954 (1970), the term "an effective amount" was held not objectionable.

6. In re Swinehart and Sfiligo, 169 USPQ 226 (1971), held that the meaning of "transparent to infra-red rays" is sufficiently clear.

7. In re Barr et al., 170 USPQ 330, 58 CCPA 1388 (1971), held that the expression "incapable of forming a dye with said oxidized developing agent," set forth definite boundaries.

706.03(d) Vague and Indefinite [R-34]

When the examiner is satisfied that patentable novelty is disclosed and it is apparent to the examiner that the claims are directed to such patentable subject matter, he should allow claims which define the patentable novelty with a *reasonable* degree of particularity and distinctness. Some latitude in the manner of expression and the aptness of terms should be permitted even though the claim language is not as precise as the examiner might desire.

The fact that a claim is broad does not necessarily justify a rejection on the ground that the claim is vague and indefinite or incomplete. In non-chemical cases, a claim may, in general, be drawn as broadly as permitted by the prior art.

The rejection of a claim as *indefinite* would appear to present no difficulties. On occasion, however, a great deal of effort is required to explain just what is wrong with the claim, when writing the examiner's letter. Although cooperation with the attorney is to be commended, undue time should not be spent trying to guess what the attorney was trying to say in the claim. Sometimes, a rejection as indefinite plus the statement that a certain line is meaningless is sufficient. The examiner's action should be constructive in nature and when possible he should offer a definite suggestion for correction.

The mere inclusion of reference numerals in a claim otherwise allowable is not a ground for rejection. But see Ex parte Osborne, 1900 C.D. 137; 92 O.G. 1797.

Alternative expressions such as "brake or locking device" may make a claim indefinite if the limitation covers two different elements. If two equivalent parts are referred to such as "rods or bars," the alternative expression may be considered proper.

The inclusion of a negative limitation shall not, in itself, be considered a sufficient basis for objection to or rejection of a claim. However, if such a limitation renders the claim unduly broad or indefinite or otherwise results in a failure to point out the invention in the manner contemplated by 35 U.S.C. 112, an appropriate rejection should be made.

Generally speaking, the inclusion of (1) negative limitations and (2) alternative expressions, provided that the alternatively expressed elements are basically equivalents for the purpose of the invention, are permitted if no uncertainty or ambiguity with respect to the question of scope or breadth of the claim is presented.

The examiner has the responsibility to make sure the wording of the claims is sufficiently definite to *reasonably* determine the scope. It is the applicant's responsibility to select proper wording of the claim, except to the extent that the selection of words makes the claims indefinite. Under no circumstances should a claim be rejected merely because the examiner prefers a different choice of wording.

Still another way in which a claim can be indefinite is where a *non sequitur* occurs. For example, a claim is inferential and therefore indefinite when it recites "said lever" and there was no earlier reference or *no antecedent* in the claim to a lever. An *indirect limitation* also affords a ground of rejection as indefinite. If a "lever" is set forth and, later in the claim, "said aluminum lever" is recited, the claim is rejected as indefinite.

Rejections for indefiniteness were affirmed in In re Cohn, 169 USPQ 95 (CCPA 1971); In re Hammack, 166 USPQ 209 (CCPA 1970); and In re Collier 158 USPQ 266 (CCPA 1968).

Rejections for indefiniteness were reversed in In re Castaing, 166 USPQ 550 (CCPA 1970); In re Fisher, 166 USPQ 18 (CCPA, 1970); and In re Wakefield, 164 USPQ 636 (CCPA 1970).

706.03(e) Product by Process [R-40]

An article may be claimed by a process of making it provided it is definite. In re Moeller, 1941 C.D. 316; 48 USPQ 542; 28 CCPA 932; In re Luck, 177 USPQ 523 (CCPA 1973); In re Steppan, 156 USPQ 143 (CCPA 1967); and In re Pilkington, 162 USPQ 145 (CCPA 1969).

When the prior art discloses a product which reasonably appears to be either identical with or only slightly different than a product claimed in a product-by-process claim, a rejection based alternatively on either section 102 or 103 of the statute is appropriate. As a practical matter, the Patent Office is not equipped to manufacture product by the myriad of processes put before it and then obtain prior art products and make physical comparisons therewith. A lesser burden of proof is required to make out a case of prima facie obviousness for product-by-process claims because of their peculiar nature than when a product is claimed in the conventional fashion. In re Brown, 59 CCPA 1036, 173 USPQ 685 (1972); In re Fessmann, 180 USPQ 324 (CCPA 1974).

The fact that it is necessary for an applicant to describe his product in product-by-process terms does not prevent him from presenting claims of varying scope, Ex parte Pantzer and Feier, 176 USPQ 141 (Board of Appeals, 1972).

706.03(f) Incomplete [R-27]

A claim can be rejected as *incomplete* if it omits essential elements, steps or necessary structural cooperative relationship of elements, such omission amounting to a gap between the elements, steps or necessary structural connections. Greater latitude is permissible with respect to the definition in a claim of matters not essential to novelty or operability than with respect to matters essential thereto. See also § 706.03(d).

706.03(g) Prolix

Claims are rejected as *prolix* when they contain long recitations of unimportant details which hide or obscure the invention. Ex parte Iagan, 1911 C.D. 10; 162 O.G. 538, expresses the thought that very long detailed claims setting forth so many elements that invention cannot possibly reside in the combination should be rejected as prolix. See also In re Ludwick, 1925 C.D. 306; 339 O.G. 393.

706.03(h) Nonstatutory Claim [R-27]

Some applications when filed contain an omnibus claim such as "A device substantially as shown and described."

Such a claim can be rejected as follows:

> Claim —— is rejected for failing to particularly point out and distinctly claim the invention as required in 35 U.S.C. 112.

For cancellation of such a claim by examiner's amendment, see § 1302.04(b).

706.03(j) Aggregation [R-34]

Rejections on the ground of *aggregation* should be based upon a lack of cooperation between the elements of the claim. Many decisions and some legal writers extend the term to include old and exhausted combinations (§ 706.03(j)). Confusion as to what is meant can be avoided by treating all claims which include more than one element as combinations (patentable or unpatentable) if there is actual cooperation between the elements, and as aggregations if there is no cooperation.

Example of aggregation: A washing machine associated with a dial telephone.

Example of old combination: An improved carburetor claimed in combination with a gasoline engine.

A claim is not necessarily aggregative because the various elements do not function simultaneously. A typewriter, for example, is a good combination. See also In re Worrest, 40 CCPA 804, 96 USPQ 381 (1953). Neither is a claim necessarily aggregative merely because elements which do cooperate are set forth in specific detail.

A rejection on aggregation should be made only after consideration of the court's comments in In re Gustafson, 51 CCPA 1358, 141 USPQ 585 (1964).

706.03(j) Old Combination [R-34]

The rejection on the ground of *old combination* (synonymous with "exhausted combination") requires the citation of a reference, but is treated here because of its relation to aggregation. The reference (not a combination of references, of course) is cited, not to anticipate the claim, but to anticipate the broad combination set forth in the claim. Moreover, the cooperation and result between the elements in the reference must be the same as it is in the claim.

A rejection on the ground of old combination should be made whenever proper. Whether subcombination claims have been presented or allowed in the same application, or whether other grounds for rejection of the combination claims exist, are not determinative of the propriety of this rejection. The rejection is proper when a single reference discloses broadly a combination of the same elements functionally cooperating in substantially the same manner to produce substantially the same results as that of the claimed combination. *Ex parte* Silverstein, 125 USPQ 238. The fact that an applicant has improved one element of a combination which may be *per se* patentable does not entitle him to a claim to the improved element in combination with old elements where the elements perform no new function in the claimed combination. In re Hall, 41 CCPA 759.

Example: An improved (specifically recited) carburetor claimed in combination with a gasoline engine. A reference is cited which shows a carburetor combined with a gasoline engine. This shows the broad combination to be old. Both in the reference and in the claimed combination, the cooperation between the carburetor and engine is the same and the end result is the same. The claimed combination is an improvement over the prior art only because of the improved carburetor. The carburetor has separate status, since entire subclasses are devoted to carburetors, claimed as such. A reference is preferably cited to show the separate status and development. (See § 904.01 (d).)

Old combination rejections ordinarily are based on 35 U.S.C. 112 (failure to point out the invention). The rejection should make it clear exactly what the combination is and why it is thought that any improved element does not modify the action of the combination. A suggested form for use in making an old combination rejection is as follows:

"Claim 1 is rejected under 35 U.S.C. 112 as being drawn to the old combination of a bell, a battery and a switch connected in series by wire conductors. This combination is shown to be old by the patent to Jones which discloses broadly the same elements functionally interrelated in the same manner to produce substantially the same results. The combination of claim 1 differs from that shown in Jones in setting forth a specific construction of the battery itself. Since the latter does not modify the action of the other elements recited in the claim in any material manner, no new combination is seen to exist. In re Hall, 100 USPQ 46; 41 CCPA 759; 208 F. 2d 370; 680 O.G.5."

See also Lincoln Engineering Co., v. Stewart-Warner Corp., 303 U.S. 545, 37 USPQ 1 (1938); In re McCabe, 48 CCPA 881, 129 USPQ 149 (1961) (discussion of claim 13); and particularly In re Bernhart, 57 CCPA 737, 163 USPQ 611 (1969).

706.03(k) Duplicate Claims: Double Patenting [R-37]

Inasmuch as a patent is supposed to be limited to only one invention or, at most, several closely related indivisible inventions, limiting an application to a single claim, or a single claim to each of the related inventions might appear to be logical as well as convenient. However, court decisions have confirmed applicant's right to restate (i.e., by plural claiming) his invention in a reasonable number of ways. Indeed, a mere difference in scope between claims has been held to be enough.

Nevertheless, when two claims in an application are duplicates, or else are so close in content that they both cover the same thing, despite a slight difference in wording, it is proper after allowing one claim to reject the other as being a substantial duplicate of the allowed claim. Also, it is possible to reject one claim on an allowed claim if they differ only by subject matter old in the art. The latter ground of rejection is set forth in the following paragraph quoted from Ex parte Whitelaw, 1915 C.D. 18; 219 O.G. 1237:

"Claim 54 is not patentable over claim 51 and claims 53, 55 and 56 are not patentable over claim 50 in view of Comstock, No. 590,657, which shows that it is old to employ an enginecasing in tools of this character. The claims held patentable are considered as fully covering applicant's invention, and applicant cannot be permitted to multiply his claims by presenting alleged combinations which distinguish from the real invention only by including elements which are old in the art and perform no new function."

This rejection (the ex parte Whitelaw doctrine) is usually not applied if there are only a few claims in the application.

Situations related to that given above are as follows:

Where there is a common assignee for two or more applications by different inventors, and the applications contain conflicting claims, see §§ 305 and 804.03.

DOUBLE PATENTING

Where there are conflicting claims in different applications of the same inventor, one of which is assigned, see § 304.

Where the same inventor has two or more applications for species or for related inventions, see Chapter 800, particularly §§ 804-804.02, 806.04(h), 822 and 822.01 for double patenting rejections of inventions not patentable over each other.

APPLICATION FILED UNDER 35 U.S.C. 121

The Commissioner has determined that under 35 U.S.C. 121, the Patent Office cannot reject a divisional application on the parent patent if the divisional application is filed as a result of a requirement for restriction made by the Office even though the requirement for restriction relates to species. In re Joyce, 1958 C.D. 2; 115 USPQ 412. See also In re Herrick et al., 1958 C.D. 1; 115 USPQ 412 where the Commissioner ruled that a requirement for restriction should not be made in an application claiming more than five species if the Examiner is of the opinion that the various species are obviously unpatentable over one another. [R-20]

706.03(1) Multiplicity [R-34]

Rule 75(b). More than one claim may be presented, provided they differ substantially from each other and are not unduly multiplied.

An unreasonable number of claims; that is unreasonable in view of the nature and scope of applicant's invention and the state of the art, may afford a basis for a rejection on the ground of *multiplicity.* A rejection on this ground should include all the claims in the case inasmuch as it relates to confusion of the issue.

To avoid the possibility that an application which has been rejected on the ground of undue multiplicity of claims may be appealed to the Board of Appeals prior to an examination on the merits of at least some of the claims presented, the examiner should, at the time of making the rejection on the ground of multiplicity of claims, specify the number of claims which in his judgment is sufficient to properly define applicant's invention and require the applicant to select certain claims, not to exceed the number specified, for examination on the merits. The examiner should be reasonable in setting the number to afford the applicant some latitude in claiming his invention.

The earlier views of the Court of Customs and Patent Appeals set forth in In re Chandler, 117 USPQ 361, 45 CCPA 911 (1958) and In re Chandler, 138 USPQ 138, 50 CCPA 1422 (1963) have been somewhat revised by its views in In re Flint, 162 USPQ 228, 56 CCPA 1300 (1969) and In re Wakefield, 164 USPQ 636, 57 CCPA 959 (1970).

If a rejection on multiplicity is in order the examiner should make a telephone call explaining that the claims are unduly multiplied and will be rejected on that ground. Note § 408. He should request selection of a specified number of claims for purposes of examination.

If time for consideration is requested arrangements should be made for a second telephone call, preferably within three working days.

When claims are selected, a formal multiplicity rejection is made, including a complete record of the telephone interview, followed by an action on the selected claims.

When applicant refuses to comply with the telephone request, a formal multiplicity rejection is made. No reference should be made to the unsuccessful telephone call.

The applicant's response to a formal multiplicity rejection of the examiner, to be complete, must either:

1. Reduce the number of claims presented to those selected previously by telephone, or if no previous selection has been made to a number not exceeding the number specified by the examiner in the Office action, thus overcoming the rejection based upon the ground of multiplicity, or

2. In the event of a traverse of said rejection applicant, besides specifically pointing out the supposed errors of the multiplicity rejection is required to confirm his selection previously made by telephone, or if no previous selection has been made, select certain claims for purpose of examination, the number of which is not greater than the number specified by the examiner.

If the rejection on multiplity is adhered to all claims retained will be included in such rejection and the selected claims only will be additionally examined on their merits. This procedure preserves applicant's right to have the rejection on multiplicity reviewed by the Board of Appeals.

See also § 706.03(k).

706.03 (m) Non-elected Inventions [R-34]

See §§ 821 to 821.03 for treatment of claims held to be drawn to non-elected inventions.

706.03 (n) Correspondence of Claim and Disclosure [R-29]

Rule 117. Amendment and revision required. The specification, claims and drawing must be amended and revised when required, to correct inaccuracies of description and definition or unnecessary prolixity, and to secure correspondence between the claims, the specification and the drawing.

Another category of rejections not based on the prior art is based upon the relation of the rejected claim to the disclosure. In chemical cases, a claim may be so broad as to not be supported by disclosure, in which case it is rejected as unwarranted by the disclosure. If averments in a claim do not correspond to the averments or disclosure in the specification, a rejection on the ground of inaccuracy may be in order. It must be kept in mind that an original claim is part of the disclosure and might adequately set forth subject matter which is completely absent from the specification. Applicant is required in such an instance to add the subject matter to the specification. Whenever an objection or rejection is made based on incomplete disclosure, the examiner should in the interest of expeditious prosecution call attention to rule 118.

When an amendment is filed in response to an objection or rejection based on incomplete disclosure, a study of the entire application is often necessary to determine whether or not "new matter" is involved. Applicant should therefore specifically point out the support for any amendments made to the disclosure.

Is subject matter capable of illustration is originally claimed and it is not shown in the drawing, the claim is not rejected but applicant is required to add it to the drawing. See § 608.01(l).

See § 706.03(z) for rejections on undue breadth.

706.03(o) New Matter [R-29]

35 U.S.C. 132. Notice of rejection; reexamination.

Whenever, on examination, any claim for a patent is rejected, or any objection or requirement made, the Commissioner shall notify the applicant thereof, stating the reasons for such rejection, or objection or requirement, together with such information and references as may be useful in judging of the propriety of continuing the prosecution of his application; and if after receiving such notice, the applicant persists in his claim for a patent, with or without amendment, the application shall be reexamined. No amendment shall introduce new matter into the disclosure of the invention.

In amended cases, subject matter not disclosed in the original application is sometimes added and a claim directed thereto. Such a claim is rejected on the ground that it is *drawn to new matter*. New matter includes not only the addition of wholly unsupported subject matter, but also, adding specific percentages or compounds after a broader original disclosure, or even the omission of a step from a method. See §§ 608.04 to 608.04(c).

In the examination of an application following amendment thereof, the examiner must be on the alert to detect new matter. The prohibition against new matter has been incorporated into the patent statute. These rejections are based on 35 U.S.C. 132.

706.03(p) No Utility [R-20]

A rejection on the ground of *lack of utility* includes the more specific grounds of *inoperativeness, involving perpetual motion, frivolous, fraudulent, against public policy*. The statutory basis for this rejection is 35 U.S.C. 101. See § 608.01(p).

706.03(q) Obvious Method [R-40]

In view of a decision of the U.S. Court of Customs and Patent Appeals, process claims should no longer be rejected on a theory that once the article or composition produced thereby is conceived, anyone skilled in the art would at once be aware of a method of making it, In re Kuehl, 177 USPQ 250 (1973).

A process may be unpatentable, however, even if the product produced therefrom is patentable, In re Kanter, 158 USPQ 331 (CCPA 1968). The mere substitution of a new starting material in an otherwise conventional process may well be obvious in the absence of some unobvious result in the process itself, In re Kanter, 158 USPQ 331; In re Neugebauer et al., 141 USPQ 205 (CCPA 1964); Corning Glass Works et al. v. Brenner, 175 USPQ 516 (D.C. Cir. 1972).

However, the use of a specific mineral oil in a process was held to be material in In re Schneider et al., 179 USPQ 46 (CCPA 1973).

706.03(r) Mere Function of Machine [R-20]

In view of the decision of the Court of Customs and Patent Appeals in In re Tarczy-Hornoch appearing at 158 USPQ 141, process or method claims are not subject to rejection by Patent Office examiners solely on the ground that they define the inherent function of a disclosed machine or apparatus.

706.03(y) Improper Markush Group [R-34]

Ex parte Markush, 1925 C.D. 126; 340 O.G. 839, sanctions, in chemical cases, claiming a genus expressed as a group consisting of certain specified materials. This type of claim is employed when there is no commonly accepted generic expression which is commensurate in scope with the field which the applicant desires to cover. Inventions in metallurgy, refractories, ceramics, pharmacy, pharmacology and biology, may be claimed under the Markush formula but it has consistently been held to be improper to extend it to purely mechanical features or process steps. It is improper to use the term "comprising" instead of "consisting of." Ex parte Dotter, 12 USPQ 382. Regarding the normally prohibited inclusion of Markush claims of varying scope in the same case, see Ex parte Burke, 1934 C.D. 5; 441 O.G. 509.

The use of Markush claims of diminishing scope should not, in itself, be considered a sufficient basis for objection to or rejection of claims. However, if such a practice renders the claims indefinite or if it results in undue multiplicity, an appropriate rejection should be made. This practice with respect to Markush claims of diminishing scope is being continued.

The materials set forth in the Markush group ordinarily must belong to a recognized physical or chemical class or to an art-recognized class. However, when the Markush group occurs in a claim reciting a process or a combination (not a single compound), it is sufficient if the members of the group are disclosed in the specification to possess at least one property in common which is mainly responsible for their function in the claimed relationship, and it is clear from their very nature or from the prior art that all of them possess this property. While in the past the test for Markush-type claims was applied as liberally as possible, present practice which holds that claims reciting Markush groups are not generic claims (§ 803) may subject the groups to a more stringent test for propriety of the recited members. Where a Markush expression is applied only to a portion of a chemical compound, the propriety of the grouping is determined by a consideration of the compound as a whole, and does not depend on there being a community of properties in the members of the Markush expression.

When materials recited in a claim are so related as to constitute a proper Markush group, they may be recited in the conventional manner, or alternatively. For example, if "wherein R is a material selected from the group consisting of A, B, C and D" is a proper limitation then "wherein R is A, B, C or D" shall also be considered proper.

SUBGENUS CLAIM

A situation may occur in which a patentee has presented a number of examples which, in the examiner's opinion, are sufficiently representative to support a generic claim and yet a court may subsequently hold the claim invalid on the ground of undue breadth. Where this happens the patentee is often limited to species claims which may not provide him with suitable protection.

The allowance of a Markush type claim under a true genus claim would appear to be beneficial to the applicant without imposing any undue burden on the Patent Office or in any way detracting from the rights of the public. Such a subgenus claim would enable the applicant to claim all the disclosed operative embodiments and afford him an intermediate level of protection in the event the true genus claims should be subsequently held invalid.

The examiners are therefore instructed not to reject a Markush type claim merely because of the presence of a true genus claim embracive thereof.

See also §§ 608.01(p) and 715.03.

706.03(z) Undue Breadth [R-32]

In applications directed to inventions in arts where results are predictable, broad claims may properly be supported by the disclosure of a single species. In re Vickers et al., 1944 C.D. 324; 61 USPQ 122: In re Cook and Merigold, 169 USPQ 298.

However, in applications directed to inventions in arts where the results are unpredictable, the disclosure of a single species usually does not provide an adequate basis to support generic claims. In re Sol, 1938 C.D. 723; 497 O.G. 546. This is because in arts such as chemistry it is not obvious from the disclosure of one species, what other species will work. In re Dreshfield, 1940 C.D. 351; 518 O.G. 255 gives this general rule: "It is well settled that in cases involving chemicals and chemical compounds, which differ radically in their properties it must appear in an applicant's specification either by the enumeration of a sufficient number of the members of a group or by other appropriate language, that the chemicals or chemical combinations included in the claims are capable of accomplishing the desired result." The article "Broader than the Disclosure in Chemical Cases," 31 J.P.O.S. 5, by Samuel S. Levin covers this subject in detail.

707.07(d) Language To Be Used In Rejecting Claims [R-36]

Where a claim is refused for any reason relating to the merits thereof it should be "rejected" and the ground of rejection fully and clairly stated, and the word "reject" must be used. The examiner should designate the *statutory basis* for any ground of rejection by express reference to a section of 35 U.S.C. in the opening sentence of each ground of rejection. If the claim is rejected as too broad, the reason for so holding should be given; if rejected as indefinite the examiner should point out wherein the indefiniteness resides; or if rejected as incomplete, the element or elements lacking should be specified, or the applicant be otherwise advised as to what the claim requires to render it complete.

See § 706.02 for language to be used.

Everything of a personal nature must be avoided. Whatever may be the examiner's view as to the utter lack of patentable merit in the disclosure of the application examined, he should not express in the record the opinion that the application is, or appears to be, devoid of patentable subject matter. Nor should he express doubts as to the allowability of allowed claims or state that every doubt has been resolved in favor of the applicant in granting him the claims allowed.

Although, not every ground of rejection may be categorically related to a specific section of the statute, § 112 is considered as the more apt section for old combination rejection than §§ 102 or 103. Ex parte Des Granges, 864 O.G. 712.

The examiner should, as a part of the first Office action on the merits, identify any claims which he judges, as presently advised, to be allowable and/or should suggest any way in which he considers that rejected claims may be amended to make them allowable. If the examiner does not do this, then by implication it will be understood by the applicant or his attorney or agent that in the examiner's opinion, as presently advised, there appears to be no allowable claim nor anything patentable in the subject matter to which the claims are directed.

IMPROPERLY EXPRESSED REJECTIONS

An omnibus rejection of the claim "on the references and for the reasons of record" is stereotyped and usually not informative and should therefore be avoided. This is especially true where certain claims have been rejected on one ground and other claims on another ground.

A plurality of claims should never be grouped together in a common rejection, unless that rejection is equally applicable to all claims in the group.

806.04 Independent Inventions [R-20]

Rule 141. Different inventions in one application.

* * *

If it can be shown that the two or more inventions are in fact independent, applicant should be required to restrict the claims presented to but one only of such independent inventions. For example:

1. Two different combinations, not disclosed as capable of use together, having different modes of operation, different functions or different effects are independent. An article of apparel such as a shoe, and a locomotive bearing would be an example. A process of painting a house and a process of boring a well would be a second example.
2. Where the two inventions are process and apparatus, and the apparatus cannot be used to practice the process or any part thereof, they are independent. A specific process of molding is independent from a molding apparatus which cannot be used to practice the specific process.
3. Where species under a genus are independent. For example, a genus of paper clips having a species differing in the manner in which a section of the wire is formed in order to achieve a greater increase in its holding power.

SPECIES ARE TREATED EXTENSIVELY IN THE FOLLOWING SECTIONS

806.04(a) Species—Genus

The statute lays down the general rule that restriction may be required to one of two or more independent inventions. Rule 141 makes an exception to this, providing that up to five species may be claimed in one application if the other conditions of the rule are met.

806.04(b) Species May Be Related Inventions

Species, while usually independent may be related under the particular disclosure. Where inventions as disclosed and claimed, are both (a) species under a claimed genus and (b) related, then the question of joinder must be determined by both the restriction practice applicable to election of species and the practice applicable to other types of restrictions. If restriction is improper under either practice it should not be required.

For example, two different subcombinations usable with each other may each be a species of some common generic invention. In ex parte Healy 1898 C.D. 157; 84 O.G. 1281, a clamp for a handle bar stem and a specifically different clamp for a seat post both usable together on a bicycle were claimed. In his decision, the commissioner considered both the restriction practice under election of species and the practice applicable to restriction between combination and subcombinations.

As a further example, species of carbon compounds may be related to each other as intermediate and final product. Thus these species are not independent and in order to sustain a restriction requirement, distinctness must be shown. Distinctness is proven if it can be shown that the intermediate product is useful other than to make the final product. Otherwise, the disclosed relationship would preclude their being issued in separate patents.

806.04(c) Subcombination Not Generic to Combination

The situation is frequently presented where two different combinations are disclosed, having a subcombination *common to each.* It is frequently puzzling to determine whether a claim readable on two different combinations is generic thereto.

This was early recognized in Ex parte Smith 1888 C.D. 131; 44 D.G. 1183, where it was held that a subcombination was not generic to the different combinations in which it was used.

To exemplify, a claim that defines only the subcombination, e.g., the mechanical structure of a joint, is not a generic or genus claim to two forms of a combination, e.g., two different forms of a doughnut cooker each of which utilize the same form of joint.

806.04(d) Definition of a Generic Claim

In an application presenting three species illustrated, for example, in Figures 1, 2 and 3 respectively, a generic claim should read on each of these views; but the fact that a claim does so read is not conclusive that it is generic. It may define only an element or subcombination common to the several species.

It is not possible to define a generic claim with that precision existing in the case of a geometrical term. In general, a generic claim should include no material element additional to those recited in the species claims, and must comprehend within its confines the organization covered in each of the species.

For the purpose of obtaining claims to more than one species in the same case, the generic claim cannot include limitations not present in each of the added species claims. Otherwise stated, the claims to the species which can be included in a case in addition to a single species must contain all the limitations of the generic claim.

Once a claim that is determined to be generic is allowed, the claims restricted to species in addition to one but not to exceed four additional species, provided they comply with the requirements, will ordinarily be obviously allowable in view of the allowance of the generic claim, since the additional species will depend thereon or otherwise include all of the limitations thereof.

When all or some of the claims directed to one of the species in addition to the first do not include all the limitations of the generic claim, then that species cannot be claimed in the same case with the other species, see 809.02(c)(2).

806.04(e) Claims Restricted to Species

Claims are never species. They are definitions of inventions. They may be restricted to a single disclosed embodiment (i.e. a single species, and thus be designated a *specific species claim*), or may include two or more of the disclosed embodiments within the breadth of scope of definition (and thus be designated a generic or genus claim).

Species are always the specifically different embodiments.

They are *usually* but not always independent as disclosed (See 806.04(b)) since there is usually no disclosure of relationship therebetween. The fact that a genus for two different embodiments is capable of being conceived and defined, does not affect the independence of the embodiments, where the case under consideration contains no disclosure of any community of operation, function or effect.

806.04(f) Claims Restricted to Species, by Mutually Exclusive Characteristics

Claims to be restricted to different species must be mutually exclusive. The general test as to when claims are restricted respectively to different species is the fact that one claim recites limitations which *under the disclosure* are found in a first species but not in a second, while a second claim recites limitations disclosed only for the second species and not the first. This is frequently expressed by saying that claims to be restricted to different species, must recite the mutually exclusive characteristics of such species.

806.04(h) Species Must Be Patentably Distinct From Each Other and From Genus

Where an applicant files a divisional application claiming a species previously claimed in the parent case, pursuant to and consonant with a requirement to restrict, there should be no determination of whether or not the species claimed in the divisional application is patentable over the species retained in the patent case.

In an application containing claims directed to more than five species, the Examiner should not require restriction to five species unless he is satisfied that he would be prepared to allow claims to each of the claimed species over the parent case, if presented in a divisional application filed according to the requirement. Restriction should not be required if the species claimed are considered clearly unpatentable over each other.

In making a requirement for restriction in an application claiming plural species, the Examiner should group together species considered clearly unpatentable over each other, with the statement that restriction as between those species is not required.

Where generic claims are allowed, applicant may claim in the *same application* species not to exceed five, as provided by Rule 141. As to these, the patentable distinction between the species and genus is not rigorously investigated, since they will issue in the same patent. However, the practice stated in 706.03(k) may be followed if the claims differ from the allowed genus only by subject matter that can be shown to be old by citation of prior art.

Where, however, an applicant optionally files another application for a different species, or for a species disclosed but not claimed in a parent case as filed and first acted upon by the Examiner, there should be close investigation to determine the presence or absence of patentable difference. See 804.01 and 804.02.

806.04(i) Generic Claims Rejected When Presented for First Time After Issue of Species [R-18]

Where an applicant has separate applications for plural species, but presents no generic claim until after the issue of a patent for one of the species, the generic claims cannot be allowed, even though the applications were copending.

806.04(j) Generic Claims in One Patent Only [R-18]

Generic claims covering two or more species which are separately claimed in two or more patents to the same inventor issued on copending applications *must all be present in a single one of the patents.* If present in two or more patents, the generic claims in the later patents are void. Thus generic claims in an application should be rejected on the ground of double patenting in view of the generic claims of the patent.

806.05 Related Inventions [R-18]

Where two or more related inventions are being claimed, the principal question to be determined in connection with a requirement to restrict or a rejection on the ground of double patenting is whether or not the inventions as claimed are distinct. If they are not distinct, restriction is never proper. If claimed in separate applications or patents, double patenting must be held, except where the additional applications were filed consonant with a requirements to restrict.

The various pairs of related inventions are noted in the following sections.

806.05(a) Combination or Aggregation and Subcombination or Element [R-25]

A combination or an aggregation is an organization of which a subcombination or element is a part.

The distinction between combination and aggregation is not material to questions of restriction or to questions of double patenting. Relative to questions of restriction where a combination is alleged, the claim thereto must be assumed to be allowable as pointed out in § 806.02, in the absence of a holding by the examiner to the contrary. When a claim is found in a patent, it has already been found by the Office to be for a combination and not an aggregation and must be treated on that basis.

Combination claims (other than combination claims which are also genus claims linking species claims) whether allowable, allowed, or not allowed and considered the subject of a proper restriction requirement should be grouped as a separate invention, see § 806.05(c).

Combination claims which under past practice may have served as a basis for joining claimed inventions are not considered to be linking claims. Likewise rejoinder of restricted inventions, should any combination claim be allowed, will not be permitted.

806.05(b) Old Combination—Novel Subcombination [R-25]

Restriction is ordinarily not proper between a combination (AB) that the examiner holds to be old and unpatentable and the subcombination (B) in which the examiner holds the novelty, if any, to reside, ex parte Donnell 1923 C.D. 54, 315 O.G. 398. (See § 820.01.)

806.05(c) Criteria of Distinctness for Combination, Subcombination or Element of a Combination—Related Inventions [R-18]

To support a requirement to restrict between the claimed inventions of two or more combinations; of two or more subcombinations; of a combination and subcombination; or a combination and an element of a combination, the Examiner must demonstrate by appropriate explanation one of the following criteria for distinctness:

(1) Separate classification thereof:

This shows that each distinct subject has attained a recognition in the art as a separate subject for inventive effort, and also a separate field of search.

(2) A separate status in the art when they are classifiable together:

Even though they are classified together, as shown by appropriate explanation each subject can be shown to have formed a separate subject for inventive effort when an explanation indicates a recognition of separate effort by inventors.

(3) A different field of search:

Where it is necessary to search for one of the distinct subjects in places where no pertinent art to the other subject exists, a different field of search is shown, even though the two are classified together. The indicated different field of search must in fact be pertinent to the type of subject matter covered by the claims.

806.05(e) Process and Apparatus for Its Practice—Distinctness [R-18]

Process and apparatus for its practice can be shown to be distinct inventions, if either or both of the following can be shown: (1) that the process *as claimed* can be practiced by another materially different apparatus or by hand, or (2) that the apparatus *as claimed* can be used to practice another and materially different process.

806.05(f) Process and Product Made—Distinctness [R-18]

A process and a product made by the process can be shown to be distinct inventions if either or both of the following can be shown: (1) that the process *as claimed* is not an obvious process of making the product *and* the process *as claimed* can be used to make other and different products, or (2) that the product *as claimed* can be made by another and materially different process.

806.05(g) Apparatus and Product Made—Distinctness [R-25]

The criteria are the same as in § 806.05(f) substituting apparatus for process.

904.01 Analysis of Claims [R-36]

The breadth of the claims in the application should always be carefully noted; that is, the examiner should be fully aware of what the claims do *not* call for, as well as what they do require. There is always danger of reading into the claim limitations imported from the specification or drawing.

904.01(a) Variant Embodiments Within Scope of Claim [R-36]

Substantially every claim includes within its breadth or scope of definition one or more variant embodiments not disclosed by applicant, which would anticipate the terms of the definition. The claim must be so analyzed and understood that any such variant encountered during the search will be recognized and selected.

In each type of subject matter capable of such treatment (e.g., a machine or other apparatus), the subject matter as defined by the claim may be sketched in order to clearly delineate the limitations of the claim. Two or more sketches, each of which is as divergent from the particular disclosure as is permitted by claim recitation, will assist the examiner in determining the claim's actual breadth or scope. However, an applicant will not be required to submit such sketches of claim structure (In re Application filed November 16, 1945, 1951 C.D. 1; 646 O.G. 5).

904.01(b) Equivalents [R-24]

All subject matter that is the patentable equivalent of the subject matter is defined in the claim, even though specifically different from the definition in the claim, must be considered.

1502 Definition of a Design

The design of an object consists of the visual characteristics or aspects displayed by the object. It is the appearance presented by the object which creates an impression, through the eye upon the mind of the observer.

As a design is manifested in appearance the subject matter of a design application may relate to the configuration or shape of an object, to the surface ornamentation thereof, or both.

A design is inseparable from the object and cannot exist alone merely as a scheme of surface ornamentation. It must be a definite, preconceived thing, capable of reproduction and not merely the chance result of a method.

1503.01 Specification and Claim [R-35]

Rule 153. Title, description and claim, oath or declaration. (a) The title of the design must designate the particular article. No description, other than a reference to the drawing, is ordinarily required. The claim shall be in formal terms to the ornamental design for the article (specifying name) as shown, or as shown and described. More than one claim is neither required nor permitted.

(b) The oath or declaration required of the applicant must comply with rule 65 except that the period of twelve months specified therein with respect to foreign applications is six months in the case of designs.

Rule 154. Arrangement of specification. The following order of arrangement should be observed in framing design specifications:

(a) Preamble, stating name of the applicant and title of the design.

(b) Description of the figure or figures of the drawing.

(c) Description, if any.

(d) Claim.

(e) Signature of applicant. (See rule 57.)

If applicant is entitled under 35 U.S.C. 120 to the benefit of an earlier U.S. filing date, the statement that, "This is a division [continuation, continuation-in-part] of design application Serial No. ———, filed ———." should appear immediately before the claim heading.

A design application cannot be considered to be a division of a utility application, and is not entitled to the filing date thereof, even though the drawings of the earlier filed utility application show the same article as that in the design application. In re Campbell, 1954 C.D. 191; 101 USPQ 406; Certiorari denied, 348 U.S. 858.

TITLE

The title is of great importance in a design application. It serves to identify the article in which the design is embodied and which is shown in the drawing, by the name generally used by the public. The title should be to a specific definite article. Thus a stove would be called a "Stove" and not a "Heating Device." The same title is used in the petition, in the preamble to the specification, in the description of the drawing, and in the claim. The title of the article being claimed in a design patent must correspond to the name of the article shown in solid lines in the drawing.

To allow latitude of construction it is permissible to add to the title—"or similar article." The title must be in the singular.

The title implies that the type of article named is old, but that the form shown is new. The title may particularize the type of article named by specifying a use "Bottle for Perfume" or by indicating a structural type—"Vacuum Bottle."

DESCRIPTION

Any description of the claimed design in the specification other than a brief description of the drawing figures is generally not necessary, for as a rule the illustration is its own best description. If there is a special description it should be of the appearance of the article. Special descriptions denoting the nature and environmental use of the claimed design are permissible where an appropriate title cannot satisfy this requirement. Special descriptions describing the construction of the claimed design are not permitted.

Where there is a particular feature of novelty in a case, this feature should be described in the specification by means of a "characteristic" feature clause, rule 71(c).

Statements in the specification which describe or suggest modifications of the design shown on the drawing are not permitted.

A disclaimer directed to any portion of the claim design invention is improper and not permitted in a design application. (35 U.S.C. 112). See Ex parte Remington, 114 O.G. 761, 1905 C.D. 761 and Ex parte Blum, 153 USPQ 177.

CLAIM

A claim is required and should be in formal terms to the ornamental design for the article (as specified in the title) as shown. Only one claim is permissible. (In re Rubinfield, 1959 C.D. 412; 123 USPQ 210.)

The claim may include the words "and described" following '"shown." If there is any descriptive or declaratory matter in the specification other than the brief descriptions or definitions of the drawing figures, the words "and described" must follow "shown."

1601 [Plant Patents] Introduction: The Act, Scope, Type of Plants Covered

The right to a plant patent stems from:
35 U.S.C. 161.

* * *

Asexually propagated plants are those that are reproduced by means other than from seeds, such as by the rooting of cuttings, by layering, budding, grafting, marching, etc.

With reference to tuber propagated plants, for which a plant patent cannot be obtained, the term "tuber" is used in its narrow horticultural sense as meaning a short, thickened portion of an underground branch. Such plants covered by the term "tuber propagated" are the Irish potato and the Jerusalem artichoke. This exception is made because this group alone, among asexually reproduced plants, is propagated by the same part of the plant that is sold as food.

The term "plant" has been interpreted to mean "plant" in the ordinary and accepted sense and not in the strict scientific sense and thus excludes bacteria. (In re Arzberger, 1940 C.D. 653; 521 O.G. 272.)

35 U.S.C. 153. Grant. In the case of a plant patent the grant shall be of the right to exclude others from asexually reproducing the plant or selling or using the plant so reproduced.

1605 Specification and Claim [R-19]

35 U.S.C. 162. Description, claim.

* * *

The specification should include a complete detailed description of the plant and the characteristics thereof that distinguish the same over related known varieties, and its antecedents, expressed in botanical terms in the general form followed in standard botanical text books or publications dealing with the varieties of the kind of plaint involved (evergreen tree, dahlia plant, rose plant, apple tree, etc.), rather than a mere broad nonbotanical characterization such as commonly found in nursery or seed catalogs. The specification should also include the origin or parentage of the plant variety sought to be patented and must particularly point out where and in what manner the variety of plant has been asexually reproduced. Where color is a distinctive feature of the plant the color should be positively identified in the specification by reference to a designated color as given by a recognized color dictionary.

A plant patent is granted on the entire plant. It therefore follows that only one claim is necessary and only one is permitted. A method claim in a plant patent application is improper.

APPENDIX E

GLOSSARY AND INDEX OF PATENT TERMS

by John D. Kaufmann

A/AN—(1) In a claim, the indefinite article A or AN connotes "one or more." (2) Also, the indefinite article A or AN is used as modifier of an ELEMENT the first time the ELEMENT is set forth (*i.e.*, introduced) in a claim. See THE. (17, *20*)*

AGGREGATION—(1) A lack of structural and/or functional co-operation between the various parts of an assembly; the opposite of COMBINATION. A non-cooperating assembly of parts (strictly speaking, NON-STATUTORY subject matter)—an inherent defect in a structure, *qua* structure, which no claim, however well drafted, can cure. (2) A COMBINATION claimed without sufficient particularity and definiteness, so that the ELEMENTS of the claim, *as claimed*, do not cooperate. A structure is not necessarily an AGGREGATION solely because all of its ELEMENTS, either in fact or as claimed, do not function simultaneously (as in a typewriter). Recent cases cast doubt on the propriety of this ground of REJECTION. See MPEP 706.03(i) and Sections 25 and 61. (*25*, *61*, 62)

ALTERNATIVE EXPRESSION—The alternative setting forth in a claim of two ELEMENTS, either (and both) of which perform the same FUNCTION in the claim, instead of a single ELEMENT

*Numerals refer to sections of the book where the term is used; *italicized numerals* indicate sections where the term is defined or discussed in detail. Solid Caps designate terms defined in the glossary.

to perform the FUNCTION. For example: "a spring *or* piston-cylinder for moving the member." Usually, there is a GENERIC word covering the ALTERNATIVE ELEMENTS, in the case of the example "means for biasing," which should be used in the claim. ALTERNATIVE EXPRESSIONS *may* render a claim INDEFINITE. In some cases, ALTERNATIVE EXPRESSIONS are permissible, if the claim is not rendered INDEFINITE thereby. For example, "one *or* more arms" (but note the connotation of A and AN). See MPEP 706.03(d) and Sections 17, 21, 33 and 47. (17, *21*, 31, 33, *47*, 55)

AMENDMENT—A change made in or to a patent application in response to (and hopefully to avoid) a REJECTION or OBJECTION by the EXAMINER. An AMENDMENT is part of a RESPONSE and may affect claims, the DESCRIPTION or the drawings. (6)

ANALOGOUS ART—A REFERENCE or some PRIOR ART directed to the same necessary FUNCTION or utility as is the subject matter set forth in a claim, either the entire claim or particular elements thereof, even though the environment differs. For example, a brick cutter shown in a REFERENCE may be ANALOGOUS ART with respect to a claimed dough cutter. See MPEP 904.01(c).

ANTECEDENT/ANTECEDENT BASIS—A claim must be consistent with the SPECIFICATION and with itself. That is, ELEMENTS recited in the claim must find ANTECEDENT BASIS in the DESCRIPTION and within the claim, if earlier recited therein. Therefore: (1) Support for; the quality of an ELEMENT which is set forth in (and supported by) the DESCRIPTION and which is then POSITIVELY recited in a claim. (2) A POSITIVELY recited, claimed ELEMENT to which later reference is made in the same (or in a DEPENDENT claim. See Sections 15 and 20. (*15* 16, *20*, 31, 33, 64)

ANTICIPATED—See FULLY MET.

APPARATUS—(1) An adjective meaning mechanical or MACHINE-like. (2) A noun meaning a MACHINE or DEVICE, including an electrical circuit, having cooperating parts and a "rule of operation" to accomplish a useful RESULT, usually some act or operation on an ARTICLE or WORKPIECE. Sometimes contrasted with an ARTICLE OF MANUFACTURE or a PRODUCT. (*Chapter III, 11,* 12, 13, 32, 37, *38,* 42)

APPARATUS LIMITATIONS IN METHOD CLAIMS—Section 38.

APPARATUS, METHOD FUNCTIONAL OF—Section 37.

ARBITRARY NAMES—Section 48.

ART—(1) A METHOD or PROCESS (pre-1952 usage). (2) Today, a field of technology, as in 35 U.S.C. § 103. See 35 U.S.C. § 100(b) and Section 33.

ARTICLE—A WORKPIECE. Distinguish from ARTICLE OF MANUFACTURE. (11, 12)

ARTICLE OF MANUFACTURE—One of the STATUTORY CLASSES of UTILITY PATENT. Broadly any product made by man and having industrial utility. Similar to an APPARATUS or MACHINE, but usually having no moving parts or "rule of operation." The same as a MANUFACTURE. It is often difficult to tell whether a DEVICE is a MACHINE or an ARTICLE OF MANUFACTURE, but this difficulty is immaterial. See Section 42. (*Chapter* V, 3, *42,* 47, 54, 61, 62)

ARTICLE OF MANUFACTURE, OBVIOUS METHOD OF MAKING—Section 36.

BODY—of a CLAIM. Narrative expository prose following the PREAMBLE of a claim and reciting the ELEMENTS of the claimed INVENTION as well as a description of how these ELE-

MENTS cooperate to make up the operative COMBINATION recited in the PREAMBLE. See Section 9. (6,7, 9, 11, 12, 31, 33, 53, 54, 56)

BROAD/BROAD CLAIM—Relates to a claim which covers or READS ON a wide range and variety of DEVICES, PROCESSES, etc., because the claim contains only few, or only general, limitations. Sometimes called "wide," especially in British practice. A BROAD CLAIM is usually entitled to a BROAD range of EQUIVALENTS. A claim may be so BROAD as to be INDEFINITE (Section 28). See NARROW. (5 6, 7, 8, 12, 13, 14, 16, 28, 31, 32, 33, 43, 46, 57, 60, 64, 65)

CATALOG—An AGGREGATION (sense (2)) as claimed. See Sections 25 and 61. (*25*, 54, *61*)

CCPA—Abbreviation for the United States *C*ourt of *C*ustoms and *P*atent *A*ppeals.

CHEMICAL CLAIMS—See Chapter VI and Sections 39, 46 and 49.

CLAIM—A description of the INVENTION (Sense 2) protected, located at the end of every patent SPECIFICATION. The protection afforded by a patent is measured by the CLAIMS which are similar to a real property deed in function, i.e., describing metes and bounds.

CLOSED-ENDED—See CONSISTING ESSENTIALLY OF and CONSISTING OF. (8)

COLON-SEMICOLON FORM—A claim format in which a colon is inserted after the TRANSITION and semicolons are used between the ELEMENTS. Such a claim format may be used; in the OUTLINE FORM; the SINGLE PARAGRAPH FORM; or in the SUBPARAGRAPH FORM. See Section 10.

COINED NAME CLAIM—A hybrid type of FINGERPRINT CLAIM in which the COINED NAME is defined and its distinctive properties, structure and METHOD of production are set forth in the DESCRIPTION (Section 50). Such a claim may be proper in the event the COINED NAME was known in the PRIOR ART before the application was filed (which occurs only rarely). (49, *50*, 51)

COMBINATION—(1) An interrelated group of ELEMENTS, structurally and FUNCTIONALLY tied together in a claim to an operative DEVICE to effect some useful FUNCTION or RESULT. Simultaneity of operation of the ELEMENTS is not necessary. See AGGREGATION and CATALOG. (2) A complete MACHINE, PROCESS, ARTICLE OF MANUFACTURE, COMPOSITION, etc., as distinguished from a SUBCOMBINATION thereof. See Sections 9, 25, 26, 27, 30-32, 33, 42 and 61. (1, 6, 7, 8, 9, 10, 12, 13, 17, *25*, *26*, *27*, 30, 31, 32, 33, 39, 42, 46, 47, 52, 53, 54, *56*, 60, *61*, 62, 65)

COMPOSITION/COMPOSITION OF MATTER—PRODUCTS wherein the chemical nature of the substances or materials used, rather than the shape or form, is the distinguishing characteristic. A COMPOSITION may be a molecule, COMPOUND, solution, mixture, alloy, atom, etc. Sometimes contrasted with ARTICLE OF MANUFACTURE. See Section 46. (Chapter VI, 3, 38, 39, *46*, 48, 49, 51, 52, 53, 54)

COMPOUND—Usually, a molecule, *per se*. See COMPOSITION. (46, 47, 49, 50)

COMPRISES/COMPRISING—TRANSITION words between the BODY of the claim and the PREAMBLE. The words mean "including the following ELEMENTS (in the BODY), but not excluding others." A claim or clause using either word is said to be OPEN-ENDED. Thus, "A COMPOSITION COMPRISING (or, WHICH COMPRISES) A, B and C" *requires* the presence of A, B and C, but does *not* exclude other components. Hence, one who produces another COMPOSITION made up of A, B, C and D would INFRINGE. INCLUDES and HAS mean the same thing. See Section 7. (7, 12, 17, 33, 47, 54)

COMPUTER PROGRAMS—Section 41.

CONSISTING ESSENTIALLY OF—A TRANSITION between the PREAMBLE and BODY of a claim. The phrase means "excluding other ELEMENTS of any essential significance to the claimed COMBINATION." More NARROW than COMPRISES, but more BROAD than CONSISTING OF. Hence, one who adds an additional component to the claimed COMBINATION may or may not INFRINGE, depending on whether the additional component substantially alters the properties of the COMPOSITION. For example, where a claim calls for "a tough, impact-resistant COMPOSITION, CONSISTING ESSENTIALLY OF A, B and C," and another adds D to the COMPOSITION, if the addition results in a COMPOSITION which is extremely brittle (i.e., non-impact-resistant) there is no INFRINGEMENT, because D's properties substantially changed the properties of the COMPOSITION. The line between CONSISTING ESSENTIALLY OF and CONSISTING OF is not clear. Use of either phrase results in what is termed a CLOSED-ENDED CLAIM. See Section 8.

CONSISTING OF—A TRANSITION between the PREAMBLE and BODY of a claim. The phrase means "excluding more than traces of other than the recited ingredients." Use of the phrase results in a CLOSED-ENDED claim. Thus, "A COMPOSITION CONSISTING OF A, B and C" *requires* the presence of A, B and C, and *only* A, B and C. One who produces a COMPOSITION of A, B, C and D would not INFRINGE. See COMPRISES, CONSISTING ESSENTIALLY OF and Section 8. (8, 47, 53)

CONTRIBUTORY INFRINGEMENT/CONTRIBUTORY INFRINGER—INFRINGEMENT arising when one (the CONTRIBUTORY INFRINGER) sells a component of a patented INVENTION, or a material or APPARATUS for use in practicing a patented PROCESS, knowing the same to be especially made and adapted for use in an INFRINGEMENT of such patent, unless what is sold is a staple article of commerce suitable for substantial non-infringing use. 35 U.S.C. 271(c).

COUNT—A claim defining the INVENTION the priority of which is being contested in an INTERFERENCE.

DEPENDENT CLAIM—A claim which refers back to and further restricts (i.e., makes more NARROW) a single preceding claim (the PARENT CLAIM), which may itself be a DEPENDENT CLAIM. 35 U.S.C. 112, Rule 75(c) and Section 53. (5, 18, 20, 33, 38, 39, 53, 54, 55, 57, 65)

DESCRIPTION—Often referred to as WRITTEN DESCRIPTION or "detailed DESCRIPTION." The SPECIFICATION of a patent or patent application is made up of drawings, a DESCRIPTION and claims. The DESCRIPTION describes the structure, composition, cooperation, function, embodiments, etc. of the INVENTION in a quite detailed, technical fashion and provides ANTECEDENT basis for the terms of the claims which define the INVENTION. (13, 15, 19, 45, 48)

DESIGN CLAIM—Section 44.

DEVICE—(1) A generalized word meaning "thing" or "item." (2) A MACHINE. (11, 12)

DOCTRINE OF EQUIVALENTS—A legal tenet holding that where a DEVICE, etc., accused of INFRINGING a claim does not include each and every ELEMENT of the CLAIM in *haec verba,* it will still INFRINGE the claim if it includes for every ELEMENT thereof such ELEMENT *or* its EQUIVALENT. See FILE WRAPPER ESTOPPEL.

DOUBLE INCLUSION—Setting forth in a claim precisely the same ELEMENT twice as two different ELEMENTS, usually under two different names. See Sections 18, 31 and 53. (*18*, 31, 53)

DRAWINGS, REFERENCE TO IN CLAIMS—Section 51.

DUPLICATE CLAIM—A redundant CLAIM. A CLAIM that does not "differ substantially" from another claim in the same patent or patent application. See Rule 75(b), MPEP 706.03(k) and Section 58. (57, *58*)

ELECTRICAL CLAIMS—Section 32. (Circuit claims.)

ELECTRICAL METHODS—Section 40.

ELEMENTS—(1) In CLAIM terminology, those things which together constitute the claimed INVENTION. In APPARATUS and ARTICLE OF MANUFACTURE claims, the ELEMENTS are the main structural parts; in METHOD claims, the ELEMENTS are steps or acts, usually GERUND phrases and clauses; in COMPOSITION claims, the ELEMENTS are chemicals or molecules. See Sections 13, 15-17, 23, 24, 32 and 34. (7, 8, 9, 10, 11, *13*, 15, 16, 17, 18, 19, 20, 21, 22, 23, 24, 25, 26, 27, 31, 32, 33, *34*, 35, 38, 42, 46, 53, 54, 56, 57, 60, 63, 65). (2) The respective parts of an assembly.

ELEMENTS, FEATURES OF—Section 22.

ELEMENTS, NAMING OF—Section 16.

ELEMENTS, NUMBER OF—Section 17.

ELEMENTS, ORDER OF—Sections 24 and 35.

ELEMENTS, PARTS OF—Section 22.

ELEMENTS, STRUCTURAL CONNECTION OF—Chapter 26.

ELEMENTS, TYING TOGETHER—Section 25.

EQUIVALENT—An ELEMENT or group of ELEMENTS that FUNCTIONS in substantially the same manner to produce substantially the same RESULT as an ELEMENT, group of ELEMENTS or INVENTION set forth in a claim. See DOCTRINE OF EQUIVALENTS. (31, 37, 51)

EUROPEAN-TYPE CLAIM—A claim format, similar to a JEPSON claim format, and common in European patents. The format followed is usually: "A (name of the DEVICE and its FUNCTION) of the type having (recitation of the PRIOR ART, usually that found in a *single* REFERENCE) characterized in that (recitation of the improvement in the claim BODY)." See Section 54.

EXAMINATION/EXAMINER—The EXAMINER, a Patent Office employee, studies in detail patent applications to determine if the applicant is entitled to a patent under the STATUTE. Such study is called the EXAMINATION. (1, 4, 63)

EXHAUSTED COMBINATION—See OLD COMBINATION. (60)

FILE WRAPPER—The official file of the Patent Office relating to the EXAMINATION of a patent application. It includes the application as filed, all formal papers and all correspondence (Office actions, RESPONSES, and the like) preceding the issuance of (or denial of) a patent. Sometimes called "file history."

FILE WRAPPER ESTOPPEL—If a patent applicant, whose claims are REJECTED (or sometimes OBJECTED to), NARROWS those claims (as by adding limiting language thereto, or, in some courts, by making arguments interpreting the claim language in a restrictive manner) and thereafter obtains allowance of the formerly rejected claims, he will be strictly limited by the additional language (or arguments), and will not be entitled to any EQUIVALENTS with respect thereto. See INFRINGE and DOCTRINE OF EQUIVALENTS.

FINGERPRINT CLAIM—A claim defining a chemical COMPOSITION in terms of its properties, such as X-ray diffraction, solubility, melting point, phase diagram, spectrum, etc., often as shown in the drawing. The use of such a claim is limited to emergency situations wherein the differences between the INVENTION and the PRIOR ART cannot be explained or described (and claimed) in the traditional terms of physical or chemical structure. Such a claim must, nevertheless, distinctly claim the INVENTION. See Sections 49, 50 and 51. (*49*, 50, 51)

FORM/FORMAT OF CLAIMS IN GENERAL—Chapter II and Section 10.

FORMAL REJECTION—A REJECTION (OBJECTION?) made by the EXAMINER to the form, as opposed to the substance (novelty and/or unobviousness), of a claim. A NON-ART REJECTION. See Chapter IX. (Chapter IX, 57, 64)

FULLY MET—A phrase used to REJECT a claim which is completely anticipated by or shown in a single REFERENCE. This type of REJECTION is properly posited on 35 U.S.C. 102, not on 35 U.S.C. 103.

FUNCTION/FUNCTIONAL CLAUSE/LIMITATION – Describing an ELEMENT in terms of what it does, as opposed to what it is (i.e., its structure). See Section 27. At times a FUNCTIONAL LIMITATION may be expressed negatively, that is, by what the ELEMENT does not do. (27, 28, *30*, 31, 42, 46, 60, 64)

FUNCTIONAL ORDER—A logical ordering of the ELEMENTS of a claim which begins with the ELEMENT which first contacts the WORKPIECE. See STRUCTURAL ORDER and Section 24.

GAZETTE—See OG/OFFICIAL GAZETTE.

GENERIC/GENUS—A GENUS is a class BROADER than, or

including, more than one SPECIES. "Primate" is a GENUS with respect to "man" and "ape" which are SPECIES thereof. A GENERIC claim includes within its SCOPE two or more disclosed embodiments (SPECIES). Such a claim must cover or READ ON what is comprehended in each of the SPECIES. See MPEP 806.02(d) and (e), and Section 55. (12, 16, 21, 31, 33, 42, 46, 47, 48, 55)

GERUND—A verbal noun expressing the action of the verb in a generalized manner; a verbal noun, ending in "-ing" and performing the function of a substantive, often taking the case phrase construction, and at the same time showing the verbal features of tense and voice, taking adverbial modifiers, and governing objects. Usually, GERUNDS are the first words of METHOD steps, the basic ELEMENTS of a METHOD claim. See Section 33.

HAS/HAVING—TRANSITION words between the PREAMBLE and the BODY of a claim. Mean the same as COMPRISES/COMPRISING. (7, 54)

HOLE—Absence of material. HOLES, unlike most ELEMENTS, should usually be claimed INFERENTIALLY (Sense (1)), as "*a* lever having *a* hole." See Section 23. (22, 23, 31)

IMPROVEMENT CLAIM—Section 54.

INCLUDES/INCLUDING—TRANSITION words between the PREAMBLE and BODY of a claim. Mean the same as COMPRISES/COMPRISING. (7, 54)

INCOMPLETE—Quality of a claim which omits essential ELEMENTS or cooperative relationships. See MPEP 706.03(f) and Section 63. (56, 63, 64, 65)

INDEFINITE—(1) Lack of proper ANTECEDENT. (2) The quality of a claim which fails to accurately define the limits or boundaries of the INVENTION for any reason. (3) Not meeting the requirements of 35 U.S.C. 112 to particularly point out and distinctly claim the INVENTION. See Section 64. (14, *20*, 21, 22, 31, 33, 47, *64*)

INDEPENDENT CLAIM—A claim that contains a complete description of the subject matter, without reference to any other claim. (See DEPENDENT CLAIM.)

INDIRECT LIMITATION—Example: First reciting "a gear" and then reciting "said plastic gear" in a claim, where the same gear is meant in both instances. "Plastic" is an INDIRECT LIMITATION rendering the claim INDEFINITE. See ANTECEDENT, INFERENTIAL and POSITIVE, and MPEP 706.03(d) and Section 20.

INFERENTIAL—(1) In reference to the form of claims as such, an INFERENTIAL claim is one wherein a new ELEMENT is introduced in the middle of a clause which introduces and describes another ELEMENT. See Section 13. (2) The term is also used to refer to the setting forth of an ELEMENT (or a limitation or feature thereof) in a claim not found in the DESCRIPTION, or an ELEMENT (or limitation of an ELEMENT) set forth definitely in the claim ("*the* arm") where not set forth earlier in the claim. See INDIRECT LIMITATION and Sections 15, 20 and 64. (3) APPARATUS limitations are usually brought into METHOD claims INFERENTIALLY in the sense of meaning (1). See Section 38. (*13*, 15, *20*, 38, 60, 64)

INFRINGE/INFRINGEMENT/INFRINGER—An INFRINGER INFRINGES a claim by making, using or selling in the United States that which is set forth in the claim without the authority of the patent owner. See 35 U.S.C. 271 and DOCTRINE OF EQUIVALENTS. Normally, the DEVICE, etc., accused of being an INFRINGEMENT must contain each and every ELEMENT of the claim. (2, 13, 31, 32, 49, 50, 52, 53, 57)

INOPERATIVE—Incapable of performing an intended purpose.

INOPERATIVENESS may reside in an INVENTION, *qua* INVENTION, or as claimed. See AGGREGATION.

IN ORDER TO—See WHEREBY. Often used in a manner different from WHEREBY in a MEANS-plus-FUNCTION clause, as: "means for rotating the wheel IN ORDER TO reciprocate the arm. . . ." Usually, "IN ORDER TO reciprocate the arm" will be considered as a STRUCTURAL/FUNCTIONAL limitation. (28)

INTERFERENCE—A proceeding in the Patent Office to determine among (a) one or more patent applicants and one or more patentees, or (b) two or more applicants, claiming the same INVENTION, which of the parties was the first inventor. The claim defining the contested INVENTION is called a COUNT. (31, 52)

INTRODUCTION/INTRODUCTORY PHRASE—"I (or we) claim" or "What is claimed is." Each claim is the direct object of a SINGLE SENTENCE beginning with an INTRODUCTORY PHRASE, which appears only once, before the first claim. See Section 4. (*4*, 11)

INVENTION—(1) As a legally significant act, the summation of conception and reduction to practice, actual or constructive. (2) Also, the thing or DEVICE invented and claimed in a patent or patent application. (3) Sometimes used (misused?) as meaning unobvious, as in "what is the invention?"; meaning, what is the novel and unobvious feature(s) defined in the claim. See 35 U.S.C. 103. (3, 13, 15, 31, 36, 46, 50, 52, 53, 55, 57, 60, 61, 64, 65)

JEPSON CLAIM—A claim format for an improvement-type INVENTION wherein the old ELEMENTS are set forth in the PREAMBLE of the claim and the new or modified ELEMENTS (or new or modified COMBINATIONS thereof) are set forth in the BODY of the claim. Similar to a EUROPEAN-TYPE CLAIM. See Section 54. (31, *54*, 56, 60). From a Patent Office decision involving an inventor named JEPSON.

LABEL CLAIM—A type of NEW USE CLAIM wherein a statement of the intended use of a COMPOSITION is set forth in the PREAMBLE as a PREAMBLE LIMITATION and is relied on for novelty and/or unobviousness. See Section 52.

LAUDATORY STATEMENTS—Words such as "novel" or "efficiently" or "long wearing" which are generally not permitted in UTILITY claims. See Section 9. Sometimes called SURPLUSAGE. Permitted in plant patent claims, see Section 45. (9, 45)

MACHINE—One of the STATUTORY CLASSES of UTILITY PATENT. Often called "APPARATUS." A DEVICE usually having moving parts and a "rule of operation." Often contrasted with ARTICLE OF MANUFACTURE. (Chapter III, 3, 11, 12, 13, 42, 54, 61, 64)

MANUFACTURE—An ARTICLE OF MANUFACTURE. (3, 12, 61, 62)

MARKUSH CLAIM—A claim using special language as a permissible ALTERNATIVE EXPRESSION for a group of materials operable therein. Generally used only in chemical claims. A contrived GENERIC expression where no true GENERIC expression exists. Example: "a metal selected from the group CONSISTING OF copper, silver and gold." Technically, but permissibly, violates the rule against ALTERNATIVE EXPRESSIONS. See Section 47. (21, 46, *47*, 55). From a case, *Ex parte* Markush.

MEANS—A generalized and very BROAD word used to describe, in appropriate situations, an ELEMENT of a claim. See third paragraph of 35 U.S.C. 112 and Section 31. (16, 18, 20, 21, 23, 36, *31*, 32, 33, 42, 46, 47, 53, 55). Properly phrased as "means for (performing a specified function)."

MENTAL STEPS—Sections *41* and 62.

METHOD—A procedure for transforming or reducing an ARTICLE, WORKPIECE or chemical substance to a different state or thing. METHOD, PROCESS and ART mean the same thing. METHOD is more common in mechanical and electrical claims; PROCESS is more common in chemical claims; ART today is more commonly used to mean "field of technology." See Chapter IV. (Chapter IV, *33*, 35, *36*, 37, 40, 41, 49, 51, 52, 53, 54)

METHOD CLAIMS, APPARATUS LIMITATIONS IN—Section 38.

METHOD, ELECTRICAL—Section 40.

METHOD FUNCTIONAL OF APPARATUS—Section 37.

METHOD OF MAKING AN ARTICLE OF MANUFACTURE, OBVIOUS—Section 36.

MPEP—The *Manual of Patent Examining Procedure*, a looseleaf booklet published by the Government Printing Office and available from the Superintendent of Documents, Box 1533, Washington, D.C. 20013. It is the EXAMINERS' "bible." (4)

MULTIPLICITY—A word connoting an indefinite number, two or more; usually a fairly large number. Often thought of as being greater than a PLURALITY. (17)

NARROW/NARROW CLAIM—A NARROW CLAIM covers or READS ON a restricted SCOPE of DEVICES, PROCESSES, etc., because it contains either many, or quite specific, limitations. A NARROW CLAIM is usually entitled only to a NARROW range of EQUIVALENTS. See BROAD CLAIM, OLD COMBINATION, PICTURE CLAIM (Sense (2)) and PROLIX. (5, 12, 13, 33, 43, 46, 57, 64, 65)

NEGATIVE LIMITATION—A claim limitation telling what an ELEMENT is not, instead of what it is; or what it does not do, instead of what it does. See Sections *14* and 42.

NEW MATTER—A term of art in Patent Law meaning any matter not "fairly" disclosed within the "four corners" (entire SPE-

CIFICATION) of a patent application *as filed*. NEW MATTER may not be introduced into an application after it is filed. (48)

NEW USE CLAIM—A claim to a METHOD involving some NEW USE of an old material or COMPOSITION, such as the killing of insects by spraying with DDT, DDT being old for *other* purposes. Traditionally (and under 35 U.S.C. 100(b)), such a NEW USE may be claimed only in METHOD terminology, and the test of patentability is the novelty and unobviousness of the METHOD. See PREAMBLE LIMITATIONS, LABEL CLAIM and Section 52. (6, 39, 42, 46, 52, 56, 60)

NON-ART REJECTION—A REJECTION of a claim based, not on PRIOR ART (i.e., not on 35 U.S.C. 102 and/or 103), but on the form of the claim. See FORMAL REJECTION and Chapter IX. Includes REJECTIONS due to: METHOD functional of APPARATUS (Section 37), improper PRODUCT-BY-PROCESS (Section 43), improper NEW USE (Section 61) and PRINTED MATTER limitations (Section 62), and other bases covered in Chapter IX. (Chapter IX, 41, 60)

NON-STATUTORY—(1) Quality of the subject matter of a purported INVENTION which is not patentable under 35 U.S.C. 101, either by the precise terms thereof, or by case-law interpretation. See Sections 3 and 62. (2) Also used as a ground for REJECTION of a claim to an INVENTION where the claim is inherently defective, as an OMNIBUS CLAIM (Section 2), the claim sets forth a RESULT only (Section 28) or the claim depends solely on printed matter for patentability (Section 62). See FORMAL REJECTION and NON-ART REJECTION. 2, 3, 28, 41, 61, 62)

NUMBERING OF CLAIMS—Section 5.

NUMERALS, REFERENCE, IN CLAIMS—Section 19.

OBJECTION—A criticism by an EXAMINER to the form of a claim, as opposed to its substance. See NON-ART REJECTION and REJECTION. (14, 28)

OFFICIAL GAZETTE/OG—A weekly publication of the Patent Office, giving abstracts of and other information on all patents granted that week, as well as other information relating to patent and trademark practice. (14) Now split into two volumes, one for Patents, one for Trademarks.

OLD COMBINATION—Quality of a claim which recites an overall COMBINATION (including a SUBCOMBINATION) wherein the INVENTION resides in the SUBCOMBINATION which does not cooperate in some new and unobvious manner with the remainder of the COMBINATION. Sometimes called EXHAUSTED COMBINATION or OVERCLAIMING. A ground for REJECTION. See Section 60. (54, 56, *60*, 63)

OMNIBUS CLAIM—A claim in formal terms, such as "My INVENTION substantially as shown and described." Not permitted in UTILITY patents under 35 U.S.C. 112. This form of claim is used in design patents, and in modified form in plant patents. See Sections 2, 44, 45, 49 and 51.

OPEN-ENDED—See COMPRISES.

ORDER OF CLAIMS—Sections 5 and 53.

OPERATIONAL EXPRESSIONS—Section 27.

OUTLINE FORMAT—A claim format in which each ELEMENT is introduced in its own SUBPARAGRAPH which is identified by a parenthesized number or letter. See Section 10. (*10*, 35)

OVERCLAIMING—See OLD COMBINATION. (28, *60*)

PARENT CLAIM—A main claim from which a DEPENDENT CLAIM depends. (20, 53, 54) The parent claim may itself be INDEPENDENT or dependent.

PERIPHERAL CLAIM—The type of claim used in the United States. It defines the outer boundaries of the INVENTION. All that is within those boundaries (including all the claimed ELE-

MENTS and their EQUIVALENTS) will be READ ON by the claim; all that is outside the boundaries is not READ ON by the claim. See DOCTRINE OF EQUIVALENTS. (2)

PICTURE CLAIM—A claim reciting all significant structure disclosed in the description, omitting only "nuts and bolts." Thus, a very NARROW claim. (51, 57)

PLANT PATENT CLAIM—Section 45.

PLURALITY—An indefinite number, two or more. See MULTIPLICITY. (17)

POSITIVE/POSITIVELY—(1) The opposite of INFERENTIAL. A POSITIVE recitation of an ELEMENT means that the ELEMENT is introduced and fully described in a clause of a claim in which no other ELEMENT is introduced (except for a HOLE). See Sections 13, 15, 20, 34, 38 and 64. (2) The opposite of NEGATIVE. See NEGATIVE LIMITATION. (13, 14, 22, 31, 33, 54, 60)

PQ—See USPQ.

PREAMBLE—The initial part of a claim the purpose of which is to name or define the thing being claimed. Often the environment in which the claimed thing will be used is set forth, as well as the WORKPIECE. See NEW USE CLAIM and Sections 6, 12, 13, and 52. (*6*, 7, 9, 11, *12*, 13, 27, 31, 33, 46, *52*, 53, 54, 56)

PREAMBLE LIMITATION—Descriptive statement in a PREAMBLE such as those related to the field of use, environment, etc. Possibly helpful in distinguishing a claim over PRIOR ART. See NEW USE CLAIM and Section 52. (*12*, 41, *52*, 56, 60)

PRINTED MATTER—See NON-ART REJECTION, NONSTATUTORY, and Section 62. (41, *62*)

PRIOR ART—All subject matter (patents, publications, etc.) bearing on the novelty and unobviousness of a claimed INVENTION pursuant, *inter alia*, to 35 U.S.C. 102 and 103.

PROCESS—One of the STATUTORY CLASSES of UTILITY PATENT. See METHOD. (Chapter IV, 3, 5, 33, 47, 48, 50)

PROCESS, CHEMICAL—Section 39.

PRODUCT—Synonomous with ARTICLE OF MANUFACTURE and COMPOSITION. (5, 46)

PRODUCT-BY-PROCESS—A type of claim defining a PRODUCT in terms of the PROÇESS by which it is made. Generally used on an emergency basis when the PRODUCT cannot be defined in more traditional terms. This type of claim covers the PRODUCT *only* when made by the specified PROCESS. Novelty and unobviousness must reside in the PRODUCT and not merely in the PROCESS. See MPEP 706.03(e) and Section 43. (28, 42, 43, 50, 53)

PROLIX—Quality of a claim which is "too complete" in that it sets forth long recitations of unimportant details which hide or obscure the INVENTION. See MPEP 706.03(g) and Section 65. (65)

PUNCTUATION OF CLAIMS—Section 10.

READ ON—To encompass, comprehend or give support to; to be within the terms of. If a claim READS ON a device accused of being an INFRINGEMENT thereof, the DEVICE does INFRINGE. If a claim READS ON a REFERENCE (or, *vice versa*) the claim is either unpatentable or invalid. A claim must READ ON the DESCRIPTION of the patent or application to which it is appended for the ELEMENTS of the claim to find ANTECEDENT basis therein. (15, 64)

REFERENCE—See PRIOR ART. Whether a REFERENCE is available as PRIOR ART depends on 35 U.S.C. and case-law interpretations thereof. PRIOR ART REFERENCES may be relied on by the EXAMINER or an accused INFRINGER to attack a claim.

REFERENCE NUMERALS IN CLAIMS—Section 19.

REJECTION—Disallowance of a claim by an EXAMINER because of its substance (lack of novelty; obvious). See OBJECTION and PRIOR ART. (14, 28, 37, 61, 63, 64, 65)

RESPONSE—An applicant's answer to an Office action. Attempts to meet REJECTIONS of and OBJECTIONS to claims either by AMENDMENT, or argument, or both.

RESTRICTION REQUIREMENT—Where the EXAMINER concludes that an application contains claims directed to more than one INVENTION, he *may* require the applicant to elect one INVENTION and to restrict his claims to such elected INVENTION. (55, 56)

RESULT—What the INVENTION is intended to accomplish. Claims setting forth only RESULTS are objectionable as too BROAD. See Sections 28 and 29. (28, 29, 31, 33)

SAID—THE. "THE SAID" is a redundancy to be avoided. (20)

SCOPE—Breadth; the limits of the boundaries of a PERIPHERAL CLAIM. See BROAD and NARROW. (Chapter VIII, 5, 6, 13, 16, 19, 22, 31, 45, 46, 53, 57, 60, 64, 65)

SCOPE OF CLAIMS, VARYING—Chapter VIII.

SINGLE ELEMENT CLAIM—A rare type of claim not to a COMBINATION but to one ELEMENT. Permissible if not a SINGLE MEANS CLAIM. (9)

SINGLE MEANS CLAIM—An impermissible claim not to a COMBINATION and having only one ELEMENT which is expressed in the form of "MEANS plus function." See Sections 31 and 33 and 35 U.S.C. 112. (31, 33, 39, 54)

SINGLE PARAGRAPH FORM—A claim format in which the ELEMENTS are not identified by indentation, letters or numerals, but are set off by commas. See COLON-SEMICOLON FORM, OUTLINE FORM, SUBPARAGRAPH FORM and Sections 10 and 11.

SINGLE SENTENCE RULE—In the United States, a claim must be a single sentence. See INTRODUCTION and Section 4. (4, 9, 23)

SO THAT—See IN ORDER TO and WHEREBY. (28, 30, 31)

SPECIES/SPECIFIC—A SPECIES is a member of a GENUS. A SPECIES is one of the two or more alternative and mutually exclusive embodiments of an INVENTION. The different SPECIES may be structures, steps, COMPOUNDS, chemicals, etc. See GENERIC/GENUS and Section 55. (16, 21, 33, 47, 53, 55)

SPECIFICATION—The drawings, DESCRIPTION and claims of a patent application or patent. See NEW MATTER. (1, 13, 15, 16, 27, 31, 33, 41, 42, 48, 49, 50, 57, 60)

STATUTE—Title 35 of the United States Code (35 U.S.C.). (Chapter I, 1)

STATUTORY CLASSES—The main categories or "pigeonholes" into which a technical subject must fit in order to be potentially patentable. These categories are set forth in 35 U.S.C. 101, 161 and 171 as interpreted by the case-law, and include PROCESS, MACHINE, MANUFACTURE, COMPOSITION OF MATTER, designs and plants. See Section 3. (3, 4)

STRUCTURAL CONNECTION—Section 26.

STRUCTURAL ORDER—A logical ordering of the ELEMENTS of a claim which begins with a base, power source or input and proceeds structurally to an ultimate ELEMENT or output. See FUNCTIONAL ORDER and Section 24.

SUBCOMBINATION—An ELEMENT or group of ELEMENTS that forms a part of a primary COMBINATION. If a SUBCOMBINATION has utility by itself, it may be claimed separately from the COMBINATION. See Section 56. (*56*, 60, 63)

SUBCOMBINATION FORMAT—A claim format for a SUBCOMBINATION: "In a (name of COMBINATION) for (COMBINATION'S FUNCTION), an X and a Y," where X, Y is the claimed SUBCOMBINATION. An exception to the "rule" that a TRANSITION should be between the PREAMBLE and BODY of a claim. (56)

SUBPARAGRAPH FORM—A claim format in which each ELEMENT is introduced and defined in its own indented subparagraph. See COLON-SEMICOLON FORM, OUTLINE FORM, SINGLE PARAGRAPH FORM and Section 10. (*10*, 11, 13, 35)

SUPPORT FOR CLAIMS IN SPECIFICATION AND DRAWINGS—See ANTECEDENT and Sections 15 and 20.

SURPLUSSAGE—See LAUDATORY STATEMENTS. (9)

TABULAR FORM—Same as SUBPARAGRAPH FORM. (10)

THE—The definite article THE is used to refer to an ELEMENT which has been introduced earlier in a claim. Alternatively SAID may be used, meaning the same thing. (*20*, 53)

THEREBY—See WHEREBY. (28, 29)

TRADEMARKED MATERIALS—Section 48.

TRANSITION/TRANSITIONAL PHRASE—Language between the PREAMBLE and BODY of a claim. May affect the SCOPE of the claim. See COMPRISES, CONSISTING OF, CONSISTING ESSENTIALLY OF, INCLUDES, HAS and Section 7. (7, 8, 9, 11, 56)

ULTIMATE SPECIES—A SPECIES which cannot be further divided into other SPECIES. (53, 55) Example: Silver is an ultimate species of the genus "conductive metals."

UNBASED COMPARATIVE—An adjective, such as "thick," "heavy," "small," etc., used in a claim wherein no basis for the use thereof (i.e., thicker, heavier, smaller than what?) is set forth. The remedy is to provide a basis or relation for comparison, such as "said second member being thicker *than* said first member." Many words, such as resilient, flexible, etc., while, strictly speaking, are UNBASED, are usually accepted without question. An UNBASED COMPARATIVE is a ground for REJECTION or OBJECTION, because its use may render a claim INDEFINITE. See Section 22.

UNDUE MULTIPLICITY—Presentation of too many claims in view of the nature and SCOPE of the INVENTION. See Rule 75(b), MPEP 706.03(1) and Section 59. (47, 50, 53, 57, 59)

USPQ—The *United States Patent Quarterly,* a magazine published weekly by BNA, Inc., and covering cases on patents, trademarks, copyrights, intellectual property, etc. The USPQ is the "official" report of the CCPA, in patent cases, as well as reporting cases from all other courts and administrative tribunes in these fields.

UTILITY PATENT—Patents defining INVENTIONS having industrial utility (METHOD, APPARATUS, ARTICLE OF MANUFACTURE, COMPOSITION OF MATTER) as distinguished from design patents (Section 44) and plant patents (Section 45). (2, 47)

VAGUE—See INDEFINITE. (22, 64)

VARYING SCOPE OF CLAIMS—Chapter VIII.

WHEREBY—When properly used in a claim, a word introducing a clause describing the FUNCTION or operation necessarily following from previously recited structure, whether a whole claim or an ELEMENT thereof. The phrase traditionally means "it necessarily follows from the foregoing that." Such a WHEREBY clause is improper when it is used to *imply* structural or cooperational relationships which are not positively recited in the claim. See Section 29. (28, 29, 30, 33)

WORKPIECE—The thing or ARTICLE operated on, altered, changed or reduced by a claimed APPARATUS or METHOD. It should be introduced in the PREAMBLE of the claim, and/or introduced INFERENTIALLY in the BODY of the claim. See Sections 12, 13 and 34. (11, 12, 13, 24, 27, 33, 34)

WRITTEN DESCRIPTION—See DESCRIPTION.

TABLE OF CASES